Approaches and theory in International Relations

Edited by **Trevor Taylor**

Longman London and New York

Longman Group Limited London

Associated companies, branches and representatives
throughout the world

Published in the United States of America
by Longman Inc., New York

First published 1978

Library of Congress Cataloging in Publication Data

Main entry under title:

Approaches and theory in international relations.

Includes index.
1. International relations--Research--Addresses,
essays, lectures. I. Taylor, Trevor.
JX1291.A67 327'.01 77-8093
ISBN 0-582-48539-8

Printed in Great Britain by
Richard Clay (The Chaucer Press) Ltd.,
Bungay, Suffolk.

Contents

Notes on contributors

David J. Dunn. Lecturer in the Department of International Relations and Politics, North Staffordshire Polytechnic. Contributor to *The Use of Force in International Relations,* ed. Northedge (Faber, 1974), and articles in *British Journal of International Studies, Bulletin of the Conflict Research Society, Millennium* and the *RUSI Journal.*

G.L. Goodwin. Montague Burton Professor of International Relations, University of London. Author of *Britain and the United Nations* (Oxford Univ. Press, 1958), editor of *University Teaching of International Relations* (Blackwell, 1952) and joint editor of *New Dimensions of World Politics* (croom Helm, 1975). Contributor to *International Organization, International Affairs, Journal of Common Market Studies, Government and Opposition.*

Michael Hodges Associate Professor in the Department of International Relations, Lehigh University, Bethlehem, Pennsylvania. Author of *Multinational Corporations and National Governments* (Saxon House, 1974), editor of *European Integration* (Penguin, 1972), contributor to *Functionalism and International Relations,* ed. Taylor and Groom (Univ. of London Press, 1975), *Policy-Making in the European Communities*, ed. Wallace and Webb (Wiley, 1977), and articles in *Current History.*

Richard Little. Lecturer in the Department of Politics, University of Lancaster. Author of *Intervention: External Involvement in Civil Wars* (Martin Robertson, 1975).

Peter Nailor. Professor of History at the Royal Naval College, Greenwich. Author of 'Medes and Persians', *Lancaster Inaugrals* (Univ. of Lancaster, 1970) and a contributor to the following volumes: *International Society,* ed. Twitchett (Oxford Univ. Press/RIIA, 1971), *European Military Institutions* (Scotland, Universities Services Study Group, 1971), *The Roles of Maritime Forces in the Security of Western Europe* (Southampton Univ., 1972), *Management of Britain's External Relations,* ed. Boardman and Groom (Macmillan, 1973), *Britain in the EEC,* ed. Evans (Gollancz, 1973) and *War in the Next Decade,* ed. Edmonds and Beaumont (Macmillan, 1975).

Robert Purnell. Senior Lecturer in the Department of International Politics, University College of Wales, Aberystwyth. Author of *The Society of States* (Weidenfeld and Nicolson, 1973). Contributor to *International Yearbook of Foreign Policy Analysis* and other hournals.

Peter Savigear. Lecturer in the Department of Politics, University of Leicester. Joint editor, *The Theory of International Relations* (Allen and Unwin, 1970) and a contributor to journals in the fields of International Relations and French government.

H. Suganami. Lecturer in International Relations, University of Keele.

Trevor Taylor. Principal lecturer in the Department of International Relations and Politics, North Staffordshire Polytechnic. Contributor to *The Use of Force in International Relations*, ed. Northedge (Faber, 1974) and articles in *International Relations, The Year Book of World Affairs* and other journals.

A.E. Thorndike. Head of the Department of International Relations and Politics, North Staffordshire Polytechnic, and a contributor to journals on Carribean and Latin American affairs.

R.I. Tooze. Lecturer in the Department of International Relations and Politics, North Staffordshire Polytechnic. Author of the Progress of International Functionalism, *British Journal of International Studies,* vol 3 no 2, July 1977.

Brian White. Lecturer in the Department of International Relations and Politics, North Staffordshire Polytechnic. Author of 'The Study of British Foreign Policy: some comments on Dr. Barber's review article; *British Journal of International Studies,* vol III, no. 3, October 1977.

Acknowledgements

We are grateful to the American Academy of Political and Social Science for permission to produce two diagrams reprinted from 'International Propaganda and Statecraft' by Bryant Wedge in volume no. 398 of THE ANNALS of the American Academy of Political and Social Science, copyright 1971, by the American Academy of Political and Social Science, all rights reserved.

Chapter 1

Introduction: the nature of International Relations

Trevor Taylor

This collection of writings is about the development of the discipline of International Relations, a subject which began to be studied formally on any scale only after 1919 but which since has grown much, both in terms of scholars involved and literature produced. By way of introduction to the analyses which follow of how International Relations has been studied and of the concepts and propositions which have been put forward, there follows a brief survey of what International Relations is, why it has been studied more and more during the course of this century and what particular problems it faces.

International Relations is the discipline which tries to explain political activities across state boundaries and, to date, it has been chiefly concerned with the political relations between governments, the official representatives of states. These political relations are seen as having a unique nature, and thus their study forms a separate branch of political science, because they are conducted in a 'political system', in a 'society', where there is no final, central authority: power, the ability to influence others, is not centralized but is spread among various human organizations, in particular, states, which recognize no superior political authority. They are 'sovereign' and, if they so wish, they may pursue their goals by using their military forces in war. Raymond Aron and George Quester are two scholars who have emphasized that international politics gains many of its unique characteristics from the constant possibility of war, which is in itself a special kind of human activity:

War is much more than simple violence, the violence which occurs in many cities, in many societies. War is violence co-ordinated and organised to a colossal degree, harnessing 'economies of scale' to make possible destruction which would be unimaginable otherwise (Quester 1974, 2).

Why study International Relations?

If the above paragraph tells something about the nature of International Relations, it tells little about why it is studied. Four arguments stand out as to why scholars should and do pay great attention to international political activity and attempt to draw up generalizations and theories as to the nature of that activity. These arguments are listed below, but in no special order of importance.

First, man's behaviour in any of its aspects constitutes an interesting and worthwhile study. This applies as much to activities in the international political arena as to economic and social matters. All aspects of social science share a fundamental concern with the same questions of why man acts as he does and what choices are open to him. In the centuries before the study of mankind was compartmentalized into the modern social sciences so as to allow specialization, philosophers intellectually roamed free, producing varied hypotheses about human behaviour, with many referring to the political activities of individuals and groups of people with regard to the world outside their own particular social organization. For centuries thinkers have been concerned with the reconciliation of order, justice and change, both within and between communities. In that political philosophers discussed the politics of an environment where there was no central authority, they were the first scholars of international politics and, in writing about the relations between the Greek city-states or between the European states of the eighteenth century, they left behind a great variety of hypotheses to stimulate the imaginations and research of contemporary scholars. Therefore, three chapters of this book endeavour to summarize the most important aspects of this mass of thinking in an attempt to rectify a sin of omission, the tendency of International Relations scholars since 1945 perhaps to neglect the contribution of political philosophers to their subject. The chapters serve as a reminder that political thinkers had much to say which was of relevance to international politics.

International Relations, then, represents part of man's effort to understand himself, but there is a second and essentially practical reason for studying it, that the findings of scholars can contribute to the formulation of foreign policy. For centuries, foreign policy steadily became a more difficult and complex task for governments and more and more personnel were allocated to it. In 1821, when Castlereagh was the British Foreign Minister, the Foreign Office had a staff of twenty-eight (Woodward 1962, 196). In 1973 the staff of the British Foreign and Commonwealth Office totalled 10,400.[1] In addition, to get an accurate idea of the number of personnel involved in Britain's foreign policy effort, it would also be necessary to take account of the civil servants in other ministries having daily concern with Britain's external affairs. These could well total a further 10,000. In 1815, according to the calculations of Small and Singer (1966), the international system consisted of just twenty-three states, about half of which were small units later integrated to become Germany and Italy. By 1973 the international system comprised over 140 states, the great majority of which were situated outside Europe.[2] In the nineteenth century, foreign policy was concerned largely with trade and security matters, but in the twentieth it spread to embrace technology, communications, culture, ideology and a whole range of economic matters with political aspects. The problem of the growing complexity of foreign policy each year grows more intense. From 1973, for example, governments in the West had to give much greater attention to the problem of securing adequate oil supplies for their economies, whereas, in previous years, they had generally been able to leave this problem to private oil companies.

In this situation of increasing complexity, the discipline of International Relations can offer substantial aid although no final solutions to foreign policy problems.

The initial contribution of the International Relations scholar is to press for propositions and assumptions, on which policy and even description must be based, to be made explicit. As Carr (1961) and de Vree (1972) among others have made clear, we cannot simply accept all facts as equal and of the same weight when we try to make sense of a situation. We select and stress some facts at the expense of others, we pick out what we see as relevant, and this is done using what are usually implicit propositions about a situation. Information not having an important place in these propositions is neglected. Two obvious sources of an individual's views about international politics are his education and his experience within the collective organization in which he operates. For instance, a foreign service official may have been taught at school that communist states were aggressive and expansionist. The majority of his colleagues at work may agree with this and so reinforce his view.

All views on and analyses of a political situation are based on hypotheses of some sort and International Relations, by concentrating on the explicit formulation of such propositions, can make a significant contribution to policy-making. For instance, the appearance of theories dealing with deterrence was an important factor in the development of the US armed forces after 1955. With the production of thermonuclear weapons, it became clear that the prime role of the US armed forces was to prevent war not win it. The Strategic Air Command adopted the motto 'Peace is our business' and, while scientists devised new weapons systems, academics such as Schelling and Boulding analyzed in depth the concept of deterrence. Their findings, specifically their emphasis on second-strike capability, represented an important argument in favour of the deployment of the solid-fuelled Minuteman missile, dispersed in hardened silos, and the submarine-based Polaris system. Chapter 8 deals in general with the place of strategic thought in International Relations. However, the International Relations theorist can rarely offer dogmatic policy advice because the propositions on which advice must be based, explicitly formulated though they may be, are not sufficiently comprehensive or sure to be satisfactory. For instance, deterrence theory has considerable logical consistency and empirical validity, but factors such as irrationality and the possibility of accidents, which it does not take into account, ensure that peace is not guaranteed even when both parties 'ought' to be deterred. Therefore the most valuable role which theory can play may be to warn against excessively straightforward approaches. The writings of Graham Allison (1971) on 'bureaucratic' and other models of foreign policy-making are not ideal, in that none of the models fits exactly with how governments behave, but they clearly have some relationship to reality and no one who has studied them could easily accept very simplistic propositions such as one which described the expansionist demands of Marxism-Leninism as the sole determinant of Soviet foreign policy. The final chapter of this book examines more closely the relationship between International Relations theorists and foreign policy issues.

Of course, not all International Relations scholars are interested in contributing directly or indirectly to policy-making and a third reason for studying International Relations may be introduced at this point – it is that awareness of the concepts, hypotheses and models of the discipline enables any student to analyse and to develop views on specific international questions.

The complexity of contemporary international politics not only makes it difficult for governments to pursue successful, coherent foreign policies, it also means that the general publics of most states find it almost impossible to understand what is going on. As a result, foreign policy-making is frequently left in the hands of ministers and civil servants influenced by a small number of interested groups. Public opinion rarely plays an important role. In this situation, International Relations, just by the provision of ordering concepts, even when of a far from adequate nature, can play an educative role. Concepts such as the national interest, power, the balance of power and imperialism, unsatisfactory though they may be for quantitative and precise analysis, do represent pegs on which individuals can hang information on foreign affairs. In the thermonuclear age, international politics appear too important to be left to politicians alone, but substantial debates of any sophistication involving the public can only occur if the public possesses the analytic tools to make sense of international political situations. It is these analytic tools which International Relations endeavours to provide and a major step forward in the development of the general educative role of the discipline would, of course, be its widespread introduction in schools.

Finally, a fourth and related reason for the study of International Relations is both moral and practical, and many see it as the most significant; it is that the discipline covers some of the most important issues with which mankind is faced today. Prominent among these issues are the questions of why wars begin, how they can be prevented and how they can be controlled. Until this century, war was seen as a normal instrument of policy or as an inevitable evil in the face of man's aggressive nature. The principal question asked by political philosophers and others was not whether wars, especially between great powers, could be banished from international politics but under which circumstances they were justifiable. Even by the time of the Reformation the question of the 'just war' had been much discussed and substantial agreement had been reached on seven criteria which included the argument that the innocent should be immune from direct attack (see

Bailey 1972, 15–16). Only a few idealists argued all war to be immoral or felt that it could be abolished.

These attitudes could be maintained because war, while by no means pleasant, was not a great evil which threatened whole societies. It was not necessary to ask how wars could be avoided. In the seventeenth century rulers fought with largely mercenary armies which were small in size because professional soldiers were rare and expensive. In the late seventeenth and eighteenth centuries, although the size of armies increased, their impact on populations was offset by the provision of organized supplies. This meant they did not need to live off the land they occupied.

The French Revolution and the rise of Napoleon changed much, for the spread of national feeling to all classes meant that large armies could be raised whose men were ready to fight and die. Technological developments in the rest of the nineteenth century, particularly improvements in the performance of hand guns and artillery, greatly increased the capacity of man rapidly to destroy his fellows, but major war between the great powers was avoided for a variety of reasons, including the limited nature of the foreign policy aims which the great powers adopted, the availability of land outside Europe for the building of empires, the ideological homogeneity of European states which enabled any state to support any other, and the desire of governments to avoid such a struggle as that which had ended in 1815.

The outbreak and course of the First World War was of consequence for International Relations in two ways. First, the matter of future war avoidance became vital in view of the unprecedented and casual loss of life which the 1914–18 conflict entailed. Every family in the combatant states was affected directly or indirectly by the heavy casualties. Total battle deaths have been estimated at 9 million (compared with 187,500 in the Franco-Prussian War of 1870 and 264,200 in the Crimean War) (Singer and Small 1972, 61–6). All-out war became for many a phenomenon to be avoided at all costs.

Second, it was far from clear why the war began. It seemed absurd that the assassination of an Austrian archduke in Bosnia could lead to a British declaration of war on Germany, ostensibly over the violation of Belgian neutrality. This absurdity could not be removed by simply blaming the Kaiser. Moreover, after the great powers' success in maintaining peace in several crises prior to 1914, it was difficult to see what was special about the issue which finally sparked off the war. Consequently, when world leaders met at Versailles in 1919 to try to establish an effective peace system, great differences of opinion appeared as to why the war had started and, related to this, how future wars could be prevented. The US representatives felt the war to be due to the authoritative nature of the governments of Austria-Hungary and Germany and to the suppression of national aspirations in Austria-Hungary. Therefore the US advocated the establishment of democratic states in Europe based on national feeling. Also, the 'balance of power' was rejected as being a device making for war and instead a collective security system organized through the League of Nations was advocated. The British government was dubious about collective security but believed that fighting had begun in 1914 partly because there was inadequate machinery for great-power consultation. Britain therefore welcomed the League as a forum where the powers could meet at short notice and discuss their differences. France, in contrast, attributed the war to inevitable German expansionism and argued that this could only be prevented in future by keeping Germany in a subordinate position in international politics. For France, the League was an instrument for the control of Germany. Because of these different approaches, international politics were poorly managed: German resentment was stimulated but no machinery for dealing with it was produced. Faced with German expansionist policies, Britain, France, the USSR and the US, states which were eventually to combine to defeat Germany, could find no common policy on the issues of which German demands should be met and what should follow if Germany pressed further demands. A common interpretation is that the German government was tempted to continue with expansionist policies by the hesitation of other governments. In 1939 it miscalculated as to the eventual consequences of an invasion of Poland and a major European war broke out again.

Technological developments after 1918 had made it even more desirable that the strongest military powers should avoid fighting each other. Hence, in the Second World War, the use of the bomber, high explosives and mobile armoured units meant that economic assets and civilians, as well as military personnel, were destroyed on a large scale. Total battle deaths have been put at 15 million (Singer and Small 1972, 61–6), but the total of deaths caused directly by the war was nearer 50 million (Calvocoressi and Wint 1974, 553). Again, the events leading to war emphasized the need for better international political theory, as the failure of British and American appeasement and neutrality policies between 1935 and 1941 illustrated that peace could not be obtained simply by the desire for it. The events of both 1914 and 1939 clearly showed that the theories about international politics held by statesmen were inadequate and inaccurate. Then, the production of nuclear weapons before the end of 1945, of thermonuclear weapons soon afterwards and of intercontinental ballistic missiles in the late 1950s gave man, for the first time, the capability rapidly to destroy himself as a species.

The development and deployment of the thermonuclear weapons and their delivery systems, coupled with frightening advances in the techniques of chemical and biological warfare, threatened the fundamental nature of international politics but did not succeed in changing it. The world remained one in which independent states dominated international politics, seeking security through the acquisition of better and more arms. The thesis of John Herz (1959) that the nation-state would disappear as a unit of social organization because it could not prevent other states from destroying its citizenry, proved invalid, as he acknowledged (Herz 1968). Yet many still feel it to be highly unsatisfactory that man has arranged his affairs so as to make his mass destruction a real and constant possibility.

Although the unsatisfactory state system remained, thermonuclear weapons meant that wars between the strongest powers became a new type of prospect. Before 1945, war could be seen as bringing an increasing amount of evil but still some good. The only permanent damage of the Second World War was to human life for, as the economic recovery of Japan and Western Europe showed, the material damage could be quickly repaired once investment funds were available. The Second World War had the effect in Britain, for example, of increasing employment, speeding the development of the welfare state and improving the agricultural system.[3] Until the mid-1950s Marxist-Leninists could believe that inevitable war between capitalist states and finally between capitalist and communist states would bring about world revolution. Yet a thermonuclear war between the USSR and the US offered the prospect only of destruction, a conflict in which neither side could gain in any positive sense.

Consequently, the purpose of strategic weapons acquired by major powers became to prevent war rather than to make 'victory' possible. Official Soviet dogma was amended so that an eventual capitalist attack on the USSR was no longer described as inevitable, and unofficially at the Geneva Summit of 1955 the USSR and the US tacitly agreed that a war between them could serve no conceivable purpose (Robertson 1966, 205).

The increasing need to avoid war served, understandably, as the greatest stimulant to the study of International Relations. Two major research institutions, the Royal Institute of International Affairs in London and the Council on Foreign Relations in New York, were set up immediately after the end of the First World War and chairs in International Relations were established on a permanent basis in Britain at the University College of Wales, Aberystwyth in 1922 and at the London School of Economics in 1923. Since then the study of International Relations has spread to many colleges and universities in the US and Britain and, although the subject is still neglected in much of Western Europe, there is increasing interest in Scandinavia where, for instance, the Stockholm International Peace Research Institute is doing valuable work, particularly on arms races and arms transfers between states. Thus, it has a similar area of concern to the London-based International Institute for Strategic Studies. In summary, International Relations now constitutes an established academic discipline.

Most involved with the problem of war was the United States, which had tried unsuccessfully to keep out of two world wars and which accepted, in 1945, that it could not return to its minor international role of before 1939. The US problem, therefore, was to act in international politics so as to promote its own interests but in a manner likely to maintain peace in an increasingly complicated international system. As a result, much International Relations writing was stimulated and, even when outwardly of a purely theoretical nature, it was often orientated towards specific prescriptions for US policy. Most notable were 'realists' such as Morgenthau and Spykman who argued that all states must maximize their power, a very clear message for US decision-makers (see Ch. 6). US policy experiences and dilemmas continued to stimulate International Relations thought and research and, much later, the impact of the Vietnam War was substantial.

However, a side-effect of the central role of consideration of possible war between major powers was that many works in International Relations concentrated on the major military powers and treated smaller powers as significant only in so far as they affected relations between the great powers. Even in the early 1970s the study of small states remained a fairly neglected area.

However, International Relations also became concerned with a range of other problems besides war and peace, chiefly because the state gained responsibility for, but apparently was unable to solve, many of the problems of the post-1945 world. These included the rising world population and resultant food shortages, the anticipated exhaustion of raw material supplies in view of their growing consumption, the management of the world economy so as to provide stability and growth, and the increasing pollution of land, sea and air. Scholars analyzed how states dealt with these problems and questioned whether there was any hope of their solution under the existing state system.[4]

Problems in the study of International Relations

The first fifty years or so in which International Relations was studied as a discipline was marked by bitter, intense but nevertheless understandable debate among academics as to the merits of their various approaches, aspirations, hypotheses and methods of verification. In many ways, debate was of real value but, at times, hostility was intense, particularly between those who claimed to be 'realists' and those they called 'Utopians', and between those who claimed to be 'scientific' and those who relied almost entirely on judgement and insight, the so-called 'traditionalists'. Explanation as to why these debates were so bitter cannot be limited to the tendency of academics to see all who disagree with them as fools, although this was perhaps a more important factor than is generally thought. In International Relations, what was probably most significant was that there are no obviously valid theories nor self-evident methods of obtaining them.

Even the content of the discipline cannot be precisely stated. Its focal point traditionally has been the political relations between states because, using Platig's argument (1967, Ch. 1), territorially based social organizations with their own governments have constituted major centres of power for centuries. In other words, it was states which had the capacity to wage war and to influence the actions of large numbers of humans by persuasion and coercion. But, especially after 1945, the central role of the state could not be taken for granted and, therefore, many International Relations scholars began grappling with the problems of whether the power of states is being eroded by the international organizations which carry out their activities with little regard for state boundaries.[5]

However, while most scholars accept that the essence of International Relations is the study of political relations between states, even though they may doubt the state's future viability or importance, the periphery of the discipline has by nature a blurred boundary.

This observation is derived from the fact that few international questions are solely the subject of one academic discipline. In practice, they are part political, part economic, part social and so on. A situation may be said to be non-political only if there is no choice available or if there is no disagreement among the parties concerned as to the ends to be achieved and as to the most appropriate action to be taken. As soon as disagreement is present, it is the political process which determines a situation's outcome. These points may be illustrated by reference to the issue of whether Britain should remain a member of the EEC. Initially, this may appear a wholly economic matter with the relevant question being whether British prosperity would be greater with Britain in or out. But further consideration introduces a whole new range of questions: What effect does EEC membership have on the distribution of income in Britain? What distribution is desirable? What non-economic price does Britain pay for EEC membership in terms of loss of national independence and the erosion of 'the British way of life'? Will British governments be better able to exercise influence and protect British interests in the world if Britain is in or out of the EEC? Clearly, then, the issue of Britain and Europe is social, economic and political. However, the specific role of politics is that political processes determine whether any changes are made in the terms of British membership of the Common Market and what decision, to stay in or leave, is finally made.

Some scholars underestimated the political content of many questions. David Mitrany, who forecast in the 1940s that the state would be eroded as a social organization as international agencies were allocated more and more of the tasks which the state performed (Mitrany 1946), assumed that governments would hand over such tasks if the new agencies could perform them better. He felt that the control of pollution, communications and the international economy, for instance, would be handed over to international organizations without demur, because he did not see them as being political issues. But, in reality, many such issues were very political, firstly because states were reluctant to give up their power over any matter, and secondly because intense disagreement arose over apparently non-controversial subjects. The goal of reducing the pollution of the Rhine was seemingly such a subject, but France refused to join in international measures to bring it about. Often, even when agreement is possible on goals, differences of opinion are usual on how best to achieve such goals and on the maximum price to be paid for their achievement. For instance, even in an area such as Western Europe, where there is substantial agreement as to the desirability of economic growth, there is also substantial disagreement as to the amount of state involvement desirable in the economic system.

Thus, International Relations suffered more than most social sciences from what is usually referred to as the unity of knowledge, the fact that everything in the universe relates to and depends on something else. It even led to the assertion that International Relations is not a discipline in its own right and, in particular, that it cannot be separated from the study of internal political systems. This claim may be met by the argument advanced earlier that international political activity, taking place in an environment where there is no central authority and where war is always possible, is inherently different from internal political activity. It is thus linked to domestic politics but has a distinct nature of its own. But a further point concerns the different sorts of questions studied by students of domestic and international politics. The focus of study in domestic political science is often the structure and operation of the system; the domestic political scientist is primarily concerned with how decisions are reached and with how pressure groups and other elements in a political system work to obtain influence. He may not be greatly concerned with the nature of the decision reached. However, the student of international politics is concerned with the decision-making process only in so far as that may also provide information about the sort of decisions which are likely to emerge. Indeed, there are still many international politics scholars who see the decision-making process as unimportant. They endorse a 'states as actors' approach which argues that all states behave in a basically similar way towards their external environments regardless of the nature of their domestic political systems. In brief, studies of domestic politics frequently discuss how governments decide; International Relations is about what they decide.

Because International Relations blends into matters concerning other disciplines such as economics, sociology and domestic politics, another factor becomes apparent, making for difficulty in producing theories of international political behaviour. This is that so many variables must be taken into account when any given act is analysed. Take, for example, the British decision to invade Egypt in 1956, an analysis of which involves weighting and integrating factors varying from Prime Minister Eden's poor personal physical condition and his experiences with Hitler and appeasement, to 'Britain's' difficulty in adapting to a smaller role in the world, to the availability of allies to take part in an invasion, the ambiguous policy of the most powerful state in the system and the apparent vulnerability of the Egyptian regime to external intervention. When more than a single act is considered, the number of variables involved becomes what James Rosenau has termed 'astronomical'. For instance, he has calculated that 'figured conservatively, what is summarily called a nation's "Latin American policy" involves attention to 89–100 continuing situations and several hundred thousand items of data' (Rosenau 1971, 35). He optimistically concludes that 'one need not be overwhelmed by such complexity' (Rosenau 1971, 37). But clearly attempts to keep track of and understand so many variables must meet enormous problems.

A related but separate problem of analysis is that on many matters the scholar does not have access to all the information needed. Governments often do not publicize how and why specific steps were taken, even though decades may have passed. For example, the full details of British and French collaboration with Israel over the Suez invasion had not been released in 1977. To a large degree, the International Relations academic always has too much information or too little.

The complexity of international politics has a number of implications for its study. In particular, it naturally provoked a search for the key variable or concept to simplify the sorting of relevant data and to make possible the explicit formulation of theory. Hence, just as in economics the premise that companies seek to maximize their profits enabled a vast amount of internally logical theory to be built up, so in International Relations it was hoped by some that the proposition that states pursue their national interest by seeking to maximize their power would also result in the build-up of theory (see Ch. 6). Academics attempting to produce theories in International Relations are always faced with what may be called the simplicity issue. Hypotheses which involve only a few variables have important virtues; in particular they are easy to understand and make very clear which data is relevant to the understanding of the essence of a situation. On the other hand, their very simplicity may cause them to lose contact with complex reality. Two-party game theory, for instance, can be criticized because it oversimplifies the situations in which decision-makers find themselves.

Hypotheses or models which incorporate a very large number of variables have perhaps even more significant disadvantages. They become difficult to understand and utilize, especially if the relevant variables are not carefully weighted and their interrelationship specifically analysed. Snyder et al. (1962) produced a scheme which claimed to incorporate all the determinants of the operation of the foreign policy decision-making process. The scheme emphasized the interaction and feedback between the 'Internal setting of decision-making', which was divided into three subcategories, the 'Social structure and behaviour' of the decision-making state, which was broken down into six subcategories, the 'External setting of decision-making' with its four subcategories, the actual 'Decision-making process' and the 'Action' taken. The model, designed as a framework for the classification of data and for the production of hypotheses, proved too cumbersome and only one major attempt (by Paige 1968) was made to utilize it, despite the fact that, in essence, it was a straightforward scheme, seeing the foreign policy process as being basically concerned with action, reaction and interaction. Theories of international integration, which in the writings of Mitrany and in the early works of Haas, were fundamentally easy to understand as they incorporated only a few key variables, steadily became more complex as academics endeavoured to make them fit reality more closely. As a result, some integration models, for instance that of George Mally (1973), which comprises eight sets of factors, which group together more than 100 categories, verge on the incomprehensible. In fairness, it should be added that Mally also gives fifteen specific hypotheses on integration and a further eight on disintegration.

While the complexity of international politics caused a search for simplicity as well as the occasional excessively complex model, it also produced an emphasis that description, explanation and prediction of events may be attempted using data derived from different layers of social organization. For example, an awareness grew up that the outbreak of war in 1939 may be attributed to the demonic personality of Hitler or to the expansionism of the totalitarian German state or to the absence of countervailing power in the international system to deter Germany, and that each of these constitutes a different type of explanation. The difficulty of deciding which kind of explanation is most appropriate or valid is immense. Discussion of this, the 'level of analysis' problem, began in the late 1950s and J. David Singer produced a paper which discussed the merits of analysing international politics at the state and international system level. He noted with regard to work done in International Relations:

*We have, in our texts and elsewhere, roamed up and down the ladder of organisational complexity with remarkable abandon, focusing upon the total system, international organizations, regions, coalitions, extra-national associations, nations, domestic pressure groups, social classes, elites and individuals as the needs of the moment required (*in Knorr and Verba 1961, 77–92*).*

In a brilliant philosophical analysis, in 1959 Kenneth Waltz published *Man, the State and War,* which dealt with the inevitability of war in the light of first, human nature, then the nature of states and finally the anarchic character of the state system.

With the work of Singer, Waltz and others the level of analysis problem was brought under control in the sense that scholars became aware of it. An explanation of the outbreak of the First World War which concentrated on the psychological condition of the Kaiser was seen as fundamentally different from one which laid emphasis on the inflexible alliances in being at the time. But the level of analysis problem was not solved in that it remained difficult to link propositions at one level with propositions at another. Generally, hypotheses at one level remained separate and unintegrated with hypotheses at other levels. However, some scholars began to offer propositions in which different levels were linked. For instance, some integration theorists moved towards the view that integration would take place through the processes of 'spillover' and attitude change if the economic and technological conditions for it were correct, that is if certain systemic pressures for integration were present, and if the states concerned had certain attributes such as a high degree of internal pluralism and similar attitudes to integration among their élites (see Schmitter in Lindberg and Scheingold 1970). The level of analysis problem is, of course, closely related to the number of variables issue; fundamentally, the lower the level of analysis selected, the more information becomes relevant to understanding the course of international politics. If we feel it is the individual which dominates, we are virtually asking the International Relations scholar to seek out the personality details of all relevant decision-makers as well as to scrutinize the environment in which they operate.

A final consequence of the complexity of international politics was the debate about what the scholar could hope to achieve and how he should set about achieving it. The debate between the 'traditionalists', who argued that accurate prediction is impossible in International Relations, and who produced explanations centred on concepts such as power, national interest and balance of power (which were often left undefined and which could not be quantified), and the 'behaviouralists', who advocated that all assumptions should be clearly spelled out and that only empirically verifiable hypotheses should be produced, was long, severe and continuing, but happily in a more restrained manner by the 1970s. James Rosenau maintained his preference for the scientific method,

As a focus of study, the nation-state is no different from the atom or the single cell organism. Its patterns of behaviour, idiosyncratic traits, and internal structure are as amenable to the process of formulating and testing hypotheses as are the characteristics of the electron or the molecule.

Yet he accepted that all International Relations scholar should study according to their own preferences, to 'play their own game' (Rosenau 1971, 17–21).

The debate between the two schools moderated, partly because it was realized that the bitterness which marked it was doing the discipline no good, but also because it was perceived increasingly that the two sides had much in common. 'Scientists' agreed that the hypotheses of the traditionalists, obtained largely through the reading of history and the use of intuition and judgement, could often be rearranged so as to be empirically testable or at least serve to stimulate the production of other hypotheses which may be tested. The scientific preference for stated assumptions became accepted by all as being desirable for logical thought and the traditionalists' argument against quantified evidence moderated to a warning that such evidence was often unavailable on important issues and that to rely on it could result in the neglect of unquantifiable factors. Such arguments do not reject quantified data outright, they simply call for care in its use. An important moderating factor was that it proved difficult to place scholars as being completely in one camp or the other. Hedley Bull (1966), in an oft-cited attack on the scientific-behavioural school, pointed out that many of the most interesting and important things which it had to say were derived from judgment and not scientific method. Certainly Morton Kaplan, for example, who is usually placed firmly in the scientific camp, makes clear in his conceptual models of international political systems that he considers military power as a, if not the most important factor in international politics. This in many ways is an essentially traditionalist viewpoint. A general point, of course, is that, in the last analysis, no theory is purely scientific in that it always owes something to judgement.[6] A final factor making for academic tolerance was that neither the scientists nor the traditionalists were sufficiently successful in the production of valid and useful theory as to be able loudly to mock the efforts of others. International Relations academics perhaps realized that people in glass houses . . .

Linked to the failure to make theoretical advances was the rise in the late 1960s of the 'post-behaviouralists': who were and are concerned mainly with peace research. This school placed less emphasis on scientific method as such and more on the need for any ideas which would reduce the incidence of war. An important feature of peace research thinking is that human conflict has a single nature and that war is but one manifestation of it. Playground fights and industrial strikes are others. Thus it is believed that the road to the understanding of the origins of war lies through trying to understand human conflict in general. Clearly, peace research threatens to break down the accepted divisions between the social sciences (see Ch. 12).

At best, there is thus something of an atmosphere of tolerance in the British and American academic communities; it is realized that different questions and issues may require different methodologies. At worst, academics agree to differ, accepting that attacking one's fellows does not, in itself, advance theory. Moreover, instead of searching for a conceptual unity for International Relations, scholars are trying to get on with the fundamental task of producing hypotheses and testing them against evidence (McClelland in Rosenau et al. 1972).

From the perspective of the early 1970s, the methodological debate among International Relations scholars may appear to have been often petty and mostly harmful. But, in all probability, it represented the unavoidable growing pains of a new discipline which, as has been shown, faced substantial methodological problems, and which, unlike the natural sciences, could not study problems which it necessarily felt could be solved. It had to study the problems which it felt needed to be solved.

International Relations is a discipline which has produced a considerable range of approaches for its study. In other words, many ggestions have been made as to what factors are important and as to how their study might be organized. But efforts to go further and produce theory– groups of related propositions dealing with the precise relevance and weight of each factor and its relationship to others – have proved less fruitful. However, the discipline is still young and perhaps it is more realistic to stress the imagination and thought shown so far rather than the failure to achieve ultimate success.

In the 1970s there is also considerable self-doubt as scholars worry that, despite five decades of effort, International Relations has not made substantial advances. There is a great awareness of the shortcomings of the propositions in the discipline about power, integration, decision-making and the like, and little enthusiasm about their good characteristics. The time, therefore, seems right to take stock, to bring together the approaches and hypotheses produced to date, to examine their intellectual origins and what they have in common and to see what their various contributions and limitations are. That is a function of this book.

International Relations prospects

In the 1960s and early 1970s many of the self-doubts which plagued International Relations scholars stemmed from their ambitious hopes for a general, empirically testable, internally logical, valid, explanatory theory of international politics with predictive powers. The search for a general theory of International Relations was much emphasized and the lack of such theory – apart from the power-politics propositions of Hans Morgenthau and others – much regretted. There was some concern that the discipline was producing only 'islands of theory' dealing with specialized topics which showed few signs that they could be linked together.

These fears represent great concern with the long-term and perhaps neglect of what is likely to be achieved in the 1970s. The ideal for International Relations may be to become 'an exact science', consisting of

a set of propositions derived from a logical argument and from which are established generalisations which 'explain' the existence and behaviour of phenomena. . . Such a theory is true if its conclusions correspond to every instance of the phenomena it seeks to explain. It is refuted if this correspondence fails to appear in any one instance (Reynolds 1973, 27).

However, such an ideal remains a remote possibility and, therefore, approaches with positive but restricted qualities must be welcomed. For instance, the communications approach of Karl Deutsch and the bureaucratic politics models of Graham Allison do not fulfil the criteria of 'an exact science', but they are fundamentally useful because they draw attention to specific and previously neglected factors affecting international political behaviour.

Furthermore, it must be recognized that problems concerning general theory are shared by many if not all social sciences. For example, a 1974 review of works on sociological theory included the statements that 'theories are nowadays demolished before the ink of their manifestos has dried or their founding fathers tactfully passed on' and 'Sociologists' contributions to the understanding of the world outside their study . . . have been remarkable for paucity not to say poverty' (Worsley 1974). Nevertheless, sociologists everywhere press on optimistically. In economics, one of the more 'scientific' of the social sciences, production continues of helpful models despite the failure to produce a quantified version of the all-important but subjective concept of utility. Theories, models and hypotheses are welcome in International Relations when they enable the scholar to amend and strengthen his views about international politics and to increase his understanding of world developments. Although the tools of analysis in International Relations may not enable him accurately to predict such developments, they should at least help him not to be surprised or baffled by specific events. Rosenau (1971, 7) may properly claim to be engaged on a 'search for certainty', but it is equally proper to accept that the search is unlikely to be fruitful in the mid-1970s and that, therefore, more modest results are still worth while. The problem which stimulated the birth and development of International Relations, the possibility of war with all its horrors, remains with us and in a much more serious form than when the discipline was born. The International Relations scholar cannot afford to be discouraged for, as Inis Claude (1962) argued, the problem of the management of destructive capabilities is the most important which mankind must solve. If solutions are not found, the outlook for all is bleak. Much responsibility, therefore, as well as academic challenge lies with the International Relations scholar and it is hoped that the chapters which follow, by examining the work done to date, may stimulate future effort.

Notes

1. A further 2,300 were employed in the Overseas Development Administration, *Civil Service Statistics* (1973, p. 9). The US State Department had a staff of 25,000 by the mid-1960s, see Crabbe (1965, 53).
2. For a list of the states in the system, see Purnell (1973, 309–14).
3. See Calder (1969, esp. 20, 132, 447, 448). The view of war as a phenomenon which ennobled the human spirit or strengthened society, which was professed by philosophers such as Hegel and endorsed by many military men, largely disappeared in the 1914–18 conflict. Churchill, a seeker of adventure in war in his youth, showed his later disillusionment in *My Early Life* (1930), 'War, which used to be cruel and magnificent, has now become cruel and squalid. In fact it has been completely spoilt. It is all the fault of Democracy and Science. . . Instead of a small number of well-trained professionals championing their country's cause with ancient weapons and a beautiful intricacy of archaic manoeuvre . . . we now have entire populations, including even women and children, pitted against one another in brutish mutual extermination, and only a set of blear-eyed clerks left to add up the butcher's bill. . . 'To Hell With It.' Quoted in Calder (1969, 104).

4. Substantial work has been done, much of it in the ecological field, including Falk (1971), Ward and Dubos (1972), Modelski (1972) and Sprout and Sprout (1972).
5. See, for example, Keohane and Nye (1970).
6. For a coherent discussion of the origins of theory see J.K. de Vree (1972, 54–93).

References and Further Reading

Allison, G.T. (1971) *Essence of Decision,* Boston, Little, Brown.

Bailey, S.D. (1972) *Prohibition and Restraint in War,* London, Oxford Univ. Press, for the RIIA.

Bull, H. (1966) 'International theory, the case for a classical approach', *World Politics,* April, also in K. Knorr and J.N. Rosenau (eds), *Contending Approaches to International Politics,* Princeton, NJ, Princeton Univ. Press, 1970.

Calvocoressi, P. and Wint, G. (1974) *Total War,* Harmondsworth, Penguin.

Calder, A. (1969) *The People's War,* London, Cape.

Carr, E.H. (1961) *What is History?* London, Penguin.

Churchill, W.S. (1930) *My Early Life,* London, Odhams Press.

Claude, I. (1962) *Power and International Relations,* New York, Random House.

Crabbe, C.V., Jnr. (1965) *American Foreign Policy in the Nuclear Age* (2nd edn), New York, Harper and Row, p. 53.

de Vree, J.K. (1972) *Political Integration: The Formation of Theory and its Problems,* The Hague and Paris, New Babylon.

Falk, R.A. (1971) *This Endangered Planet,* New York and Toronto, Random House.

Goodwin, G.L. (1973) 'International relations and international studies' *The Year Book of World Affairs, 1973,* Vol. 27, London, Stevens and Sons.

Herz, J.H. (1959) *International Politics in the Atomic Age,* New York, Columbia Univ. Press.

Herz, J.H. (1968) 'The territorial state revisited', first published in *Polity* 1 (1), since published in J.N. Rosenau (ed.), *International Politics and Foreign Policy,* New York, Free Press, 1969, 76–89.

Kaplan, M. (1957) *System and Process in International Politics,* New York, Wiley.

Keohane, R.O. and Nye, J.S. (1970) *Transnational Relations and World Politics,* Cambridge, Mass., Harvard Univ. Press.

Knorr, K. and Verba, S. (eds) (1961) *The International System,* Princeton, NJ, Princeton Univ. Press.

Lijphart, A. (1974) 'The structure of the theoretical revolution in international relations', *International Studies Quarterly,* **18** (1) (March).

Lindberg, L.N. and Scheingold, S.A. (1970) 'Regional integration, theory and research', *International Organisation,* xxiv (Autumn).

Mally, G. (1973) *The European Community in Perspective,* London, Lexington.

Mitrany, D. (1946) *A Working Peace System,* London, Royal Institute of International Affairs.

Modelski, G. (1972) *Principles of World Politics,* New York and London, Collier-Macmillan.

Paige, G.D. (1968) *The Korean Decision,* New York, The Free Press.

Pfaltzgraff, R., Jr. (1974) 'International relations theory', *International Affairs,* **50** (1) (January).

Platig, E.R. (1967) *International Relations Research,* Santa Barbara, Calif., Clio Press, for the Carnegie Endowment for International Peace.

Porter, B. (ed.) (1972) *The Aberystwyth Papers,* London, Oxford Univ. Press.

Purnell, R. (1973) *The Society of States,* London, Weidenfeld and Nicolson.

Quester, G. (1974) *The Continuing Problem of International Politics,* New York, Holt, Rinehart and Winston.

Reynolds, C. (1973) *Theory and Explanation in International Politics,* London, Martin Robertson.

Robertson, C.L. (1966) *International Politics Since World War II,* New York, Wiley.
Rosenau, J.N. (1971) *The Scientific Study of Foreign Policy,* New York, Free Press.
Rosenau, J.N., Davis, V. and East, M.A. (eds.) (1972) *The Analysis of International Relations,* London, Collier-Macmillan.
Singer, J.D. and Small, M. (1972) *The Wages of War,* New York, Wiley.
Small, M. and Singer, J.D. (1966) 'The diplomatic importance of states, 1816–1940', *World Politics,* xviii (January).
Snyder, R.C., Bruck, H.W. and Sapin, B. (eds.) (1962) *Foreign Policy Decision-Making: An Approach to the Study of International Politics.* New York, Free Press.
Sprout, H. and M. (1972) *The Politics of the Planet Earth,* New York, Van Nostrand.
Waltz, K.N. (1959) *Man, the State and War,* New York, Columbia Univ. Press.
Ward, B. and Dubos, R. (1972) *Only One Earth,* Harmondsworth, Penguin.
Woodward, Sir Llewellyn, (1962) *The Age of Reform 1815–70,* Oxford, Clarendon Press.
Worsley, P. (1974) *The Guardian* (13 June).
Wright, Q. (1955) *The Study of International Relations,* New York, Appleton-Century-Crofts.

Chapter 2

Theoretical approaches to International Relations: the contribution of the Graeco-Roman world

Robert Purnell

A Lack of Theory

We must start by admitting frankly that at no period of their history do Greek and Roman thinkers appear to have developed anything approaching a comprehensive and consistent theory of International Relations. Greek thought, most notably in the brains of Plato and Aristotle, certainly theorized elaborately about the state: its nature, scope, norms, potential for excellence, necessity to the living of a complete human life, its pathological forms and much else. But Greek philosophy had little to say about relations between states. Lidia Storoni Mazzolani (1970, 16) roundly declares:

In the political thought of the ancient world there is no systematic legal basis for coexistence between nations. The rights and duties of citizens, both towards each other and towards the State, were exactly and strictly regulated; but relationships between one people and another interested neither the theoretician nor the legislator. The outer world was only significant if it threatened invasion or promised plunder.

This state of affairs may seem surprising in view of the complex pattern of relationships between them that, in practice, characterized the ongoing collective life of sovereign political communities in the Graeco-Roman world. War, diplomacy and trade between states, perhaps on the whole in that order of importance, preoccupied citizens and their leaders in all the major *poleis* (and most of the lesser ones) in ancient Greece, as they did in the political communities of Italy until the decisive hegemony and then *imperium* of Rome was achieved.

How are we to account for this virtual absence of active theorizing about interstate relations? Two considerations may be suggested. Firstly, there is the sheer weight of intellectual demand made by political thought about the state upon that tiny minority of Greeks who actually theorized about politics at all. We must avoid any temptation to believe that the mass of Greek herdsmen, cultivators and artisans, even when free men, spent their days grappling with large philosophical themes or problems. They bore the burden of life, participated as the constitution and their avocations might allow in policy-making, and hoped that the state would provide such essential protection as would enable them to keep going from day to day and year to year. Still, Greeks collectively demonstrated a greatness which is still freely attributed to them in being pioneers of political thought and consequent practice. In a sense the Greeks may be said to have invented politics, at least in so far as politics implies decision-making about what is to be done pursued by processes of public debate. Both their political thought and the structures which embodied it – and frequently attracted trenchant criticism – represent a tremendous achievement. But just as the political vitality and power of the Greek city-states declined, so it may not be too fanciful to suggest that the intellectual effort involved in developing, virtually *ex nihil,* such elaborate conceptions of citizenship and its rights and duties as the emergence and history of the *polis* illustrate proved as much as the creative mind of the Greek people could compass in that particular field. We must not forget how intensely curious and active thought was in so many other areas of human enquiry and attainment through much of Greek history. It embraced science, art, philosophy beyond its more strictly political form, the cherished skills of rhetoric and, not least, in later Greek times certainly, the intricacies of a highly complex theology. Mental energy is limited among peoples as in individuals. When we survey what the Greeks did accomplish in the intensely exacting field of conceptualization we may feel like murmuring, 'Lo, it is enough'.'

The second reason is perhaps more prosaic. Greek literature, however uniquely various and splendid it may seem to be among the ancient literatures of the world, is still as it has come down to us only a fragment. Very much was produced that has been lost. Though it may seem unlikely, we cannot be sure that important theoretical approaches to interstate relations were never made by Greek political thinkers and subsequently lost. Sophocles, for instance, wrote apparently some 123 plays, all highly successful – he was placed first and second in the drama festivals but never third – yet we have only seven extant with some fragments of others. Time winnows harshly. On the other hand, even had a substantive theoretical work disappeared, some abstract, digest, summary or reference would probably have survived. So we may conclude that so far as the Greeks are concerned we shall be obliged, in seeking to deduce their conceptual approach to interstate relations, to rely heavily on implications drawn from how the *poleis* actually tended to behave towards each other. And we may be permitted, too, to extrapolate elements of interstate theory from the complex theories the Greeks did develop about political relations between citizens.

Moreover, when, from the third century BC onwards, Hellenistic philosophers quite specifically thought beyond the city-state to envisage types of *cosmopolis,* emphasis lay on the conception of a more or less unified world order and of the *individual's* place in it. International Relations in terms of coexisting multiple sovereign units was thus transcended. Cosmopolitan thought was to be profoundly influential, and take several forms, finding a sanction both in an advanced paganism and a highly institutionalized Christianity. This concept of a world order envisaged a kind of 'world-city', coextensive with the human race itself, and of which, as a natural consequence, individual men were citizens. Clearly such a conception, however tentative or but partially realized in actual institutions, would transform any existing notions about an international system of the conventional kind, and about international law conceived as a means of regulating relations between states.

In some respects the Romans represent a separate case from the Greeks. In their practical if derivative way they took over the body of Greek theory about the state and such thinking as there was concerning interstate relations. This is not the least important aspect of the profound cultural debt owed by the ultimately dominant Romans to the Greek people they came to govern. Cicero's *Republic,* for instance, is not very much more than a respectful plagiary of Plato's great Dialogue. However, political necessities arising from the growth of Roman power, and the attainment by the city-state on the Tiber of the *imperium* of the whole Mediterranean littoral, did give rise to important ideas concerning the relations of the Roman state – strictly the *res publica,* the 'public thing' managed by the Senate and people of Rome – with other political communities within and beyond the area of Roman jurisdiction.

A whole complex of 'international relations' thus developed between Rome and her federated allies (*foederati*), her *municipa* (cities within the Empire enjoying local self-government), client states along the Roman borders in varying conditions of allied dependency, enjoying Roman protection and contributing to Roman security, and not least the independent powers beyond the frontiers; this last a relationship as often of 'cold war' or active hostilities as of peaceful coexistence.

Such a political experience gave rise to a body of 'international law' (*ius gentes*), which evolved in response to the need to provide norms and precedents for the regulation of relations between political communities. Such a 'law of peoples' implicitly represented a recognition that, whatever pretensions to world rule imperial Rome might be supposed to entertain, the world was not, and might never become, a monolith of political unity. However, reflections by jurisconsults upon prescriptive legal relations between peoples coexisted with persistent visions of a genuine world order, embracing in theory the whole of human society. In the fourth century AD St Augustine envisaged such an order in the form of two interrelated and complementary aspects. These were both aspects of an ultimately monistic 'City of God'. The spiritual order sanctified the temporal order, which, however imperfect, lay under divine government, and fulfilled divine purposes. As an instrument of God's will the temporal order, 'the world', the City of Men, rightfully demanded their allegiance. Thus the *cosmopolis* of Hellenistic sages became theologized into a divinely ordained world order, existing indeed amidst the evil of original sin, and in its manifestations sharing in that sinfulness, yet also providing the essential context in which, and at least partly the means by which, men could seek and attain their salvation.

St Augustine's conception is, in fact, a special case of the instrumental view of the state which sees it as providing the means by which men may be enabled to lead the Good Life. In this respect Augustinian thought derives from and develops in a particular theological direction a fundamental element in Platonism. What St Augustine does not do, because his political monism excludes it, is to develop a theory of norms to govern relations between sovereign states. The concept of sovereignty had become in effect monopolized by the Roman *imperium*. However much Alaric the Goth in sacking Rome in AD 410 might be regarded as a manifestation of evil inherent in a fallen world, or an instrument of providential retribution for the sins of Romans, or a sign of the anger of the tutelary gods of the Roman state at their abandonment in favour of the religion of Jesus Christ, he was not regarded as a fellow-sovereign with the Roman Emperor, or as representing a component of an international system. The concept of what we might call 'the singularity of legitimacy' in respect of the Roman state lingered on in men's minds long after the formal ending of the Western Empire with the deposition in AD 476 of Romulus Augustulus. The barbarian successor kings in Italy usually sought formal ratification of their office by the remaining Emperor at Constantinople, and often regarded the title of 'Patrician' conferred upon them by the Eastern Emperor as the most significant and prestigious of their titulary honours.

The Homeric Concept

Let us return to the Greeks. There is in Homer no conception of an international system. Instead we have hints of a form of paramountcy, entitling and enabling Agamemnon to summon a great coalition of chiefs and their contingents to a major military enterprise: the war against Troy.

The leaders so allied are warrior *hetairoi*, 'companions', both of each other and also of the nobles whom they led. Stress is laid by Homer on the warrior virtues of courage and prowess, and on the rights attaching to honour. (When Agamemnon refused to allot the girl captive, Briseis, to her captor Achilles, as custom prescribed, the latter's honour was insulted and he skulked in his tent.) Of a clearly defined network of reciprocities between what were evidently the princely representatives of autonomous political communities there is scarcely a trace. Nor is there of any theory to explain relations between the 'states' contributing their contingents (which Homer carefully lists) to the Trojan campaign. Even the fighting itself, protracted as it has been, seems spasmodic, haphazard and pursued by no clear strategic principles or even much in the way of tactical planning (Andrewes 1971).

Of course with Homer we are in the realm of epic, not political analysis. Still, we do obtain a picture of a collectivity of states of a sort, acknowledging some sense of mutual obligation, in regard to concerted military action at least, and functioning as a loose confederation for a specific purpose under a recognized 'High King' who, pre-eminent in dignity as he may be, does not derive or confirm his authority by any pre-eminence in feats of arms.

We can then, hardly seek in Homer for even a nascent conception of international politics in any sense that modern political scientists would regard as substantive. However, in a broader context we may be struck by Rex Warner's (1972, 174) considered judgement that Homer's world, 'in which everyone is good and everyone may be unfortunate, where . . . difficult questions of personal or communal morality simply do not arise' remains none the less 'perhaps the most perfect, satisfying and, in a sense, true world ever created or described by man'.

The Classical City-State System

As distinct from the political institutions and processes of the Mycenean age as dimly remembered and anachronistically distorted by the poets of the Homeric period, Classical Greece is a very different matter.

Here there is the familiar complex of city-states, some 1,500 of them, ranging in size and importance from great, powerful and sometimes luxurious cities to tiny fortified settlements at the heads of remote valleys, all assertively sovereign until conquered or destroyed, or laid under the subjection of a stronger city, all pursuing interstate relations more or less continuously on a larger or smaller scale. Yet, as we have suggested, the Greeks of the Classical age, for all their acute sense of politics and their correspondingly exuberant and elaborate practice of it, and the lively interest of thinkers and rhetoricians in the phenomena of statehood, did not create anything closely approaching a systematic analysis of interstate behaviour or a developed explanation of it.

But there is something. If Homer's legendary heroes had an obsessive preoccupation with warriors' honour, the Classical Greeks (who retained something of that) were passionately interested in the notion of justice. One suspects that many Greeks would have agreed with Michael Oakeshott in contesting the conception of *Justice* as an absolute value in itself, or as constituting an actual condition of things. But justice as a sense of what is felt to be fair, in a given situation, and a given condition of society, mattered to the Greeks greatly. Thus Thucydides in Book V of his *History of the Peloponnesian War* deals with the issue of relations between Athens and Melos in terms which indicate that certain norms of interstate behaviour enjoyed a measure of recognition in the fifth century BC and that expectations could be flouted. Melos, a small island state, an old Spartan colony, was making difficulties about paying tribute to Athens as a member of the Delian League. The Athenians proposed to reduce the recalcitrant Melians by force, with complete disregard for any 'justice' there might be in the Melian case. The ambassadors from Melos are represented by Thucydides as pleading for fair play in interstate relations, which the Athenians dismiss with the argument, expressed by the great historian in epigrammatic form, that 'fair play' is in fact determined by those able to impose their will; that the powerful do what they can and the feeble bear what they must.

This insistence is echoed by Thrasymachus in Plato's *Republic* when in his famous discussion with Socrates he is made to argue that history shows justice to be the will of the stronger. This kind of 'realism' is akin to the grim assertion of Karl Marx that actual political values and state institutions are maintained to preserve the power and privileges of ruling classes. The merit of such realistic interpretation of political behaviour is that it undermines *naïveté* and exposes humbug. Its danger lies in an implied totality of explanation which gives insufficient place to genuine scruples and the observance of norms which may actually constrain the mere assertion of self-interest. In a world of alleged ruthless *realpolitik,* small and weak political communities do in fact survive for long periods: indeed, as in ancient Greece and contemporary international society, they may tend to proliferate. And the context of their emergence and survival by no means suggests that they emerge and survive merely or always as a function of mutual deterrence on the part of great powers. Something analogous to a 'right to life' is customarily attributed to states which have achieved an institutional presence in the world. At the same time Bertrand Russell's (1940) insight as expressed in his study of *Power* remains relevant, whether in reference to the modern world or to the competitive city-states of the Graeco-Roman world, namely, that states on the whole desire to maximize their power (for a variety of purposes) and tend to extend their power outwards to the limit at which the countervailing power of other states acts as an effective check. So far as crude territoriality is concerned, this tendency was more evident in the ancient world than in ours, where the sophistications of modern economic and political penetrability may safeguard or enhance power without any question of actual territorial expansion.

Competitive Power versus Stable Order

In general it seems necessary to stress that the Greek preoccupation with justice was precisely *not* a concern with equality. Aristotle with somewhat unnerving candour declares, for instance, that there is an inherent quality of slavishness characterizing certain men. This justifies their actual enslavement. Justice is thus rendering to each man according to his deserts. It is as unjust to treat unequals equally as to treat equals unequally. As between men, so between sovereign cities. It then becomes not only unrealistic but actually unjust for a small, weak and backward city to expect the kind of consideration from its neighbours which is to be shown, both from motives of propriety and doubtless prudence as well, to great and powerful cities. Admittedly, this frank recognition of the highly unequal distribution of power and hence of political opportunity is qualified in the minds of both Plato and Aristotle by a conception of optimum size for a *polis.* To both men Athens in reality represented a dangerous departure in scale from the 5,000-strong collectivity of citizens envisaged as approximating to the ideal. However, a consequence of the divergence of the real world from an ideal world was a recognition, regretful or otherwise, that the strong would normally strive to grow stronger and the weak seek to avoid becoming weaker. Underlying all the complexities of trading links and diplomatic negotiations, and evident in the prevalence of warfare, the characteristic relationship of the *poleis* with each other was one of competitive coexistence, to borrow a phrase contributed to the vocabulary of political discourse by the precepts and practice of the Soviet Union in international relations. In interstate politics no less than in most other aspects of their daily life the brilliant and inventive Greeks remained intensely competitive. Paradoxically the fear and hatred Greeks entertained towards the effective hegemony of any one city were an expression of their political competitiveness equally with the actual tendency of the greatest cities to attempt to achieve it.

There is evidence, too, of a real division between cities in the matter of observing understood norms and usages of international behaviour. While some accepted that their conduct of relations with other cities should remain subject to that body of perhaps rather vaguely defined constraints known as *Nomos,* a 'moral law', so others pressed for the disregard of the bindingness of formal treaties and even for the abandonment of 'unwritten laws of decency and fairness'. (Sinclair 1961, Ch. 6). Indeed the temptation to de-moralize interstate relations was bound to be strong in an environment which laid such normative stress on the principle of autonomy. If the collective 'virtue' of a city lay mainly in its independent status, what could it well do other than seek its own advantage? And for some Greeks who accepted the sharp logic of this situation advantage would come to be less and less compromised by the means of its attainment. A moral rejoinder to this kind of naked *Machtpolitik* was the belief put forward in Corinth that the great Hellenic powers had a duty to check a drive to domination by any one city or any combination of cities: a faint prefiguring perhaps of a notion of collective security.

Thucydides,[1] while he did not produce a developed theory of interstate relations, revealed a piercing vision of the consequences attendant upon the fighting of a great and prolonged war between the principal states of Greece and their respective alliance systems. These consequences included the overturn of received values, the increased incidence of treachery, a catastrophic fall in the level of honesty, kindliness and restraint and the general prevalence of *stasis,* or disorder. This was most sombrely typified by a condition in which responsible men found themselves powerless and powerful men acknowledged no responsibility. Thucydides's masterpiece, though never completed, has the wholeness of a consistent vision; essentially a tragic vision. He adduces no prescriptions from his data. He seems instead to assume that men tend to behave badly and that when they do evil effects naturally follow. We might almost conclude that a recognition of the likelihood of *stasis* as characteristic of relations between fiercely competitive sovereign cities *was* Thucydides' theoretical approach to the interstate system he knew.

The Domestic Determinants of Inter-state Behaviour

It is notorious that Plato was an anti-democrat. Both the late R. H. S. Crossman (1959) and Sir Karl Popper (1962), from their differing points of view, have authoritatively qualified Plato's greatness on this ground. The peculiar charm of the dialogue method of exposition as handled by Plato, and his seductive style, prompted some liberal idealists, among them perhaps Goldsworthy Lowes Dickinson and Sir Richard Livingstone, if not to misunderstand him at least to discount his stern critique of democratic politics. To redress the balance Plato has been equally laid under contribution by prescriptive authoritarians. Dictators of the Left and Right, in their philosophic moments, have appealed to the sanction of Plato. It seems probable enough that though Plato was primarily concerned with the state in regard to its structure and internal political relations, as we have suggested all the Greek political theorists essentially were, his mistrust and resentment towards the rule of the many in part derived from what he believed to be ignorant, ill-conceived and wrong-headed mob judgements in the field of foreign policy. It was democratic decision-making under the persuasion of often demogogic leaders which determined strategic policy during the Peloponnesian War. This proved a chastening experience which seems to have influenced the young Plato in ways that were reflected in his thinking throughout his life.

Where political norms were concerned, as distinct from any method of conducting international relations, it seems likely that Plato's contempt for the democracy reflected his belief that common men were but too prone to reveal a collective coarseness of moral sensibility in keeping with their tendency to be stupid and vicious. And in this regard Plato may well have been as much concerned with a conception of international decencies as with the problem of justice between men: decencies only too liable to be ignored or even denounced by vociferous representatives of the *Ecclesia,* seeking to determine policy in meeting-days on the Agora. The mature philosophers who were to be trained to rule and to be the guardians of the state and all its interests in Plato's prescriptive scheme would be expected to exercise in their conduct of interstate relations the same calm wisdom and unshakable virtue which was intended to characterize Platonic government within the state. Yet implicitly Plato kept his feet on the ground, however his Republic might be 'laid up in the heavens', by insisting on the continuing need, whatever norms of international behaviour might be desired to prevail, to train and maintain a warrior caste: men with their own special *arete* or virtue, who represented the *spirited,* courageous quality of the organic state, and who thereby could defend it against assailants from without. At no point is the possibility of the Platonic state being involved in war excluded. This at least reflected a prevailing reality in the interstate politics of Greece.

Indeed, during the decades of Plato's most fruitful intellectual activity – he was born about 427 BC – from somewhat before the euphemistically named 'King's Peace' of 387 to around 350 the international system of Hellas was as disturbed, confused, violent and filled with inter-city belligerency as at any time in Classical history. After the defeat of Athens near the close of the fifth century, first Sparta then Thebes wrestled for the hegemony. The Greek cities generally grew more exhausted. Mercenary armies, comprising impoverished but able-bodied citizens from many states, abounded. *Stasis* was in many respects the salient characteristic of the time. And to *stasis,* Plato may fairly be presumed to believe, democracy, with its inherent qualities of excitability and unpredictability, made its own distinctive contribution.

The wonder remains that despite *stasis,* and largely in reaction to it, impressive and often profound intellectual analysis of men's collective predicaments continued. Not in conditions of prevailing peace, calm and prosperity, but rather in the opposite were the great insights and most significant prescriptions of Greek political thought developed. If *The Republic* is in some respects an ideal state, Plato had no grounds in terms of contemporary experience to imagine that it would be delivered from the hard necessities of self-defence. Plato even hints that the Republic might justifiably employ its warriors in offensive action on behalf of state interests held to be legitimate. Certainly in the context Plato conceived for his city he nowhere appeared to suppose that war was a mere aberration, an abnormality. On the contrary Plato remained firmly representative of the collective Greek mind in apparently recognizing that war remained a central, if tragic, feature of international life.

Meta-diplomatics Undeveloped

A real block to the development of a sophisticated theory of international relations among the Greeks may be found in their habit of referring to actual city-states as a body of people rather than a named political unit. We are familiar with what C. A. W. Manning (1962) called the 'meta-diplomatics' involved in attributing individuality and personality to states. This usage is reinforced by the theory of international law, which defines international personality as a function of state sovereignty, and provides that sovereign states are individual subjects of international law. Thus we quite accurately, in terms of diplomatic and legal theory, speak of 'Prussia' invading 'France' in late July 1870, or of 'England' (itself a synonym here for the United Kingdom of Great Britain and Ireland) presenting 'Germany' (i.e. the German Empire) with an ultimatum in early August 1914. Similarly it was 'Britain', not the British, who joined the European Economic Community in January 1972. The Greeks in their commentary upon interstate affairs did not indulge in such abstractions. Their *myth* of international relationships was less developed. For them 'the Athenians', not Athens, went to war with 'the Spartans' sometimes called more broadly 'the Lacedaemonians', not Sparta. It was 'the Megareans', not Megara, who had the decrees issued against them, which action by the Athenians was a precipitant of the Peloponnesian War. This was more than a mere point of semantics. The Greeks had an intense conception of personality. They were immensely interested, as Herodotus shows in his *Histories,* in the observed or believed play of personal factors in political outcomes. But they did not, as we do, attribute personality, and therefore, by natural extension, volition, moral sense and good or ill will to states themselves. This limited the degree to which they could theorize about relations between states as such.

Here again the Roman experience is somewhat different. The Greeks vividly personalized their gods. Athens, the city, was seen as firmly under the protection of its tutelary deity, Pallas Athene. This had many consequences. Continued protection was to be guaranteed by collective and elaborate acts of public worship. The goddess herself, rather than simply the state, or 'the Athenians', was represented in the persons of accredited heralds and ambassadors. This was in a manner analogous to that in which, in later diplomatic practice, European ambassadors represented their respective sovereigns, and, through that representation, their sovereigns' respective patrimonial states. Similarly, as diplomatic immunity came to express the norm of international behaviour whereby representatives of a sovereign could expect to be treated honourably as the sovereign in person would expect to be treated, so the embassies of antiquity expected to enjoy the kind of deference and safety from maltreatment that would be shown to the divine persons on whose behalf they exercised their diplomatic function. So sacredness attached to the persons of ancient heralds, in their role as such, and to insult or mishandle them was a form of sacrilege. But the Greek state itself was not divine, although it was indeed as much of a religious as a political institution. However, in the case of the Romans there came to be a measure of sacred, even divine, personality ascribed to the Roman state as such. *Roma* was personified as herself of at least quasi-divine nature. As the Roman sense of mission and 'manifest destiny' grew in the period of the late Republic, and was fully articulated under the aegis of the monarchical Empire, altars were raised and rites established to provide for the religious observance of the divine claims of the city itself, and of the genius of Rome. This practice existed side by side with and powerfully reinforced the attribution of divine status to the emperors.

Although Augustus forbade emperor-worship within the city, and discouraged it throughout Italy, he sanctioned it as a unifying practice in the provinces, and certainly encouraged all Romans to pay divine honours to *Roma*.

However, this divergence from Greek habits did not lead among Romans to a developed attribution of diplomatic personality to states generally. *Roma* was unique. She presided with a majesty that was, in its political as in its religious connotations, *sui genesis*, over the relations of the Senate and people of Rome with other political communities both within and beyond the imperial spheres of influence.

Realism, Idealism and the 'World State'

We may finally envisage a political spectrum. One pole represents 'realism' of an absolute and therefore unattainable kind. Here international behaviour is totally self-regarding. Considerations of expediency alone determine policy. No rights whatever are attributed to other members of international society. Moral scruples have no admissibility at all. The assertion of self-interest by means of the instrumentalities of power is wholly untrammelled. At the other pole lies an absolute idealism. Here all policy is directed to self-abnegation and the subordination of all self-regarding claims totally to the claims of others.

On such a continuum we may feel that such evidence as we have requires us to locate the conceptions and intuitions of the ancients, so far as their international relations were concerned, somewhere towards the realist pole. This we may suggest indicates a marked similarity with the conceptions prevailing in contemporary international society.

Such a location does not of course obliterate a real distinction between the collective experience of Greeks and Romans. In the case of the former the preoccupation with power – its manifestations, acquisition, extension and uses – was linked to a passion for particularism. There was the acknowledgement of a certain ethnic unity in Hellas. Greeks observed a general devotion to a number of pan-Hellenic religious cults and festivals. These undoubtedly played a major part in Greek collective life. Greeks certainly indulged a sense of shared cultural and political superiority to the barbarians dwelling beyond the perceived if somewhat imprecise bounds of Hellas as a whole; those whose speech was unintelligible and who were not 'free men'. Despite all this, intra-Hellenic particularism was never significantly transcended, even by the Leagues of Classical and Hellenistic Greece. Unity was only imposed, not achieved, although as ultimately a Roman province Hellas continued to enrich that Mediterranean civilization which the Roman *imperium* so magnificently defended.

When we come to Rome we find from an early date a willingness to practise *realpolitik* as exuberant as that of the Greeks. But Rome almost from the beginning used such power as she commanded both to conquer and to conciliate. By such means Rome developed a characteristic drive towards a wider and wider hegemony, first in Italy and then beyond. If, in the proud words Thucydides puts in the mouth of Pericles, Athens was the school of Greece, she never mastered it, and her short-lived imperial phase was always equivocal. Rome became the undisputed queen of the Mediterannean world. It was as such that, through her political practitioners, her administrators and, above all perhaps, her lawyers, she developed a vision of a universal order bringing the benefits of a high civilization to many diverse peoples: an order, however partially and imperfectly realized, of which the instrumentalities of power were, in principle at any rate, the servants, and to which the harsh demands of *realpolitik* were, in aspiration at least, essentially subordinate.

These two linked yet distinctive historical experiences of the Greek and Roman peoples have some relevance to contemporary political conceptions, if only to illustrate aspects of the human predicament, which, from one form and period of world order to another, retain suggestive similarities. Both in respect of the eventual cosmopolitan vision of the later Greeks and the imperial Romans, as of the significant failure of the Greeks to attain a political union by consent, the experience of the Graeco-Roman world and the rudimentary theorizing about International Relations to which that experience gave rise remain timely, and find, we may suggest, an appropriate if minor place in the present work.[2]

Notes

1. For a satisfactory version of *The Peloponnesian War* see Crawley (1910).
2. The finest version of Plato in English is still probably the monumental work by Jowett (1892) with analyses and introductions. There is an excellent version of Aristotle's *Politics* in Penguin Classics, 1962, translated and introduced by T.A. Sinclair. Other books which may be profitably consulted include Balsdon (1965), Levi (1965), Ryder (1965), Burn (1968), Hooper (1968), Grant (1970) (admirable on Thucydides), and Mossé (1973).

References and Further Reading

Andrewes, A. (1971) *Greek Society,* London, Pelican Books.
Balsdon, J.P.V.D. (ed.) (1965) *Roman Civilization,* London, Penguin Books.
Burn, A.R. (1968) *The Warring States of Greece,* London, Thames and Hudson.
Crawley, R. (trans.) (1910) Thucydides, *The Peloponnesian War,* London, Everyman's Library.
Crossman, R.H.S. (1959) *Plato Today* (rev. 2nd ed.), London, Unwin Books.
Grant, M. (1970) *The Ancient Historians,* London, Weidenfeld and Nicolson.
Hooper, F. (1968) *Greek Realities,* London, Hart-Davies.
Jowett, B. (1892) *The Dialogues of Plato,* 5 vols. (3rd edn.), London, Macmillan.
Levi, M.A. (1965) *Political Power in the Ancient World,* trans. J. Costello, London, Weidenfeld and Nicolson.

Manning, C.A.W. (1962) *The Nature of International Society,* London, Bell.
Mazzolani, L.S. (1970) *The Idea of the City of Roman Thought,* trans. S. O'Donnell, London, Hollis and Carter.
Mossé, C. (1973) *Athens in Decline,* London, Routledge and Kegan Paul.
Popper, K.R. (1962) 'The spell of Plato' in *The Open Society and Its Enemies,* Vol. 1 (rev. 4th edn.) London, Routledge.
Russell, B. (1940) *Power,* London, Basic Books.
Ryder, T.T.B. (1965) *Koine Eirene, General Peace and Local Independence in Ancient Greece,* Oxford and London, Oxford Univ. Press.
Sinclair, T.A. (1961) *A History of Greek Political Thought,* London, Routledge paperback.
Warner, R. (1972) *Men of Athens,* London Bodley Head.

Chapter 3

European Political Philosophy and the theory of International Relations

P. Savigear

The theory of the state in Europe, from its beginnings in the High Renaissance, spawned a theory of International Relations. Yet the predominance of the theory of the state in the writings of European political thinkers has left the thought about the relations between states in some obscurity. The fate of this thought has been reminiscent of that of prose in the life of Monsieur Jourdan, Molière's *Bourgeois Gentilhomme* (Act 2, scene 4): 'Par ma foi! il y a plus de quarante ans que je dis de la prose sans que j'en susse rien.' The study of political thought from the time of Machiavelli reveals a rich corpus of references to and consideration of the international behaviour of states, so that the question begged by Martin Wight over ten years ago, 'Why is there no international theory?' (Butterfield and Wight 1966), could have been most amply embellished from four centuries of political thought, letters and commentaries on the relations of the European states. However, in so far as the political theorists and philosophers of Europe from Machiavelli to the First World War concerned themselves with these relations, they presented this for the most part as an extension of the arguments about the nature of the state. The 'classical' theory of International Relations had, in common with the theory of the state, a close connection with the evolution of philosophy and with the actual growth and history of the strong state. International Relations was then seen as a consequence of the nature of the state, a subordinate branch of political theory. Too often thought about International Relations was lost in the argument about the state and the individual.

Nevertheless the peculiar quality of the relations between states was revealed when attention was turned explicitly to the world of states. The understanding of the relations of states in this body of theory found its dynamic, the impetus providing the persistent foundations for theorizing, in two features of the political landscape, the constitution of the state and the need to change the world for the better. These two contrasting points provided a tension and required a theory in order to reconcile their conflicting demands.

International Relations were essentially interstate relations, and thought about these relations has been conservative of the state because without the state the basis of this body of writing disappeared. The state which lay at the core of 'classical' theory was the central state, independent in its command over the means of defence and attack, in the public control of the economy through the minting of money, and the centralization of law by which the people were governed.[1] The terrible consequences of such power, contrasting with the legalistic preoccupations of the medieval period, were first seen in fifteenth-century Italy and Burgundy and thence spread through the rest of Europe in the creation of dynastic empires, the absolutist states of the eighteenth century and the complex political organisms of the nineteenth and twentieth centuries. The morphology of the state, the necessity which it imposed upon the statesmen and peoples, obliged any speculation about International Relations to meet the argument that no relations were possible between such entities. Politics, in short, could only exist within the states and not between them, and that therefore there could not be a theory of disorder in which no regular relations were discernible. The very strength of the state presented theorists of International Relations with their starting-point, to show how such relations could emerge, and this obligation is as important for T. H. Green and Heinrich von Treitschke writing about the behaviour of states in the late nineteenth century as it was for Machiavelli at the beginning of the sixteenth. The world of chaos between states was the so-called world of states described by Thomas Hobbes, where '. . . Kings, and Persons of Soveraigne authority, because of their Independency, are in continual jealousies, and in the state and posture of Gladiators; having their weapons pointing, and their eyes fixed on one another; that is, their Forts, Garrisons, and Guns, upon the Frontiers of their Kingdomes; and continuall Spyes upon their neighbours' (Ch. 13, p. 89–131). Some conception of order had to be demonstrated for International Relations to exist as a theory. The 'classical' theorists retained the integrity of the state and sought conceptions of order consistent with the state. Where this presupposition was rejected, a quite distinct body of thought developed, that of the revolutionary thinkers.

The second element in the philosophy of the relations between states was an ethical one. Drawing on the ideas of justice and morality, observers of the facts of interstate relations were led to inject a desire for change and improvement in the apparently single-minded concern of the state and of its spokesmen for power and the relations founded on power. The tension that was thereby generated, between the description of the state and the necessary results of its nature for the world of states, and the desire to provide that world with a moral basis and to sustain an argument about choice, and therefore the possibility of taking the 'right' choice in the policies of states, this tension served as a continual motor driving the theory of International Relations.

The legacy left to the theory of International Relations from the 'classical' political philosophy of Europe is thus most immediately found in the mass of separate works, both distinguished and the rather mundane, which poured from the presses from the period of the Italian Renaissance. Nevertheless some attempt has been frequently made to ascribe some form to this seeming hotch-potch of writings linked only by the thin thread of attention to the external policy of states. Some such attempts have tried to go beyond a straightforward account of a chronological kind which implies a direct lineage from one author to the next. Most distinguished of such commentators in recent years has been Martin Wight. He sought to isolate 'Western values in international relations' (Butterfield and Wight 1966, Ch. 5, p. 91). He selected four 'figures in the pattern', namely international society, the maintenance of order, intervention and international morality. The focus of this exercise was to establish a tradition. He hoped to show that 'this pattern of ideas is persistent and recurrent. Sometimes eclipsed and distorted, it has constantly reappeared and reasserted its authority, so that it may even seem something like a consensus of Western diplomatic opinion' (Butterfield and Wight 1966, 90).

Yet the attempt to isolate themes, however recurrent and persistent, opens a gulf between the thoughts of the original writers and the mind of the commentator. The question is begged how far such themes are being imposed upon the literature. We are in a difficulty about the nature of the 'coherent pattern of ideas' which are seen to exist through so many texts; are they no more than a scheme imposed from outside, an attempt to make these works respond to an order to which they are alien? We cannot know. There is a question, however, to which some answer can be made and which enables some qualitative judgement of the texts devoted to International Relations to be made, namely why do such patterns persist? No matter whether the particular four selected by Martin Wight or whether another series are perceived working through the body of thought, how is it that there should be any constancy at all? The answer is that thought about the international world is wedded to the state in a way more fundamentally than any other branch of political theory.

The thought about interstate relations is in essence of the same kind. The ideas return always to the state, the state understood in a crucially similar way, a way established by the political writers of late medieval Italy, from Marsilio di Padua to Machiavelli and the publicists of the later Renaissance. Once this basis of thought in the central state was abandoned, then the entire conception of International Relations changed, and this abandonment did occur in the nineteenth and twentieth centuries. Others then rejected the state altogether, or sought to explain International Relations by constituting a political order superior to the state, or indeed seeking to explain away the state as a structure or system corresponding to some carefully delineated political model.[2] All this thought was different in kind from that which dominated the previous 400 years, and in which all other ideas were reconciled to the idea of the state or the attempt was made so to reconcile them. To say that International Relations as a strain of ideas was conservative in the European tradition is to say something about its very nature. Higher moral considerations, history, all other ideas that developed in the intellectual vocabulary and in the minds of political philosophers, had to be accommodated to that of the state as the foundation of International Relations. The state was thus accepted and not questioned in the thought about International Relations. Thus there seems to be a difference between the body of writing about International Relations and that devoted to the government and the internal ordering of the state.

The state has changed – the precise form of that change may be in dispute, some would say from dynastic to absolutist and to democratic for example – and the philosophy of the state has changed with it. Thought about International Relations, and indeed International Relations themselves, have not so changed. This thought, in all the many pieces of writing, returns again and again to the same point, the state, which it cannot allow to be destroyed. There is not the same sense of moving forward through the history of thought that characterizes the traditional presentation of political theory because in a way there *was* a progression in the changing nature of the relationship between ruler and ruled and the consequences for that relationship of the introduction of new ideas, like that of the General Will for example. The conception of the state was thus eroded from within by the theorists of the internal ordering of the state, but this did not happen for those writers who drew their arguments about International Relations from political philosophy. Their commitment to the state was stronger, and their first principle was to reconcile how the state is and how it ought to be. It is with the state and the political world in which the state operated that the theory of International Relations is thus concerned, and was to remain so until the state itself came under attack, for the most part from the political 'Left', and from those whose arguments sought to demonstrate the erosion of the notion of the independence of the state and the inevitability of this process. This chapter is about those theorists who assumed that the integrity and sovereignty of the state was a necessary part of International Relations and who wrote about the politics of those relations.

The existence of the state and the creation of relations with other states did not therefore pass unobserved by those attempting to philosophize about the nature of the political world as they saw and lived it. The task of many of the first political theorists looking at the state was to urge the primacy of that institution at the expense of other, older political forms like the guilds and feudatories. The state did not simply exist as a set of institutions, but made a claim upon the loyalty and service of the citizens which meant that the state took on moral quality which demanded priority and obedience. The state in the minds of the theorists of International Relations was a moral entity whose 'right' could be defined and defended against other moral claims.

Machiavelli was clearly one of the strongest proponents of this argument in urging that the ruler's duty was to the political entity and its security and not to any other moral code. The distinction between the public and the private realm was taken, from the outset, into the body of international thought and was not a central issue of debate as with many political theorists of the state. International Relations could not be conducted if the state itself could not possess moral force and the emergence of the subject was dependent upon this. If private moral considerations could override the moral force of the state and the public realm, then International Relations would be subordinated to the moral dictates of conscience, and judgements between political organizations made on the basis of ideas coming from outside politics. The public realm acquired a rightful authority which could stand up to the right of private conscience. Machiavelli was adamant about this. Politics had to be judged from a political standpoint, as much in the relations between states as within the state. It was this conviction that led him to give primacy to the external strength of the state: 'The main foundations of every state, new states as well as ancient or composite ones, are good laws and good arms; and because you cannot have good laws without good arms, and where there are good arms, good laws inevitably follow, I shall not discuss laws but give my attention to arms' (*The Prince,* Ch. 12, p. 77). The criteria by which the militarized state was to be judged were than quite distinct from the moral quality by which the individual might wish to regulate his own life. It was on these grounds that Machiavelli defended the murder of Remus by Romulus, that the security of the state depended upon it (*The Discourses,* Bk. 1, Ch. 9, p. 132). The position of the state as a moral force could only come with the advent of this more secular view. The construction of a theory about the behaviour of states one to another was the counterpart of the secular politics of Marsilius of Padua. Private conscience and the Church were not the sole criteria by which political actions could be judged. He was clear that the state as a whole makes demands on the citizen and required him to look after its defence.

Much of Machiavelli's writings were specifically directed to the organization of defence. Every reader of *The Prince* knows that he had much to say about mercenaries. But he went further than this and established the world of states with its own patterns and demands made upon the rulers, directing these latter to set all other considerations to one side in their adjustments to the international position of their state. He was thus adamant about the folly of neutrality and the naïve belief that one state can be excluded from the totality of the international order. Neutrality was an illusion, a futile attempt to deny the international system. The interrelatedness of the states, particularly those of the Italian peninsula, transformed the notion of interest of the political community. The ruler was obliged by the circumstances of the state that could never be alone but grew with the other states, to qualify his policy and his view of the interest of his state by reference to the interstate environment, or so at least Machiavelli argued.[3] The international world of the Renaissance state was one of interests working in relation to each other. The state was not defined solely by its internal ordering or by its territory, but also by an understanding of the interests of other states.[4] This is what was implied by the conception of the interrelatedness of the European order of states. An essential presupposition about International Relations retained by subsequent theorists, even if modified and developed, was thus made explicit by Machiavelli, that the international world was indivisible, and that therefore peace and war were equally indivisible.

Machiavelli, writing at the birth of modern European theory about the political world, established the two key elements in the theory of International Relations for the next 400 years, and the themes which have become universal in this philosophy of the external relations of the state, that the state is a moral force and that the international world exists and has structure. The implications of the moral ordering of the state, and the precise form of the structure have been the substance of most of the subsequent literature.

The introduction of an idea of political interest in the behaviour of rulers which drew its direction in part from the international circumstances in which the ruler found himself, affected also the evaluation of war, which underwent a transformation from the medieval doctrine of the Just War. The rightness of the cause was explicitly rejected as the most important factor by writers following Machiavelli's presuppositions about the state and in its place came, firstly the efficiency of the campaign as a means of ensuring the continuity of the state, and secondly the political orientation of war. Total victory was replaced by the notion of a politically successful war, not necessarily directed towards the complete destruction of the opponent and his state. Whatever the extent of the precedents for such an approach during the later Middle Ages, the statement of the truly political war was only to accompany the other new conceptions of which Machiavelli was the clearest exponent.

Such a change in the attitude towards war required this more profound change in the moral assumptions by which political action was judged. Christianity could no longer provide a ready answer to the problem of political strife in which neither side held a monopoly of the right. Just as religious war *within* the state eroded the traditional religious judgements and made ultimately for toleration, notably in France and Germany, so traditional moral assessments of war between states were subject to an important change. International Relations were not only political but pre-eminently secular. The counterpart in International Relations to the arguments of Bodin in France and Richard Hooker in England came with the writings of the Italian Protestant, Alberico Gentili.

Gentili embraced the view that relations between states should be regarded in no way other than the secular. His starting-point was the continued religious warring of the European powers and particularly the civil and religious wars in France. His arguments were designed to show that emphasis on religious difference was to miss the salient feature of the international landscape.

If men in another state live in a manner different from that which we follow in our own state, they surely do us no wrong. Therefore, since war against them will be either vindictive or positive, it can in neither event be just; for we have not been injured, so that we can justly take vengeance, nor are they our subjects, so that it is our part to chastise them (Bk 1, Ch. 9).

What then became the basis of relations between states if the element of the religious crusade and the personal conscience had been removed, or placed in this new secular light? The matter of the just causes of war was made central to International Relations. Gentili here also was clear about the position of the state. The justice of a cause in war was not confined to one side, with a monopoly of right, and with no element of justice on the other, as had been the view with regard to the crusading war. Both parties could share an element of justice; the just war could be waged on both sides. 'But if it is doubtful on which side justice is, and if each side aims at justice, neither can be called unjust' (Bk 1, Ch. 6). The arguments of Gentili made war a matter of political and not moral or religious concern. The sort of pressures which Gentili envisaged would lead states into war were not of a religious kind but political in the sense that they were the result of compromise and arrangement between states, arrived at through interest and not divine retribution or reward. Thus he argued, 'I add here the cases in which one renders aid to allies, friends, kindred, neighbours and others whom one is under obligations to assist' (Bk 1, Ch. 6). The nature of International Relations was thus set in a new mould and clearly understood to be so by these early theorists of interstate behaviour.

This secular view of International Relations and the accommodation of war in the regular relations between states created a new approach to politics, that of *realpolitik*. The implication was that despite the reciprocity and interrelatedness of the states, these political units did not constitute a 'society' in the sense of a body amounting to more than the sum of the individual states. The diplomacy of *realpolitik*, of Machiavelli, was one of immediate arrangement with little or no broader view than the handling of the immediate situation. The expression of this *realpolitik* was a gloomy but concrete vision of International Relations and its diplomacy. All states were caught irrevocably in the same system and hence came their inevitable suspicion and hostility, as Machiavelli observed: '. . . the natural hatred which neighbouring princes and neighbouring republics have for one another . . . is occasioned by the ambition which moves states to dominate one another, and by their jealousy, . . . and this rivalry and competition have made it difficult, and will continue to make it difficult, for one to seize the other' (*The Discourses,* Bk 3, Ch. 12, p. 441). The resolution and maintenance of order came from the pursuit of interest and the recognition of the interest of others. The result was the contrivance of diplomatic deals, the secrecy which protected this mutual acknowledgement of interests and the spirit of judgement replaced by one of compromise between states and statesmen. The new presuppositions about International Relations did not therefore include a coherent advocacy of an international society. It was a starker world of blatant interest now regarded from its own moral standpoint. The notion of an improvement or bettering of this world was not automatically suggested by this kind of argument, yet there remained room in the theory for a moral force of a different kind.

The stumbling emergence of the European centralized state from the legal order of medieval Europe brought with it a fresh conception of Europe. Consideration of the relations between these new political entities rested upon the description of 'Europe' as an ordered world of states. Some political writers denied the very existence of any such order. Others gave it scant treatment, regarding any international order as dependent upon and subordinate to the internal ordering of the states, and therefore to be understood only in terms of the separate aims, structure and policies of those states. A few, those who were truly theorists of international politics, turned their attention to the way in which the European system of state relations worked, to the question of how far the order was an organic one, how to achieve peace (asserting itself inevitably, regardless of the nature of the constituent states and their governments) and to the formulation of rules by which Europe, understood as an international order, could be maintained. The result of this speculation was a body of ideas, not always coherent and often contradictory, which can be described as the classical theory of International Relations. Even Hobbes suggests an element of order between states. The situation is not one of war, but 'a posture of War'. The very vigilance of the state is itself a modification of a world of total chaos and implies, in however rudimentary a form, some order in the world of states. The idea of the strong state existing in an ordered world of states gave rise to the idea of the interrelatedness and interdependence of states, and did so at the very moment of the emergence of the doctrine of the strong state. John Locke drew a sharp distinction between the state of war and that of nature, 'and all Commonwealths are in the state of Nature one with another' (Ch. XVI, para. 183). He urged the difference between 'the State of Nature, and the State of War, which however some Men have confounded' (Ch. III, para. 19). The possibility of 'Good Will, Mutual Assistance and Preservation' which constituted that state of Nature (Ch. III, para. 19), provided a basis for politics between states, and for a positive attempt to order those relations, although Locke did not develop the implications of his argument for International Relations. It was left to others to seek the means of ordering those relations. Whereas *realpolitik* did not seek explicitly to improve the international environment, a view of international politics as an improving force attempted precisely that. The tasks of morals and International Relations were thus associated, and the writer who most strongly represented this tendency was Hugo Grotius, writing in the early seventeenth century.

Grotius went further than those writers who had perceived both the unity of the international system as depicted by those theorists writing at the time of the Italian High Renaissance, and also required that the order was a moral system embodying and not destroying the civilizing elements of humanity. International society was thus a moral entity in the theory of Grotius, although all states did not at all times necessarily uphold that moral order. He urged moderation in the treatment of enemies, and the acceptance of the rules of war because such precepts would advance the morality of international society by giving it order. He was thus able to reintroduce a concept of the "just war", fought for reasons which could be accepted as just in terms of international society. For Grotius wars could be regarded as just for a precise reason: 'No other just cause for undertaking war can there be excepting injury received' (Kelsey, Bk 2, Ch. 1). War and International Relations had to be understood through genuinely international criteria. Once engaged, wars were to be conducted by clear rules. The key question is why? Grotius is clear; International Relations should conform to the law of nature, 'violence is characteristic of wild beasts, and effort should be put forth that it be tempered with humanity, lest by imitating wild beasts too much we forget to be human' (Kelsey, Bk. 3, Ch. 25). 'We desire rather to restrict the unrestrained licence of war to that which is permitted by nature' (Kelsey, Bk 3, Ch. 12).

The confidence that International Relations in Europe were not simply a war of all against all produced a conception of 'Europe' which invited detailed explanation of the methods by which the order was sustained. Was it induced by the craft of statesmen, as suggested by the policies and *Testament Politique* of Richelieu, or was it a spontaneous operation of political compromise holding the states together? The notion of Europe required the further elaboration of how that political entity was organized, but the acknowledgement of such a political unity was the common element from the moment of the decline of a religious commonwealth of Christianity. The secular approach did not destroy ideas of unity and such concepts recurred constantly, from that of Suarez, writing of the moral and political ties of the human race,[5] to Edmund Burke looking to 'the secret, unseen, but irrefragable bond of habitual intercourse' which held men and nations together 'even when their perverse and litigious nature sets them to equivocate, scuffle, and fight about the terms of their written obligations' (Burke 1796).

Interrelatedness and reciprocity were the striking aspects of the European order of states, and the differences between writers came over their understanding of how these operated. There is a real tension in Grotius' political theory of international behaviour between the world as it is and the rules dictated by international morality. He is not as assertive as Pufendorf that the rule comes directly from natural law, but sees a multiplicity of laws bearing upon the interstate world, in which natural law has a central place. Nevertheless there remains a lack of clarity in Grotius about how it is that states are to be obliged to conform to the moral standard and rules which he suggests are the safeguards of international harmony. With the seventeenth century, and above all with Grotius, the dilemma of the theorists of International Relations is in the open; how should consciously applied rules of international behaviour be reconciled with the view of an inevitable logic inherent in the international system, forcing the relations of states whatever the wishes, attitudes and policies of the governments? If there was an international order or society, was it immune to the follies and incompetence of statesmen, or was it necessary deliberately to control the system? This became the major problem to which theorists of International Relations addressed themselves. *Realpolitik* smacked of a rationally induced world, a diplomacy conforming to clear rules and productive of order between states. The Cartesian mind of the seventeenth and eighteenth century applied itself to diplomacy and produced rules and a theory of International Relations. The contemporary obsession with mathematics and geometry stimulated the adoption of the concept of the balance of power as the description of International Relations, but did not always clarify the extent to which this balance was indeed a description of International Relations or a prescription for statesman and a theory which provided rules by which policy was to stabilize the relations between states.

The notion of balance became very deeply embedded in the thought about and description of International Relations during the eighteenth century. Lord Chesterfield, not one of the most quoted writers on international politics, was to describe an application of the balance in a letter (1775, No. 128, 30 Aug. 1748, 289) to his son: 'Different Powers must now unite to make a balance against France; which union, though formed upon the principle of their common interest, can never be so intimate as to compose a machine so compact and simple as that of one great kingdom, directed by one will, and moved by one interest. . .' The limited scope and the diplomatic necessity of the balance of power are here described: a device for the satisfactory ordering of the European states. The idea of the policy of balance dug deep. David Hume, in his essay on the balance, traced the origins of the idea of balance to the world of the Greek *polis.* Robertson, writing his biography of the Emperor Charles V, made the case for the balance as a creation of the Italian states of the fifteenth century. Whatever the period, it remained necessary to explain how far the balance was a deliberate contrivance, and how far it was the spontaneous result of the juxtaposition of powers. Clearly the conception implied the defence of territorial integrity and a certain continuity of relations irrespective of ideology.[6] The difficulty was to indicate how this was achieved: to disentangle international law from the prescriptive element in natural law theory and to explain how the dictates of natural law were to be impressed upon the state and its rulers. Grotius remains unclear. Giovanni Botero had been among the earliest writers to seek to depict a reason of state. His argument moved in the direction of diplomatic theory and practice as the means of creating a balance. Machiavelli had pointed out the indivisibility of the international community, but it required later writers to pick this up and to develop the implication that the international order itself imposed constraints and policies upon governments whatever their particular ideological standpoint.

Although Wolff, Vattel, Hume and others expounded doctrines of power and balance of power, their views retained an element of confusion because they took over so much from diplomatic practice of the eighteenth century. The structure which they described was both descriptive and prescriptive. How could such opposed approaches be reconciled? The tendency was to keep the theory of International Relations in the realm of law and prescribe rules for the conduct of relations between states. Not until the awareness of history and the notion of progress through the dialectic of history was this theory released from the inhibitions of prescriptive law and a legalistic view of international society and order. Until such a notion of the relativity of time and place had been accepted by European thinkers at the end of the eighteenth century, the concept of a universal reason retained its prominence, applying equally to all mankind, and leading directly to prescriptions for the ordering of the world. The *Law of Nations* was thus significantly the title of Vattel's popular work, in which the position of the state was clarified from the standpoint of international law. His contribution was to develop the idea of the independent sovereign state. Vattel provided a much clearer view of the special field of International Relations than many previous writers. He picked up the obscurities in the writings of previous commentators, notably Grotius, and sought to define the peculiarity of the interstate world. 'Hence it follows that the natural Law of Nations is a special science which consists in a just and reasonable application of the Law of Nature to the affairs and the conduct of Nations and of Sovereigns' (Fenwick 1964, Preface). Thus this special category of the law of nations 'gives rise among Nations even to an exterior obligation', here contrasted with the laws binding on the consciences of statesmen which Vattel regarded as the view of Grotius, 'independent of their will' (Fenwick 1964, Preface). The sole writer, concludes Vattel, who had achieved the distinction between the application of the law of nature in general and its application to the problems of International Relations was Wolff (Fenwick 1964, Preface). However, Vattel was less impressed both with the style, 'it is written after the method and systematic form of treatises on geometry', and some of Wolff's detailed deductions, 'Mr Wolff concludes that the Law of Nature permits the use of poisoned weapons in warfare. This conclusion shocks me . . .' (Fenwick 1964, Preface).

The basis of the international society for Vattel is the sovereignty of each state, 'Each independent state claims to be, and actually is, independent of all the others' (Fenwick 1964, Intro.). Vattel already begins to bring out the differences between the states and individuals, thus qualifying the too easily made analogy between individuals and states, which is an assumption of Hobbes and other political theorists of the state. 'It is clear that there is by no means the same necessity for a civil society among Nations as among individuals' (Fenwick 1964, Preface). The European theory of International Relations is thus found moving towards the creation of a special category of laws and rules for the state, founded on twin pillars; that the state is independent, and that it is not the individual writ large. How then do these units communicate with each other? The answer to this question for Vattel was the balance of power. The development of this theory, although by no means founded by Vattel, was given a theoretical precision by him which moved the argument on to a much more coherent level. International society was composed of two different and conflicting elements, the independent state on the one hand and the necessity for relations on the other, this latter point is a restatement of the view of Machiavelli that International Relations are indivisible. Vattel therefore envisaged Europe as 'a political system in which the Nations inhabiting this part of the world are bound together by their relations and various interests into a single body' (Fenwick 1964, Bk 3, Ch. 3). The object of this ordering now coming to the fore in the theory of International Relations was the creation of 'an arrangement of affairs so that no state shall be in a position to have absolute mastery and dominate over the others' (Fenwick 1964, Bk 3, Ch. 3). The enunciation of this aim brought also the discussion of the nature of the balance, should states be approximately equal? how can this be achieved? Vattel exposed this dilemma. His answer is 'to have recourse to the method . . . of forming alliances . . . to act as a mutual check'. The apparent contradiction between the independence of states and their necessary relations through the device of alliances and arrangements was reconciled by this balance which was 'maintaining the liberty of Nations' (Fenwick 1964, Bk 3, Ch. 3). Vattel argued that this operation was not inevitable but contrived by the scheming and policy of the sovereigns for whom he was writing. 'Let us, therefore, leave to the conscience of sovereigns the observance of the natural and necessary law in all its strictness' (Fenwick 1964, Bk 3, Ch. 12). There were in addition other rules for the conduct of International Relations. These were referred to by Vattel as the *voluntary* laws of nations. Such law was applied by the statesmen, it was thus a prescription. The diplomat was thereby constrained within 'the bounds of a law whose princples are consecrated to the safety and welfare of the universal society of Nations' (Fenwick 1964, Bk 3, Ch. 12).

A more or less mechanistic view of the balance of power disposed eighteenth century authors to stress the controllable quality of diplomacy and they were optimistic about interstate relations. This established a firmly *realpolitik* view of International Relations, offering the prospect of minimal agreements and a clear division of interest among the states. The arguments stemming from international law, from Grotius and Pufendorf, were perfectly reconcilable with this *étatist* picture of the world of states. The consequence was the total acceptance of the point made by Gentili that no party possessed a monopoly of justice, and that therefore war must itself be regarded as a part of the political life of states. A sharp division could thus be exposed in the approaches of political thinkers to the question of the nature of International Relations. Some remained repelled by the continuing lack of form of those relations and retained a faith in the rational capacity of man to amend this situation. These turned to arguments based on the necessity of changing the nature of the state itself and supplanting it by some form of world government. Such thinkers tended not to be found among the more recognized and established political philosophers, and their 'Utopian' schemes did not demand a persistent consideration from later generations of thinkers, although many, like the Abbé St Pierre, received some notoriety in their time. The tradition of international thought which found a greater degree of sympathy among the truly philosophical writers on the state moved in a quite different direction.

The dissatisfaction of the philosophers derived from the contradiction which appeared to exist between the actual fact of the power of the state and its disposition to war, and the necessity felt by them to create a better world. The contradiction was sharply delineated by Jean-Jacques Rousseau in the short account which has been left of the international world, usually known as *The State of War*.

Reciprocity allied to the concept of the balance of power produced a different kind of explanation of the events of International Relations. The balance was now an 'unseen mover' in the relations between states, because states were obliged to react and respond to each other. The enunciation of this view, largely unread and unappreciated in his day, was the great contribution of Rousseau to the theory of International Relations.

Rousseau, like Immanuel Kant writing a few years later, recognized the pressures which pushed states into war. They both began from the most pessimistic view of the role of the state, and rejected any direct and easy resolution of the difficulty of the interstate conflicts. Rousseau in expounding his stark view of the state and its relations was able to give a truly international 'definition' of the state. He understood the state as an international phenomenon, relating itself not to an absolute standard, or the approximate equality as was the case with man – 'The State on the other hand, being an artificial body, has no fixed measure' (Forsyth et al. 1970, 170) – but to other states. The state 'is forced to compare itself in order to know itself' (Forsyth et al. 1970, 171). The interrelatedness of the international world, as described by Machiavelli, was thus reinforced by the more sophisticated view of the state: 'it depends on its whole environment and has to take an interest in all that happens' (Forsyth et al. 1970, 171). But Rousseau was unable to see a way out of the warring and hostile posturing of the states, and he presented the thesis of the state with no logic by which the condition of international politics could be seen to alter from one of war.

This was not so for Kant, starting from a similarly pessimistic view that the states were obliged to hold themselves ready for war, thus 'the full development of the capacities of mankind are undoubtedly retarded in their progress' (*Idea for a Universal History,* 'Seventh Proposition') a view apparently close to that of Rousseau. However, Kant established a remedy for international ills through the logic of the international system itself, and he did not try to overcome these ills by a rationalist attack from outside as it were, either by asserting the necessity for change *a priori* or by rational juggling with the aims and conduct of governments. He attempted to reconcile the prescriptive and the descriptive by associating them. In so doing he planted the theory about International Relations as it was treated by the European philosophers firmly in a conservative mould, contrasting with the then more radical suggestions of Grotius or Vattel, or the prescriptions of the Abbé St Pierre.

For Kant the logic of the international world was to be found in its evil; 'the very evils which thus arise, compel men to find out means against them. A law of Equilibrium is thus discovered for the regulation of the really wholesome antagonism of contiguous States as it springs up out of their freedom' (*Idea for a Universal History,* Seventh Proposition). The result was his argument that there would be 'a united Power', so constituted that 'there is introduced a universal condition of public security among the Nations' (*Idea for a Universal History,* Seventh Proposition). His argument thus saw 'perpetual peace' emerging through the wars and evils of the conflicting states, resulting in the constitution of a 'pacific federation' which would permit the liberty of each nation as well as the renunciation of war. This contrasted with those formulae deriving from Grotius and Vattel which, according to Kant, had not 'the slightest legal force' (*Perpetual Peace,* Sect. 2, Definitive art.). This was a conservative theory in the sense that it worked through the established order and did not wish to change it into something which it could not be. Kant rejected those theories which asked the states to transform themselves without explaining the necessity for them so doing. His description of the states and their mutual relations was thus able to lead to a prescriptive formula by his understanding of the *nature* of their relations. Kant's argument developed the consequences of the idea of peace and the idea of the state, and he did not need to rely on history to show how things would change. This theory of the development of International Relations was thus founded upon his philosophical understanding of the logic of the idea of the state, similar to Rousseau and yet so much more far-sighted in arguing through the consequences of understanding the nature of the state.

Not all philosophers, however, moved in precisely this direction. Kant wrote at the very moment when European thought was to undergo a transformation which affected particularly both political thought and conservative doctrine. He wrote without historical understanding. Some of those thinkers who were his contemporaries or who immediately followed him approached the same issues but from a historical point of view, namely Burke, Gentz and Hegel,[7] the most representative of these thinkers. History was now an understanding of the impact of circumstances and the relativity of historical time, and of philosophy itself. These two qualities, the philosophical and the historical, dominated the European thought about International Relations for the next 100 years.

Gentz was to use the balance of power as the key to the logic in an international order. His view was conservative because he wished to see the balance operate to ensure the *status quo,* or to re-establish it. If any disturbance occurred this was absorbed and a new *status quo* accepted. One could not actually go back. Thus the partitions of Poland at the end of the eighteenth century had become part of a new *status quo* in Europe, regrettable but irreversible:

The fate of Poland is long ago decided, not only in fact but in *right . . . by a number of treaties of peace and conventions concluded between the partitioning powers, and all the other European states, their old and new possessions are recognized and guaranteed; the former Polish provinces are now so completely united and incorporated with their old territory as to make it impossible to separate the one from the other; the reestablishment of Poland is therefore impracticable, either in* fact *or* right (Gentz, Ch. 22).

Gentz envisaged the necessity of war in order to maintain this balance of power, or counterpoise as he preferred to call it. Coercion was part of the system which he perceived in Europe. The balance was at once the logic of the system and the policy to be applied. Throughout the two elements, the descriptive and the prescriptive, coexist. The balance of power was both the actual and the necessary structure of the relations between states, and this balance had to be deliberately created and fostered by the statesmen of Europe. War was both a sign of the erosion of the balance, by an aggressive power like Napoleonic France for example, and a sign of the activity of restoring the balance, by means of alliances. Gentz thus resented the 'apathy of the spirit' which led to the destruction of the *status quo* and to the 'apathy of form' to which this feeble diplomacy gave rise. The balance of power would work if it were encouraged to do so by the activities of the statesmen, and Gentz gave them rules of thumb to assist this diplomatic work, his 'maxims' forming 'a practical basis, which was not to be deviated from' (Gentz, Ch. 1).

The fruitfulness of this conception of the balance of power was such that it could serve as the explanation of the history of International Relations in the era of the central state, as was achieved by Leopold von Ranke writing of the *Great Powers.* The domestic and the external policy of the European states were there seen in terms of response to the international environment. The power of France was necessarily the driving force of this international system composed of similar states which were indeed trying to compare each other, and by responding in this way the notion of 'counterpoise' indicated by Gentz, was given specific content. The essay by Ranke remains one of the most outstanding monuments to theory which had evolved steadily in the works of European thinkers about the state and its relations since the emergence of the central, unitary state. However, emphasis on balance and *realpolitik* appeared to reduce or at least subordinate morality to the demands of the structure and its balance. If the structure of the system required one arrangement of powers, how was any question of morality or progress towards a more moral international order to be realized? The evolution of the theory of International Relations in the nineteenth century was to bring together the historical understanding of the interstate world and the attempt to invest the order with a moral direction.

Hegel appeared to be at once placing all the emphasis on the development of the state as the source of morality in history and denying the existence of a distinct international society which was in some way above that of the individual states. The history of the state and the understanding of that history as an unfolding rational process was the central issue. Peace was not the culmination of the historical process, but this process was the realization of the state, with its integrity and its moral force. The consequences for the thought about International Relations, not always explicit in Hegel, was to accept the opposition of the states to each other and to make the principal task of political theory that of understanding the internal ordering of the state. Hegel, it seems, subordinated International Relations as an academic study to the study of the state, and thereby destroyed its autonomy. Political thought is about rule and therefore about the state. International Relations were merely the consequences of rule.

This view was consistent with the conservative trend in thought about International Relations as it emerged from the eighteenth century. The integrity of the state was the *raison d'être* of International Relations, whether in the form of war or of peace treaties. The argument was akin to that of Kant, that the political order would embody the moral order, but the stress was totally upon the *internal* moral ordering of the state, which had not been true of the theory followed by Kant. Hegelian philosophers of the state, for example T. H. Green in England, were concerned not with International Relations in the first instance but with the constitution of the state at home. War is thus a product not of international society or an international order, but of the wrong ordering of the state.[8] The reconciliation of the 'is' and 'ought' of classical political theory as it applied to the phenomena of interstate relations, was in the improved constitution of the state and not in the international juxtaposition of states.

The emphasis on the state as the fundamental element in the political ordering of Europe reinforced the doctrine of those who believed that the only acceptable policy to follow in International Relations was one consistent with that tradition handed down as 'Machiavellism'. There seems thus to have been a consistency between the arguments of Hegel and the practice of statesmen like Lord Palmerston and Bismarck. The principle of this statesmanship was the maintenance of stability through practical arrangement, whether the Concert of Europe or the secret diplomacy of the last two decades of the nineteenth century. The diplomacy of *realpolitik* was precisely the assertion that agreement between states was possible by virtue of their common political basis *as* states. Political agreement was possible, although war might also be consistent with the security of the state. The philosophical theory of the state thus led to a position in which the European political philosophers could be radicals at home and conservative in their view of international affairs, and this was the case with much of the theory of the moral basis of the state. Each author might vary in the precision of his position and the extent of his liberalism, thus Heinrich von Treitschke was less liberal at home than T. H. Green, but was more conservative in his view of foreign affairs; whereas Bernard Bosanquet was more liberal than Treitschke in his argument about domestic politics but no less conservative of the integrity of the state in its external aspect (Savigear 1975). Their principal concern was everywhere the same, the preservation and development of moral values within the state, and the protection of the unity and independence of the state in International Relations in order to permit the development of morality. The contradiction on which 400 years of international politics had been based was thus exposed; International Relations were grounded on the autonomy of the state in order to claim that there was indeed an international order at all, yet the fundamental position of the state accorded that political form a primacy which in turn subordinated the world and logic of International Relations. The interests of the state were served by the international environment, not the other way about. Treitschke carried this argument to its extreme in his *Lectures on Politics* by arguing that war was itself creative of the moral order, the creation of which he saw as the prime duty of politics. The moral international order was the achievement of war and the strife of states. Here was the ultimate demonstration of the moral worth of the state, that it could both fight a war and adhere to a moral law of war. The forms of this morality to which he pointed in International Relations were the rules governing the conduct of war and the treatment of prisoners, and also those associations between states which their varying strengths required (Bk 4, Ch. 28). Meaning in the international world came from the association of morals and politics, much as Kant had already indicated. The problem was to be clear about the connection. The crucial question was whether good could arise from evil. Hegel had appeared to suggest that this was possible, and even T. H. Green who seemed to insist that evil will always and only engender evil, was at times less clear, at least as regards the side-effects of evil: 'Wars have been a means by which the movement of mankind, which there is reason for considering a progress to higher good, has been carried on' (1906, 473). Nevertheless, the basis of such reasoning remained the state. We are in fact little further than Machiavelli who had distinguished between the public and private realm in order to be able to relate the apparently evil conduct of public life to the preservation of the good of private morality. Both for Green and for Machiavelli, wrong-doing remains wrong-doing although the position is complicated by political life, which necessitates such 'evil', and nowhere is this so manifest as in the unconstituted world of International Relations.

A different emphasis came with the attempt to do away with the state as the agent of moral improvement in International Relations. The origins of such a 'tradition' in European political thought were deep and respectable, in the Abbé St Pierre and the 'imperial society' as described by Dante. The argument had indeed been found in Kant, but it was never to destroy the philosophy of the state which explained the process in his argument. The difficulty was to provide a satisfactory reason for the erosion of the state, and attempts were thus to flounder and remain open to criticism, as was the case with the Abbé St Pierre,[9] or to fall back on the state, as with Henri de Saint-Simon whose reorganization of European society rested on the leadership and example of France and England.[10] Here was therefore a reassertion of the primacy of the state. This was a weakness in all such 'federal' arguments for the alteration of the basis of International Relations. The failure to explain the 'withering away' of the state left only a resort to the looser bonds of European society, the 'identity of religion, of moral standard, of international law' (Rousseau, *Abstract* of the Abbé St Pierre's Project for Perpetual Peace). It was this which constituted the tradition of pacifism which drew support from but provided no really political argument about the state (Hinsley 1967, 16ff) until it was associated with an argument drawn from economics which transformed the level of this otherwise optimistic and not truly philosophical debate.

Where the democratic state had not offered any new approach to the state and the tension between reality and morality in interstate relations, economics at least suggested such a progression. Whereas the proclamation by Lamartine in 1848, that the Second Republic would not change the bases of French foreign policy, demonstrated that this 'revolutionary' and republican policy was as conservative as that of Prince Metternich, commerce implied an international community which subordinated the state to other factors. The development of economic links, through trade and monetary policy as well as the exploitation of countries outside Europe, suggested that the interconnectedness of the states would be vastly extended, to that point where the states were no longer sovereign bodies. Two arguments were produced. The first was to urge that the development of such ties would reduce the prospect of war and conflict in International Relations because it would no longer be in the interest of the states to risk damage to their trade. The second argument was that this should be followed by more extensive contacts between states in order to civilize the international world and create a social community of international ties, going beyond the purely economic. But radicalism in foreign affairs conformed to many of the presuppositions of the mainstream of diplomatic thinking. This was not simply because the argument for free trade was formulated as a policy to be controlled and implemented by independent states, an assertion of their independence as much as of their interdependence and thus an old theme in the thought about interstate relations. The radicalism of foreign policy, and in particular that which became associated with writers like Mill and Cobden in England, and statesmen like Gladstone and Michael Chevalier, was not founded upon the idea of the collapse of the state under the impact of economic forces now liberated, but upon a desire to make the state itself more moral, and therefore International Relations also more moral. The morality of international society was not the only issue, but the moral and civilizing quality of the state itself. Cobden was appalled at the moral consequences of an association with what he regarded as barbarous powers, like the Ottoman Empire, and he wished, like Bentham before him, to see the sovereignty of law apply in the relations between states. His arguments for free trade were thus a consequence of his moral, indeed pacifist argument – 'he worked for free trade because he wanted peace, not for peace because he wanted free trade' (Hinsley 1967, 96). As with Grotius, the desire to improve the world through the acceptance of a more moral international law had only to be shown to be consistent with the nature and morphology of the state. This they could not do, and the argument was left in mid-air until the erosion of sovereignty was linked to the creation of international organizations, to economic interdependence and to international law. Such writings, although derived from the tradition established by the political theorists of the state, demanded the transformation of the state as strongly as those 'revolutionary' arguments coming from the socialist 'Left' in European political thought. All represented a departure from the theory of the state as it had been handed down, rephrased and modified since the High Renaissance.

The First World War discredited those ideas based on the political theory of the state. Such ideas were regarded as Germanic, as in many respects they were, and they fell with the German Empire (Muirhead 1915). Fascism and the revamped theory of the state as embodied in Mussolini and delineated by Gentili turned this theory of state derived from Machiavelli into a more destructive mould and added the final blow to that moral theory of the state which had been developed by Kant, Hegel and T. H. Green. Ironically however a Bismarckian view of *realpolitik,* of the possibility of reason of state operating through minimal agreements between states, has survived the critique of the moral state with which this view had for so long been associated. The same could be said of the theory of war as an inevitable and consistent part of the theory of the state. This was the nub of that theory of war developed in detail by von Clausewitz; war was a reciprocal act and its theory had to show how war was related to politics and the totality of the political situation. These were lessons in conformity with the diplomacy of *realpolitik* perfected over centuries of negotiation.[11]

The twentieth century has seen new approaches to International Relations, prompted by the persistent disillusion following the wars of the first fifty years. What therefore remains of the so-called classical theory of International Relations? If some left-wing commentators have noted the extraordinary capacity of capitalism to survive its apparently crippling crises, others now observe the equal resilience of the state, and therefore the relevance of the theory of the state as it has been passed to us over the last 400 years with its corollaries of balance of power, *realpolitik* and intervention as a consequence of interrelatedness. Although often obscure and seemingly tangential, this body of ideas still provides any statement about International Relations with a set of criteria by which it can be judged. The achievement of the theory of International Relations as it had emerged through four centuries was to accept the blemishes and not to try to make the international world what it was not, and yet to see that a moral stability had come about through the operation of the international system itself. The conservative element in the theory was thus retained, associated with a more historical appraoch to International Relations than had characterized the earliest European discussion of the nature of relations between states. The state was a moral force and therefore the world of the state and its relations had to be developed not destroyed. This was the legacy of the European tradition of political philosophy: 'The tasks of morals and of international politics are different in principle, though the end to which they cooperate is the same. The immediate task of morals is to live a life, that of international politics is to provide a world within which life can be lived' (Bosanquet 1915, 137).

Notes

1. The power of 'making and unmaking law' was the quality which comprehended all the rest of the attributes of sovereignty, or so argued Jean Bodin in his *Six Books of the Commonwealth,* Ch. X, 'The true attributes of sovereignty'. The inclusion of 'appreciating or depreciating the value and weight of the coinage' is given particular stress by Bodin because 'there is nothing of more moment to a country, after the law, than the denomination, the value, and the weight of the coinage', and a subject on which he had written a number of treatises.
2. See below: chapters on these different approaches to international relations.
3. '. . . it is impossible for a state to remain for ever in the peaceful enjoyment of its liberties and its narrow confines; for though it may not molest other states, it will be molested by them', *The Discourses,* Penguin Classics ed, Bk 2, Ch. 19.
4. Machiavelli went further and argued that the constitution of the state was in some measure a response to its international environment, thus, 'It was Rome's neighbours who in their desire to crush her, caused her to set up institutions which not only enabled her to defend herself but also to attack them with greater force, counsel and authority' Ibid., Bk 1, Ch. 34.
5. 'The human race, though divided into no matter how many different peoples and nations, has for all that a certain unity, a unity not merely physical, but also in a sense political and moral', *De Legibus,* Bk 2, Ch. 19, Sect. 9.
6. Thus William Roscoe J. McCreery (1806, p. 5, note a) writing of the creation of the balance, and referring to both Robertson and David Hume, remarked 'the idea of a

systematic arrangement for securing to states, within the same sphere of political action the possession of their respective territories and the continuance of existing rights, is of modern origin'.

7. The distinction lies between those who argued that progress came logically, from the very nature of things, and those who saw it coming through the actual events in history and explained this by a historical account. It was the French Revolution which focused this latter approach on the questions of international relations, when French armies swept across Europe.
8. 'There is no such thing as an inevitable conflict between states. There is nothing in the nature of the state that, given a multiplicity of states, should make the gain of the one the loss of the other. The more perfectly each one of them attains its proper object of giving free scope to the capacities of all persons living on a certain range of territory, the easier it is for others to do so; and in proportion as they all do so the danger of conflict disappears' (Green 1906, Sect. 163, 476–7).
9. There is a full discussion of these theories and pacifist tradition in Hinsley (1967).
10. 'De la réorganisation de la société européenne'.
11. Theory, wrote Clausewitz (1940, Vol. 3, p. 78) 'should show the relation of things to each other'. Diplomacy and war were thus closely related in his famous observation that 'War is only a continuation of state policy by other means' (Vol. 1, p. xxiii). Cf. the description of *realpolitik,* by Hedley Bull, *Diplomatic Investigations,* p. 52 – states 'are capable of agreeing only for certain minimum purposes'.

References and Further Reading

Bodin, Jean (1955) *Six Books of the Commonwealth,* Ch. X, abridged and translated by M.J. Tooley, Blackwell, Oxford.

Bosanquet, B. (1915) 'Patriotism in the perfect state', *The International Crisis in Its Ethical and Psychological Aspects,* London, Oxford Univ. Press.

Burke, Edmond, (1796) *Letter . . . On Proposals for Peace with the Regicide Directory of France,* London, F. and C. Rivington.

Butterfield, H. and Wight, M. (eds.) (1966) *Diplomatic Investigations,* London, Allen and Unwin.

Chesterfield, Lord (1775) *Letters to His Son,* Dublin, Stanhope.

von Clausewitz, G. (1940) *On War,* London, Kegan Paul.

Fenwick, C. (ed.) (1964). Emmerich de Vattel, *The Law of Nations,* New York, Oceana.

Forsyth, M.G., Keens-Soper, M. and Savigear, P. (eds.) (1970) *The Theory of International Relations: The State of War,* Allen and Unwin, London, p. 170.

Gentili, A. (1964) *De Juri Belli Libri Tres,* trans. G.J. Laing, New York, Oceana.

Gentz, F. (1806) 'Fragments upon the present state of the political balance of Europe', in M.G. Forsyth et al. (eds.), *The Theory of International Relations,* London, Allen and Unwin, 1970.

Green, T.H. (1906) *Lectures on the Principles of Political Obligation,* London, Longmans, Green.

Hinsley, H. (1967) *Power and the Pursuit of Peace,* Cambridge, Cambridge Univ. Press.

Hobbes, Thomas, (1651) *Leviathan.*

Hoffmann, S. (1965) *The State of War,* London, Pall Mall.

Holbraad, C. (1970) *The Concert of Europe: A Study in German and British International Thought. 1815–1914,* Harlow, Longman.

Kant, Immanuel, (1970) *Idea for a Universal History from a Cosmo-political point of view,* and *Perpetual Peace,* in M.G. Forsyth et al. (eds.) *The Theory of International Relations,* London, Allen and Unwin.

Kelsey, F.W. (trans.) (1964) Hugo Grotius, *De Juri Belli ac Facis Libri Tres,* New York, Oceana.

Locke, J. (1963) *The Second Treatise of Government,* P. Laslett, (Ed.) London, Cambridge Univ. Press.

Machiavelli, Niccolo, (1961) *The Prince,* London, Penguin Classics.
Machiavelli, Niccolo, (1970) *The Discourses,* London, Penguin Classics.
Muirhead, J.H. (1915) *German Philosophy and the War,* London, Murray.
Remec, P.P. (1961) *The Position of the Individual in International Law According to Grotius and Vattel,* The Hague, Nijhoff.
Roscoe, W. (1806) *Life of Lorenzo de Medici,* London, McCreery.
Saint-Simon, Henri de (1952) 'De la réorganisation de la société européenne', F. Markham, (ed.), *Saint-Simon, Claude Henri de Rouvroy,* Oxford, Blackwell.
Savigear, P. (1975) 'Philosophical idealism and international politics: Bosanquet, Treitschke and War', *British Journal of International Studies.*
Suarez, Francisco, (1964) *De Legibus,* selections trans. Gwladys L. Williams, New York, Oceana.
von Treitschke, H. (1914) *Lectures on Politics,* selection trans. A. Gowans, London, Gowans and Gray.
Wolfers, A. and Martin, L. (1956) *The Anglo-American Tradition in Foreign Affairs,* New Haven, Yale.

Chapter 4

The revolutionary approach: the Marxist perspective

Tony Thorndike

The Marxist doctrine is omnipotent because it is true.
Lenin

It is said that Mrs Marx observed at the end of a long and rather bleak life that how much better it would have been if dear Karl had made some capital instead of writing so much about it.
Harold Macmillan at the United Nations, 26 April 1962

It has been occasionally fashionable to argue that, in any consideration of Marxism, the phenomena of International Relations presents both a problem and a puzzle. Generally expressed in empiricist terms, it is seen as a problem in as much as the state-centric international system apparently persists in the face of a Marxist logic that dictates an eventual stateless world. The puzzle follows from the problem, since there is an enthusiastic acquiesence in this by the socialist states. But the admitted logical contradiction of such socialist states *qua* states which do not 'wither away' must not arrest any attempt to analyse the contraposition of the equation: that when considering International Relations, Marxism itself presents a problem and a puzzle. However, the problem here is not so much empiricist as methodological in nature, in that as viewed through the basically Hobbesian state-centric perspective of the international political system, Marxism is regarded as an ideology of the more messianic kind. The dominant questions then revolve around whether such an ideology can be adapted to socialist states and how far their policies express its imperatives. Once again, there is an admitted logical contradiction (which in this case also compounds the one previously identified), as such an employment of Marxism is totally antithetical to Marx's argument. To him, ideology originates in the material conditions of life and is thereby a 'false consciousness' and 'a screen for reality', expressing an intimate and by inference, often regressive, relationship between policy and group interests. Flowing from this is the puzzle that, despite its significance, the study of International Relations has rarely been framed in a true Marxist manner, for when correctly employed as a *methodology* and a conceptual framework, it may be utilized to formulate – and answer – questions that appear to be important. It also suggests intellectually profitable lines of enquiry and speculation and identifies real and concrete problems in the world that are long overdue for analysis.

Furthermore, only recently has the popular reductionist tradition in International Relations of concentrating upon the state been effectively challenged by new theoretical approaches of which the transactions model (e.g. Burton 1972, Keohane and Nye 1972, Rosenau 1971) plays a prominent part, despite attacks on it for its 'tired myths' (Northedge 1976). It is increasingly apparent that International Relations can no longer be defined simply in terms of interstate relations. The concept of traditional legal sovereignty is now an increasing obstacle to analysis for a growing multiplicity of actors defy the juridical state, such as class alliances, multinational corporations and liberation movements. Described by Keohane and Nye (1972, xi) as 'the contracts, coalitions and integrations across state boundaries that are not controlled by the central policy organs of government', traditional analysis either does not account for them or does so inadequately. As if to stress the point further, Burton's parallel concern with 'world society' and what he terms the 'linkages' within it also recognizes this inadequacy:

The conventional map of the world is a physical one: it shows geographical relationships, over which are drawn political boundaries. It does not tell us much about processes or behaviour. . . (It does) not give us much information about behaviour, or more particularly, about transactions and links that exist. . . What we really need to have, either in map form or conceptually, is an image of world society that shows behaviour by showing these linkages (Burton 1972, 35).

Then there is the welcome upsurge in interest in the study of international political economy, although possibly owing to the pressures of 'relevance' than to any entrepreneurial urge to seek academic boundaries as such. To date, there has been a sharp tendency in the literature to deal with the economic aspects of foreign policy (e.g. Gardner 1956, Strange 1971, Knorr 1975) rather than with the evolution and process of the international economic order (Kindleberger 1970). But there is a strong case for arguing that its study may lead to a deepening of understanding in International Relations and of world affairs, so long as it does not merely consist of applying the insights provided by economics and International Relations on a mutually discrete basis to selected issues and problems. After all, in the real world, 'economic and political forces and factors are constantly interacting and are extremely hard to disentangle one from the other' (Strange 1976, 337).

The significance of Marxist methodology is that its utilization makes for a deeper degree of scrutiny – and for a greater relevance – in the pursuit of such alternative and non-traditional *Gestalten.* Although it has been criticized that, as far as its identity with international political economy is concerned, all the stress in its analysis is on the economic system as the established, determining structure leaving the political as only the short-term process (Strange 1976), this misses the point of the utility of Marxist[1] theory. It is this theory, resting on its methodogical foundation, which in fact gives a sense of unity, direction and order to such important studies. In other words, by utilizing its own mode of analysis of man in society through time, it has created a new paradigm[2] of International Relations. In the spirit of the pioneering detection of new paradigmatic parameters, not only are new ideas and insights involved but also the role of new actors considered. In the case of the application of Marxist methodology, an exciting impetus is provided with the identification of class as a transnational actor, and the concept of class struggle and the indentification and resolution of contradictions in society as providing the dynamic. Through this is seen a world divided not into states but into class antagonisms and a dichotomy of riches and poverty, with imperialism and economic and political asymmetrical penetration affecting the fortunes of millions of people. It is, after all, only through the categories of a methodology and the propositions and assumptions within an associated theory may any supposed reality be perceived, or as Burton (1972, 43) clearly puts it, 'the model we have in the back of our minds determines our interpretations of events, our theories and our policies'.

Any new paradigm, besides suggesting new lines of enquiry, also brings a new significance to acknowledged problems. A prime example of this is the North–South (or rich consumer–poor producer) division of the world and all the issues inherent in it. Made further complex with the emergence of China and Cuba as influential purveyors of ideas and potential power, it has on its own account attracted the attention of many Marxists. Few scholars of International Relations would dispute its significance as an issue area and as a possible source of world conflict but, despite the clearly displayed evidence of world poverty, and riches for the few, many do not regard it to be at the *very least* of equal importance to other problems and enigmas. What is worse, few others than Marxists or the non-Marxist left in International Relations attempt a theoretical analysis of cause and effect and, in doing so, stress its central importance. In this and in other areas of attention, Marxist methodology provides both tools of analysis and an explanatory framework (or *Auschauungweisse*) of the phenomena involved.

What it ultimately amounts to is that Marxism is fundamentally revolutionary in terms of International Relations, not so much because of the concerns to which it draws attention, but rather because, above all, it does not accept the traditional state-centric model of world politics. Not only does it reject this model (thus directly challenging much of the base of existing international theory), it also presents its own methodology, that of historical materialism, using the dialectic both as a form of logic and as a crucial tool in the analysis of society through time.

It is this denial of the primacy of the state that puts the Marxist perspecive into a category on its own. It may also help to explain why International Relations, as a discipline, has never had an identifiable (and honourable) Marxist tradition compared with other social sciences, notably politics, sociology and economics. Such a direct challenge to what constitutes to many how the world *is* invites ridicule, being 'plainly contrary to all, or almost all, the evidence of the senses' (Northedge 1976, 27).

Further barriers to a Marxist tradition in International Relations

In International Relations, Marxism is primarily treated as an *ideology* in the formation of the foreign policies of particular states, notably the Soviet Union and the Warsaw Pact countries and, latterly, China and Cuba. Alternatively, it is considered for its role in motivating Third World revolutionary movements.[3] But rarely is asked the obvious question: Can the Soviet Union or any other society be conveniently labelled communist, or should they be considered as Marxist?

Further, in much of the literature devoted to ideology, the easy conclusion is often expressed that, in a state-centric world dominated by considerations of national interest and power, and with war as always a potential possibility, ideology plays a relatively trivial role in the operationalization of foreign policy, although perhaps not in its genesis.[4] This allows for the dismissal of Marxism as undoubtedly interesting but somewhat irrelevant to the *real* world. It should be noted, of course, that this use of Marxism effectively Hegelianizes it, whereas Marx expressly attempted to overturn Hegel. Hegel's idealist philosophy had stressed the motive force of ideas in society, seeing history as a series of *geists,* of conscious sensibilities, leading to the thesis that one's social existence was determined by different modes of comprehending the world; in other words, that social reality was ancillary to the mind. Marx, on the other hand, strenuously argued that it was the other way around, with the existence of matter being *independent* of human consciousness. Put another way, one's consciousness was substantially determined by the objective conditions of social and material existence. In Marx's words, . . . 'The mode of production of material life conditions the general character of the social, political, and spiritual processes of life. It is not the consciousness of men that determines their existence but, on the contrary, their social existence that determines their consciousness.'[5]

This is the very base of materialist philosophy which was a direct challenge to Hegel. Therefore, the reduction of Marxism to a system of ideas which may or may not rationalize and justify the foreign policy process or the operation of revolutionary movements ought at best be considered a secondary concern. Indeed, it may be precisely this stress on materialism which has resulted in the diminution of those heirs to the Hegelian tradition who would argue for the primacy of ideas. Therefore, in concluding the philosophical aspect of the argument, the paradoxical fact is that the heritage of Marxism since 1917 is that of a dogma, expressing the power of ideas in determining action. Hence, it is logical that a consideration of this lies more properly with policy studies than with Marxist methodology.

A rather different approach to Marxism as an ideology is to identify major concerns of International Relations such as war and peace, nationalism, international law and morality, and the state and then to examine what contributions, if any, Marxism had made to their analysis and operationalization. In the content of the discipline this can be a valuable line of enquiry, but with two fundamental conditions. These are, firstly, that the concerns be discussed and made intelligible within the terms of the paradigm that give them birth, i.e. based upon the foundations of materialist philosophy and the *economic* substructure of society, to which *all* phenomena in society are subsidiary. Secondly, that they must be examined in conjunction with other problems such as imperialism and the transnational class struggle, which the methodology identifies as worthy of analysis. In other words, because the Marxist analysis of International Relations is not state-centric, it largely ignores traditional issues in the discipline and, more importantly in this context, when it does mention them, they are within a completely different paradigm. With these caveats in mind, it is nevertheless true that Marxist analyses of these concerns have never been adequate, although some of Lenin's comments on war in society, and its causation, are of considerable significance. On the other hand, nationalism is markedly poorly served, Marxism never having the time to develop a sufficient structure of theory to explain the extraordinary potency of this historical phenomenon. Overwhelmed by the catastrophies of 1914 and the Stalinism of the future, it 'represents Marxism's great historical failure' (Nairn 1976, 3) although of course this judgement is disputed by others.

However, it is again unfortunate that, in discussing the contribution of Marxism to these 'traditional' concerns, the bulk of the literature has treated it in terms of specific relationship to the requirements of Soviet et al., foreign policy which once again, allows for its dismissal. In sum, therefore, only when important questions have been asked (such as what is the precise methodological contribution of Marxism, and what does it identify as significant areas of analysis and how does it proceed to analyse them) and tentative answers offered may the ideological dimension be considered. In sum, the fact of the October Revolution of 1917 and the subsequent 'nationalization' of Marxism should not divert the student of International Relations in his consideration of the Marxist perspective.

Finally, there are other obstacles in the way of the development of Marxist tradition in International Relations. For instance, there is the continuing difficulty of divergent interpretations of Marxism itself, the problem of exegenis by neo-Marxists faced with contemporary conditions and the continuing heritage of the pre-Leninist conception of the state and subsequent revisionism.

It is well known that Marx's theory continues to be a source of considerable controversy because his breadth of intellectual vision made his theories very flexible for purposes of historical interpretation, and as guides to action. His many writings and abstract concepts are also often obscure, incomplete and unsystematic. Much of what he – and later, Lenin – wrote was polemical in tone, criticizing the ideas of his socialist and anarchist contemporaries. As a result, it is no wonder that the 'reinterpretation' of Marxism began immediately after his death, beginning with Engels, in order to explain what Marx was trying to say and to defend it. In doing so, Engels almost succeeded in emasculating parts of the Marxist analysis and sometimes watered down its revolutionary content as, for instance, concerning the nature of the future international society. Thus he set the problem for constant reinterpretation, often with results which would have surprised Marx. Such exercises, near inevitable in the circumstances, lent some credence to the subsequent claims of social democrats, syndicalists, insurrectionists and many other diverse groups to be Marxist, having shed much intellectual baggage in the process of political evolution. To many (for instance, Althusser 1969, Anderson 1976), the current interpretations of Marx in contemporary Western and Eastern Europe are largely revisionist in content, justifying the reformist rather than the revolutionary tendencies in the European workers' movement. This contemporary debate within Marxism may be dated from 1956, and is perhaps best illustrated by Althusser's theory of the 'epistemological break'. It was in 1956 that Khruschev denounced Stalinism in his secret speech to the Twentieth Congress of the Communist Party of the Soviet Union (CPSU), giving evidence for the first time of the atrocities committed during the period of Stalin's rule. The whole catalogue of terror, murder and repression was revealed and the effect of his speech, and that of the invasion of Hungary later in the same year, reduced even further the attractiveness of Marxism and Soviet communism for Western audiences. Marxism had gained little ground in Western Europe, with the exception of France and Italy, and an improvement was unlikely now that it was associated with Stalinism and economic determinism. Left-wing intellectuals were thus faced with a choice: either to abandon Marxism altogether, or take control of Marxism and its development from the state ideologues of the CPSU. In the event, the answer was to turn to Marx's Early Writings in order to develop a critique of both Western capitalism and Soviet communism.

The Early Writings, heavily influenced by Feuerbach's critique of Hegel, focus primarily upon the theme of alienation, defined as the separation of man from his essence, from his 'species being'. Man, his needs and his potentiality and the nature of his being, was the focus of analysis. Hence, the Early Writings were more humanist in outlook, rather than as constituting a theory of political economy. Louis Althusser, the theoretician of the then heavily pro-Soviet French Communist Party, objected to this 'uncritical Feuerbachism' and with his theory of the 'epistemological break', attempted to demonstrate that there is not one Marx but at least two. In other words, that the Early Writings are written by a young and politically naïve Marx, and that only in the later works such as the *Grundrisse* and *Capital* does Marxism as a science emerge. Marxism, for Althusser, is a theory of political economy based on the methodology of historical materialism, and not a theory of human essence. Hence, an overemphasis on the latter leads to intolerable ideological deviation and distortion. The debate within contemporary Marxism, therefore, should be seen not only as a legitimate argument over correct interpretation and the tactical considerations, reformist or revolutionary, that follow therefrom, but also as a political conflict over the hegemony of the International Communist Movement.

This perennial problem of interpretation is incapable of solution. Furthermore, it is reinforced by the relative lack of reference in the vast store of his – and Engels' – writings of direct relevance to International Relations. Whereas, for example, the emphasis on class directly challenges the state-centric model, there is no comprehensive theory of war and peace except on some broad lines suggested by Lenin – and even then subsequently amended in the light of direct Soviet and Chinese experience. Where specifically *Marxist* concepts of war and peace coincide with non-Marxist ones unfortunately is rarely considered, such is the emphasis upon such experience. But as one observer has pointed out, 'Marxism is an open system that develops in the content of the future development of objective reality and the process of cognition of the world, and, if no attempt was made to develop Marxist theory further, its sense and content would be negated' (Kara 1968, 1).

It is not often appreciated that the use of the dialectic ensures this open-endedness and so it would be illogical if no attempt *was* made to develop Marxist theory. By developing thesis and antithesis, it extends itself: and as materialism is the methodological base, these theses constantly emerge from ever-changing objective conditions, and the emergent contradictions present intellectual challenges. It was this that enabled other areas of interest to be developed after Marx's death, some with a considerable degree of perceptive analysis and equanimity, such as imperialism and exploitation in a global and world-economy framework (e.g. Bukharin 1918, Horowitz 1969, Magdoff 1969, Baran and Sweezy 1968, Jenkins 1970). This, of course, is not surprising given its central importance to Marxists, resting on the premise that the foundation of society is an economic one, based on production.

But, the problems of exegesis extend further, for essentially Marxist theory was concerned with the analysis of society *within* the bourgeois state. But the theoretical difficulties involved in linking the national and international economies have been exaggerated for, as will be seen, Marx observed the expansive nature of capitalism and in particular, its propensity towards internationalization. Admittedly, however, it was left to Lenin in his *Imperialism* (1916) both to recast and reinforce this factor by illustrating the intensification of this process as expressed through colonialism, the export of investment capital and imperialist policies generally. In doing so, he utilized the tools of Marxist analysis and considerably extended the scope of Marxist theory; whether this constitutes 'revisionism' as some of his critics claim is therefore open to great doubt.

Marx's thoughts, however, in no way extended to the theoretical problems produced by the continuing presence of bourgeois states which did not 'wither away' in the post-revolutionary era. Therefore, further refinements of his theory were necessary, and appeared with Leninism. Derived from his insistence of 'putting politics in command', this is defined as meaning the ideology of *organization* popularly associated with Lenin's name, where the political and military capacity of opposition élites are decisively elimated by a tightly disciplined and led 'vanguard'. The subsequent institutionalization of this by the CPSU and its (and also Stalin's) attempts to interpret Marx in the content of a Russian socialist state, goes to the extremes of exegesis. This effectively brings the student of International Relations back to the first and fundamental barrier which was suggested as preventing a fair discussion of Marxism in the content of the discipline.

The significance of the Marxist analysis

However, following the identification of these obstacles, an appreciation of the intrinsic significance of the Marxist perspective becomes possible. Its importance may be postulated as being applicable at two levels: upon International Relations as an academic discipline and also with reference to the objective facts of international affairs. Taking the latter empirical level first, its impact is patently obvious, for not only do over half the world's population now live under regimes which embrace a Marxist approach to policy in varying degrees of strength and stresses, but also that to many sections of the remaining world population it enjoys support, particularly when sloganized in the pursuance of a struggle for equality or other human 'rights' or translated into schemes for rapid economic and social development. Much of his emotion and enthusiasm appears to emanate in the Third World, but the currently fashionable concentration upon this area should not blur an appreciation of its continuing and expanding appeal in developed areas, including the post-Vietnam USA.

However, to the student of International Relations its theoretical and methodological contributions are more important. In considering this, the student must see the broad vision of the theory and its *Weltanschauung*[6] covering state, interstate and transnational behaviour as plumbing depths of analysis which, as indicated earlier, only now are non-state centric models of international transactions beginning to explore. In short, it is a theory which, *qua* theory, provides a broad-based vision of society in all stages of development; at its base lies the fundamental importance of production and from there, the economic substructure of society and the crucial role of class. By the use of the dialectic – adapted from Hegel – Marx was able to present a picture of continuing contradictions in society. These contradictions were seen to exist both within and between classes at different stages of their development, and also between the constantly developing forces of production – new manufacturing and distribution methods, growth of capital accummulation and monopolies, etc. – and the existing social relations of production, such as social classes and legal structures. By their dialectical resolution, which created new contradictions, the distinction between diagnosis and prognosis was dissolved. Therefore, an appreciation of these contradictions at different levels of society, times and intensity is essential. To Mao Tse-Tung, 'to imagine that none exist is a naïve idea which is at variance with objective reality'. In his analysis, an important distinction is drawn between two types of social contradictions:

those between ourselves and the enemy and those among the people themselves. The two are totally different in their nature. . . The contradictions between ourselves and the enemy are antagonistic contradictions. Within the ranks of the people, the contradictions among the working people are non-antagonistic, while those between the exploited and the exploiting classes have a non-antagonistic aspect in addition to an antagonistic aspect. There have always been contradictions among the people, but their content differs in each period of the revolution and in the period of social reconstruction.[7]

As the role of production and the importance of the dialectic are inseparable from any study of Marxism, a brief summary is necessary.

Marxism, production and the dialectic

Being a theory of social science, Marxism ultimately devolves upon a conception of man and his role in society in which Marx insisted was pursued in a scientific manner. He began by explicitly rejecting the notion of a universal human nature, for 'every century has its own peculiar nature, so does it engender its own peculiar natural man' (Marx 1842).

'Natural' human rights and natural law theories being bogus, it follows that man is neither 'naturally' aggressive nor peaceful. However, as he presently exists in the epoch of capitalism, capitalist man portrays the characteristics of that mode of production as outlined by Hobbes: power-seeking and competitive aggression. However, there are in this vision two universal characteristics of man, or twin interdependent ontological assumptions. Together, they constitute what he termed man's 'species-being' (*Gattungswesen*). The first is that man must labour and produce in order to exist for

The first premise of all human existence, and therefore, of all history is

the premise that man must be in a position to live in order to 'make history'. But life involves alone all else, eating and drinking, a habitation, clothing and many other things. The first historical act is thus the production of the means to satisfy these needs, the production of material life itself.[8]

It therefore follows that, "Labour is the workers' own life-activity, the manifestation of his own life."[9]

Secondly, 'he is not only a social animal, but an animal that can individualize himself only within society'.[10] The propensity of man to group with others is therefore natural. However, although the focus on production and the productive process is explicit, social relationships are implicit in these processes. Therefore, the question eventually arises as to when and how the existing 'mode of production' (i.e. the sum of the forces, and social relations, of production) conforms to or *distorts* man's 'species-being'. In other words, has that mode of production which collectively describes all that which characterizes an epoch determined certain social, political, legal and economic processes ('relations of production') which are *detrimental* to man and society, whether in the so-called domestic or international spheres? This question must be considered as the relations of production are largely determined by the nature of the forces of production. If such a detrimental situation is perceived to have been established (as Marx argued that it was under capitalism), then the concept of alienation is of critical importance. Not to be considered as a mere psychological reaction to the inhumanity of the production process, alienation arises when man has lost to someone or something an essential part of his 'species-being', i.e. when what he, or others before him, have created then slips from his control and instead, dominates him. While the role of religion in society is certainly viewed within this framework by Marxists, this is above all where the significance of capital lies. After having been created by man through the extraction of surplus value from his labour, it becomes a force independent of himself and as such, determines the manner by which society will be organized. Beset by this, and by the use made by the exploiters of capital of the socially regressive division of labour, and of the pre-capitalist heritage of the principle of private property, man is thus alienated on two counts: firstly, he no longer controls his own labour being at best a 'wage-slave', while secondly, the social factor is also affected as his human relationships become exchange relationships (determined by money) and power relationships (determined by capital). All the surplus value which he produces in the productive process is, of course, expropriated.

The analysis of the nature, condition and consciousness of man as being determined by his relationship to the mode of production rather than to the state or nation is allied to a further factor: that the history of the world is characterized by a series of epochs, each following the other. These epochs are, to Marx, ancient, Oriental, feudalist, capitalist, socialist and communist, each representing a definite stage of social development and economic organization. In each, 'we find almost everywhere a complicated arrangement of society into various orders, a manifold graduation of social rank'.[11] The order in which Marx put them was more a product of his observations of the course of world history than as representation of any 'law of history',[12] although there is the notion of the progressive development of society through to the final goal of communism, with all its connotations of a higher order. Materialism is the key to this progression for, as man's interests and consciousness are rooted in material considerations, therefore, 'the history of all hitherto existing society is the history of class struggles'.[13] Their dialectical resolution, of course, in resolving the class antagonisms of each epoch, ensures such progression.

Conflict, therefore, is a characteristic of society, being a creation of class consciousness and the clashing of interests. But as Mao Tse-Tung's words illustrated (see p. 62) it does not necessarily mean that it will be expressed as violence, as conflict is broadly defined as including argument and collective bargaining. But the main point remains: a period of social revolution consequent upon an increasingly intolerable structure of contradictions in the productive process, and the sharpening of class consciousness, will render a change in the economic foundation. When that happens, 'the entire immense superstructure is more or less rapidly transformed'.

The superstructure which Marx refers to is, in essence, the state. As it is materialism and not nationalism which is of central importance, the state is but a reflection of the underlying mode of production. In his classic words:

In the whole productive process to which men devote their lives, they enter into definite relations that are indispensable and independent of their will; these relationships based on production correspond to a definite stage of development of their material powers of production. This sum total of these relationships constitutes the economic structure of society – the real foundation, on which rise legal and political superstructures and to which correspond definite forms of social consciousness.[14]

The implications of this are enormous for not only are states a reflection of the 'definite stage of development' (and Marx naturally concentrated upon what he termed the bourgeois era of capitalism) but that the 'existing production relationships', i.e. the dominance of the bourgeoisie, is 'but a legal expression' for their exploitative power which the state protects. It therefore follows that the dominant class can, and will, employ the legal, administrative and coercive machinery of the state to protect its interests. In the crushingly powerful language of the hastily-written *Manifesto:* 'The executive of the modern State is but a committee for managing the common affairs of the bourgeoisie'.

Later, it was to be put more delicately by Engels, and to be linked logically to political action by the proletariat against the bourgeois state. Noting that the state was created by society to safeguard its *common* interests against internal and external attacks, he was to argue that, as an organ of ideological power over man, it 'makes itself independent *vis-à-vis* society; and indeed, the more so, the more it becomes the organ of a particular class, the more it directly enforces the supremacy of that class. The fight of the oppressed class against the ruling class becomes necessarily a political fight, a fight first of all against the polititical dominance of this class.' He then goes on to warn that, 'the consciousness of the interconnection between this political struggle and its economic basis becomes dulled and can be lost altogether'.[15]

Liberation, therefore, from this ever more oppressive situation would only come through a revolution by the proletariat to create an eventual communist society, where production would finally be for the market and for the satisfaction of people's needs, rather than for class profit (although, of course, surplus value must still be created for wealth: the difference would be not in its production but in its distribution). In so far as the state is concerned, the logic is obvious: states would assume only administrative purposes and, as the social revolution progressed towards full equality in the fullness of time, everybody would, in effect, be an administrator and the state – as we know it – would wither away. In Engels celebrated, if enigmatic, phrase in the *Anti-Dühring* (1886 edition), 'the government of man will become the administration of things'. Additionally, as the invidious division of labour which was forced upon man enslaves him instead of being controlled by him, it will be abolished as

'*. . . in communist society, where nobody has one exclusive sphere of activity, but where each can become accomplished in any branch he wishes, society regulates the general production and thus makes it possible for me to do one thing today and another tomorrow, to hunt in the morning, to fish in the afternoon, rear cattle in the evening, criticise after dinner, just as I have a mind, without ever becoming hunter, fisherman, shepherd or critic.*'[16]

At this highest stage of human development, therefore, no antagonistic contradictions are assumed to exist. However, whatever the obvious and enormous difficulties presented by the theoretical nature of this future society when considered from the perspective of International Relations, some commentators have cogently argued for the continued existence of contradictions given the nature of modern industrial life characterized as it is by commercial interdependence and mass production (e.g. Avineri 1968, Berki 1971). Engels himself hinted at a continuing concern about this future state of affairs for, 'all successive historical systems are only transitory stages in the endless course of development of human society moving from the lower to the higher'. He went on to point out the apparent illogicality of an end of contradiction in a dynamic world, for '. . . if all the contradictions are once for all disposed of, we shall have arrived at so-called absolute truth – world history would have been at an end. And yet it has to continue although there is nothing left for it to do – hence, a new, insoluble contradiction'.[17]

However there is no *real* problem here as Engels, using the materialist conception of history, sees 'history' as being determined by the mode of production in society. Therefore, and confounding his critics, as these modes of production have been developed through a dialectical process through time in response to evolving concrete conditions, it is only *this* usage of history that ceases to be operative. The society has reached a totally new and higher stage, with a totally and fundamentally new consciousness based upon the new social reality of communism. To the end, therefore, the Marxian analysis of society and the emphasis upon prescription is rooted in its relation to objective reality and so to practice: central to this is the well-known concept of *praxis,* or the unity of theory and practice. This is clear in the attack by Marx and Engels on idealism and in particular, the use of the base of materialism to arrive at an idealist position of abstraction by such philosophers as Feuerbach, perhaps best summed up by the *Second Thesis on Feuerbach:*

The question whether objective truth can be attributed to human thinking is not a question of theory but is a practical *question. In practice man must prove the truth, that is, the reality and power, the this-sidedness of his thinking. The dispute over the reality or non-reality of thinking which is isolated from practice is a purely* scholastic *question.*

This conviction is further expressed by the often misinterpreted *Eleventh Thesis*: 'The philosophers have only *interpreted* the world, in various ways; the point, however, is to change it'.[18] The point here is not that philosophers themselves should change the world, but rather it is an appeal for philosophy to be linked with social reality. To Marx, it had been abstracted from its social context by two ways: not only by idealism and the general Hegelian notion of speculation where reality tended to be ancillary to the mind, but also by the then current emergence of the empiricist tradition by which description and explanation were more important than prescription. The notion of *praxis,* therefore, was that philosophy must not be socially abstracted but be committed: in other words, that the criteria of truth in philosophy should be in its social utility and relevance. It obviously follows that, 'Theory is only realized in a people only in so far as it is a realization of the people's needs', which further begs the question, 'Will the theoretical needs be directly practical needs? It is not enough that thought should strive to realize itself; reality must itself strive towards thought.'[19]

The philosophical (as opposed to the ideologically dynamic bond between Marxism and the mass revolutionary struggle) implications are clear and have imprinted themselves on many subsequent Marxist philosophers. For Gramsci, for instance, his nomenclature of Marxism was that of a 'philosophy of praxis' (Anderson 1976, 67).

Class, capital and state

This rather simplified version of Marxian analysis does indicate several factors which underline its relevance to the study of International Relations. First and foremost, as materialism and not nationalism is the basis of society, the key unit of analysis is class. One commentator has expressed this succinctly, whereby classes, 'are the basis units in history, and the struggle between classes, instead of interstate conflict, occupies the centre of attention' (Berki 1971, 81).

However, at this stage the motor force is the *internal* contradiction within society where the state or nation, as clearly observed, is merely contiguous to the development of the bourgeoisie. If Marx's analysis had remained at this simple stage where all exogenous variables are, in effect, neglected, then it would have effectively precluded any useful contribution to International Relations. Essentially, Marx never promulgated a theory of the state as such but only talked about it in terms of its relationship to class. References to his thought on the relationship between capital and state, and the idea of territoriality are sketchy, but Marx himself admitted that his great project, of which *Capital* was only the first of six books, would include such considerations. This series of seven rough-drafted work-books (*Grundrisse,* 1857–8) contain the basic outline of this entire opus, of which much was uncompleted, including that on 'The State' (Book 4), 'International Trade' (Book 5) and 'World Market' (Book 6). Additionally, his notes and outlines of the latter two volumes written in 1854–5 remain in Moscow and, as yet, unpublished (Nicolaus 1973, 54). But this problem notwithstanding, it is widely accepted that the analysis of a closed national economy was but a simplifying assumption, particularly in Volumes I and II of *Capital.* In Volume III the world market and the internationalization of capital is mentioned, and linked to credit and banking systems although with a warning that such matters were not part of this, the first book, but rather belonged to a later stage.

However, as previously acknowledged, the open-endedness of his theory permits its development. Following the methodological foundations laid by him,

the tendency is to take the national economy – the developed, monopoly capitalist system in which the capitalist mode of production is universal, the development and socialization of the means of production has gone furthest, and the dominance of capital and its movement is most clear – and then to analyse the forces projecting out from *this system into the outside world' (Radice 1975, 16).*

These forces can be generally summed up as the internationalization of capital and imperialism; as objective historical trends of capitalism their analysis represent further concretizations of Marxist theory of particular relevance to International Relations.

At this juncture, therefore, it is important to be reminded that, when Marx recognized the immense growth of productive forces unleashed by the Industrial Revolution, he was thinking of *class* rather than capital. The dominant class made strong by this historic development, the bourgeoisie, was not only responsible for intensifying exploitation because of the increased opportunities offered it, but also because it had a need for a constantly expanding overseas market for its products. Above all this class, while stoutly retaining its national identity, has 'through its exploitation of the world market given a cosmopolitan character to production and consumption in every country'.[20] On the other hand, a new class of proletarians were born out of this process, whereby, 'big business created everywhere the same relations between the classes of society, and thus destroyed the peculiar individuality of the various nationalities . . . while the bourgeoisie of each nation still retained separate national interests, big industry created a class, which in all nations has the same industry and with which nationality is already dead'.[21] From this two factors immediately emerge: firstly, the transnational characteristic of class, especially that of the proletariat, and which led Marx provocatively to state that, as the human victims of capitalism, it knew no particular country,[22] and secondly, the interdependence of nations. This latter implication was in complete contradiction to the narrow framework of nation-states which contemporary statesmen such as Mazzini, Kossuth and Bismarck were trying so hard, and largely successfully, to establish.

The question of the relationship between *capital* and the state was, at least in chronological terms of Marxian analysis, to come later. By adding to class the observation of the transnational and international characteristics of capital and its immutable link with the capitalist state and the development of imperialism, the essential framework of the Marxist paradigm of International Relations was made. At the same time, the continuing process of consolidation of the state by the national bourgeoisie created a contradiction which, given the nature of bourgeois world politics, could end in mass bloodshed. This risk, to Marxists, was a very real one for just as the state solidified and made concrete the interest of the national bourgeoisie in their competitive worldwide pursuits of profits, so this itself tended to increase national antagonisms and hence, potential war. This was but a logical consequence of the imperialist struggle to control markets, the exploitation of one nation by another, and the cultivation of chauvinism to create mass support for aggressive war.

The bourgeois state and imperialism are, therefore, closely linked. What then distinguishes the modern state in the Marxist paradigm? It is that the state is an effect of class, and not its cause. It can, therefore, be recognized as a *derivative* actor within the dialectical relationship between the proletariat and bourgeoisie. As a product of such class antagonism, it is not a prime actor as the more traditional power-political model would suggest. That is not to argue it is unrecognized as an objective reality by Marxists. On the contrary, in view of its role in promoting and popularizing aggression, as a provider of succour for the imperialistic activity of multinational companies, and as a refuge for ill-gotten transnational gains, this would be totally unrealistic. In fact, in parentheses, despite Engels' exhortation to 'throw the entire lumber of the state onto the scrap heap'[23] many neo-Marxists have interpreted Marx's philosophical concept of *aufhebung* as not meaning *only* 'abolition' but transcendance to a higher state of social authority. The legitimacy of this would lie in popular internal identification rather than in coercion and a need for external defence (Avineri 1968): thus is the importance of some state functions recognized. Nevertheless, as the tool of the élite through the epochs, it is ultimately transitory in its present form. Originally evolved by society for purposes of its own administration, it is now the master of the proletariat which, in Marxist terms, is alienated from it.

The question then arises as to whether the reality of the state in International Relations can be reassessed in terms of Marxist methodology and its paradigm. In the pre-revolutionary period, its reality and continuing momentum remains a constant – consequent upon the development of capitalism – but its *nature* can be all the better analysed and clarified as an immensely powerful class organization and instrument which almost has a life of its own. In the post-revolutionary phase, it ultimately poses questions relating to popular legitimacy and the 'irreducible minimum' of administrative functions. Rather, and more importantly, the Marxist methodology poses questions and problems in the period of coexistence between capitalist and socialist states in contemporary International Relations, a period in which Marxist logic would dictate as being one of gradual transition from one to the other. Lenin, speaking in 1919 as head of state, did express a Marxist position when he predicted international conflict between the two[24] – although the sole inference of *violent* conflict was not necessarily methodologically correct. But inasmuch as he was perfectly justified in this opinion in view of both the Allied intervention in 1919–20 and a continuing stance of hostility from the capitalist states to the new Soviet Union, the claim that the subsequent use of the available (and potential) instruments of state control and coercion by the new ruling élite was Marxist is more debatable. Admittedly, Marx in his *Critique of the Gotha Programme* (1875) had suggested the need for strong assertive action by the revolutionary authorities during the transitional stage of the 'dictatorship of the proletariat'. The debate then ultimately rests upon the question of whether the Bolshevik regime was, particularly after Lenin's death in 1924, attempting such a 'dictatorship'. Certainly the increasing distortions associated with Stalinism, resulting in militarism, the personality cult and stultifying bureaucratization, so penetratingly exposed by the exiled Trotsky in his *The Revolution Betrayed* (1936), made the debate increasingly unreal and sterile. The at times convenient alliance between the Russian national interest and the exigencies of Marxism-Leninism where external territorial, military or economic expansion (or 'social imperialism' in neo-Marxist terms) and increased social regimentation may be justified in terms of the furtherance of the revolution lends credence to the claim of the Trotskyite Fourth International that the Soviet Union is a degenerate workers' state. The particular experience of Russia, therefore, indicates a deviation from the conception of the state with a regime which, it is claimed, is Marxist in orientation and practice.

World society

If the transnational characteristic of class as dominant actor, with the state as derivative, is accepted, then world society must be the overall focus, or the level of analysis. The economic and commercial interactions, with their political implications and consequences, must be studied with their fundamental implications for *peoples* wherever in the world, resulting in inequality, relative deprivation and economic dependency distortions. It follows, therefore, that the Marxist conception is uncompromisingly internationalist and this has been echoed by his followers and state ideologues, as for instance, 'in building socialism, the Soviet people are carrying out their internationalist duty to the world revolutionary movement' (Suslov 1975, 109), although it should be added, *en passant,* that the ideology of 'proletarian internationalism' implied above is not quite in itself of the same essence of what Marx really intended. To Marx, the goal was a new proletarian humanism and consciousness, a far more radical concept where the whole of humanity is the meaningful totality (Löwy 1976).

The 'law' of the class nature and struggle in society, and the determining requirements of production, besides indicating the internationalization of capital, also leads to an attempt to comprehend the nature and operation of imperialism. It is important here to remember from the outset that the causal factor as dictated by Marxist methodology is the requirements of production, and not the ideology of the imperialist state and its institutions or the acts of individuals of the character of, for instance, Clive, Rhodes and Rockefeller. The operationalization of this in terms of an international mode of production, which in turn rested upon an understanding of the existence of a world economy, was provided by the theory of imperialism. Written by Marxists of the early twentieth century, it is still being developed. The two major contributions were by Bukharin and Lenin, but that is not to diminish the importance of others. Taken as a whole, the statements, arguments and debates show a large and complex body of hypotheses emerging through the application of Marxist methodology.

Imperialism

Bukharin's work, written in 1915 but not published until 1918, remains very important in contemporary terms with its development of the concept of the world economy and its considered analysis of the combined effect of two trends simultaneously at work in capitalism – the internationalization of capital and its nationalization with the fusion of capital and state. The former, he argued, acted through the latter and was illustrated by annexations and overt attempts to control other national economies. But it was to be Lenin's booklet published in 1916 which became by far the most influential and best known on the subject. Despite its polemical style and the lack of truly original insights by the author, it was of fundamental importance. Not only did it become the basis of all subsequent official (i.e. Soviet) ideology on the subject, but it provided the basis for a theory of international political economy. In terms of International Relations this was the most important and fundamental result: in other words, *praxis* was brought to an international level.

The point of departure was provided by the observation by J. A. Hobson (1902), a British liberal economist, that capitalism was increasingly, in his eyes, a victim to the self-interest of such elements in society as arms dealers and financiers and that the growth in export capital following the effective 'nationalization' of the world through colonialism could and would lead to conflict in the highly competitive atmosphere among national groups of capitalists. Since he saw this exodus of capital as resulting from a lack of investment opportunity at home due to widespread poverty, his remedy was to improve living standards. To the Marxist this would be quite impossible under capitalism given, on one hand, the nature of exploitation and on the other, Marx's 'iron law of wages' whereby monopolist capitalists would be in an increasingly strong position to force down wages in the interests of profits, even to the extent of collaborating with each other to ensure this. Thereafter, concern with the phenomena was taken over by Marxists, the most influential being Bauer, Hilferding and Luxemburg; from all Lenin was to draw. In Kiernan's (1974, 37) words:

He singled out Hobson and Hilferding as having given the best lead, but as suffering from political errors. He himself as a Marxist thinker was not a great originator, but rather a great systemizer: one of those minds, also indispensable, that deepen and consolidate a body of thought and given it firmer anchorage. It was a talent that went with his genius for practical organization.

Its influence, of course, owed much to the triumph of the Bolshevik Revolution and, given Lenin's position, it was elevated to the level of a canonical text and for a considerable period stifled all serious research into the subject.

Karl Kautsky, as early as 1901–2, established a causal connection between the capitalist mode of production and its corollary, the bourgeois state, and the increasingly great propensity for war among the then colonial powers, actual or potential. His contributions, along with the several other variants, represented an attempt to protect Marxist orthodoxy against revisionist attacks by accounting in Marxist terms for developments within the capitalist economy unforeseen by Marx who, after all, had died before the so-called 'golden age' of colonialism of 1884–5. Marx, therefore, had not been in full possession of the facts which would account for the failure of both the wages thesis to manifest itself, and of the predicted even development of capitalist economies. On the other hand, the Marxists of the period could see that the exploitation of the masses in one country by another resulted in the level of wages in the imperialist country being maintained and that also, some countries would exploit more successfully than others and so develop more quickly. Kautsky, in his *The Road to Power* (1909), seeing a link between imperialism and prosperity, was far more concerned with the results of imperialism than with the crucial theoretical question as to whether capitalism as an *economic* phenomenon had an ineradicable urge towards imperialism. Also, he denied any close link between banking and finance on one hand, and industrial interests on the other, as each had different motives in capitalist society. The important convergence of these two wings of capitalism was to be made by Rudolf Hilferding in his *Das Finanzkapital* (1910). Both he and Bauer believed firmly in the importance of capital exports and the role of capital in forging virtually unbreakable bonds between banks and industries, to form cartels. Such rapacious cartels, he believed, do not believe in the harmony of capitalist interest and 'in the place of the ideal of humanity steps that of the might and power of the State' (quoted in Horowitz 1969, 53). But the logic of cartels dictated a line of thought leading to the possibility of an equilibrium in capitalism, both domestically and internationally, and in tentatively developing this, Hilferding, as with many others, moved towards the reformist camp.

This concept was subsequently taken up by Kautsky in a short article in *Die Neue Zeit* in late 1914 where his theory of 'ultra-imperialism' emerged. Forecasting an agreement amongst capital-imperialists to forgo their struggles in favour of a peaceful division and exploitation of the world for their own benefit, he could point to contemporary evidence of implicit understandings between the developed powers on their respective spheres of influence, and to cooperation against outbreaks of colonial resistance. However, he also went on to delimit the definition of imperialism to colonialism, its *alter ego*. While there was some substance in his charge that imperialism, as a term, was being treated too loosely, and that it was not an ultimate stage of capitalism but rather an expression of it at a particular stage of its development, his definition became too narrow and, to all intents and purposes, had little theoretical utility.

Against this reformist position stood Rosa Luxemburg, Lenin and Bukharin. To Luxemburg (1913), capitalism could *not* function as a closed system 'but only through interaction with a realm outside itself' (quoted in Kiernan 1974, 17). In other words, her theory strongly emphasized that modern capitalism had *never* existed in isolation on purely economic grounds. To her, such was the pressure of the economism in her theory that it led her to see a world where centres of capitalism were multiplying in a frenzy and as such, that they were approaching an automatic breakdown. Collapse must come 'inevitably, as an objective historical necessity' since imperialism was 'the final stage of its historical career' (quoted in Kiernan 1974, 20). The collapse could be from a variety of causes, such as a war resulting from the arms race between capitalists or the impoverishment of the masses causing a breakdown in law and order resulting in revolution. Theoretically, therefore, there was the unmistakable conclusion that imperialism and capitalism were absolutely inseparable and that one could not be removed without the other. Indeed, their positions in society were so entrenched that a violent revolution was impossible to avoid.

Lenin, on the other hand, rejected both this thesis and that of Kautsky, although he fully accepted the unbreakable bond between capitalism and imperialism, and agreed with Kautsky that the only cure for the world's increasingly manifest ills was the total abolition of capitalism. He also rejected the increasing tendency of the German-dominated Second International to endorse the leading ideas of anti-imperialism while simultaneously moving to compromise with colonial policies, especially those of Imperial Germany. Several times he attacked their notion of some kind of condominium between workers and capitalists over colonial areas (Haupt 1972) where big business would act as a benevolent force and be against governmental militarism. Such reformism and 'cupidity' had to be met by heightening the controversy through polemical publications of which his 1916 pamphlet was typical.

It is through these rejections that his ideas may be viewed. For instance, his argument against Rosa Luxemburg's restriction of imperialism as being only relevant to underdeveloped (or, to her, pre-capitalist) areas was that 'the characteristic feature of imperialism is precisely that it strives to annex, *not only* agrarian territories, but even most highly industrialised regions' (Lenin 1970, 109). He also challenged her breakdown theory, not only because it appeared to justify a sit-back-and-wait policy, which was anthema to him as a member of the militant Left, but also because more fundamentally, she was in methodological error. While he recognized that the proletariat, in sharing some of the super-profits made by imperialism, would fall to the twin dangers of a confused class consciousness and 'social chauvinism', the fact remained that the exploited proletariat in their wretched state would act on its own behalf. Workers' consciousness of their situation would lead them to interact with each other across national boundaries, just as the bourgeoisie had done. The main thrust would come from the colonial areas, which were in the most wretched state of all, and they would shame the proletariat of the developed states into action along with themselves, and so fulfil the historic mission of the proletariat. Therefore, no automatic breakdown was possible, and, as for her theory that armaments underpinned capitalism by providing it with a special, artificial market which would create and inflame tensions, get out of control and destroy the system, he replied that armaments were only one factor leading to potential revolutionary situations which the proletariat would exploit and purposefully turn to their advantage.

Kautsky he resoundingly denounced as misleading the masses and 'distracting their attention from . . . sharp antagonisms' (Lenin 1970, 143). He insisted Kautsky was in fundamental error: as the instruments of imperialist dominance were ultimately the concern of powerful state machines (although not necessarily under their control), competition among states would be such that the Kautskian alliances could only, by definition, be temporary because they were imperialist. The relentless logic of the system dictated the accentuation of predatory domination and violence (Dobb 1970) by states to control and exploit the assets of other nations. Just as the bourgeoisie had done this to the proletariat, the ultimate result would be war. In this way, capitalist competition is transferred to the realm of interstate and not just interclass conflict:

Capitalism has grown into a world system of colonial oppression, and of financial strangulation of the overwhelming majority of the population of the world by a handful of 'advanced' countries. And this 'booty' is shared between two or three powerful world marauders aroused to the teeth . . . who also involve the whole world in their *war over the sharing of* their *booty (Dobb 1970, 5–6; original italics).*

Hence, just as Marx had shown that capitalism had polarized internal class structures, so imperialism was shown by Lenin to have polarized international relations. However, it may be argued that his prediction of the inevitability of war between imperialists was coloured by his own contemporary experience, trapped as he was in Switzerland while the 'predator' states fought it out in the Flanders mud. Also, there was his anxiety to undermine the position of the German Left who, before the war, had insisted upon the impossibility of a world war and then upon its declaration, had almost unanimously supported Germany and its 'imperialistic' war aims. His polemical language towards the 'despicable renegade' Kautsky may be seen in the same context of the 'disintegration and decay' of the Second International which he broke up in 1914, whose 'bourgeois and democratic prejudices' could be traced, in his mind, to a few ex-Marxist opportunists overtaken by chauvinism and above all, revisionism.

Class and imperialism as variables

The Marxist paradigm has, therefore, a foundation comprising two different variables: class as actor, and imperialism as a motive force in world society. Since the Marxist methodology is *historical* materialism, it is thereby important to remember that both variables act in a defined historical context – that of the epoch where capitalism is the dominant mode of production. Although the concept of class may be utilized as a key to the understanding of any social framework throughout human history, class as actor in International Relations is restricted in time. Only the capitalist mode has created transnational class and with it, worldwide class consciousness and antagonisms. Similarly, only the capitalist epoch is characterized by a world economy. The same general comment applies to imperialism also for, as capitalism and the entrenchment of the capitalist state drew attention to imperialism, so this phenomenon itself represents only a particular stage of the development of society in history.

Lenin's ideas, of course, were related to a set of objective conditions operating in the early years of the twentieth century. Thus, while there is no doubt that his theoretical contributions have provided many essential insights, historical developments in the world economy since 1916–18 have required much additional analysis to the extent that some parts of contemporary Marxist theory on imperialism is becoming near unrecognizable as 'Leninist'. The main studies developed since then centred the question of the inevitability of war in imperialism, and its different impact on developed and underdeveloped areas. These have involved work on neo-colonialism, modern multinational companies (qualitatively different from the trusts and cartels of Lenin's day) and capitalist regional economic organizations. The extent of current research into such contemporary manifestations seems unlikely to diminish.

Further studies have attempted to move away from Lenin's excessive economism which virtually ignores political and socio-psychological aspects of imperialism (Schumpeter 1919, Strachey 1961, Kiernan 1974). All these contributions show that, in the continuing response to the evolution of the structure and operation of the world economy, imperialism is developing both quantitively and qualitatively. It therefore appears that it manifests itself in very different ways according to the diverse economic, political and geographical conditions as exist in the world. As such, as there is an *a-priori* situation of uneven development in the world, it is not so much *the* highest stage of capitalism but rather a series of developing stages corresponding to steps in the progressive evolution of capitalism in different areas – a thesis which the much-maligned Kautsky hinted at. In other words, since capitalism as a mode of production is in simultaneously different stages of evolution in the different political systems in which it is the economic base, imperialism must be regarded in the same light. Naturally, whatever the multifaceted manifestations of imperialism, the Marxist methodology which permits its analysis remains intact.

But whatever the redrawn intellectual frontiers suggested by the paradigm, the central question has still to be asked: *does the operationalization of the two variables – class and imperialism – characterize contemporary International Relations?* In so far as capitalism is the dominant mode of production in the world and as some facets of economic and political organization in the socialist bloc also allegedly exhibit capitalist characteristics, there is a strong case for its relevance. Above all, the picture of the international political economy which the theory of imperialism presents is not one which is seen solely to operate in the context of national commercial and financial policies, nor of international economic theory associated with the state-centric paradigm. Instead, it draws attention to capital operating regardless of national boundaries, the increasing centralization of capitalism in certain monopolist economies, and the interpenetration of national and international capital.

The proof of the pudding: The role of class as Actor

Such general comments should be seen as being precursive for the proof of any pudding is in its eating. As the Hobbesian pudding is unacceptable, what contemporary features of the international political system would the application of the Marxist paradigm, with its twin foundations of class as actor and imperialism as motive force, see as being worthy of investigation?

As regards the role of class, this is manifest in many ways. Most importantly, there is the objective existence of transnational working-class and associated revolutionary movements. There has been a subtle change over the years from *inter*national to *trans*national as, until the recent past, the most apparent expression of this revolutionary solidarity was identified with moral and material support given by the various socialist countries, although to continue to see it in this light is not only inaccurate but also pernicious. However, such a sentiment may be understandable in view of the poor opportunistic image given to such sustenance in the past. It was doubtless distorted in the post-Lenin days of the 'Comintern' (1919–43), which was originally formed as the Third International to rally all those on the extreme Left against the moderating influences of social democracy, and which rapidly became the vehicle to harness this support for the Russian national interest and, in some instances, for Stalin's own personal purposes. In this posture it reached its height in the period 1939–41 although, of course, it could be (and was) argued that the protection of the first fledgling socialist state against imperialist predators and other counter-revolutionary elements was a natural priority. But despite this, and despite the breakup of the monolithic International Communist Movement which survived the dissolution of the Comintern in 1943 and which, *inter alia,* orchestrated the 'peace struggle' between 1948 and 1952, the existence of the fraternity spirit cannot be in doubt. Although now in a far more emotional and cultural rather than institutional framework centred on one state, it expresses itself in a variety of ways, such as the near-simultaneous response from 'progressive' European and American elements to take up arms against Franco in 1936. Indeed, it may be said that the International Brigade was the first transnational army ever formed. Inspired by this was the little-known 'Caribbean Legion' of

1945–8 which, composed of an army of rebels from throughout the Spanish-speaking area of the region, attempted to invade Costa Rica and the Dominican Republic to overthrow the dictators who had seized power there in the aftermath of the Second World War. Less dramatically, it has been seen in uncoordinated but nevertheless effective pressure upon governments on certain key issues such as decolonization, anti-racialism and anti-apartheid, Vietnam and the American presence, and the interests of the so-called 'Third World' countries.

Another materialization of class as actor, and certainly very observable, is the significance which it accords to national liberation movements. Support for them by the revolutionary movement is imperative; theoretically, they symbolize not so much a reaction to specific reactionary national conditions but, more fundamentally, as representing the struggle of all oppressed *peoples* of the world whatever the national boundaries may dictate. In the Maoist variant, this is further developed within a town–country context (which is certainly not divorced from the thinking of the early Marx, albeit in a different context) with the oppressed being the undeveloped rural areas. To Mao, just as the revolution moves from the countryside into the town, so Africa, Asia and Latin America as representing the rural areas of the world, will bring revolution to the developed countries, or 'cities'. Arguably one of the most original geopolitical concepts ever to emerge, it reflects the currently fashionable division of the world by analysts of International Relations into the North–South dichotomy. However, while the Marxist methodology may suggest such a view, the role of the peasant so presented is not part of Marxian analysis and 'is no more than an illegitimate generalisation from the actual course of the Chinese revolution and a futuristic projection. . .' (Claudin 1975, 174).

Certainly, the importance of these movements as an expression of class struggle has not diminished in the least, as witness Khruschev's statement of 1961:

Liberation wars will continue to exist as long as imperialism exists. These are revolutionary wars. Such wars are not only admissible, but inevitable . . . the peoples can obtain their freedom and independence only through struggle, including armed struggle. We recognize such wars and will help the peoples striving for their independence. . . The Communists fully support such just wars and march in the front rank with peoples waging liberation struggles (quoted in Wolfe 1969, 357).

It should be added that such support was not only ideologically determined but an integral part of the policy of peaceful coexistence proclaimed in 1956. Inaugurated as a response to the zero-sum thermonuclear problem and the establishment of mutual deterrence, there still remained the goal of world socialism and later, communism. This will be achieved not through war between socialist and capitalist states but through, on one hand, the gradual internal transformation of capitalist societies through the work of progressive forces *but also* through the repulse of imperialism, using force if need be.

Viewed through the Marxist methodology, these wars are 'just' but under certain conditions. First and foremost, they must not involve secession from a socialist state as, according to the Leninist theory of national self-determination, the internationalist unity of the proletariat precludes any concession to nationalism which undermines the democratic struggle and the proletarian revolution (Löwy 1976, 98). Also, they must be against a bourgeois or feudal subjugator, and for 'genuine' independence, now less narrowly restricted as meaning something exclusively socialist. But the problem remains of the Soviet Union being a state within a society of states, and a self-proclaimed 'peace-loving' one at that. The theoretical questions which national liberation wars raise have; therefore, been virtually ignored in Soviet literature (Vigor 1975, 56) and, in practice, 'fraternal aid' is granted when and where circumstances permit. The actual results illustrate this, for actual Soviet commitment to, and involvement in, such wars has been very limited compared, for instance, to that of the USA. Not only that, there is also evidence to show that in the Angolan and Rhodesian crises, Soviet intervention has been an expression of anti-Chinese as much as anti-Western imperialist motives, taking the form not of direct action but of arms supplies, the use of proxy troops and training. This example itself, therefore, should act as a warning against confusing Marxism as an analytical framework supporting a paradigm of International Relations, and its application as a politico-ideological tool in international affairs.

Marxism and race

There is yet another aspect of class as actor which has pressing significance for International Relations: that of race and the world racial question. The racial (defined as 'colour') factor, so far as International Relations is concerned, can be said to constitute one of its most urgent current concerns; not only on the empirical level with its appearance in issues of decolonization, Africa and the 'racial boundaries' of the Zambezi and Limpopo rivers, the Caribbean and Black Power and recently, in the Vietnamese War and its racial undertones, but also conceptually because, in the final analysis, this new and growing constituent of world politics has a transnational character. But within the framework of Marxist methodology, it presents problems of exegesis as, to Marx, the phenomenon of race stood outside the categories of historical materialism and, in present terms, he could certainly be termed a racialist. He believed, for instance, in the inferiority of the Negro race[25] and that slavery, therefore, was as much a function of the mode of production as the assertion of an abler race imposing its will upon the 'lesser breeds', to employ Kipling's phrase. Ultimately, the racial factor in history was independent of the historical progression of society and so the notion of a separation of society by race, cutting across the orthodox economic layers of society was and still largely is, unexplored by Marxist philosophy. A major contribution to the debate has been provided by Frantz Fanon who, obsessed by his position as a coloured Francophone West Indian in French society, rejected the concept of *négritude*. This, following the initial inspiration of Césaire and Leopold Senghor, advocated the revival of Negro racial consciousness and civilization as a counterweight to the smothering application of French culture. To do this within a Marxist intellectual framework, he employed the concept of the dialectic of *négritude*.

Basically, its source lay in Sartre's *Orphée Noir* (1948) where he

had argued that the subjective, existential, ethnic idea of Négritude passes, in the Hegelian sense, into the objective, positive, exact idea of the proletariat. The affirmation of white supremacy provides the thesis; Négritude as an authentic value was the moment of negativity; the creation of a humanity without 'races' would be the synthesis. Négritude is hereby viewed as the minor term of a dialectic progression (Caute 1970, 26).

For his part, Fanon readily observed that in Martinique, his birthplace, the birth of proletarian politics coincided with the birth of black awareness. He also perceived that *négritude* was a feature of French West Indian intellectuals with their atypical social heritage and of 'assimilated' Africans in voluntary exile in Paris: as such it was almost wholly divorced from this 'real' Africa. For this reason alone, he saw its claims to offer a lead to Africa to be nothing short of pretentious. Rather, his concern was to argue that, despite the colonialist-inspired barriers between races corresponding to politico-economic status where 'the zone where the natives live is not complementary to the zone inhabited by the settlers. The two zones are opposed, but not in the service of a higher unity. Obedient to the rules of pure Aristotelian logic, they both follow the principle of reciprocal exclusivity' (Fanon 1967, 31). What was wanted was a revolutionary de-mystification of race, and the achievement of this higher unity. To do this in Marxist terms, he readily admitted in *The Wretched of the Earth* (1961) that 'Marxist analysis should always be stretched every time we have to do with the colonial problem' (Fanon 1967, 30). So, as Marx saw an awareness of class deprivation and class antagonism as preludes to the ultimate transcendance of class, Fanon argued that racial identity are preludes to the transcendance, and abolition, of race.

There is a further point in his argument, perhaps more quasi- than neo-Marxist in that not only does he see a grand division of the world between colonized (black) and colonisers (white), but that violence would be the only method of its resolution. This would be utilized not only by the black people as a whole as a route to social revolution and the building of a new, decolonized community, but also for the 'moral regeneration' within black societies with the recognition of the 'disinherited' groups within them.

The peasantry is systematically disregarded for the most part by the propaganda put out by the nationalist parties. And it is clear that in the colonial countries the peasants alone are revolutionary, for they have nothing to lose and everything to gain. The starving peasant, outside the class system, is the first among the exploited to discover that only violence pays. For him there is no compromise, no possible coming to terms; colonisation and decolonisation are simply a question of relative strength. The exploited man sees that his liberation implies the use of all means, and that of force first and foremost . . . colonialism . . . is violence in its natural state, and it will only yield when confronted with greater violence (Fanon 1967, 47–8).

A further development of the racial theme in neo-Marxist literature is provided by the Guyanese radical, Walter Rodney. Again, a product of the Caribbean where, perhaps as in no other area in the world, the question of race and of graduated pigmentation as a sociological and psychological factor is all-important, he sees 'black' and 'white' as purely abstractions of the colour names. Race, as such, blurs the class struggle for 'black' refers to the poor and oppressed and 'white' to the oppressor: to him, those blacks who have taken political power in capitalist (and in the context of the Third World, neocolonialist) countries such as Jamaica are 'white-hearted'. But he flounders on the rocks of black consciousness for 'the colour of our skins is the most fundamental thing about us' (Rodney 1969, 16).

In other words, that however much 'black' may be seen as an abstraction, it is a concrete fact and he, in common with other adherents of Black Power, can offer neither an anodyne nor a theoretical prescription.

The proof of the pudding: Imperialism as the central dynamic

What of the realization of the paradigm as regards imperialism? The unity between capitalism and imperialism lays the foundation for a wide-ranging concept of international political economy of which only an outline can be suggested here. In essence, it centres attention on the political problems of three selected contemporary international economic issues: multinational companies, transnational financial flows and economic dependency. This is not to deny the validity of other issues but suffice to say that they too can be viewed through the analytical framework presented by the paradigm.

Just as the international political paradigm is different from that of the 'orthodox', so is the economic methodology. Capitalist economic theory, resting largely on Keynesian macro-economics, is essentially an operational body of descriptive analysis and policy prescription limited to the management of the national economy through government interventionist policies. Therefore, not only are states *the* actors 'in the market', but orthodox theory, when confronted with powerful commercial and financial forces which not only underwrite the increasing economic interdependence of the world but which also act over and above national policies, attempts to make these forces actors on a par to, or substituted for, nation-states (Radice 1975, 13–14). The theoretical difficulties produced are then largely ignored, with the economist simply looking at the impact of these actors on national economies and, on the other hand, attempting to describe their structure and market behaviour disregarding their essentially different character from that of the state. As a *world-economy view* is not adopted, it is difficult to explain why poverty and underdevelopment persist at this level and why, in national economies, economic monetary and fiscal management become ever more difficult. The case for alternative frameworks of international political-economic analysis is a valid one and, although partially taken up by the so-called 'Cambridge School' (e.g. Robinson and Eatwell 1973, Levitt 1970), with a greater emphasis on pragmatism and a recognition of the essentially political nature of much economic policy, has not been wholly provided except through a Marxist analysis.

This analysis is rooted in an appreciation of two laws of motion. Firstly, there is the process of capital accumulation within a national economy (or rather, a series of such economies) where a developing surplus cannot be accommodated unless reconstituted at a world level leading to the internationalization of capital. This is expressed by worldwide trade, financial flows and a developing international division of labour as capital incorporates the resources, and commodities, over the world as a whole. Secondly, there is the law of uneven development, originally developed by Lenin in the theory of imperialism, translated in terms of the world-economy view as under development and economic dependency. In other words, the internationalization of capital creates, in its wake, a hierarchy rather than an equality of benefits. The Marxist critique of political economy would, furthermore, not just present a rather bleak portrait of these hierarchies and patterns of exploitation, but also would attempt to analyse them in terms of the contradictory relationships between international capital and the nation-state, and the class nature of, and struggle within, both capital and the state. Also, however, it would illustrate the historically *progressive* spirit of capitalism in breaking down old and socially retrograde political and social relationships in the process of modernization of the world economy, particularly in the Third World.

Multinational corporations

The study of multinational companies in this framework is particularly rewarding, and general interest in their study has been growing from a variety of Marxist and non-Marxist viewpoints. The importance of the multinational company, defined as being a commercial organization with production facilities in more than one country,[26] is summarized by Hymer,

The multinational corporation, because of its great power to plan economic activity, represents an important step forward over previous methods of organising international exchange. It demonstrates the social nature of production on a global scale. As it eliminates the anarchy of international markets and brings about a more extensive and productive international division of labour, it releases great sources of latent energy. However, as it crosses international boundaries, it pulls and tears at the social and political fabric and erodes the cohesiveness of national states (in Bhagwati 1972, 138).

It is clear from this that the multinational corporation is both a cause of, and response to, economic interdependence, and, at another level, it is again both a cause of the decreasing power of the state to manage and stabilize its economy (particularly in the areas of aggregate demand and exchange controls), and a creature of governmental policies freeing the obstacles facing world trade and financial transactions. They can also be both beneficial and predatory. In Marxist terms they can be progressive and also even revolutionary in bringing to an end 'all feudal, patriarchial, idyllic relations. It has pitilessly torn asunder the motley feudal ties that bound man to his 'natural superiors'. . .[27] And if under governmental tax and legal controls, and in selected areas, such companies can make very useful contributions to development; one observer, writing from the non-Marxist left, takes the criteria of the needs of the underdeveloped countries as the basic standard by which their impact may be judged, and the answer is not unsympathetic (Turner 1974).

On the other hand, there is the concrete evidence available from the hearings of the United States Foreign Relations Committee, subcommittee on multinational companies in 1973–4, the celebrated case studies of the United Fruit Company and Union Minière, the price and supply policies of the oil corporations during the 1973 oil crisis and, more recently, the closely documented activities of ITT in Chile. In all these cases, the basic contradictions were made sharply clear: that not only is there conflict between the aims of these companies and those of states but also that as privately owned institutions their actions are motivated only by a dialectical interplay of growth and profit stimuli, their outlook characterized by limited socio-political horizons, and their societal impact dysfunctional in the longer term.

In the underdeveloped and, to a lesser extent, semi-developed areas, their initial stimulation and then undermining of indigeous development leads to the creation of a new bourgeois class and a small skilled sector of the working class. By doing so, not only is class consciousness heightened (or in Marxist terms, class struggle promoted) but also the condition of both personal and general economic dependency so created results in the state's room for manoeuvre being substantially reduced in the face of this cosmopolitan force. However, in the developed world, the expansion of state economic activities has largely matched the growing size of firms whereby their very scale and their reliance on a foreign exchange market free from controls allows for their manipulation, to a greater or lesser extent, by the states concerned. But in Marxist terms, this is to miss the point. The state-centric scenario implicit in this analysis would be questioned and, instead, the crucial role of class would be emphasized. In the less-developed areas generally, the government élite and small bourgeoisie would be seen as being willing to cooperate with the operations and transactions of the companies, with the masses of peasants and unskilled workers being exploited by both transnational and national capitalist forces, and with agriculture squeezed to finance urban growth. In the developed world, the sentiment would be the same but with a different emphasis: given that the capitalist mode of production is the dominating force permeating *both* the nation-state and the multinational companies, the developed state institutions are both superimposed by, and are in partnership at different levels with, the companies. Despite the sharp contradictions created, the highly sophisticated methods of manipulation of the working classes by the media and of the processes of political socialization by the national and transnational bourgeoisie – and aided and abetted by social democratic opportunistic political interests – enable these antagonisms to be obscured.

Transnational financial flows

The Marxist methodology would provide much the same analysis when applied to another characteristic of international political economy, that of transnational financial flows. Here, there is a difference from multinational companies in qualitative terms as no production is concerned: also the amounts of capital involved are, as the scanty but available evidence suggests, larger. They are linked, of course, in that profits net of investment and distribution do constitute part of these flows, being entrusted to brokers for speculative purposes in the short-term capital markets of the world.

Briefly summarized, these flows were negligible prior to 1939, the world financial system suffering from a severe lack of loan funds. The first major indication of the existence – and effect – of widespread disposable funds came in 1949 when, in the peculiar circumstances caused by the post-war 'dollar shortage', there was a dramatic run on the British pound in 1949 following its forced convertibility by US pressure (Gardner 1956), resulting in an economic crisis, severe cutbacks in governments' social expenditure and a massive devaluation. After approximately 1965, a combination of a near-constant US balance-of-payments deficit, the incapacity of some oil producers to absorb huge influx of funds (particularly after 1973–4) and an increasingly high level of government interest rates which attracted both residual commercial profits and the huge reserves of the insurance and pension funds, has meant the gradual development of a huge and largely immeasurable amount of so-called 'hot' money moving via the various financial markets of the world. In Bell's (1973, vi) words,

The collapse of Bretton Woods was largely determined by the inability of the system to deal with the problem of the balance of payments imbalance of the United States vis-à-vis *the rest of the world. At the same time, the underlying malaise of the system was brought into both sharp relief and up to breaking point by the weight of short-term capital movements emanating from the Euro-currency markets.*

The link between the US deficit and the Euro- and Asian-dollar currency[28] funds is a crucial one, for although starting from quite different foundations, their combination results in an important contemporary issue in International Relations, and particularly so when viewed through a Marxist framework. Although such flows of short-term capital are not necessarily destructive and not wholly of a speculative nature, their potential for so being is very high. The long-term problem presented by such flows is twofold. Firstly, a complete absence of a 'lender of last resort' means high risk and potential illiquidity in a major financial crisis. Second, their power as founts of international inflation is such that national monetary and fiscal policies may be effectively undermined. Only a very powerful state operating in the capitalist international financial market can hope to exert some influence, as witness the impact of US domestic monetary policy on the Euro-dollar market in 1970–1 during the financial boom caused by the Vietnam War (de Cecco 1976). An enormous boost to the funds' influence over states was provided by the introduction of floating exchange rates, and the evidence of the increasing inadequacy of the Smithsonian parities of 1971 would help to support this contention. Combined with the ineffectual application of competing interest rates and manipulation of spot and forward markets by governments, the political effect of such pressures are, in the least, considerable.

A Marxist analysis would utilize the world-economy view and see the victims once again as the working class throughout the capitalist world, trapped in a financial vortex beyond comprehension and control, and having to pay the Keynesian price of social wage cuts and unemployment. Given the circumstances of this internationalization of capital, the manipulators of these funds are seen as being in close collusion with the national bourgeoisie who both personally benefit and help to operate this international and transnational financial system. Governments, again despite the very clear contradictions, also willingly cooperate, for they wish to attract such money to fund government debt; indeed, they have no choice. They themselves have an ideological stake in the system, or in Marx's words, they are part of the 'legal and political superstructure'. Therefore, whereas the orthodox economist would stress the need for a re-creation of a sound world monetary base that Bretton Woods (1944) aimed for, together with fixed exchange rates, Marxists would argue otherwise. To them, unless visited by a fundamental socialist revolution – which, if only on a national scale, would probably entail a protective seige economy in the short term, it is a system that states and their populations cannot avoid.

As an organized class response to these developments, the Marxist view would be to stress trade unionism as a long-term route to this socialist revolution. But its growth has been marked by feebleness and fissiparousness and a true internationalist social consciousness has far from emerged, due to bourgeois-inspired chauvinism and a false sense of self-interest. Not only is unionism heavily divided internally, i.e. within the national economy, by craft and other largely bureaucratic interests, it is also heavily parochial in its external outlook: the attitude of protest by US unions to the jobs which American multinational companies have allegedly exported abroad is an example (Flanagan and Weber 1975). Also, the political emphasis of unions vary considerably from country to country, as a generalized comparison between the CGT of France and the AFL–CIO of the USA will illustrate. Cooperation over boundaries is largely restricted to fraternal conferences and, so far as the underdeveloped world is concerned, training programmes. Furthermore, the unions of these areas suffer from the problem of representing only a very small sector of the population, and their activities drew a scathing comment from Fanon (1967, 97):

> *... the trade unions realise that if their social demands were to be expressed, they would scandalise the rest of the nation: for the workers are in fact the most favoured section of the population, and represent the most comfortably-off fraction of the people. Any movement ... to fight ... for the betterment of living conditions ... would ... run the risk of provoking the hostility of the disinherited rural population.*

The general literature on the subject is little, reflecting the subject, and further studies appear to run up against the law of diminishing returns. But there are some isolated instances of transnational union action as in the case of the Ford and Dunlop–Pirelli industries in Europe, and in the US–Canadian automobile industry. There is also the consistent support given by British unions to better social conditions overseas (beginning perhaps with Sir Walter, now Lord, Citrine, in the British Caribbean in the late 1930s) and currently, to organizations representing black workers in South Africa. But even in this case there is a contradiction, as such expressions of proletarian brotherhood are within the context of capitalism: as union pressure is applied to British companies with assembly facilities in South Africa to recognize indigenous organizations, the risk of antagonizing the government is high to the extent that closure would be possible, and hence a loss of British jobs.

Contradiction, therefore, is rooted in interdependence but the problem – defined as such in Marxist terms – goes deeper in significance than that. The synthesis and application of the two laws of motion within the Marxist analysis of the international political economy – the internationalization of capital and uneven development – results in an understanding of the deeper and more profound contradictions within the most apparent phenomena in international affairs, that of dependency, and the spectre of widespread mass poverty affecting 75–80 per cent of the world's population (Worsley 1964).

Dependency

Dependency is popularly viewed at two levels. One equates it with neocolonialism which, first identified by Lenin, has been sketched by Nkrumah (1965, ix): 'The essence of neocolonialism is that the State which is subject to it is, in theory, independent and has all the trappings of international sovereignty. In reality its economic system and thus its internal policy is directed from outside.' While this clearly indicates a socio-economic structure dependent upon imperialist powers to which it is an economic and social appendage, it is far too wide in scope with its implication that *all* political policy is determined elsewhere. In effect, it ignores the counteravailing power rooted in increased solidarity between underdeveloped nations in international relations whose effect is to provide a base to attack imperialism, and to work towards the realization of a new economic order. This wide and commonly accepted definition of neo-colonialism is also unsatisfactory as it is largely seen as being applicable only to underdeveloped areas, whereas dependency, like imperialism, is much more comprehensive in its coverage. A simpler and more useful definition could therefore be suggested as describing a situation where the control of the major variables within the economy rests with external forces.

Another, and less obvious, view of dependency links it with the question of equitable resource allocation and exploitation. Resting on the fact that the population of the developed states (20–25 per cent of that of the world), heavily dominated by the mass-consumption and high-income economy of the USA, both control and consume 75 per cent of the world's realized wealth, it indicates not only deprivation but also ecological dislocation to the disadvantage of the already disadvantaged, with the impact of the high technology of this developed world (Ward and Dubos 1972).

Neither view really reaches to the heart of the matter in Marxist terms, and to present an adequate perspective of the problem of international equality within the paradigm, certain salient variables already identified need to be applied: a transnational world-economy view, the internationalization of capital, class as actor and state as derivative actor. From this, a picture of 'asymmetrical penetration' may be constructed.

This concept rests on three assumptions. Firstly, that there are transnational linkages affecting both rich and poor,[29] producing networks of complex relationships between states, between multinational companies and other nonstate actors and above all, between classes; this ultimate relationship subsumes all others. Secondly, that simply to say that these social, economic, political institutional units of varying significance are economically independent is not enough: they are transnational linkages where the network of relationships involve asymmetries and inequalities. In other words, the gains of one actor or its derivative arising out of these linkages are unequally related to that of the other, whose greater economic power and command of resources mean that the linkage relationship involves much greater cost in terms of autonomy and dependency for the weaker and exploited actor. The superior means of mobilization of resources and the power of the strong, characterized by the bourgeoisie and their commercial, financial, legal, administrative and coercive tools, allow for a greater control of the content and direction of these transnational linkages. This power therefore provides a greater potential for insulation against adverse pressures than is possible for the weaker, with important consequences for the nature of the interaction between penetrated economies and their hapless proletariat in international relations. Thirdly, that the situation of nuclear stalemate has forced a widening of the concept of security in the capitalist countries, especially within the USA beyond traditional state-based military cognition. Now a wider definition of national security needs (and by extrapolation, security for international monopoly capital) includes both areas in which the cooperation of the underdeveloped world and its bourgeois élites is considered vital, and, specifically in the Marxist view, the successful management of the environment, and the capitalist international economic system for trade, finance, production and distribution of food, fuel and commodities (Erb and Kallab, 1975).

Given these three assumptions, three meaningful conclusions may be drawn. First and obviously, both the nature of capitalism, and the actions of its agents, inevitably produces dependency or more exactly, the penetration and hence control of those elements in society that it has the opportunity to exploit in order to survive and develop. Consequently it is only logical to assume that, for instance, political influence is therefore the *sine qua non* of economic (i.e. non-military) aid unless proven otherwise. As Teresa Hayter (1971, 9–10 remarks:

Aid can be regarded as a concession by the imperialist powers to enable them to continue their exploitation of the semi-colonial countries; it is similar in its effects to reforms within capitalist countries, in the sense that the exploiting classes relinquish the minimum necessary in order to retain their essential interests. . . It may also help to create and sustain, within Third World countries, a class which is dependent on the continued existence of aid and foreign private investment and which therefore becomes an ally of imperialism. . . It may enlarge the overseas markets for the private companies of the imperialist powers; and it can be used to secure the creation of facilities such as roads, harbours and training institutions, to commit the Third World's own resources to such projects, and thus to make the operations of these companies more profitable.

Whereas the motives of national (or 'bilateral') donors may be viewed in this framework, the conventional wisdom dictates that 'multilateral' aid (i.e. from international institutional donors) are a form of 'disinterested international munificence'. This is not so, for her study argues that not only do both forms of aid involve 'leverage' or irresistible pressure against a recipient's domestic policies if they are regarded as unfavourable, but the principal world monetary agencies are bound very largely by orthodox economic analysis and methodology. Therefore, it follows that their priorities are quite different from the human priorities which could be embodied in an aid programme, particularly as they concern the vast mass of the peasant population who are left virtually untouched by the developmental process except as victims of increased taxation and lost opportunities.

This conclusion about the nature of capitalism has led to a neo-Marxist (Jenkins 1970) to develop the concept of International Relations as a 'feudal structure'. An international political system that is feudal is defined as one where there are a group of powerful states who interact on a considerable scale with each other, each of whom dominate and penetrate a poorer area (or areas) according to historical heritage or to more contemporary exigible motives. 'Tribute' is extracted from these areas in return for 'protection'. In this scenario, there are three such 'metropolises' (USA, Britain, France) and each are linked with other rich states such as Japan, South Africa and West Germany, which differ only in terms of their non-possession of nuclear weapons. The USSR and China are two other metropolises, but each are mutually separated from the capitalist 'core'. Whereas China is seen as not acting as a feudal lord, the USSR is. Despite the qualitative and quantitative difference of Soviet expansionism, it has been 'traversing the road back to some form of state capitalism' and by disengaging from the transnational class struggle, it ultimately enforced its feudalism by military force in Eastern Europe. The picture which Jenkins (1970, 84) thus draws is 'rather like an octopus, the head being the rich metropolis and the tentacles representing the ability of the metropolis to suck surplus out of the poor nations. Each tentacle is known as a 'sphere of influence'. In terms of power, communication and influence, this is what the world looks like'. This, he concludes, results in very strong and powerful structural restraints preventing effective cooperation between the poorer states, let alone between peoples, due to these different 'vertical' spheres of influence.

Nevertheless, the second conclusion emanating from a consideration of the three assumptions about asymmetrical penetration is more sanguine. While it is undoubtedly true that the expressions of capitalism are transnational, whereby powerful business enterprises, and the state forces that support them, act to reinforce the rich, the poor have also responded with the adoption of transnational ideologies and strategies to combat and resist penetration. This process, already referred to, is aptly named 'collective decolonization' by Mittelman and which 'can be regarded as a strategy for asserting local control, exercising leverage in international affairs, and bargaining with major concentrations of power and wealth. [It] alludes to mutually sponsored effects to co-ordinate indigeneous resistance against colonial domination with the activities of various international support groups' (Mittelman 1975, 12). Such activities as multilateral declarations of intent, regional alliances, commodity trading organizations and producer associations, support of liberation movements acting either nationally or transnationally (i.e. when their resolution is carried beyond national borders in the face of imperialist recalcitrance), and the active use of the United Nations and its agencies, are indicative.

Thirdly, the ever pressing need for resources, particularly food and fuel, has led underdeveloped countries to take control – at least nominally – over key economic assets, in the name of the people. Whether this, plus the modicum of economic and technical advancement achieved, and a growing political sophistication will allow for a greater capacity realistically to resist asymmetrical penetration, remains unclear. So far as the poor areas of the world are concerned, the examples of Cuba and China, both theoretically operating through a Marxist framework and continuing to experience a socialist revolution, are at least worthy of sympathetic consideration with their progressive rebuttal of penetration. The answer of the more developed areas to penetration has not been to work through socialism for its eventual demise but, as the case of the EEC demonstrates, to unite in terms of economic production, distribution and exchange to face all the more effectively the penetrating forces of US and Japanese capitalism. Not only this, but the European bourgeoisie and their business interests have been able to utilize their stronger base to intensify their asymmetrical penetration relationships with other social units, whether internal or external to the Community, which are weaker and open to exploitation by their reinvigorated capitalism.

The progressiveness of Marxism in International Relations

Marxism, then, is a structured attempt to understand the dynamics of the social system that now encompasses the world. Although some practical problems militating against the study of this perspective have already been suggested, it is also a truism that a more fundamental reason for its neglect by students of International Relations outside the socialist world lies deep in the labyrinths of the sociology of knowledge. The long-standing intellectual tradition of the atomistic model based on the paradigm of state power politics is to many an attractive *status quo,* particularly for a descriptive and historical analysis, however much it has been amended and refined by the behavioural school. But the interpenetration of economic interests between states alone, leaving aside transnational factors, produces enormous and virtually insoluble theoretical problems for this model. To change models, and in this case to discard the notion of the nation-state as the major focus of analysis, requires fundamental rethinking of assumptions as well as radical retooling. The result, nevertheless, of such an intellectual substitution not only acts as a stimulus towards a deeper and clearer understanding of International Relations but, by the adoption of the basic tenets of the transnational model, it enables the products of Marxist analysis to be accommodated within the discipline. With transnational interactions as the focus of attention, the commonality engendered enables Marxists and non-Marxists to meet on a mutually productive meeting-ground, despite their different views on causality (Mittelman, 1975).

Together with its attempt to revolutionize and recast thinking in International Relations by the adoption of transnational class relations as a basic unit of analysis, its notion of progression distinguishes it totally from all other analytical conceptual frameworks which have been applied to the discipline. Whereas the state-centric power model concentrates upon the actions of states with a somewhat sterile and dismal scenario of power reacting against power in a never-ending Darwinian saga, the Marxist paradigm presents a far more progressive picture. Clearly, it recognizes world politics as being dominated by an international political economy, itself characterized by a vista of international class contradictions and by powerful state machines working at the behest of ruling-class interests concretely based on, and reacting to, the basic imperatives of production. It also sees worldwide patterns of market distortion and dislocation resulting from asymmetric penetration and the activities of transnational commercial and financial forces. But there is more than just 'hope' of radical change, for the progressive metamorphosis of society towards the eventual new order of production and production functions is rooted in a scientific theory of the place of man in society through the aeons of time.

This transformation of society is wholly rooted in Marxist analysis which, rather than accept that states coexist at different levels of economic and political development in various points of the world (Rostow 1960), dismisses this as an apology for imperialism, and incorrect. Instead, the Marxist would recast this in terms of evolutionary epochs through which *all* societies are progressing. As the historical epochs of primitivism, slavery and feudalism have passed, the working of the dialectic dictates that one is logically bound to argue that in world history, the world political economy is moving from the subsequent and contemporary epoch of capitalism – characterized, *inter alia,* by imperialism – to the higher one of socialism. Contemporary international relations are, therefore, dominated by the economic, political and militaristic efforts of capitalism and the ruling classes to maintain their privileged position. In turn, there is ensured the inexorable evolution of the epoch of socialism through various stages of revolutionary social change to that of the final stage of communism.

Marxism and international theory

Finally, what is the place of the Marxist paradigm in the whole spectrum of international theory? In terms of the popular threefold conception of thought developed by Martin Wight, described as 'the debate between three groups of thinkers: the Machiavellians, the Grotians and the Kantians – or, as he sometimes called them . . . the Realists, the Rationalists and the Revolutionists' (Bull 1976, 104) Marxism occupies a unique place to the extent that the theoretical conception developed by Wight and used so extensively by subsequent scholars needs to be amended to account for it. In this context, no comment need be made about the realists to whom a true description of international politics is that it is an anarchy marked by conflict between sovereign states and where the idea of international society is at best suspicious and at worse, fictitious. For the rationalists, it was about a mixture of conflict and cooperation among states while for the revolutionists

it was only at a superficial and transient level that international politics was about relations among states at all; at a deeper level it was about relations among the human beings of which states were composed. The ultimate reality was the community of mankind, which existed potentially, even if it did not exist actually, and was destined to sweep the system of states into limbo (Bull 1976, 105).

However wide Wight intended this category to be, it may be argued that Marxism might be considered as the sole 'revolutionist', all other possible contenders being, at the very least, by comparison simply insignificant in their scope and social scientific vistas. But according to Wight, this pattern of thought divided international society into horizontal rather than vertical lines and was represented by three revolutions in history, the Protestant, the French and the Communist. He also argued that it was embodied in the counter-revolutionary reactions to these: the Catholic, international legitimism and Dullesian anti-communism. It is, therefore, the latter two categories of thought – rationalist and revolutionary – that need recasting to accommodate Marxism and to avoid a distortion of its niche in international theory.

In the first place, Wight's own conception of Marxism was not only sceptical with regards to its impact on international theory but also that he did not see it as a paradigm and so confused it with international *affairs,* and with Soviet foreign policy:

It is a theory of domestic society, a political theory, which since Russia after Lenin's death came to acquiesce for the time being in remaining the only Socialist state in international society, has been tugged and cut about to cover a much wider range of political circumstances than it was designed for... Neither Marx, Lenin nor Stalin made any systematic contribution to international theory... The absence of Marxist international theory has a wider importance than making it difficult to recommend reading to an undergraduate who wants to study the principles of Communist foreign policy in the original sources. It creates the obscurity, so fruitful to the Communists themselves, about what these principles actually are... (Butterfield and Wight 1966, 25).

Secondly, the revolutions in history to which he referred were concerned with the emancipation of ideas and intellectual speculation, and more seriously attempted to formulate an international system where states were not the focus of attention. Only one theoretician of the Bolshevik Revolution, Trotsky, steadfastly and sincerely held this view and was prepared to work for its realization; as is well known, this resulted in exile and eventual assassination by agents of the Soviet state. This episode and its cryptic warning itself isolates the Marxist analysis of International Relations, apart from a serious consideration of the 1917 Revolution as being 'revolutionist' in the terms of Wight's conception.

Thirdly, the Kantian doctrine cited by Wight admittedly saw international morality in terms not so much as rules of 'good' behaviour applicable to states but rather as providing revolutionary imperatives that required all men to work for a new order of human brotherhood or 'cosmopolitanism'. But in constructing his concept of a union of peoples or *Völkerbund* which would replace the state system in which was inherent (*Völkerstaat*), Kant did not say how it would be constituted, although he did rule out federations and world government as impracticable. As a product of his time, he wrote in the grand universalizing tradition of the European Enlightenment, reflecting the forward view that progress meant a process of steady acculturation of, and with it, transfer of responsibilities to, the people. As such, he praised national divisions in Europe as they prevented despotism, particularly of the feared Turkish variety. In the future, middle-class trade, the spirit of commerce and the 'dependable' power of money would compel the ruling classes to pursue policies of peace. To reinforce these pacific forces, he suggested a *modus operandi* of law and '*good* neighbourliness'. But the question of law (as opposed to moral consciousness and search for absolute values) presupposes in these circumstances a foundation at best an absolute degree of consensus or second best, a system of administration and the application of fiat (Friedmann 1967). Furthermore, Kant wrote before the Industrial Revolution which not only revolutionized the structure of society but made the prospects for its metamorphosis into a community of mankind (or *civitas maxima* in Kantian terms) a fundamentally different proposition in qualitative terms alone.

Lastly, there is the further question of anarchism being 'revolutionist' in Wight's terms, although he did not include this intellectual tradition within his conception of the category. His reluctance to do so is understandable for it is very largely a desire to abolish International

Relations rather than to revolutionize them. Nevertheless, as it was associated with the development of the Marxist methodology and that, *prima facie,* it exhibits several similarities with it, its omission in any discussion on Marxism generally, or relating to its place in the spectrum of thought in International Relations, would be erroneous. Both rejected capitalism and its unity with the state and its coercive machinery, both endorsed the use of force to achieve revolutionary ends and both shared a vision of future society free from exploitation and inequality. Yet the fundamental difference between them went a considerable way in accounting for the short-lived existence of the First International (1864–72) – of which both were members – and the near disastrous split in the early history of the international working-class movement. Anarchism, for instance, had no consistent theory and exhibited a deliberate avoidance of systematic thought: Bakunin's complaint that 'Marx is ruining the workers by making theorists of them' (Joll 1964, 86) is characteristic. There was also a romanticized attachment to the peasantry as a society untainted by industrialization, and a great stress upon libertarian individualism. The somewhat inchoate view of post-revolutionary international society is one of anarcho-communism, being loosely based upon the freedom of the individual and a system of self-sufficient communes.[30] It follows, therefore, that there is a complete rejection of power and authoritarianism and, so far as Marxism is concerned, of the analysis of class and the post-revolutionary dictatorship of the proletariat. Furthermore, it suffered from such leaders as Bakunin who 'succeeded in making a revolutionary mentality rather than a revolutionary organization' (Joll 1964, 114), while other theoreticians like Kropotkin, whose analysis of the state was intellectually brilliant, suffered from the poor image so produced. But in the final analysis, anarchism was essentially parochial and may only be realistically considered as internationalist in the sense that its rather crude analysis of society and its apocalyptic visions were meant to be generally applicable worldwide.

Taking these elements of critique together, they suggest that a truer and more realistic picture would be to argue that Marxism is indeed the sole constituent of the 'revolutionist' category, for feasible alternatives continue implicitly to recognize the state or some other centralized political institution as basic actor in the modern world, and rely only on ideas to motivate thought. As such, Wight's 'rationalists' should become part of a wider category of 'reformists'. This group would then comprise all those who argue in terms of alternative goals and values to those suggested by *realpolitik* and who, in the final analysis, advocate methods of transcending what are perceived as the twin evils of the state as a war machine, and as a catalytic agent making manifest aggressiveness in man (whether considered latent or not). By accepting that 'anarchy' does not necessarily mean disorder but simply a lack of centralized international authority, they work for a reform of the existing system. Some, as with functionalists, would go so far as to ultimately work towards the replacement of the state by some other political and/or legal institution more suited, in their view, to the *real* needs of the world. Such a teleological doctrine, and the view of its protagonists that structures exist to perform functions may be superficially attractive, but it does not ask what gives rise to these functions. This is borne out by the omission of fundamental *social* changes to accompany such political metamorphoses, other than a progressive lessening of nationalist policies and feelings. In Marxist terms, only the 'superstructure' would change, not the crucial economic substructure.

This wide category of thought would therefore encompass theories which, at one end, appear to suggest an acceptance of the basic assumptions of the Clausewitzian struggle for survival but where the emphasis is upon the analysis of existing and *implicit* forces of order in the system, along with an assessment of the prospects for the accretion of a minimum 'modicum of order' (Bull 1977) to those more radical. As already indicated, these would be largely characterized by notions of functional cooperation and the progressively greater reliance upon international institutions as providers of welfare (Mitrany 1933, 1943; Haas 1964), the security function of states being undermined and finally buried in the face of such a rational and orderly distribution of the world's resources. Alternatively, they would include the construction of a universalist legal order, with a radical reordering of the subjects and objects of international law (Jenks 1958, Clark and Sohn 1960) in an evolutionary manner; for all, the attainment of peace, human rights and approximations to equality are the collective goals.

What then remains of the 'revolutionist' school? Nothing but Marxism whose methodology and analytical insights make for its effective isolation. In this situation, perhaps Marx's lifelong friend, Engels, should pronounce the valedictory in proclaiming that Marx had 'showed us the way out of the labyrinth of systems to real positive knowledge of the world'.[31] All scholars, by definition, have a desire to understand; this desire E. M. Forster believed to be the deepest in human nature far outpacing any other. That being so, then it is doubtless apposite for the Marxist paradigm of International Relations to be treated seriously and studied as a tool of understanding. For if Lichtheim's claim that 'to some extent, we are all Marxists now' (Curtis 1970, 11) is a correct one, then that alone should make scholars of International Relations stop and think, and invite the Marxist perspective to come out of the cold.

Notes

1. Strictly speaking, the generic term 'Marxist-Leninist' should be used in recognition of the fundamental importance of Lenin in developing Marxist theory. But since it is the methodology of Marx which is considered as being central to the analysis of International Relations, and as Lenin developed his theories of imperialism and of the state through the analytical framework derived from the methodology, only the term

'Marxist' will be used except where a theory, etc. is expressly attributed to Lenin.

2. 'Paradigm' has, in recent years, apparently developed a bewildering number of meanings (Lakatos and Musgrave 1971). For the purpose of this analysis, Rosenau's (1971, 107) interpretation has been used: 'A general orientation towards all events, a point of view or a philosophy about the way the world is.'
3. Many commentators have argued that the 'hierarchy of struggles' have been reversed, whereby the primacy of the struggle between the proletariat and the bourgeoisie in the Western world has given way to that between colonial and neo-colonial peoples against their imperialist masters. Trotsky was the first to observe this, and coined the phrase about the path to London and Paris lying through Calcutta and Peking. (Deutscher 1954, 457–8).
4. A notable attempt to seriously discuss this is Brzezinski. But he is eventually led to the conclusion that '... politics has a way of catching up with intellectual insight, and some practitioners of power have already realized that their unifying ideology has become a domestic liability to them' (Brzezinski 1967, 512). In a study by Triska and Findlay (1968), the techniques of content analysis are applied to foreign policy analysis, particularly that of the Societ Union. By doing so, it stresses the great importance of the *Weltanschauung* (see note 6), but shows that in the operationalization of the policy, the ideology is by no means a determining factor.
5. Preface to a contribution to the *Critique of Political Economy* (1859) in Feuer 1969, 84.
6. There is no adequate translation of this word into English (*conception du monde* in French). Unfortunately, it is sometimes used to connote ideology but this, of course, is quite incorrect.
7. *On the Correct Handling of Contradictions Among the People* (1957), in Mao Tse-Tung 1971, 433–4.
8. *The German Ideology* (1846) in Marx and Engels 1970, 48.
9. Ibid., 42.
10. *Introduction to a Critique of Political Economy* (1859) in Marx and Engels 1970, 125.
11. *The Communist Manifesto* (1848). Marx and Engels 1967, 80.
12. Hobsbawm (1964, 19–20), makes this explicit with his comment that 'the general theory of historical materialism requires only that there should be a succession of modes of production, though not necessarily any particular modes, and perhaps not in any particular order'.
13. *Manifesto,* op. cit., 79.
14. Preface, etc. (1859), in Feuer 1969, 85, 84.
15. *Ludwig Feuerbach and the End of Classical German Philosophy* (1888), in Marx and Engels 1968, 617.
16. *The German Ideology* (1846) in Feuer 1969, 295.
17. *Feuerbach,* op. cit., in Marx and Engels 1968, 588.
18. *Theses on Feuerbach* (1845), in Marx and Engels 1968, 28, 30.
19. *Introduction to the Critique of Hegel's Philosophy of Right* (1843–4), in Marx, 1975, 252.
20. *Manifesto,* in Marx and Engels 1967, 82–3.
21. *The German Ideology,* in Marx and Engels 1970, 78.
22. Not only did that statement provide unpromising grounds from which a general Marxist theory of nationalism could grow, but in his later writings he became increasingly concerned by what he termed 'embourgeoisment'. This he meant to mean the identification of the proletariat with the bourgeois state and its values. The concept was later taken up by the theorists of imperialism who saw imperialism as an explanatory model devised to explain such reactionary qualities. The answer thereby offered was the well-known one, that the living standards of the proletariat were rising due to subsidies obtained from the extraction of profits elsewhere, and which in turn gave the bourgeois state a continuing image of social progressiveness.
23. *Preface* to the 1891 edition of Marx's *Civil War in France,* in Marx and Engels 1968, 258.
24. 'We are living not merely in a state but in a system of states and the existence of the

Soviet Republic side by side with imperialist states for a long time is unthinkable. One or other must triumph in the end. And before that end supervenes, a series of frightful collisions between the Soviet Republic and the bourgeois states will be inevitable. That means that if the ruling class, the proletariat, wants to hold sway, it must prove its capacity to do so by its military organisations' (quoted by Stalin 1940, 156). In fact, Lenin did not specify whether the predicted clash would result from revolutionary war or from a counter-revolutionary attack on the USSR. Also, contrary to many commentator's views, this new thesis of inevitable conflict between imperialism and socialism was *not* a conversion from his theoretical conclusion of inter-capitalist wars consequent upon imperialism. Although Lenin never confused the two, Khruschev certainly did at the Twentieth Congress of the CPSU when he formally made peaceful coexistence, and not conflict, the official policy of the USSR. In fact, 'coexistence' was recognized by Lenin as a necessary fact of international life within the operational parameters of the state-centric paradigm, almost simultaneously with his famous statement above. For a discussion of this, see Burin 1963, and Vigor 1975.

25. Feuer 1969, 25. In 1866, Marx followed the theories of the French anthropologist Trémaux: 'the common Negro type was a degeneration from a quite higher one' was quoted by him approvingly.
26. There is a continuing debate over the exact definition of the multinational company in that a spectrum exists between those which are decentralized, with an international shareholding subscription and a registration in a 'tax haven' such as the Cayman Islands, to those which are monolithically organized and owned with a registered and fully operational headquarters in one country, and subsidiary production plants overseas in a direct line of control. For the purposes of this brief study, a simple definition has been adopted.
27. *Manifesto,* in Marx and Engels 1967, 82.
28. Euro-dollars may be in any convertible and 'hard' currency, and be resident anywhere where exchange controls permit. Hirsch (1967, 169) quoted a definition from the Bank of International Settlements 1964 Report: 'The activity of the Euro-dollar market could be looked on as "the acquisition of dollars by banks located outside the United States, mostly through the taking of deposits but also to some extent through swapping other currencies into dollars, and the re-lending of these dollars, often after re-depositing with other banks to non-bank borrowers anywhere in the world" – noting specifically that the currency swapping can come before the re-lending as well as after.'
29. Compare the conclusion to Keohane and Nye (1972, 388): 'If transnationalism has become the ideology of some of the rich, nationalism remains the ideology of the poor. In many of the new states transnational processes are (or seem to be) remnants of colonial rule.'
30. This interpretation is both original and modern. Marcuse (1964) has, for instance, merged both anarchism and Marxism with his concept of a non-repressive society made possible by the removal of the 'repressive' elements of modern industrialized society, and thus enabling the transformation of human instincts.
31. *Ludwig Feuerbach,* (1888) in Marx and Engels 1968, 590.

References and Further Reading

Althusser, L. (1969) *For Marx.* London, Allen Lane.

Anderson, P. (1976) *Considerations on Western Marxism,* London, New Left Books.

Avineri, S. (0000) *The Social and Political Thought of Karl Marx*, London, Cambridge Univ. Press.

Baran, P. and Sweezy, P. (1968) *Monopoly Capital,* Harmondsworth, Penguin.

Bell, G. (1973) *The Euro-Dollar Market and the International Financial System,* London, Macmillan.

Berki, R.N. (1971) 'On Marxian thought and the problem of International Relations', *World Politics* (October).

Bhagwati, T. (ed.) (1972) *Economics and World Order from the 1970s to the 1990s,* New York, Collier-Macmillan.
Brzezinski, Z.K. (1967) *The Soviet Bloc, Unity and Conflict,* Cambridge, Mass., Harvard Univ. Press.
Bukharin, N. (1918) *Imperialism and World Economy,* London, Merlin Press, 1972.
Bull, H. (1976) *The Anarchical Society,* London, Macmillan.
Bull, H. (1977) 'Martin Wight and the theory of international relations' (The Second Martin Wight Memorial Lecture), *British Journal of International Studies,* **2,** (2), July.
Burin, F.S. (1963) 'The communist doctrine of the inevitability of war', *American Political Science Review,* **57** (2), June.
Burton, J. (1972) *World Society,* London, Cambridge Univ. Press.
Butterfield, H. and Wight, M. (eds.) (1966) *Diplomatic Investigations,* London, Allen and Unwin.
Caute, D. (1970) *Fanon,* London, Fontana.
Clark, G. and Sohn, L.B. (1960) *World Peace Through World Law.* Cambridge, Mass., Harvard Univ. Press.
Claudin, F. (1975) *The Communist Movement,* Harmondsworth, Penguin.
Curtis, M. (1970) *Marxism,* New York, Atherton Press.
de Cecco, M. (1976) 'International financial markets and US domestic policy since 1945', *International Affairs,* **52,** (3), July.
Deutscher, I. (1954) *The Prophet Armed,* London, Oxford Univ. Press.
Dobb, M. (1970) 'Lenin and imperialism', *Marxism Today,* April.
Erb, G.F. and Kallab, V. (1975) *Beyond Dependency: The Developing World Speaks Out.* Washington, DC, Overseas Development Council.
Fanon, F. (1961) *The Wretched of the Earth,* Harmondsworth, Penguin, 1967.
Feuer, L.S. (ed.) (1969) *Marx and Engels,* London, Fontana.
Flanagan, R.J. and Weber, A.R. (eds.) (1975) *Bargaining without Boundaries. The Multinational Corporation and International Labour Relations.* Chicago, Chicago Univ. Press.
Friedmann, W. (1944) *Legal Theory,* London, Stevens, 1967.
Gardner, R.N. (1956) *Sterling-Dollar Diplomacy,* Oxford, Clarendon Press.
Haas, E. (1964) *Beyond the Nation State,* Stanford, Calif., Stanford Univ. Press.
Haupt, G. (1972) *Socialism and the Great War: The Collapse of the Second International,* Oxford, Clarendon Press.
Hayter, T. (1971) *Aid as Imperialism,* Harmondsworth, Penguin.
Hilferding, R. (1970) 'Das Finanzkapital' in Fieldhouse, D.K. (ed.) *The Theory of Capitalist Imperialism,* London, Longman, 1967.
Hirsch, F. (1967) *Money International,* London, Allen Lane.
Hobson, J.A. (1962) *Imperialism: A Study,* London, Allen & Unwin, rev. edn. 1948.
Hobsbaum, E. (ed.) (1964) *Introduction to Pre-Capitalist Economic Formations,* Londonn, Lawrence and Wishart.
Horowitz, D. (1969) Imperialism and Revolution, London, Allen Lane.
Hymer, S. (1972) 'The multinational corporation and the law of uneven development', in J. Bhagwati, (ed.), *Economics and World Order from the 1970s to the 1990s.* New York, Collier-Macmillan.
Jenkins, R. (1970) *Exploitation,* London, MacGibbon and Kee.
Jenks, C.W. (1958) *The Common Law of Mankind,* London, Stevens.
Joll, J. (1964) *The Anarchists,* London, Methuen.
Kara, K. (1968) 'On the Marxist theory of war and peace', *Journal of Peace Research,* No. 1.
Kautsky, K. (1902) *The Social Revolution,* Chicago, Chicago U.P.
Kautsky, K. (1970) 'Ultra-imperialism', *New Left Review,* **59,** Jan-Feb.
Keohane, R.O. and Nye, J.S. Jr., (1972) *Transnational Relations and World Politics.* Cambridge, Mass., Harvard Univ. Press.
Kiernan, V.G. (1974) *Marxism and Imperialism,* London, Arnold.
Kindleberger, C.P. (1970) *Power and Money. The Politics of International Economics and the Economics of International Politics,* London, Macmillan.

Knorr, K. (1975) *The Power of Nations: The Political Economy of International Relations,* New York, Basic Books.
Lakatos, I. and Musgrave, A. (1971) *Criticism and the Growth of Knowledge,* London, Cambridge Univ. Press.
Lenin, V.I. (1916) *Imperialism The Highest Stage of Capitalism,* Peking, Foreign Languages Press, 1970.
Levitt, K. (1970) *Silent Surrender.* London, Macmillan.
Lowy, M. (1976) 'Marxists and the national question', *New Left Review,* **96,** (March–April).
Luxembourg, R. (1973) *The Accumulation of Capital,* Routledge and Kegan Paul, 2nd edn. 1965.
Mao Tse-Tung (1971) *Selected Readings,* Peking, Foreign Languages Press.
Magdoff, H. (1969) *The Age of Imperialism,* New York, Monthly Review Press.
Marcuse, H. (1964) *One Dimensional Man,* London, Routledge and Kegan Paul.
Marx, K. (1842) 'The historical school of law', *Rheinische Zeitung* (9 August).
Marx, K. (1857–8) *Grundrisse* (introduced by M. Nicolaus), Harmondsworth, Penguin, 1973.
Marx, K. (1875) 'The critique of the Gotha programme', in Fernbach D. (ed.), *The First International And After,* Harmondsworth, Pelican, 1974.
Marx, K. (1975) *Early Writings* (introduced by Lucio Colletti), Harmondsworth, Penguin.
Marx, K. and Engels, F. (1848) *The Communist Manifesto* (introduced by A.J.P. Taylor), Harmondsworth, Penguin, 1967.
Marx, K. and Engels, F. (1968) *Selected Works* (in one volume), London, Lawrence and Wishart.
Marx, K. and Engels, F. (1970) *The German Ideology,* C.J. Arthur, (ed.), London, Lawrence and Wishart.
Mitrany, D. (1943) *A Working Peace System,* London, RIIA.
Mitrany, D. (1933) *The Progress of International Government,* London, Allen and Unwin.
Mittelman, J. (1975) 'International relations theory and transnationalism: A framework for evaluating decolonisation', *International Studies Notes,* **2** (2), Summer.
Nairn, T. (1975) 'Marxism and the modern Janus', *New Left Review* **94** (November–December).
Nicolaus, M. (ed.) (1973) Marx *Grundisse* (Foreword), Harmondsworth, Penguin.
Nkrumah, K. (1965) *Neocolonialism: The Last Stage of Capitalism,* London, Heinemann.
Northedge, F.S. (1976) 'Transnationalism: The American illusion', *Millenium,* **5** (1) (Spring).
Radice, H. (ed.) (1975) *International Firms and Modern Imperialism,* Harmondsworth, Penguin.
Robinson, J. and Eatwell, J. (1973) *An Introduction to Modern Economics,* New York, McGraw-Hill.
Rodney, W. (1969) *The Groundings with my Brothers,* London, Bogle-L'Ouverture Publications.
Rosenau, J.N. (1971) *A Scientific Study of Foreign Policy,* New York, Free Press.
Rostow, W.W. (1960) *The Stages of Economic Growth: A Non-Communist Manifesto,* London, Cambridge Univ. Press.
Sartre, J.P. 'Orphee Noir' in Fell, J. *Emotion in the Thought of Sartre,* New York, Columbia U.P., 1965.
Schumpeter, J.A. 'Imperialism and capitalism' in Sweezy, P.M. (ed.), *Imperialism and Social Classes,* Oxford, Blackwell, 1951.
Stalin, J.V. (1940) *Problems of Leninism,* Moscow, Foreign Languages Press.
Strachey, K. (1959) *The End of Empire,* London, Gollancz.
Strange, S. (1971) *Sterling and British Policy,* London, Oxford Univ. Press for the RIIA.
Strange, S. (1976) 'The study of transnational relations', *International Affairs,* **52,** (3) (July).

Suslov, M.A. (1975) *Marxism–Leninism: The International Teaching of The Working Class,* Moscow, Foreign Languages Press.
Triska, J.F. and Findlay, D.D. *Soviet Foreign Policy,* New York, Macmillan.
Trotsky, L. (1936) *The Revolution Betrayed,* London, Pathfinder Press, 1937.
Turner, L. (1974) *Multinational Companies and the Third World,* London, Allen Lane.
Vigor, P.H. (1975) *The Soviet View of War, Peace and Neutrality,* London, Routledge and Kegan Paul.
Ward, B. and Dubos, R. (1972) *Only One World,* Harmondsworth, Penguin.
Wolfe, B.D. (1969) *An Ideology in Power,* London, Allen and Unwin.
Worsley, P. (1964) *The Third World,* London, Weidenfeld and Nicolson.

Chapter 5

The 'peace through law' approach: a critical examination of its ideas

H. Suganami

The 'emergence' of the approach

There is a degree of artificiality in E. H. Carr's thesis that those thinkers of the interwar years who saw international law and organization as representing the road to peace were, so to speak, the 'alchemists' in the field of international relations. His argument, which appears in the first chapter of his well-known book, *The Twenty Years' Crisis,* can be summarized along the following lines.

Logically, we ought first to collect, classify and analyse facts and draw inferences from them: we shall then be ready to investigate the purpose to which our facts and deductions can be put. However, the human mind works in the opposite direction. Purpose, which should follow analysis, is required to give it both its initial impulse and its direction. As purpose thus precedes and conditions thought, it is natural that when a new field of study is created, its initial stage is characterized by the strong element of wish and purpose. In the case of the science of international politics, the passionate desire to prevent war, from which it took its rise, determined the whole initial course of the study. In this respect, this science followed the pattern of other sciences, and has been markedly Utopian: it has attempted, as it were, to make gold out of lead (Carr 1946, 1–8). Such an explanation seems too schematic and requires some qualification.

Although it is true that the science of international politics as an academic discipline was in its infancy in the period after the First World War, it is certainly not the case that the idea of peace through law was then also in its infancy. This idea did not so much 'emerge'; *it was there.*

It was there when in 1814, as a congress assembled at Vienna, Saint-Simon, a French socialist and eccentric, found 'no salvation for Europe except through a general reorganization' of the European society (Markham 1952, 33–4). The peace and prosperity of Europe required, in his view, *first,* the establishment of a common government which was to be in the same relation to the different peoples as national governments were to individuals, and *second,* the application of the best possible constitution to the common government as well as to the national governments (Markham 1952, 32, 39).

It was there when Kant, the great German philosopher, in his *Zum Ewigen Frieden* and other related writings, saw in the late eighteenth century that the fate of the citizen of a state depended, not only upon the internal organization of the state, but also upon its relationship with other states, and asserted that the subordination of international relations to a rule of law is a moral imperative (Klinke 1951, 112–22).

It was there when Grotius, the father of international law, as he is often (though somewhat inaccurately) called, asserted in his *De Jure Belli ac Pacis,* written in the middle of the Thirty Years War, that there was a common law among nations which was valid alike for war and in war (in Forsyth et al. 1970, 54), and went on to elaborate what he believed this common law prescribed.

And *it was there* not only in theory but also in practice, albeit on a regional scale, when in the late thirteenth century the three forest communities of Switzerland formed a perpetual league, which was at once a collective defence system against an external enemy and a collective security system among themselves (Newton 1923, 41–3). *It was there* even among the Greeks who, in their intercity relationships, developed procedures for resolving conflicts short of war such as arbitration and conciliation, but who again were not the inventors, in the literal sense, of such methods: they were there already (Holsti 1974, 51 n. 37).

The 'emergence' in the period after the First World War of the 'peace through law' approach should be regarded primarily as an instance of this long tradition, in thought and practice, and not merely as an infantile disease of a new-born academic discipline. This tradition had existed long before it occurred to some people that it might make sense to subsume that tradition under a new category of intellectual exercises.

On the other hand, there is no doubt that the outbreak of the First World War precipitated the massive production of proposals for the revision of the then existing international legal system. Not only the eccentric, the great philosopher, and the international jurist of world-wide renown, but also statesmen, intellectuals and common citizens joined the chorus. The idea of peace through law 'emerged' in the sense that far more people came to adhere to the doctrine far more enthusiastically, and expressed their allegiance to it far more frequently, than ever before in the history of mankind.

In addition to his explanation of the 'peace through law' approach as an infantile disease of the science of international politics, Carr also offers another explanation of the process through which this approach emerged. While the first explanation is sociological and psychological in nature, the second is historical.

Carr points out that nearly all popular theories of international politics between the two world wars (the 'peace through law' approach being their primary example) were reflections, seen in an American mirror, of nineteenth century liberal thought. His argument, more specifically, is that though liberalism had lost its support in Europe by the end of the nineteenth century, its half-discarded assumptions reappeared in the special field of international politics through the influence of the United States where these assumptions were still held to be valid. He writes:

Just as Bentham, a century earlier, had taken the eighteenth century doctrine of reason and refashioned it to the needs of the coming age, so now Woodrow Wilson, the impassioned admirer of Bright and Gladstone, transplanted the nineteenth century rationalist faith to the almost virgin soil of international politics and, bringing it back with him to Europe, gave it a new lease of life (Carr 1946, 27).

This is a figurative description of the actual historical process and in that sense somewhat artificial: one should not be led to think that the 'peace through law' approach in the field of International Relations was literally introduced from America to Europe in the sense in which tobacco was, or to imagine that a rationalist tradition had not existed in European ideas about the relation of states. There is no doubt that America, as personified by Wilson, was strongly influential in moulding the *Zeitgeist* of the period after the First World War in the field of International Relations. However, the Wilsonian influence should not be exaggerated. It seems more appropriate to say that the popularity of the 'peace through law' approach was largely the result of spontaneous reaction to the experience of the war in the minds of many thinking individuals, of whom Wilson was a symbolic and influential one.

In fact, the wave of proposals for the revision of the then existing international legal system can be seen both as an extension of the nineteenth century pacifist–internationalist movement and as a reaction against the sanguine attitude underlying that system of law.

The nineteenth century pacifist–internationalist movement, on which there exists a considerable body of literature, (e.g. Hinsley 1967, 92–113). had culminated in the Hague Peace Conference of 1899 and 1907 J. B. Scott, an American international lawyer and ardent supporter of the Conferences, described them as 'the first truly international assemblies meeting in time of peace for the purpose of preserving peace, not of concluding a war then in progress' (1920, v). They marked, in his view, an epoch in the history of international relations, for they 'showed on a large scale that international cooperation [w]as possible and they created institutions – imperfect it may be, as is the work of human hands, – which, when improved in the light of experience, will both by themselves and by the force of their example promote the administration of justice and the betterment of mankind' (1920, v–vi).

The improvement and perfection, rather than a radical alteration, of the existing system of international law on the basis of the Hague achievements was the keynote of the 'peace through law' approach before the outbreak of the First World War. However, the traumatic experience of the war brought home to many thinkers that a radical alteration was required if international law was to remain a relevant factor in International relations. The Hague Peace Conferences, which were the culminating point of the nineteenth century pacifist–internationalist movement and the achievements of which were regarded by some as the starting-point for the perfection of the international legal system came to be seen by many as having produced a wrong kind of law altogether: the *Peace* Conferences did not pave the way to peace, but by codifying rules of warfare, condoned war; the Hague system did not 'outlaw' war, but attempted merely to regulate it (c.f. Vollenhoven 1919, 40–58).

Thus the 'emergence' of the 'peace through law' approach can be said to consist not merely of a numerical increase of the supporters of this approach: more significantly, it consisted of the formation of a new consensus of opinion as to the minimum standard which international law must satisfy. The adherents of this approach generally held that the right of states to go to war must be legally restricted and that international law must embody the principle of collective security. This point can be well illustrated by looking at the metamorphosis of Oppenheim's conception of the ideal content of international law before and after his experience of the First World War.

Oppenheim, the author of 'probably the most influential English textbook of international law' (Wight in Butterfield and Wight 1966, 172) is regarded by some as a potential political 'realist' among the many idealistically minded international jurists (Bull in Butterfield and Wight 1966, 53 n. 1). While it is true that he was not so radical a Utopian as to advocate the replacement of international society by a world state, he was idealistic enough to formulate a scheme for an improved organization of international society. His proposal of 1911, four years after the second Hague Peace Conference and three years before the outbreak of the First World War, included the establishment of an international court of justice endowed with the authority of compulsory jurisdiction, international courts of appeal and an international quasi-legislature (Oppenheim 1921, esp. 23–55).

Oppenheim's 1911 plan, however, did not include an international executive authority or any form of coercive mechanism. He regarded this omission as a distinctive and important feature of his proposal. His rejection of the necessity to establish a coercive mechanism in international society is based on a very optimistic assumption. Thus he argues as follows:

In the internal life of states it is necessary for courts to possess executive power because the conditions of human nature demand it. Just as there will always be individual offenders, so there will always be individuals who will only yield to compulsion. But states are a different kind of person from individual men; their present-day constitution on the generally prevalent type has made them, so to say, more moral than in the times of absolutism. The personal interests and ambition of sovereigns, and their passion for an increase of their might, have finished playing their part in the life of peoples. The real and true interests of states and the welfare of the inhabitants of the state have taken the place thereof. Machiavellian principles are no longer prevalent everywhere. The mutual intercourse of states is carried on in reliance on the sacredness of treaties. Peaceable adjustment of state disputes is in the interests of the states themselves, for war is nowadays an immense moral and economic evil even for the victor state (Oppenheim 1921, 54).

Oppenheim's optimism, so vividly expressed in these lines, which was by no means peculiar to him in his time, was soon to be shattered. In his letter of February 1919 addressed to Theodore Marburg, one of the organizers of the League of Nations movement in America, Oppenheim confesses his conversion:

As regards the question which you raise in your letter namely 'whether it is necessary to provide for enforcing the judgement of the Court', before the war I was of opinion like you that, if we only got the International Court of Justice established, no enforcement of its verdicts would be necessary. . . .

However, the war has changed everything,. . . *in case a party against which a verdict of the Court has been given disobeyed the verdict and resorted to hostilities, there is no doubt that the* [proposed] *League would have to take the side of the attacked party* (Latané 1932, 615 emphasis added).

This can be regarded, by implication, as the advocacy of a collective security system. While it is difficult to assess the actual number of instances in which such a conversion took place, the fact that an influential international lawyer did go through such a metamorphosis is by itself significant. As Judge H. Lauterpacht has noted, 'Liszt, the author of the well-known German text-book' of international law, also went through a radical change of attitude as regards the place of compulsion in international law after the experience of the First World War (H. Lauterpacht 1933, 432 n. 3). One may also note O. Nippold's book, *The Development of International Law After the World War,* in which he compares his own writings before and after the outbreak of the war to show his conversion as regards the question of sanctions (Nippold 1923, 33–6). These writings illustrate in a symbolic manner the way in which the experience of the First World War gave rise to a new climate of opinion, which is commonly noted as the 'emergence' of the 'peace through law' approach in International Relations.

The analysis of the approach: (I) its assumptions

As Josef Kunz has clearly described in his article, 'The swing of the pendulum', the immense popularity of the idea of peace through law after the First World War has been replaced since the breakdown of the League of Nations by a popular notion that international law is largely irrelevant (Kunz 1950, 135–40). This alleged irrelevance of international law is often confused with the so-called Utopian nature of the 'peace through law' approach.

It is therefore essential to point out at the outset that the following discussion is *not* concerned with the relevance of international law, *either* as a system of rules deemed to be binding upon the conduct of sovereign states as a matter of the 'orthodox' doctrine of international relations (Manning 1962, 101–13), *or* as a branch of an academic discipline subsumed under the general category of Law or International Relations.

The relevance of international law as a system of rules in international society is a matter for the Sociology of International Law to determine on the basis of empirical investigations combined with conceptual clarifications. The relevance of international law as a branch of an academic discipline is a matter of opinion, perhaps most reliably judged by academics and practitioners of wide knowledge and experience. Although there is a close link between the relevance of these two things in that the value of an academic discipline depends to a considerable extent upon the practical importance of the subject-matter, they should not be confused. Nor should the relevance of either of them be confused with that of the subject-matter of this essay. Our concern here is not international law in either of those two senses, but an international theory about the place of law in international society and, more specifically, about the ideal content of law for the organization of mankind.

As a theory of international relations, the 'peace through law' approach is *prescriptive,* and not *explanatory:* it consists of recommendations, not hypotheses. It does not intend to explain why things are as they are in international society: but it assumes that the lack of sufficient orderliness in international society is due to the poor quality of law by which that society is organized. In other words, it takes it for granted that the legal structure of international society is chiefly, if not solely, responsible for the predicament of that society. To use the well-known trichotomy of international theory popularized by Kenneth Waltz, the 'peace through law' approach therefore falls into the category of the third image analysis of international relations.[1]

The assumption that the poor quality of law is responsible for the poor quality of life in international society can be contrasted with two other assumptions.

One is the view that the poor quality of law is but a manifestation of the poor quality of life in international society. Those who take this view tend to emphasize that a change in the content of law, which takes place in the sphere of 'ought', will not necessarily create a corresponding and desired change in the pattern of actual life, or in the sphere of 'is'. According to this view, a proposal for the reorganization of international society is merely an exercise in constitution-mongering at the international level.

The other is the view that the poor quality of law is not necessarily detrimental to the quality of life in a society in which it is deemed to be valid. According to this view, the quality of law cannot be judged in an *a-priori* fashion. For instance, one tends to assume in an *a-priori* manner that a clearly and unambiguously codified system of law is intrinsically better than that which is loose and vague. However, within a society where its members are not very cooperative in the first place, it might very well be that a loosely and vaguely formulated system of law susceptible of multiple interpretations is more conducive to keeping the modicum of orderliness that exists in that society: a clear and unambiguous law may simply exacerbate the situation in such a society by making it too clear to its members that a flagrant violation of law has taken place while its members remain unable to take any effective measures against the violation. In other words, a clear and unambiguous law may have an unintended result of embittering the original difference between the contenders by 'adding a charge of bad faith to the original cause of difference' (Westlake 1904, 344), just as a man and a woman might perhaps enjoy a longer period of harmony than a man and his wife.

However, the 'peace through law' approach of the post-First World War variety, on the whole took the view (*a*) that the improvement of international law would create a better international order, and (*b*) that the quality of an international legal system should be judged by the degree to which it corresponded, in its essential aspects, with a domestic legal system. In short, this approach was based on the assumption that the more closely analogous the international legal system would become in a number of aspects to a domestic legal system, the more peaceful and orderly would be the society of nations. The belief in the validity of this domestic analogy, therefore, is the central pillar of the 'peace through law' approach under consideration.

At the base of this pillar lies a set of more fundamental assumptions: the belief in the progressive nature of human history and in the harmony of 'true' national interests.

The belief in progress and that in the harmony of interests are intertwined in that the goal of mankind's progress is held by its believers to be a harmonious world in which states act in accordance with their 'true' interests. Indeed, unless such a specific goal is envisaged, it does not make sense to talk of a 'progress', for, in Walter Schiffer's words, the 'idea that mankind is steadily advancing is conceivable only if it is assumed that there exist criteria which make it possible objectively to measure the advance' (Schiffer 1972, 142). The stage of development of human history, therefore, is to be judged by the closeness of the real to the ideal world, or by the degree of peace and well-being attained in the world.

As Schiffer points out, the roots of such beliefs or assumptions are to be found in the rationalist tradition going at least as far back as Grotius. Before the outbreak of the First World War, it seemed possible for the adherents of such beliefs to refer to a number of factors apparently justifying their assertions. We have in fact caught a glimpse of such assertions in the passage we quoted in the previous section from Oppenheim's 1911 proposal. The principles of liberal-democratic government had been applied to an increasing extent. Technological advancement stimulated an expansion of industry and commerce, leading to an increase of international economic intercourse, and the improved means of communication and transport brought the peoples into closer contact. The growing mutual interdependence of peoples seemed to indicate the absurdity, and hence the unlikelihood, of a war. Indeed, since the end of the Napoleonic Wars, there had been no general conflict of similar magnitude, and the states' willingness to submit their differences to arbitration seemed to be increasing steadily. It was therefore not unnatural that the condition of the world appeared to some to be better than it had ever been in the history of mankind and that they believed in the possibility of further improvements in the future (Schiffer 1972, 142–8).

The belief in the harmony of 'true' national interests was popularized, as Carr points out, chiefly by the *laissez-faire* school of political economy created by Adam Smith. Just as individuals are thought, by pursuing their own good, to enhance the good of the whole community, so nations in search of their 'true' interests are assumed by the upholders of this belief to serve humanity as a whole (Carr 1946, 41–62). In fact, as Carr notes, there was a special reason for the ready acceptance of the doctrine of the natural harmony of interests in the international sphere. He writes as follows: 'In domestic affairs it is clearly the business of the state to create harmony if no natural harmony exists. In international politics, there is no organized power charged with the task of creating harmony; and the temptation to assume a natural harmony is therefore particularly strong, (Carr, 1946, 51).

As exemplified by Oppenheim's assertion quoted earlier, it was commonly held before the First World War by the adherents of the 'peace through law' approach that not only was there no 'true' conflict of national interests, but also that states were acting increasingly reasonably and thus in accordance with their 'true' interests. This explains the relative unpopularity of the idea in the nineteenth century that an orderly social life required compulsion in the international sphere. It has, however, been pointed out in the previous section that one of the consequences of the experience of the war was the radical change of attitude among thinkers as regards the place of compulsion in international law. It had now come to be argued not only that there was no 'true' conflict of national interests, but, more emphatically, that those who resorted to force were therefore acting irrationally and wrongfully.

The belief in the harmony of 'true' national interests had survived the war. What had now been added was a felt need for a legal mechanism which not only provided a pacific substitute for war, but also prevented states from taking that irrational course of action. The attempt at the creation of such a mechanism through the establishment of the League of .Nations' collective security system was now held to constitute a progressive step in the history of the legal organization of mankind.

The analysis of the approach: (II) Its prescriptions

It has been pointed out in the previous section that the 'peace through law' approach is prescriptive and that the central pillar of this approach is the use of a domestic analogy. It follows that the actual content of prescription depends upon the way in which the domestic analogy is used. An analysis of this analogy, therefore, is essential to the understanding of the 'peace through law' approach and its various prescriptions.

Hedley Bull explains the domestic analogy as follows:

> [*It is*] *the argument from the experience of individual men in domestic society to the experience of states, according to which the need of individual men to stand in awe of a common power in order to live in peace is a ground for holding that states must do the same. The conditions of an orderly social life, on this view, are the same among states as they are within them: they require that the institutions of domestic society be reproduced on a universal scale* (in Butterfield and Wight 1966, 35).

This explanation of domestic analogy is admirably succinct. However, it contains within it two ambiguities, which must be clarified at the outset.

First, it is not clear how much significance Bull intends to attach to the definite article when he refers to '*the* institutions of domestic society' in the above quotation. Can one be said to be using domestic analogy *only* when one advocates the reproduction on a universal scale of all the essential institutions of domestic society, including the legislature, the judicature and the executive? Can one consequently claim that one is *not* using domestic analogy if one merely advocates the necessity for an international legislature and judicature, for instance, but not an executive?

This is in fact the line of argument adopted by Oppenheim as regards his 1911 proposal. He thinks that his proposed organization is unstate-like, because it lacks the executive organ (Oppenheim 1921, 16, 21–2). However, it seems somewhat contradictory to say that Oppenheim does not use domestic analogy *at all* when in fact he very clearly bases his advocacy for the establishment of the international court and courts of appeal upon the experience of the judicial system in domestic society (Oppenheim 1921, 14, 51–2). It seems more appropriate to consider him as using domestic analogy *in part.* There is after all nothing unnatural in the idea of reproducing on a universal scale only those institutions of domestic society which it is useful to reproduce: in other words, resorting to domestic analogy *selectively.*

Secondly, the expression, the reproduction 'on a universal scale', is not without ambiguity. The reproduction can be done in two different ways: first in such a way that the reorganized world can still be said to constitute an 'international' society; second in such a way that the reproduction renders the idea of an 'international' society an obsolete one. In other words, by using domestic analogy, one may *either* make a proposal that does not alter the fundamental structure of international society (i.e. the society of sovereign states), *or* produce a scheme according to which the existing international society is to be replaced by a global domestic society. In the first case, the reorganized world would be analogous in its structure to a domestic society, but, as such, could not be regarded as constituting one. In the second case, the reorganized world as such would count as a domestic society. One way of illuminating this distinction is to point out that the use of domestic analogy in the first pattern is based on 'internationalism' and the second on 'cosmopolitanism', as distinguished, for instance, by Christian Lange (Schiffer 1972, 118).

In a world reorganization proposal based on the use of domestic analogy in the second way, i.e. envisaging the establishment of a global domestic society, the existing sovereign states are bound to lose their sovereignty. Sovereignty can be defined in this context as 'constitutional insularity or self-containedness' (Manning in Porter 1972, 308) or *Völkerrechtsunmittelbarkeit* in the expression of Verdross and Kunz (Bernier 1973, 20).[2] In such a society, the existing states would turn into bodies equivalent to provinces of a unitary state or member states of a federal union. There, for instance, law regulating the conduct of individuals would be enacted directly by the legislature of the world government.

Advocacy of such a drastic reorganization of the global society is in fact extremely rare; much rarer than the common tendency to label an international reorganization scheme as a 'world government' scheme would have us believe. Thus Theodore Marburg, in his survey of leading American and European plans for international organization formulated between 1914 and 1919, remarks as follows:

Of course the ideal instrument to realize the fundamental aim of peaceful settlement of disputes is a super-State, dominating the various nations just as the Federal Government dominates the individual States comprising the American Union. Few men, however, believe that this ideal is realizable in the present stage of world opinion and prejudice, though certain French and English writers would go far in that direction (Latané 1932, 767).

In fact, a closer examination of the proposals put forward by those 'few men' noted by Marburg, such as H. Lepert and P. Otlet, reveals that, though their proposed organizations may go farther in the direction of a super-state than those envisaged by other writers, those proposed bodies cannot justifiably be described as constituting a state (Latané 1932, 767–8).

What is in fact far more common than the advocacy for the establishment of a global domestic society is the use of domestic analogy in the other fashion, i.e. on the basis of the idea that states are fundamental units unlikely to be eliminated, or on the basis of the personification of states.

That the development of international law depended heavily upon the idea that states are persons has commonly been noted. Perhaps the most exhaustive and systematic treatment of this aspect of international law is found in H. Lauterpacht's book, *Private Law Sources and Analogies of International Law.* It seems undeniable that private law analogies played an important role in the formative period of international law. Lauterpacht expresses this by saying that 'international public law belongs to the *genus* private law' (H. Lauterpacht 1927, 81).

However, the analogy between private law and international law breaks down in one vital point. Within a domestic legal system the use of force is generally prohibited, while in contrast, in the international system, the right of states to use force had traditionally been regarded as outside the concern of positive law. As a consequence, the acquisition of territory by conquest (or more widely, the validity of treaties made under duress) has been recognized by the traditional system of public international law, while private law (of the *species* domestic, in Lauterpacht's manner of speech) does not know of any such mode of acquiring property.

In Lauterpacht's view, however, this lack of analogy should not be regarded as an inevitably permanent feature of international law reflecting the 'specific' nature of international society. Thus characteristically he describes this lack of analogy as a 'missing link' of the two systems of law, and maintains as follows:

The development of international law towards a true system of law is to a considerable degree co-extensive with the restoration of the missing link of analogy of contracts and treaties, i.e. of the freedom of will as a requirement for the validity of treaties, and with the relegation of force to the category of sanctions. The Covenant of the League of Nations, which, in its Article 10, safeguards the political independence and territorial integrity of the Members of the League from acts of external aggression, may be regarded as containing in gremio, *the elements of this development* (H. Lauterpacht 1927, 166–7).

It has been pointed out that the adherents of the 'peace through law' approach generally held since the experience of the First World War that the right of states to go to war must be legally restricted and that international law must embody the principle of collective security. Lauterpacht is no exception and is undoubtedly glad to see the progressive development of international law made by the creation of the League of Nations.

However, as regards the much-debated question of the necessity for a more effective system of sanctions, or more centralized mechanism of enforcement than is embodied in the League's collective security system, Lauterpacht takes a somewhat conservative view. He remarks that the 'provisions in the matter of sanctions embodied in Article 16 of the Covenant of the League of Nations marked the first step' (E. Lauterpacht 1970, 19) in the way towards the collective enforcement of the law.

He does believe that the continued legal and political integration of international society will develop the nature and the scope of sanctions available to international law. However, he maintains that the problem of enforcement is not so acute in international law for a somewhat paradoxical reason: the question of enforcement arises normally in relation to rights ascertained by an impartial tribunal applying rules of law, but there is as yet, in principle, no compulsory jurisdiction of international tribunals (E. Lauterpacht 1970, 16–20). In other words, in Lauterpacht's view, the perfection of the judicial system is of primary importance, which would then both necessitate and perhaps lead to the creation of a better-organized system of sanctions than that with which the League of Nations was equipped.

It is on this question of the compulsory jurisdiction of international tribunals that Lauterpacht has contributed another major work, *The Function of Law in the International Community*. The importance of this book as a good example of the Utopian thinking is noted by E. H. Carr (1946, 195 n. 1). Lauterpacht's uncompromising adherence to the 'peace throgh law' approach and the typically comprehensive nature of his work justify a detailed analysis of his mode of thought as expressed in this book.

The major aim of Lauterpacht's book is to denounce the doctrine that there exists a certain category of disputes in international relations which is inherently non-justiciable. This doctrine he calls that of the inherent limitations of the judicial process in international law. In denouncing this, his reliance on domestic analogy is both absolute and explicit.

It is Lauterpacht's belief that for a system of law to fulfil its primordial duty of preserving peace it must not refuse to adjudicate upon a particular claim, 'at least to the extent of pronouncing that violence must not be used for the purpose of enforcing it' (H. Lauterpacht 1933, 64). He argues that in a civilized country all disputes are deemed to be 'justiciable' in the sense that domestic courts can either pronounce on the merits or definitely dismiss the claim on the ground that it is not entitled to protection and enforcement by the law. In the latter case, the court disposes of a dispute definitely 'by the implied prohibition of enforcement of the claim through recourse to violence, or by the refusal to lend the aid of the State in enforcing it' (H. Lauterpacht 1933, 21).

Lauterpacht extends his idea of law into the international sphere and argues that international law, in order to become a true system of law, must not allow the concept of an inherently non-justiciable dispute. To Lauterpacht, the existence of such a concept appears to be a defect of international law, and he thinks it is misleading to consider such a defect as a manifestation of the 'specific' character of international law. As has been noted earlier, he does not think that there ought to be anything 'specific' about international law. Thus he argues:

It is better that international law should be regarded as incomplete, and in a state of transition to the finite and attainable ideal of a society of States under the binding rule of law, as generally recognized and practised by civilized communities within their borders, than that, as the result of the well-meant desire to raise its formal authority qua *law, it should be treated as the perfect and immutable species of a comprehensively diluted* genus proximum *(1933, 432).*

It is important to note that Lauterpacht's idea of the place of law in international society is thus inextricably intertwined with his conception of law and with his determination to take domestic law as the paradigm of law.

Lauterpacht is aware of some arguments against his belief in the near omnipotence of the judicial process in settling international disputes: two of these may be noted. (The following is based on H. Lauterpacht 1933, 245–69).

One argument is that the jurisdiction of international courts ought to remain limited because there is no legislature in international society. The upholders of this view stress the static character of international law and maintain that a controversy may arise for which a judicial decision, giving effect to an existing international right, may be manifestly unjust. According to their argument, judicial decisions might be so little in accord with the changes continually taking place in international society that they would have the unavoidable effect of perpetuating injustice and friction.

Lauterpacht's defence of his belief consists of a number of interesting assertions which can be summarized in the following points.

First of all, he contends that international law in the present stage of development is not liable to be affected in a decisive manner by economic and other changes, for it does not regulate the relations of its subjects in the same intensive and pervading manner as does municipal law. In his view, only 'when the political organization of the international community has undergone a fundamental change, so as to regulate in detail the life of its individual members in its internal aspects – only then will it be possible to speak of a constant flux of changes necessitating legislative remedies' (H. Lauterpacht 1933, 249–50).

Secondly, he criticizes the view that the growing power and influence of a state must be translated into its legal rights.

This view, according to him, 'ignores the fact that one of the not least important functions of the law is to protect the weaker members of the community against the physical preponderance of others, and not invariably to give effect to it' (H. Lauterpacht 1933, 250). In this single statement, one may see a crystallization of the idea of peace through law.

Thirdly, he maintains that although the existing legal *status quo* may be a source of friction, there is no certainty that legislation devised to alter it may not prove even more dangerous to the cause of peace. No legislative action can, according to him, remove such sources of friction as one due to the desire for changes in respect of certain territories with racially mixed populations. He argues that only neighbourly arrangements, conceived in a spirit of accommodation, can in such cases provide a satisfactory and lasting solution.

And finally, he points out the function of courts as an instrument for adapting the existing law to changed conditions. Here in fact Lauterpacht resorts to a different kind of domestic analogy, namely, the analogy from the domestic experience as regards the development of a legal system. Citing a passage from Sir Henry Maine's *Ancient Law,* Lauterpacht argues that in a less developed system of law, judicial law-making plays an important part, and that only in an advanced phase of its legal organization, a community can rely fully upon legislation as a means of changing the law.[3]

The other argument against Lauterpacht's belief in the decisive role the judicial process can play in settling international disputes is one which emphasizes the role of international conciliation.

Lauterpacht does indeed recognize the importance of conciliation, but does not think that its importance ought to outweigh the value of judicial settlement. He acknowledges the view 'that the eventual right to demand a judicial decision may render illusory the advantage of conciliation' (1933, 268). This view is based on the consideration that if a state believes itself to have the law on its side and is determined to insist rigidly on its formal right, it may be disinclined to show the spirit of accommodation and broad-minded appreciation of the equitable aspect of the controversy, while such a spirit is an essential condition for the successful settlement of a dispute by conciliation. Lauterpacht points out that such a line of argument was in fact advanced in Australia by those opposed to the compulsory arbitration of industrial disputes. However, he does not forget to stress the existence of the opposing view, i.e. that unless there is in the background a court endowed with compulsory jurisdiction, little respect is paid to the conciliator. Thus here again Lauterpacht is found to justify his position, or at any rate attempt to do so, by reference to the experience of domestic legal problems.

Lauterpacht's ideas have been discussed in some considerable detail because his theory of the place of law in international relations is undoubtedly one of by far the most thoroughly constructed and by far the most substantial among those formulated by the adherents of the 'peace through law' approach in the interwar period. In fact, one may go a little further and maintain that Lauterpacht's works constitute one of a few permanently valuable exceptions among the 'idealist' literature massively produced during and after the First World War: this bulk of literature is on the whole not much worth reading now except for the light it throws upon the history of ideas.

While Lauterpacht is perhaps the most radical among the adherents of the 'peace through law' approach in so entirely denouncing the doctrine of the inherent limitations of the judicial process in international law, it has been seen that he is less than enthusiastic about the establishment of a legislature in international society. As regards the problem of strengthening the system of sanctions available to international law, it has been noted that in Lauterpacht's view compulsory adjudication does not necessarily presuppose a centralized executive authority.

Such a position may be contrasted with a more spectacular assertion as regards the necessity for the establishment of an international police. *The Problem of the Twentieth Century* by David Davies is one such example.

It is not necessary here to examine the project elaborated in extreme detail in this almost 800-page book. One may be impressed by the irony of history (as Dr Brian Porter once pointed out to me) more than by the author's ingenuity when one reads in his proposal that Palestine is to become the first freehold territory of the international authority where the projected international police is to have its headquarters and that the bulk of devastating weapons, such as submarines, aeroplanes, tanks and poison gas, is to be stored there (Davies 1934, 433–66).

Nor is it necessary to quote actual instances of his explicit use of domestic analogy. This in fact occurs so frequently that even a very cursory reading will enable one to select a few examples in those pages. It is sufficient to point out that the author has no hesitation in exhibiting his belief in the validity of domestic analogy as if it were an axiomatic truth. He expresses this by saying that it is in accordance with human nature that legislative, judicial and executive institutions be introduced from the domestic into the international sphere as the final step in the development of the legal organization of mankind (Davies 1934, 159–60).

The following passage, however, requires attention particularly in relation to Lauterpacht's position as regards the necessity for a centralized executive authority:

The prevention of war . . . involves the creation of machinery for securing international justice; justice, in turn, is dependent upon disarmament; disarmament cannot be obtained without security; and security cannot be purchased without the establishment of sanctions. These are the links in the chain which must be welded together during the next fifty years if the world is to be saved from annihilation (Davies 1934, 3).

By 'the establishment of sanctions', Davies means the creation of an international police force, which together with the constabularies and the national armies completes the system of sanctions necessary for the legal community of mankind (Davies 1934, 363). For Davies, in contrast to the case of Lauterpacht, the creation of an international police force is of primary importance, a *sine qua non* for the successful substitution of war by the judicial machinery.

Not all those who adhere to the 'peace through law' aproach resort to domestic analogy as clearly as do Lauterpacht and Davies. In fact there are a few international lawyers writing after the outbreak of the First World War who put stress more on the limit of domestic analogy than its utility. However, they are a minority, it seems safe to say, and moreover, they do not expose the limit of this analogy in a sufficiently articulate fashion. They generally do not go further than giving a warning in a rather vague manner against an uncritical reliance on it (see, e.g. Dickinson 1916–17, 591 and Brown 1923, Ch. 10–11, esp. 115ff).

At this point it is pertinent to refer to Oppenheim's division of his contemporary international lawyers into the legal and the diplomatic schools. The legal school desires international law to develop more or less on the lines of municipal law, 'aiming at the codification of firm, decisive, and unequivocal rules of International Law, and working for the establishment of international Courts for the purpose of the administration of international justice'. On the other hand, 'the diplomatic school', says Oppenheim, 'considers International Law to be, and prefers it to remain, rather a body of elastic principle than of firm and precise rules'. According to him, the diplomatic school opposes the establishment of international courts, 'because it considers diplomatic settlement of international disputes, and failing this arbitration, preferable to international administration of justice by international Courts composed of permanently appointed judges' (Oppenheim 1912, 82).

There are in fact some doubts as to whether these two schools of thought really existed among Oppenheim's contemporaries in such a clear-cut fashion as he would like us to believe. A closer examination of the history of legal thought at the turn of the century would seem to indicate that there were enough borderline cases to make the suggested distinction somewhat artificial.

However, the important thing to note in the present context is that the diplomatic school as defined by Oppenheim was clearly on the wane among the adherents of the 'peace through law' approach in the interwar years, and that some undoubted members of the legal school in this period were advocating more far-reaching revision of the international legal system than Oppenheim himself would have liked to see at the turn of the century.

What is interesting to note is Oppenheim's belief that the progress of international law 'depends to a great extent upon whether the legal school of International Jurists prevails over the diplomatic school' (Oppenheim 1912, 82). It may be said that in the interwar years the legal school was indeed far more predominant than the diplomatic school. Whether such a state of affairs in the history of international thought was a desirable phenomenon is another matter. In the final section, therefore, some attempt will be made at the evaluation of the 'peace through law' approach of the interwar years.

The evaluation of the approach

The 'peace throgh law' approach of the interwar years is *prescriptive, deductive* and *analogical.* It does not offer explanatory hypotheses derived by an inductive reasoning from empirical data. It neither aspires nor pretends to be a scientific theory. It is not fruitful for an amateur philosopher to indulge in speculating about the status in human thought and the value for human action of non-scientific prescriptive theories in general. In the present context, we must be satisfied with an examination of some of the major weaknesses of the 'peace through law' approach in particular.

First, the two basic assumptions must be examined: the belief in the harmony of 'true' national interests, and that in the progressive nature of human history.

What is important to note about the first belief is that it hides a normative element. To maintain that it is in the 'true' interest of a state to avoid a war is tantamount to saying that it *ought to* formulate its interest in a manner harmonious with that of other states. To say that the maintenance of peace is the 'true' interest common to all states is equivalent to saying that states *ought to* give priority to peace. When a state pursues its interest in a manner contrary to that of other states, giving priority to its own egoistic interests, and resorts to war, it is said to be ignoring its 'true' interest, which is just another way of saying that it is behaving in the way it *ought not to.* Moreover, even when two contending states are being compelled by a prudential calculation to avoid going to war, they cannot be said to find 'true' interest commonly in peace, for, as Carr (1946, 52–3) points out, such a situation merely masks the fact that one of the contenders desires to maintain the *status quo* without having to fight for it, while the other wishes to change the *status quo* without having to fight in order to do so.

The belief in the progressive nature of human history, or, in the present context in particular, the idea that the world is becoming more and more peaceful, does not seem derivable from an empirical generalization, in spite of the fact that the upholders of this belief before the First World War attempted to justify their claim by pointing out some factors which indicated the improved condition of human life. It was not unnatural for optimistic nineteenth century men to adhere to this belief. However, whether their belief was anything other than one of many possible *Weltanschauungen* was not asked by them.

However, to say that the foundations of the idea of peace through law consist of a normative statement and a *Weltanschauung* is not the same as saying that the idea is unfounded. On the contrary, it is possible to argue that no prescriptive theory is possible without a set of necessary presuppositions.

Furthermore, it may be held to be possible to defend the validity of the two presuppositions under consideration on the basis of their utility. It may be thought possible to argue that the frequency of conflict could never be lessened, and its intensity never mitigated, unless we acted on the assumption that it is within our power to lessen its frequency and mitigate its intensity. Similarly, it may be argued that unless we acted on the assumption that human history is progressive, it could never make any progress.

According to this position, it is not even necessary to attempt to verify those assumptions empirically. Nor is it necessary to try to show those assumptions as valid *a priori.* It is sufficient to point out that those assumptions are necessary for the good of mankind.

Here, in fact, lies the most fundamental question. Do those assumptions really serve the good of mankind? The answer must be in the affirmative *only if* it can be shown that what is referred to as 'the common interest in peace' is truly equivalent to the common interest of mankind. As Carr (1946, 80–5) points out, the so-called 'common interest in peace' tends too frequently to be the interest of the stronger, the contented and the more conservative; the believer in law and order.

However, even if we assume that peace is the highest ideal of mankind, the question remains whether the 'peace through law' approach of the post-First World War variety can be understood properly to have made a contribution to the progress of mankind towards that goal. This is closely linked with the question of the validity of domestic analogy, because the adherents of the 'peace through law' approach tended to identify the progress of international law with that of the community of mankind, and moreover, they tended to measure the degree of international law's progress by reference to its affinity to domestic law. The progressive development of international law meant to them both the progressive development of international society and the growing similarity between international and domestic legal systems.

Here seems to lie the weakest point of the 'peace through law' approach of the interwar years. The prescriptive theory offered by this approach is of doubtful value, not primarily because it is prescriptive or deductive, but because it is analogical in its structure. The idea that the optimal legal organization of mankind must be based on a domestic constitutional model is at best unwarranted; at worst it can be positively harmful.

One could even argue that the desire to transfer domestic legal conceptions and institutions into the international sphere is a manifestation of an unimaginative fastidiousness or of an obsession with a schematic tidiness in ideas about law and society. This can be seen in Lauterpacht's uncompromising determination to take domestic law as a paradigm of law and his single-minded desire to develop international law into a 'true' system of law by endowing it with the qualities distinctive of domestic law, though it seems almost blasphemous to talk of this lofty idealist as being unimaginative or obsessed.

Moreover, the belief in the validity of domestic analogy reflects an optimistic and vastly simplified image of domestic politics, particularly when that analogy is used in advocacy of a centralized executive organ or an international police force, as we have seen in the case of Davies. This point has been discussed in depth by Inis Claude in his *Power and International Relations.*

Claude (1962, 260) argues that the conception of government as 'a legislature, a code of law, a policeman, a judge, and a jail' is utterly unsophisticated and schoolboyish. Few actual governments, he says, are very government-like in the way in which the adherents of the 'peace through law' approach imagine them to be. Claude does not in fact reject domestic analogy entirely: he warns against the use of this analogy in a one-sidedly legalistic manner. What we can fruitfully learn from our domestic experience is, in his view, not how a government deals with individual robbers, but how, through 'a sensitive and skillful operation of the mechanism of political adjustment' (Claude 1962, 271), it deals with the problems of maintaining order among conflicting groups.

Another danger in using domestic analogy in relation to the enforcement of law is that international society does not appear to possess that degree of consensus and solidarity which is necessary for the collective enforcement of law. Thus, as Hedley Bull maintains, following closely, if not explicitly, the line of argument put forward by an eighteenth century international lawyer, Vattel, the system of law restricting the right of states to use force and embodying the principle of the collective enforcement of law may not merely be unworkable, but positively harmful to the working of the society of nations. Such a system of law, which Bull (somewhat inaccurately) terms 'Grotian', may not only widen the gap between law and reality, diminishing as a result the credibility of legal constraints and the respect for law, but also have the effect of intensifying and prolonging a conflict.

This is the case, so it is said, because as an inevitable consequence of the lack of consensus among nations, each nation claims to have justice on its side. Therefore, under a system of international law, restricting states' right to use force and favouring the victim and the third parties as against an aggressor, each nation (according to Vattel) will end up in arrogating to itself all the rights of war: it will claim 'that its enemy has none, that his hostilities are but deeds of robbery, acts in violation of the Law of Nations, and deserving of punishment by all Nations' (in Forsyth et al. 1970, 121–2).

Against these penetrating criticisms, the advocates of peace through law could try to defend their position only by resorting to a negative argument or to agnosticism.

Against Claude's argument they might willingly concede that 'a sensitive and skillful operation of the mechanisms of political adjustment' is indeed what is required for peace and order at the international level. However, they might require Claude and his supporters to analyse the necessary ingredients of such 'mechanisms', and might further ask if such mechanisms do not necessarily presuppose a legal framework. If these mechanisms are said to presuppose a legal framework, the adherents of the 'peace through law' approach might then ask Claude and his supporters to determine the optimal degree of analogy with a domestic legal system which must be contained in such a legal framework. As we have seen in the previous section, Lauterpacht in effect resorts to such a tactic when he engages himself in a hypothetical battle against the supporters of conciliation as a more suitable mechanism than adjudication for the settlement of international disputes.

Against Vattel's line of argument, the adherents of the 'peace through law' approach could resort to an agnostic position. It does not seem very easy to prove empirically that the harm done to the society of nations by the introduction of domestic legal conceptions and institutions is necessarily larger than its beneficial effect. One can never be certain, for instance, that the legal restriction upon the right to go to war does indeed decrease the frequency of war, or that it has the side-effect of thereby intensifying or prolonging a war. It would be even more difficult to judge whether this side-effect outweighs the intended positive effect of lessening war's frequency. Therefore, the adherents of the 'peace through law' approach might, as their last line of defence, resort to agnosticism and maintain that their position is empirically no more or no less valid than the position of their opponents.

It has been argued earlier that domestic analogy can be used *selectively*. Some particular selective use of domestic analogy in the development of international law, quite regardless of whether such a selection can be proved to be theoretically sound, may, in practice, result in producing *a* desirable, if not necessarily *the* desired, state of affairs. This, however, is not the concern of this essay. What is important to point out finally is that the use of domestic analogy to its fullest extent by the adherents of the 'peace through law' approach, leading to advocacy of the establishment of a legislature, judicature and executive is likely to be based on a careless misunderstanding.

Within a domestic society, the existence of these three organs has its theoretical basis in the idea of the separation of power. Within a state, the power had already been centralized, and it merely had to be separated. Those who use domestic analogy in advocating the necessity of the establishment of the three organs in the international sphere tend to forget this vital fact. In international society, there is no centralized power which can be separated into the three organs, or from which any of these powers can be extracted. The 'peace through law' approach has its inherent weakness in this respect. It takes little note of the fact that in international society power is decentralized, the recognition of which is in fact the starting-point of the so-called 'realist' approach to international politics.

It is an obvious, but nevertheless important, truth, as Hans Kelsen (1967, 11) insists on pointing out, that it does not make sense to have a rule of law which it is either impossible to observe or impossible not to observe. It is inherent in the nature of law that it has certain tension with political reality: law is by nature different from the prudential rules of politics. It is only natural that a tension persists similarly between the adherents of the 'peace through law' approach who think of politics as a function of law, and the so-called 'realists' who think of law as a function of politics.

One may be disinclined to adhere to the 'realist' position for a number of reasons. One may nevertheless hold the view, against Lauterpacht and the school of thought he represents, that it is 'more realistic to see international law as law of a different species, than as merely a more primitive form of what is destined some day to have the nature of a universal system of non-primitive municipal law' (Manning in Porter 1972, 319).

Notes

1. According to Waltz, the causes of war can be discussed at three different levels: that of man's nature, of a state's internal structure and of the nature of international society. He terms the investigations of International Relations at those levels the first, second and third image analyses, respectively (Waltz 1954).
2. Bernier translates *Völkerrechtsunmittelbarkeit* as 'international immediacy'. This means the state of being in a direct or 'immediate' contact with international law.
3. This type of domestic analogy is in fact frequently used by the adherents of the 'peace through law' approach. See, for instance, Williams (1929, 33 n. 3). He is, however, more sceptical than Lauterpacht of the role the judiciary can play by itself in settling international disputes. See Williams (1929, 33–5). See also Kelsen (1944, 21) and his earlier works referred to in Kelsen (1944, 14).

References and Further Reading

Asterisked items make up a short bibliography of works of particular importance to this chapter.

Bernier, I. (1973) *International Legal Aspects of Federalism,* London, Longman.

Brown, P.M. (1923) *International Society: Its Nature and Interests,* New York, Macmillan.

*__Butterfield, H. and Wight, M.__ (eds.) (1966) *Diplomatic Investigations: Essays in the Theory of International Politics,* London, Allen and Unwin.

*__Carr, E.H.__ (1946) *The Twenty Years' Crisis 1919–1939: An Introduction to the Study of International Relations,* first published in 1939, 2nd edn, London, Macmillan.

*__Claude, I.L. Jr.__ (1962) *Power and International Relations,* New York, Random House.

Davies, D. (1934) *The Problem of the Twentieth Century: A Study in International Relationships,* London, Benn.

Dickinson, E.D. (1916–17) 'The analogy between natural persons, and international persons in the law of nations', *Yale Law Journal,* **26,** 564–91.

*__Forsyth, M.G.__ et al. (eds.) (1970) *The Theory of International Relations: Selected Texts from Gentili to Treitschke,* London, Allen and Unwin.

Hinsley, F.H. (1967) *Power and the Pursuit of Peace: Theory and Practice in the History of Relations between States,* Cambridge, Cambridge Univ. Press.

Holsti, K.J. (1974) *International Politics: A Framework for Analysis* (2nd edn.), London, Prentice-Hall.

Kelsen, H. (1944) *Peace Through Law,* Chapel Hill, Univ. of North Carolina Press.

Kelsen, H. (1967) *The Pure Theory of Law,* trans. from the 2nd German ed. by M. Knight, Berkeley, Univ. of California Press.

Klinke, W. (1951) *Kant for Everyman,* trans. from the German by M. Bullock, London, Routledge and Kegan Paul.

Kunz, J. (1950) 'The swing of the pendulum: From overestimation to underestimation of international law', *American Journal of International Law,* **44,** 135–40.

Latané, J.H. (ed.) (1932) *Development of the League of Nations Idea: Documents and Correspondence of Theodore Marburg,* Vol. 2, New York, Macmillan (2 vols).

Lauterpacht, E. (ed.) (1970) *International Law, Being the Collected Papers of Hersch Lauterpacht,* Vol. 1. Cambridge, Cambridge Univ. Press (2 vols).

Lauterpacht, H. (1927) *Private Law Sources and Analogies of International Law (With Special Reference to International Arbitration),* London, Longmans, Green.

***Lauterpacht, H.** (1933) *The Function of Law in the International Community,* Oxford, Clarendon Press.

***Manning, C.A.W.** (1962) *The Nature of International Society,* London, Bell.

Markham, F.M.H. (ed. and trans.) (1952) *Henri Compte de Saint-Simon (1760–1825): Selected Writings,* Oxford, Blackwell.

Newton, A.P. (ed.) (1923) *Federal and Unified Constitutions: A Collection of Constitutional Documents for the Use of Students,* London, Longmans, Green.

Nippold, O. (1923) *The Development of International Law After the World War,* trans. A.S. Hershey from the German published in 1917, Oxford, Clarendon Press.

Oppenheim, L. (1912) *International Law: A Treatise,* 2nd edn, London, Longmans, Green (2 vols). Vol. 1. *Peace.*

Oppenheim, L. (1921) *The Future of International Law,* first published in 1911 in German, trans. J.P. Bate, Oxford, Clarendon Press.

***Porter, B.** (ed.) (1972) *The Aberystwyth Papers: International Politics 1919–1969,* London, Oxford Univ. Press.

***Schiffer, W.** (1972) *The Legal Community of Mankind: A Critical Analysis of the Modern Concept of World Organization,* first published in 1954 by Columbia Univ. Press, Westport, Conn., Greenwood.

Scott, J.B. (ed.) (1920) *The Proceedings of the Hague Peace Conferences: Translation of the Official Texts, The Conference of 1899,* New York, Oxford Univ. Press.

Vollenhoven, C. van (1919) *The Three Stages in the Evolution of the Law of Nations,* The Hague, Nijhoff.

Waltz, K.N. (1954) *Man, the State and War: A Theoretical Analysis,* London, Columbia Univ. Press.

Westlake, J. (1904) *International Law,* Part I, Peace. Cambridge, Cambridge Univ. Press.

Williams, Sir John F. (1929) *Chapters on Current International Law and the League of Nations,* London, Longmans, Green.

Chapter 6

Power politics

Trevor Taylor

Origins and scholars

Although, to my knowledge, no research has been done in the way of counting words written or weighing books published, it can be reasonably asserted that the majority of International Relations literature has given a prominent place to power, a much-defined concept meaning fundamentally, in its social science context, the ability to influence or change the behaviour of others in a desired direction. This consideration alone presents a problem for the analyst of the power politics school; from such a volume of literature it must be decided what distinguishes 'power politics' thought from the rest, what are its central features.

It is the position of this chapter that the power-politics school contains a series of shared beliefs about international politics which centre around the proposition that it is the nature of the state to acquire as much power as it can, because of the dangerous and anarchic world in which it exists. It is merely a self-evident aspect of power-thinking that what a state can do in international politics depends on the power it possesses. What is significant about power-politics theory is that it goes further and suggests that if a state is to succeed, it has little choice but to make the acquisition of power its central, immediate aim. In so far as this represents a suggested universal rule of state behaviour, power-politics thinking must be accepted as an effort to produce a general theory of International Relations.

Of the various features of power-politics thinking, some are emphasized more by some authors than by others. Some authors stress parts of power-politics theory and neglect or even reject others. However, the latter course presents major intellectual difficulties because power-politics theory is, as I hope to show, a connected whole. Damage to part of it damages all of it. So, while I have quoted as freely from 'partial' adherents to power-politics thinking as I have from the 'founder members' (such as Schuman, Schwarzenberger, Spykman and Morgenthau), I have done so only when their contribution epitomizes the power-politics position. To examine this position, rather than to compare the various authors who have contributed to it, is the role of this chapter.

From the beginning power-politics writers were situated on both sides of the Atlantic. Britain's early major thinkers and the dates of their important publications were Carr (1939), Schwarzenberger (1941) and Wight (1946) while in the US the most prominent names were Schuman (1933), Niebuhr (1936 and 1959), Spykman (1942) and Morgenthau (1948). Although the standing of these authors reached a peak in the early 1950s, after which they were increasingly attacked on intellectual grounds, because of the weaknesses of their concepts and methodology, and on empirical grounds, because they offered little hope for the future, new editions appeared of their major works and they continued to publish. Moreover, they were followed by a group of distinguished scholars, for example, Aron, Organski, Rosecrance, Spanier, Thompson and Waltz, who thought and wrote basically within a power-politics framework. Thus power-politics has held a sustained and substantial position in International Relations and it is worth while to consider why.

A combination of factors may be cited to account for the rise and perseverance of power-politics thinking. There is Carr's point that power-politics constituted a natural development of International Relations as a new discipline. He argued that all disciplines go through an initial stage of wishful thinking, of concentrating on how things ought to be, before attention is focused on how things actually are. Arguing that new disciplines arise because new problems require solutions, Carr (1946, 5) observed that 'when the human mind begins to exercise itself in some fresh field, an initial stage occurs in which the element of wish or purpose is overwhelmingly strong, and the inclination to analyse facts weak or non-existent'. In this view, power-politics marked the end of the wishful-thinking stage in International Relations, of 'Utopian' thinking. Power-politics analysed the world in being and was thus 'realist' in nature.

Certainly in the 1930s the inadequacies of Utopian prescriptions for international politics were exposed by the policies of Germany and Japan. Utopian thinking appeared increasingly irrelevant. By the 1940s the most convincing arguments for how the Second World War could have been avoided were those which had proposed rearmament and a firm alliance of anti-fascist states in order to deter aggression (e.g. F. E. Jones 1938 and R. P. Dutt 1936). The lesson of the 1930s was that state behaviour could not be reformed; it had to be controlled.

Also, during the course of the Second World War, it became increasingly clear that the United States would be in a new position at the end of the war. So some power-politics writing, favouring a substantial US world role, emerged as part of the debate on what US policy should be (see especially Spykman 1942). But power-politics thought went further than mere prescription, seeking also to explain and justify; for instance, in presenting a view of the state system in which the balance of power, a much-criticized concept in the US, played a permanent and stabilizing role, it made US participation in world politics more acceptable. Power-politics theory made the balance of power an inevitable feature of international politics, not an evil feature. In 1951 Morgenthau, using realist theory, tried to show not only what US foreign policy should be, but also that it was actually a state's moral *duty* to pursue but 'One Guiding Star', *In Defense of The National Interest* (1951, 242).

So political realism, utilizing principles expounded by earlier philosophers and (so realists claimed) practised by the wisest statesmen, arose to fill a theory and a policy need in a period of crisis and prolonged uncertainty between 1930 and the mid-1950s. It sought to provide reasoned general propositions which could serve as the basis for successful policy, in contrast to Utopian theory, whose application would (and did) lead to policy disaster. In fact, as is discussed later, the relationship between power-politics theory and policy is not clear cut because the uncertain nature of 'power' allows the theory to justify and explain many policies. Yet political realism has survived this weakness in that it is still widely studied and endorsed.

Three points can be offered as to why this should be so. First, although power is a poor concept for scientific analysis, many writers have found it impossible to conceive of politics without it. Schuman (1958, 23), adapting Lasswell's (1958) definition, summed up politics as 'the science of who gets what, when and how. It is also the process by which people compete for control of the instrumentalities of favours, frauds and force that are the essence of government'. Almond defined a political system as 'that system of interactions to be found in all independent societies which performs the functions of integration and adaptation (both internally and *vis-à-vis* other societies) by means of the employment, or the threat of employment, of more or less legitimate physical compulsion' (Almond and Coleman 1960, 7). Duncan summed up a common viewpoint when he said, 'All politics are, of course, power-politics in the sense of being a struggle for power in a conflict of wills' (in Wallace 1957, 249). If power is accepted as an integral part of politics, it is extremely difficult to remove it from International Relations, the discipline concerned with the study of international politics, whatever its faults as a concept.

Second, a consequence of the use of power as a central concept is that it is impossible to prove power-politics theory right or wrong. Again, this is expanded on later, but here it is enough to observe that power-politics theory may live indefinitely because its validity and utility is a matter of subjective judgement. To date, its value is still widely accepted.

The third consideration may partially account for this. As an effort to explain all state behaviour with regard to its external environment, political realism has few rivals. As is clear from other chapters here, International Relations has developed a wealth of approaches and methods of study as well as a good many propositions about specific types of action, but general theory remains scarce. To an extent, power-politics theory has survived in the evolution of International Relations because no new theory has appeared to displace it.

Methods and assumptions

It was observed that some of the more damaging criticisms of realist thinking focused on their methodology and this is not surprising in view of the fact that, with the notable exception of Morgenthau (1946), few realists appear to have paid much attention to their methods, at least until the methodological debate in International Relations in the 1950s rather imposed such attention on them. However, some general methodological points can be made. For instance, history has important roles. On the one hand, its study serves as a source of inspiration for hypotheses; thus Schwarzenberger (1964, 14) talks about power-politics as 'an abstraction reached inductively by the study of International Relations of the past and present'. On the other hand, history's role is to show the accuracy of hypotheses presented. Power-politics writers use carefully selected examples to add weight to their arguments. Frequently a proposition is followed by a historical case. A section from Morgenthau (1973, 211) illustrates this – here he discusses the dynamics of the balance of power:

Yet the very act of redressing the balance carries within itself the elements of a new disturbance. The dynamics of power-politics as outlined previously make this development inevitable. Yesterday's defender of the status quo is transformed by victory into the imperialist of today, against whom yesterday's vanquished will seek revenge tomorrow. The ambition of the victor who took up arms to restore the balance, as well as the resentment of the loser who could not overthrow it, tend to make the new balance a virtually invisible point of transition from one disturbance to the next. Thus the balancing process has frequently led to the substitution of one predominant power, disturbing the balance, for another one. Charles V of Habsburg was thwarted in his aspirations for a universal monarchy in France, only to be succeeded by Louis XIV of France, whose similar aspirations united all of Europe against him. Once the balance had been restored against Louis XIV, a new disturbing factor arose in Frederick the Great of Prussia.

Morgenthau goes on to give two more examples, but enough was quoted to show how he uses history. Aron's *Peace and War* (1966) is particularly rich in historical material and the reader cannot fail to be impressed by the range in time and place of events cited to back the author's points.

Some realist writers see the role of history as being to verify propositions. Rosecrance (1973, 25) says 'history is a laboratory in which our generalisations about international politics can be tested'. Yet the earlier power-politics writers rarely used history in such a rigorous way. They did not test a proposition against events in a randomly selected period. Rather they selected historical cases to illustrate their points as well as to reinforce them. Cases are given as a demonstration of the meaning and application of an abstract proposition. The weight of such a proposition, it can be argued, rests on the premises and reasoning from which it was derived.

In seeking propositions to present about international politics, realists looked to political philosophy, with which in many cases their education had made them familiar, and which contained a wealth of ideas (see Ch. 3) rather than to natural or other social sciences. They were most obviously attracted to thinkers such as Hobbes and Machiavelli, whose works emphasized the dark side of human behaviour, but it is important that many political philosophers endorsed the basic model used by realists, revolving around sovereignty, the consequent international anarchy and the competitive nature of interstate relations. Lijphart stresses it as constituting the 'traditional paradigm' in International Relations. He observes that theories which do not seem to fit it 'turn out either not to deviate far from the traditional paradigm or to be rather marginal to the main body of theoretical thinking. . .' (Lijphart 1974, 49). Realism, then, is an adaption of much earlier thinking and clearly owes much to it.

It is not easy to say much more about realist methodology in terms of its general features. Morgenthau, whose views are shared by many writers in this context, is very specific about certain points. For instance, while he says that it is possible to present viable theories of state behaviour, he rejects the notion that prediction is possible in International Relations (Morgenthau 1973, 21) because the scholar can only guess which of the several tendencies inherent in a political situation are likely to prevail. Elsewhere (in Fox 1959, 21–2) he argues that social scientists can never reach absolute truth because they cannot be wholly objective, even in their choice of problem to study. More contentious is Morgenthau's view that politics can be studied in isolation from other disciplines and that there are positive advantages attached to doing so:

Political realism is based upon a pluralistic conception of human nature. Real man is a composite of 'economic man', 'political man', 'moral man', 'religious man', etc. A man who was nothing but a political man would be a beast, for he would be completely lacking in moral restraints. A man who was nothing but a moral man would be a fool, for he would be completely lacking in prudence . . .

Recognising that these different facets of human nature exist, political realism also recognises that, in order to understand one of them, one has to deal with it on its own terms (Morganthau 1973, 14).

The appeal of this position is apparent. By concentrating on 'political man', whose concern was purely with power, the political realist could build a theory of 'rational action' based on making progress towards a single goal. The concept of 'economic man' had aided the construction of economic theory: political man could do the same for International Relations theory.

It is so quite consistent that, on the whole, power-politics writers were not among those who argued that International Relations should look to other social and natural sciences for useful techniques and concepts. However, there are some notable exceptions, for example Schuman (1954) uses considerable material from psychology and sociology. Deutsch and Singer (1964) adapted the sociological concept of cross-cutting loyalties in their argument that multipolar systems in international politics gained stability from the likelihood that two states, although they may be enemies over one issue, would be friends over another.

Basically, in the great debate between traditionalists and behaviouralists, political realists, while largely in the camp of the former, have occasionally stood with at least one leg in the latter. Power-politics writers are frequently among those who condemn model-building as an International Relations exercise, yet perhaps the most well-known models published to date are those of Morton Kaplan (1957). The reasoning of political realism figures large in many of his models. In the debate on the utility of quantitative data, political realists have scarcely been among those who have had high hopes of quantified evidence. Singer is a great advocate of quantification yet some of his ideas fit within a power-politics framework. Also, in the works on power and status published in the early 1970s, complex statistical efforts were made to produce indicators of power (see especially Wallace 1973 and Ferris 1973).

The most significant features of realist methodology are perhaps the assumptions made in order to develop propositions. The departure point is the view that the state can be treated as an actor, that it has a similar sense of purpose and direction as an individual and that it is capable of rational action. Carr argues that it is impossible, given the continuity of institutions and other considerations, to analyse international politics without attributing personality to the state. Thus, while it is impossible to prove personality, to postulate it is 'a necessary fiction or hypothesis' (Carr 1946, 148–9).

Like several features of political realism, this point cannot be proved but must be accepted on faith, and works by Allison and others in the field of foreign policy analysis have undoubtedly measured the case, both for the point that the state does act as a single unit and, that it is necessary to assume it does in order to study international politics.

Given state personality, political realists assume that every state in any political situation has a 'national interest' which benefits the whole rather than just part of the state. The national interest is often identified with security because the latter is viewed as the prime goal of foreign policy. The realist argument runs basically to the effect that, unless a state is secure, it cannot be sure that it will survive and, if it does not survive, it will not be able to fulfil any other goals favouring its citizens' welfare. Schuman's (1969, 279) view that 'Since survival is the first law of life, the first duty of diplomats is the promotion of national security' is accepted in much power-politics literature.

Morgenthau argues slightly differently in that he stresses power rather than security as the central content of the national interest. Yet for others this is not a significant distinction. Thus Crabb finds it hard to distinguish between the two: 'At its most primitive level', he says, 'power is the ability of the state to maintain its own existence' (Crabb 1968, 12).

The view that security is the main goal of foreign policy and the most important aspect of the national interest is, of course, shared by those who believe that the primary purpose of the state as an institution is to provide the citizen with protection against internal and external danger.

A further assumption is the belief that it is possible to discern where the national interest, whether it be defined in terms of power or security, lies. The scholar is expected to be able to see what the statesman ought to do or ought to have done in a particular situation. This is the implication of Morgenthau's second principle of political realism which reads: 'We assume that statesmen think and act in terms of interest defined as power and the evidence of history bears that assumption out. The assumption allows us to retrace and anticipate, as it were, the steps a statesman – past, present or future – has taken or will take on the political scene (Morgenthau 1973, 5).

The impact of this assumption is substantial for, by making the acquisition of power the unambiguous goal of action, it theoretically makes it possible to build models of behaviour based on 'rational action'. Just as in economics the assumption that firms maximize their profits allows the production of theory about how firms behave, so it is believed that the power acquisition thesis will do the same for International Relations.[1] 'The relatively constant and at present insoluble relationship between power and the national interest is the basic datum for the purposes of both theoretical analysis and political practise' (Morgenthau in Fox 1959, 26).

For critics of political realism, these two concepts represent a shaky foundation for theory. The weaknesses of power have already been mentioned but the national interest follows as a related and vague concept. The adherents of power-politics theory argue it is possible to discern where the objective national interest lies. 'Unbelievers' state simply the opposite – that an assessment of the national interest cannot be more than subjective judgement based on selected and limited information.

Underlying much of what realists argue is obviously their view of human nature. Basically they emphasize the worse aspects of human behaviour and so stress that those who wish to be successful must protect themselves against the evil which others may and probably will commit. The power-politics view is that of Machiavelli who, in advising the Prince not to keep agreements which have ceased to be in his interest, says: 'If men were all good, this precept would not be a good one; but as they are bad and would not observe their faith with you, so you are not bound to keep faith with them' (1950, 64).

Particularly of interest to realists is man's supposed love of power for its own sake. Schwarzenberger (1964, 42) sums up his view of *homo sapiens* by saying that 'love, fear and lust for power are his perennial companions'. Aron (1966, 73) says that 'the more strength he has, the less risk a man runs of being attacked but he also finds, in strength as such and in the capacity to impose himself upon others, a satisfaction which needs no other justification'. Russell (1938) and Schuman (1954) are among those who argue that the lust for power varies with individuals, but that those who most seek power become politicians. Thus the leaders of states are almost invariably those who most enjoy power for itself.

Thus power-politics thinking starts from the position that at root one's fellow man is a dangerous and untrustworthy creature. Moreover, there is little expectation that his interests and others will be complementary. The realist view is that the world is made of clashing interests and the belief that a global harmony of interests exists is rejected. Carr pointed out that such a belief had credibility in the nineteenth century because of expanding markets and the availability of territories for colonization. But from the start of the twentieth century there were fewer and fewer markets and states struggled to maintain their prosperity against foreign threats: 'The complex phenomenon known as economic nationalism swept over the world... The hollowness of the glib nineteenth century platitude that nobody can benefit from what harms another was revealed. The basic presupposition of Utopianism had broken down' (Carr 1946, 62). In the 1930s realists could talk about 'the hard and even repellent facts of world conflict' (Brown et al. 1939, 5).

Internationally, the realist expects the wishes and interests of a state to be opposed by others. The things that men and states want, such as wealth, prestige and, of course, power, do not and cannot exist in sufficient quantities for all to be satisfied and conflict is the inevitable result. Hobbes' observation is relevant: 'Moreover, considering that men's appetites carry them to one and the same end; which end sometimes can neither be enjoyed in common, nor divideth, it followeth, that the stronger must enjoy it alone, and that it must be decided by battle who is the stronger (in King and McGilvray, 1973, 87).

For the realist, conflict is natural. Schwarzenberger (1964, 12) said that states have 'an instinct of repulsion'. Schuman (1954, 27) quoted Alexander Hamilton, 'the causes of hostility among nations are innumerable'. Dutt (1936, 26) described relations between states as 'ceaseless conflict, sometimes breaking out into open war'...

Propositions

From the above foundations, a considerable body of theoretical propositions has been obtained and the most central of these is that states have no choice but to maximize their power because of the anarchic political system in which they have to operate. In more detail, because the international political system or the society of states (both phrases were popular at different times) has no central authority to resolve disputes and to allocate scarce resources, it is up to each member to obtain what it can for itself and to hold on to it. The state has to rely on itself for protection against external threat.

In this situation, it is argued that all states must seek power because only with it will they be able to protect themselves and advance the well-being of their citizens. 'All nations are united in their dependence on national power and in their use of it to achieve policy goals' (Crabb 1968, 26). Power is thus a means to an end but it is also an end in itself, at least in the short term, because only with power will a state be well placed to pursue other goals such as prosperity and peace.

Power-politics writers as a rule do not see power as the only goal of states and some, such as Carr (1946) and Niebuhr (1936), discuss the moral foundations of other goals, but the overall message of their writing is that states have to concentrate on power and can rarely devote much time to the issue of the purposes for which it is obtained (Morgenthau 1958, Bull 1969). Thus Modelski (1962, 150–1) argued that a successful foreign policy is basically one which increases a state's net power resources.

It is important to emphasize that state behaviour is seen as being induced by the system; regardless of culture or ideology, all states must act similarly, selfishly seeking to increase their own power. Wight saw power politics as an inevitable feature of a political system without a central authority and he thus made the two almost synonymous. He observed, 'Power politics means the relations between independent powers' (Wight 1946, 7).

The 'system' argument above about power says essentially that the nature of the system does not provide the state with protection or help. The contribution of the realists' beliefs about the lack of harmony of interest in the world and about man's capacity for evil and his thirst for power is, therefore, to reinforce the system argument: not only do states not have protection, they are also in danger and so need it.

This viewpoint emphasizes International Relations as basically conflictful. It leads to the opinion that states should place minimum reliance on the word of others and should constantly be alert for threats or potential threats. As Schwarzenberger (1964, 142) and Schuman (1969, 272) stressed, states should prepare to deal with the worst possible situation. They should guard against the capabilities of others rather than the intentions. Under the power-politics view, international politics becomes a continuous, perpetual game where the object is to win as much power as possible. John Spanier's introductory textbook is aptly titled *Games Nations Play* (1972). Cooperation is possible, but only when it serves the national interest defined in terms of power. A state will cooperate, it is argued, only if doing so improves its overall power position.

Given the view that states should seek power, the statesman must decide where power lies. Many power-politics writers saw people and territory as important sources of power and argued that states expand their area whenever possible. Schuman (1969, 272) analysed how a state will behave: 'If it possesses sufficient power to do so, and others lack sufficient power to resist the effort, it will, with almost mathematical certainty, proceed to subject them to its own authority.' Schwarzenberger (1964, 49) is similarly straightforward: 'If any power finds a political vacuum on its doorstep, it is likely to fill it before other powers can establish themselves there.' Butterfield believed that states did what they could get away with. He argued that 'aggressiveness is always latent, and is even mathematically proportioned to the degree to which a state can misbehave with impunity' and so 'those who establish openings for aggression are helping almost inevitably to create another aggressor' (Butterfield 1953, 64). States are seen as expanding, not according to a plan or to a sense of justice, but according to opportunity. 'The broad rule is that a state conquers what it can' (Russell 1938, 110). Expansion is also seen as frequently pre-emptive, that is, to prevent others from expanding and so becoming an increased danger.

These observations about expansion and territory lead to a further feature of realist thinking, that in international politics it is military strength which is the most important source of power. The use of force is viewed as the ultimate and the most serious type of state action. Carr (1946, 109) observes: 'The supreme importance of the military instrument lies in the fact that the *ultima ratio* of power in International Relations is war. Every act of the state, in its power aspect, is directed to war, not as a desirable weapon, but as a weapon which it may require in the last resort to use.'

Schuman (1969, 272) stresses the contrast with domestic politics:

Power per se *is 'the ability to win friends and influence people', to evoke sympathy, to command obedience, to employ effectively all the devices of coercion, propaganda and material indulgences and deprivations likely to induce respect and cooperation. But the power which is of prime importance to sovereignties in dealing with other sovereignties is a quality at once simpler, more limited and more uncertain than the power which concerns politicians, parties, pressure groups, lobbies and voters acting within the framework of organized government... The ultimate* ratio regum *of sovereigns in dealing with other sovereigns is force.*

The belief that military strength is the most important aspect of power is also implicit or explicitly stated in the works by Spiegel, Wallace, Ferris, Midlarsky and others whose assessments of a state's 'power capability' are essentially geared to its ability to wage war or effectively to threaten it. Moreover, while writers such as Brown (1974), Knorr (1973) and Kindleberger (1970) stress the rising importance of other types of power, particularly economic power, the military emphasis remains dominant. Some writers do not see this as an inevitable situation but one resulting from the opinions of decision-makers themselves; C. Wright Mills (1959, 27) wrote that 'small ruling circles in both superstates assume that military violence and the whole supporting ethos of an overdeveloped society geared for war are hard-headed, practical, inevitable and realistic conceptions'.

Belief in the importance of military strength is derived from the expectation that a state whose armies have conquered the enemy's forces and have occupied its territory can then impose its will on the defeated people. The conqueror is seen to have what Russell called 'naked power' – 'the kind that involves no acquiescence on the part of the subject. Such is the power of the butcher over the sheep, of an invading army over a vanquished nation, and of the police over detected conspirators' (Russell 1938, 57). Others would not go so far but would go along with Waltz (1967, 227–8) that 'Strong states cannot do everything with their military forces, as Napoleon acutely realized, but they are able to do things that militarily weak states cannot.' Probably the most coherent work emphasizing the utility of military strength even in the nuclear age is Osgood and Tucker's *Force, Order and Justice* (1967).

Given the importance of military might in foreign policy, it follows that the nature of military might and its distribution among states will be a most important determinant of the course of international politics. Writing on these considerations is usually done under the heading 'the balance of power' and their importance is summed up by a comment by Liska that 'the key structural guarantee of minimum order in a pure multistate system is the distribution of antagonistic power in a reciprocally countervailing pattern' (in Romani 1972, 234).

Since the seventeenth century, when the state system centred on Europe, there have been two basic distributions of power. First, until 1945 there were at least five states of roughly equal strength among the stronger units in the system. Second, since 1945 two states have emerged as having much greater strength than any of their rivals. The first situation is usually designated a multipolar system, although confusingly it is also sometimes called *the* balance-of-power system, mainly because of Kaplan's work (1957). The second is called a bipolar system. Partly by coincidence, the period of the multipolar system was one in which, although weapons were of increasing and eventually enormous destructive power, for one great power to make war on another could still be seen as a rational action. With the development of nuclear weapons and their delivery systems in the bipolar age, this ceased to be the case because, in an all-out war between the strongest states, both would lose much more than they could gain.

Multipolar and bipolar systems, both in general and in particular, have been studied at length by International Relations scholars. Realists believe that no state would go to war if it knew it would lose more than it would gain and that all wars could be avoided if their outcome could be discovered in advance – the loser-to-be would give in without suffering the expense of fighting. But they have had great difficutly in agreeing on the proper distribution of power, particularly in a multipolar system, which would have the effect of abolishing or minimizing war.

Obviously, if peace is seen as depending on the predictable outcome of war, the most peaceful situation should be one where one side is clearly superior. This is the view of Organski (1958), Gelber (1950), Jones

(1938) and Dutt (1936), among others. However, against this view is the argument that, if all states are expansionist, the superior side will take advantage of its strength until it finally provokes its desperate opponents into war. The superior side may even initiate war. To counter this point realists usually argue that the side with superiority should be 'our side' (since 1945, the United States and its allies), whose expansionist tendencies are moderated by its particular qualities. Gelber (1950) argues that the institution of democracy prevents Western expansionism. Left-wing writers in the 1930s, who wrote within a basically realist framework, felt that socialist states were not inherently expansionist.

Other power-politics writers, on the other hand, have argued that the ideal distribution of power is one where there is equality of strength, believing that no state will resort to war unless it is sure of victory. Thus Speer and Kahler (1939, 26) concluded that 'the events of 1938, the Czechoslovakian crisis as well as the Japanese–Russian clashes in the Changkipend area . . ., seem to indicate that opponents which are practically equal in strength are especially reluctant to fight'. The logical strength of this argument would seem to rest on the costs of war involved, which in turn depend on the nature of military strength concerned. If war, as it was in the eighteenth century, is a relatively inexpensive activity involving comparatively little destruction, it may be undertaken even when the chances of winning are minimal. If, however, a war is expensive and may result in the mass destruction of one's people, it will not be undertaken so casually.

The construction of deterrence models which require that both sides have a 'second-strike capability', an ability to retaliate against an enemy who has struck first to the extent that he will suffer 'unacceptable damage', is a way out of the debate about superiority and equality as sources of peace. Instead retaliatory capacity is stressed. But few realists believe that international war can be entirely abolished; even mutual nuclear deterrence can break down by accident. Gelber (1950, 4) described any peace based on military strength as 'peace with risks', and it is a common view that 'Men who live without government live inescapably by the ways of violence' (Schuman 1954, 485). The most that the distribution of power can do is to minimize the number of occasions in which war is used and to minimize the level of destruction in war.

Moving from the nature and operation of the state-dominated international political system to its future prospects, power-politics reasoning leans heavily to the view that no major change is likely. Yet change is accepted as possible in theory because man is a creature of free will and may do with his world as he chooses. Thus the state system may end if 'we cease to cling fearfully to the ways of darkness and raise our eyes to the sunlit heights' (Schuman 1954, 494).

The state system could be overthrown or reformed in several conceivable ways. A single state in the system could acquire ever-increasing power and come to dominate the whole. A world empire would then be established. Functionalist theorists argue that states will gradually lose their power to international organizations, which will perform more and more of the tasks of states as the world becomes increasingly interdependent. States may volunteer to give up their sovereignty and to establish a world government because they feel that the existing 'international anarchy' makes war too probable and costly. Of more modest apparent impact, states may reform their behaviour so that war is virtually abolished; they could obey a wide-ranging and binding international law, establish a collective security system and institute general and complete disarmament. The state system might be eroded by transnational forces such as the growing power of companies with global interests and resources or the rise of a dynamic, all-encompassing ideology. A world war could occur, destroying not only the state but also civilization as we know it.

But the reasoning of the political realist makes none of these appear to be very probable. The rising power of one state will provoke fear among others, who will band together to resist it. Wight (1946, 47) says that such behaviour represents 'as nearly a fundamental law of politics as it is possible to find', and it is important that in history no state has ever been able to conquer all others. Welfare considerations are not likely to destroy power-politics either because, quoting the same author, 'every power has an interest greater than welfare, an interest on which it believes that welfare depends and to which welfare must in the last resort be sacrificed – the maintenance of power itself' 'Wight 1946, 67). Fundamentally, states accustomed to struggling for power cannot be expected to give it up voluntarily as they would fear the vulnerability which would follow. They will neither trust other states also to give up their power nor allow other bodies (such as international organizations) to look after the interests of their citizens on a permanent and irrevocable basis. Hence, while international organizations may be given important tasks, states will reserve the right to control such bodies and to cease participating in them if necessary.

Nor is it foreseen that the power of the state will be taken from it forcibly. As has been argued, no one state can establish a world empire. Other bodies, such as international corporations, which threaten the might of the state, will be controlled because of the state's monopoly of the legitimate use of force, because of the loyalty it can command from its citizens and because of the propaganda, educational and other resources which it can use to keep that loyalty. The state is seen as having power, not wishing to give it up and not being vulnerable to having it taken away. Some scholars subscribe, almost subconsciously, to a Hegelian view that the sovereign state represents the ultimate form of human political and social organization. Certainly they find it hard to imagine anything which could replace it.

A related theme in much power-politics writing is that the overthrow or reform of the state system might, in itself, mean little. Wars, it is stressed, usually occur because of conflicts of interests between groups.

While such conflicts exist, global peace is unlikely because some groups will be willing to use violence to try to get their way. Thus the establishment of a world government might mean a simple replacement of 'international' war with 'civil' war. Even 'general and complete disarmament' would not substantially affect this situation because man, if he wishes, can fight with sticks and stones, or even his bare hands. To summarize the considerable range of realist literature on the reform or destruction of the state system, power-politics thinking emphasizes the drawbacks and obstacles to change rather than the advantages.

Such attitudes are understandable. Power-politics writing, initially a reaction against Utopian belief that mere publication of a 'good idea' would result in its acceptance and implementation, is at pains to stress the factors and pressures making things as they actually are. Such factors and pressures serve also to explain why things are not already different. Political realism is the explanation (and often the justification) of the state system, of the *status quo*. Being a realist means almost that the elements reinforcing the *status quo* are made prominent while those making for change are neglected. Placing substantial limits on the possibilities for improvement in behaviour in the international political system, political realism is a conservative and may even be called a reactionary school of thought. Hopes and suggestions for a better world can be rejected, not as harmful to established vested interests, but as impractical and unrealistic. Wight (1946, 68) encourages 'high ideals' and discourages 'foolish expectations', yet power-politics logic may be used to transform expressions of the former so that they appear as the latter.

Critique

The conservative nature of power-politics thinking is but one of the criticisms which can be made of it. A central point, mentioned earlier, is that the basis of realist thinking, the concept of power, is an unsatisfactory basis for theory. The theory of power maximization envisages power as a commodity of which one can have more or less. In fact, power, defined as the ability to change the behaviour of others, becomes manifest only within the terms of a specific relationship. Who possesses it will depend on the parties and the item at issue. Most people would have assessed the US, with its great military and economic resources, as more powerful than North Vietnam, but it was the latter which was more able to get its way in South Vietnam in the 1960s and early 1970s. What is powerful depends on the circumstances, as is easily illustrated by the children's game of paper, scissors and stone, where the rules are that paper can wrap up (defeat) stone, stone can break scissors and scissors can cut paper. A player chooses one of these resources without knowing his opponent's choice. Which of these resources yields the most power?

The power of a state is essentially an unquantifiable phenomenon and no amount of debate about definition and redefinition can change this. All that can be counted are those resources which, like men under arms, seem likely to prove useful in future specific situations. However, there is no guarantee that they will prove so and thus they remain at best indicators of power, guides as to where perhaps it will lie. Thus in practice, states cannot maximize their power, they can only try to acquire resources which they think will prove useful. There is no basis for the power-politics assumption that the statesman (and the scholar) can discern where a state's interest, defined in terms of power, lies. Both can only use judgement based on the information available. Clearly, as time unfolds, assessments as to who was correct regarding past interests can be expected to change. In the 1920s trade barriers were seen by many governments as serving their countries' interests. Yet, by the 1950s, it appeared that most states in the 1920s would have done better to relax trade restrictions. Within another thirty years, views may have changed again.

A most important consequence of the complex and unquantifiable nature of power is that power-politics theory cannot be empirically tested to see how close states are coming to the ideal behaviour of the power model. This is to say that, although it may *appear* that state action is directed towards maximizing power, this cannot be proved. The reverse is also relevant; when a state *appears* to be neglecting its power, it cannot be shown conclusively that it is so doing. For Morgenthau, when a state claims to be acting for moral reasons, it is simply covering up its true power motives. Also, some authors stress that a reputation for moral behaviour is a useful asset for states. Schuman (1969, 279) states that a state which 'repeatedly breaks its word, betrays its allies, and exhibits no decent respect for the opinions of mankind will win many rounds of the contest, but will lose in the end because no others will treat with it or trust it . . .'. So, to maximize its power, a state must act morally to a certain extent.

When these considerations are introduced, it can be seen that both a state breaking a treaty and a state keeping one can be used to support the power-politics case. The position can be ambiguous even with regard to military strength; it can be said that a state which neglects its armed forces is still building up its power in the long run because resources which could have been devoted to the armed forces were instead used to build up the economy and, in future years, the economy will produce more resources for the armed forces. Any state action may be interpreted as increasing state power. Thus, not only is it impossible to discern whether a government is maximizing its state's power, it is also impossible to discern whether it is trying (or not trying) to do so.

Clearly it is not the case that power-politics theory has no policy application. Indeed realists like Morgenthau and Kennan have been very concerned to give policy advice and have used their theory to support their recommendations. The trouble lies in the fact that power-politics theory can be used to justify almost any policy.

Reflecting these considerations, the relationship between realist theory and policy is ambiguous; the most straightforward version of the theory says that states must get as much power as they can because of the nature of the anarchic and dangerous system in which they operate. Yet when political realists criticize individual government policies, they often argue that a government is neglecting its state's power. There is an obvious problem – if states must maximize their power, how is it that sometimes they do not. In other words, power-politics theory is basically determinist, but a rather ambiguous place is left for voluntarism. Analysis and prescription are uncomfortably blended.

From a realist, there is an answer that governments which are careless about power will eventually see their states destroyed. But surely this will not be the case if all the governments concerned are also negligent? Canada and the United States have successfully not defended against each other for more than 150 years. Since the end of the Second World War, the states of the North Atlantic area have given up the threat and use of force in their relations with each other. They thus form what Deutsch has called a pluralistic security community.

However, the accuracy or otherwise of power-politics theory is less important than its ambiguity. We cannot know whether or not it is correct. The discovery of ways in which a theory is incorrect at least throws some light on a problem and, hopefully, the researcher can go further and amend the theory so that it better matches reality. Were power-politics theory testable, it could be used as a yardstick against which reality could be judged. But this is not the case. Power-politics propositions can be accepted as valid and/or useful or rejected, but the course chosen will be selected through judgement and, in the end, faith.

As was noted, the root of the problems about political realism lies in the concept of power itself. What can be said in defence of this much-maligned term? Certainly its persistence in social science generally indicates that it must have some perceived merit. In psychology and anthropology power has an important place and Martin (p. 240, 1971) described it as 'one of the most central and yet problematic concepts in sociological theory'. Within International Relations, in the 1960s and 1970s the concept of power was used increasingly, particularly in the general area of conflict and peace research. Despite a movement away from power-politics theory and towards a behavioural and interdisciplinary style of analysis, it proved to be difficult meaningfully to discuss international politics without using the concept of power. One needs only to look at Carroll's article, 'Peace research, the cult of power' (1972), which surveyed the sizeable body of writing concerned with power published in the *Journal of Conflict Resolution,* a journal closely associated with behaviouralism. Increasingly it seems that the concept of power may not be incompatible with behaviouralism; Ferris (1973) and Wallace (1973) are just two authors who, by looking at the impact on behaviour of gaps between a state's power and its status, try to deal with power in a scientific manner. Overall, the resilience of power in the social sciences may be used as evidence for the view that, if it is not an ideal concept, it is the best available to date. Certainly power and propositions about it remain a central feature of International Relations. Conceivably, it could be that power-politics theory can be refined and amended to suit behaviouralist techniques along the lines suggested broadly by Fox (1959, 37): 'the significant question might be transformed from whether or not states seek to maximise power to what kind of power states seek to maximize under what conditions'.

Power-politics thinking, with its positive features such as its effort to explain all state behaviour and its negative aspects of conceptual weakness, commands a central place in the evolution of International Relations thought. In conclusion, two points should be made in its favour. First, in so far as power-politics does claim to constitute a general theory of International Relations, it is largely without a rival (although Deutsch may be said to have made a start on producing such a rival by suggesting that communications are the basic determinant of international politics). That no other general practical theory of International Relations has been produced is a reflection of the problems involved. In a way, it is also a tribute to the intellectual effort spread over centuries which produced political realism.

Second, power-politics, by studying different distributions of military power, represents a positive attempt to minimize the dangers attached to the existence in the world of great destructive military capabilities. As noted in Chapter 1, the management of military power may be the greatest problem facing mankind, and power-politics, with its propositions about the balance of power and deterrence, offers positive suggestions for how that management should be approached. Though these suggestions are not ideal, for they leave war as a possibility, they help to make it unlikely, and we must be grateful for that. But when concentrating purely on war, power-politics blends into a subdivision of International Relations, a subdivision in which many political realists have a place, that of strategic studies (see Ch. 8).

Notes

1. For an analysis of the analogy between money and power, see Baldwin (1971, 578–614).

References and Further Reading

Asterisked items make up a short bibliography of major works on power-politics.

Alcock, N.Z. and Newcombe, A.G. (1970) 'The perception of national power', *Journal of Conflict Resolution,* **14,** (September) 335–43.

Almond, G. and Coleman, J.S. (eds) (1960) *The Politics of Developing Areas,* Princeton. NJ, Princeton Univ. Press.

***Aron, R.** (1966) *Peace and War,* London, Weidenfeld and Nicolson (first published in French in 1962).

Baldwin, D.A. (1971) Money and power, *Journal of Politics,* **33** (August), 578–614.

Brown, F.J., Hodges, C. and Roucek, J.S. (eds) (1939) *Contemporary World Politics,* London, Wiley.

Brown, S. (1974) *New Forces in World Politics,* Washington, Brookings Institution.

Bull, H. (1969) 'The twenty years crisis: Thirty years on', *International Journal,* **24** (4), 626–37.

Butterfield, H. (1953) *Christianity, Diplomacy and War,* London, Epworth Press.

***Carr, E.H.** (1939) *The Twenty Years Crisis, 1919–1939,* London, Macmillan.

Carr, E.H. (1946) Op. cit. (2nd edn.).

Carroll, B.A. (1972) 'Peace research: The cult of power', *Journal of Conflict Resolution,* **16** (December) 585–619.

***Claude, I.L.** (1962) *Power and International Relations,* New York, Random House.

Crabb, C.V., Jnr. (1968) *Nations in a Multipolar World,* New York, Harper and Row.

Deutsch, K. and Singer, J.D. (1964) 'Multipolar systems and international stability', *World Politics,* **16** (April, 390–406).

Dutt, R.P. (1936) *World Politics 1918–36,* London, Victor Gollancz.

Ferris, W.H. (1973) *The Poower Capabilities of Nation-States,* London, Lexington Books.

Fox, W.T.R. (ed) (1959) *Theoretical Aspects of International Relations,* Notre Dame, Univ. of Notre Dame Press.

***Gelber, L.** (1950) *Reprieve from War: A Manual for Realists,* New York, Macmillan.

***Gulick, E.V.** (1967) *Europe's Classical Balance of Power,* New York, Norton (first published 1955).

***Haas, E.B.** (1953) 'The balance of power: Prescription, concept or propaganda', *World Politics,* **5** (July), 442–77.

***Hawtrey, R.G.** (1930) *Economic Aspects of Sovereignty,* London, Longmans, Green.

Healy, B. and Stein, A. (1973) 'The balance of power in international history', *Journal of Conflict Resolution,* **17** (1) (March), 33–61.

***James, Alan,** (1964) 'Power politics', *Political Studies,* **12** (3) (October), 307–26.

Jones, F.E. (1938) *The Battle for Peace,* London, Gollancz.

Kaplan, M. (1957) *System and Process in International Politics,* New York, Wiley.

Kindleberger, C. (1970) *Power and Money,* London, Macmillan.

King, J.C. and McGilvray, J.A. (eds) (1973) *Political and Social Philosophy,* New York, McGraw-Hill.

Knorr, K. (1973) *Power and Money,* London, Macmillan.

Korpi, W. (1974) 'Conflict, power and relative deprivation', *American Political Science Review,* **68** (4), (December), 1569–78.

Lasswell, H. (1958) *Politics: Who Gets What, When, How,* New York and Cleveland, World Publishing (first published by McGraw-Hill, 1936).

Lijphart, A. (1974) 'The structure of the theoretical revolution in International Relations', *International Studies Quarterly,* **18** (1) (March), 41–74.

Machiavelli, N. (1950) *The Prince and the Discourses,* New York, Modern Library.

Martin, R. (1971) 'The concept of power: A critical defence', *British Journal of Sociology,* **22** (3), 240–56.

Midlarsky, M.I. (1974) 'Power, uncertainty and the onset of international violence', *Journal of Conflict Resolution,* **18,** (3) (September), 395–431.

Mills, C. Wright, (1959) *The Causes of World War Three,* London, Secker and Warburg.

Modelski, G. (1962) *A Theory of Foreign Policy,* London, Pall Mall.

***Morgenthau, H.J.** (1946) *Scientific Man versus Power Politics,* Chicago, Univ. of Chicago Press.

***Morgenthau, H.J.** (1948) *Politics Among Nations,* New York, Knopf.

***Morgenthau, H.J.** (1951) *In Defense of the National Interest,* New York, Knopf, 1951.

***Morgenthau, H.J.** (1958) *Dilemmas of Power,* Chicago, Univ. of Chicago Press.

Morgenthau, H.J. (1973) *Politics Among Nations,* New York, Knopf (5th edn.).
Morgenthau, H.J. and Thompson, K.W. (eds) (1950) *Principles and Problems of International Politics,* New York, Knopf.
***Niebuhr, R.** (1936) *Moral Man and Immoral Society,* New York, Charles Scribner's Sons.
***Niebuhr, R.** (1959) *Nations and Empires,* London, Faber and Faber.
***Organski, A.F.K.** (1958) *World Politics,* New York, Knopf. (2nd edn. 1968).
***Osgood, R. and Tucker, R.** (1967) *Force, Order and Justice,* Baltimore, Johns Hopkins Press.
Reynolds, P.A. (1975) 'The balance of power: New wine in an old bottle' *Political Studies, xxiii (2) and (3) (June/September), 352–64.*
Romani, R. (ed) (1972) *The International Political System,* New York, Wiley.
Rosecrance, R.N. (1966) 'Bipolarity, multipolarity and the future', *Journal of Conflict Resolution,* x (3), 314–27.
Rosecrance, R.N. (1973) *International Relations: Peace or War,* New York, McGraw-Hill.
Rummel, R.J. (1972) *The Dimensions of Nations,* London, Sage.
***Russell, B.** (1938) *Power,* London, Allen and Unwin.
***Schuman, F.L.** (1933) *International Politics,* New York, McGraw-Hill.
Schuman, F.L. (1958) *International Politics,* New York, McGraw-Hill (6th edn.).
Schuman, F.L. (1969) Op. cit. (7th edn.).
***Schuman, F.L.** (1954) *The Commonwealth of Man,* London, Hale.
***Schwarzenberger, G.** (1941) *Power Politics,* London, Stevens.
Schwarzenberger, G. (1964) Op. cit. (3rd edn.).
Sertel, A.K. (1972) 'Images of power', *American Anthropology,* **74** (June), 639–57.
Spanier, J. (1972) *Games Nations Play,* New York, Praeger.
Speier, H. and Kahler, A. (eds) (1939) *War in Our Time,* New York, Norton.
Spiegel, S.L. (1972) *Dominance and Diversity: The International Hierarchy,* Boston, Little, Brown.
***Spykman, N.** (1942) *America's Strategy in World Politics,* New York, Harcourt Brace (also Connecticut, Archon Books, 1970).
Thompson, K.W. (1960) *Political Realism and the Crisis of World Politics,* Princeton, NJ, Princeton Univ. Press.
Wallace, V.H. (ed) (1957) *Paths to Peace,* Melbourne, Melbourne Univ. Press.
Wallace, M.D. (1973) *War and Rank Among Nations,* London, Lexington Books.
Waltz, K.N. (1954) *Man, The State and War,* New York, Columbia Univ. Press.
Waltz, K.N. (1964) 'The stability of a bipolar world', *Daedalus,* (Summer).
Waltz, K.N. (1967) 'International Structure, national force, and the balance of world power', *Journal of International Affairs,* xxi (2), 215–31.
***Wight, M.** (1946) *Power Politics,* London, RIIA.
***Wolfers, A.** (1962) *Discord and Collaboration,* Baltimore, Johns Hopkins Press.
Wright, Q. (1964) *A Study of War,* Chicago, Univ. of Chicago Press, (abridged version, original version, 1942).
Zilliacus, K. (1944) *The Mirror of the Past,* London, Gollancz.

Chapter 7

Decision-making analysis

B.P. White

This approach, with its emphasis on 'decisions' and 'decision-making processes', offers an analytical focus which is distinctive in the context of this book. Like other schools of thought, described and evaluated elsewhere, this approach is relevant to the whole study of International Relations. The seminal monograph on decision-making in the field[1] was written in the hope that it would serve as 'the core of a frame of reference for the study of international politics' (Snyder et al. 1962, 17). However, as the authors of this study admit, their immediate objective was 'to identify some of the crucial variables that determine *national* responses to concrete situations' (Snyder et al. 1962, 2, my emphasis). As far as this subject is concerned, the major impact of the decision-making approach has been on foreign policy analysis, the important area of study within International Relations which attempts to explain the external behaviour of states from the analytical perspective of the state rather than the international system (Singer 1969). A preliminary description of this approach, therefore, would stress the fact that it focuses the attention of the analyst on the behaviour of the human 'decision-makers' who are involved in the formulation and execution of foreign policy. For the purpose of this chapter, the approach will be related primarily to foreign policy analysis.

Historical setting and development

In order to establish a context within which to evaluate the decision-making approach, this section will attempt to assess the contribution of the approach to the study of foreign policy by locating it within both an historical and a methodological framework. To facilitate this, the year in which the original Snyder scheme was published (1954) will be taken as a convenient date around which to develop a historical overview. Thus, developments in the approach will be considered in terms of broader developments in the study of foreign policy. Hopefully, any insights produced by this overview will serve to justify the generalized interpretation which follows.

Clearly, the impact of the original formulation cannot be assessed without reference to the 'state of the discipline' in the early 1950s. Without implying any general consensus on the appropriate mode of analysing foreign policy prior to 1954, it can be argued (following Wagner 1974), that most studies of foreign policy, as of international politics, took as their starting-point two related assumptions which were rarely made explicit. The first assumption was that states can be regarded as the most important actors in international politics and, therefore, relations between states constitute the prime object of study. Secondly, it was assumed that the activities of governments which operate on behalf of states in the international arena, can be analysed as if they were unitary, monolithic actors. These two assumptions, taken together, provided the foundations of what several writers have referred to as a 'state-centric', 'state-as-actor' or 'billiard-ball' model of International Relations, though not always with identical connotations (see, *inter alia,* Wolfers 1962, Keohane and Nye 1972, Wagner 1974, Nye 1975). To avoid confusion, the distinction suggested by Wagner will be adopted here. The first assumption will be referred to as 'state-centric'; the second, unitary assumption will be labelled 'state-as-actor'. This latter assumption in particular, by treating governments as aggregations, fostered the tendency to account for state actions by analogy with the behaviour of purposive individuals. Such analyses resulted not only in the reification but often the personification of the state as an international actor. (In this context, see the 'rational actor' or 'classical' model, characterized by Graham Allison 1969 and 1971).

As Wagner suggests, the pervasiveness of this traditional state-centred analysis, apart from promising to be a theoretically productive simplification, appears to have resulted from (and indeed it is difficult to separate) the harnessing of these basic assumptions to what is termed a realist conception of International Relations. As the last chapter made clear, the realist critique was concerned to stress the permanence and the inexorable nature of certain characteristics of International Relations. A key assumption, expressed in a variety of different ways, is that International Relations, because of mutual insecurity and the absence of a superior political authority, is characterized by anarchy and, therefore, the ever constant danger of war between states. Foreign policy then, in this conception, is essentially security policy. The first and most difficult task of government is to ensure the survival of the state in a hostile, violent, Hobbesian environment. To focus on the need to maintain the autonomy of the government and, thereby, the integrity of the state against the dangers of military defeat, is to assert the primacy of security interests and security politics (for the elucidation of a 'security politics paradigm', see Puchala and Fagan 1974, 244ff). From this it is an easy, though not necessarily a logical, step to assume that all governments are internally united by the desire for military security and externally preoccupied with threats to it (Wagner 1974, 438). This sort of analysis suggests that realist assumptions have reinforced the two basic assumptions outlined above. This would seem to be implied by Lijphart's (1974, 43) assertion that 'the traditional paradigm in International Relations revolves around the notions of state sovereignty and its logical corollary, international anarchy'.

Having made these important assumptions explicit, it should now be possible to characterize the mode of analysis and explanation which can be said to have typified studies of foreign policy before the publication of the Snyder scheme. Employing primarily a historical–descriptive methodology, such studies tended to explain the external behaviour of the state in terms of what Pettman (1975, 34) has called the 'contextual imperatives': the geographical, historical, economic and political 'realities' of the environment external to the state boundary. Thus, 'external' rather than 'internal' factors are taken to be the important determinants of state behaviour. By assuming that the prime task of the state is survival in a hostile environment, it also followed that the means by which the state might survive provide another focal point for analysis. Hence, the space allotted in many of the traditional textbooks to the so-called 'elements of state power', which highlight not only the range of military–strategic and other policy instruments, but also geographical position, indigenous resources, size of population, gross national product and other 'elements' assumed to be relevant to state performance.

It should be noted here that the relating of state power to contextual imperative often produced, to a greater or lesser extent, deterministic accounts of state behaviour, such was the pressing nature of one or more of these external 'realities'. Statesmen were regarded as having little choice but to respond to international events, by utilizing the traditional skills of statecraft in order to manipulate, more or less successfully, the finite power of the state. Similarly, it was assumed that the purposes of state action were most evidently constrained if not shaped by these same external factors. If the observer could locate these factors, he could also identify the goals that statesmen were attempting to pursue. It would seem apparent, then, that a systemic perspective pervaded traditional analysis of foreign policy (Singer 1969, 22–3); this, in turn, produced an homogenized image of the nation-state in its external relations, which is clearly reflected in the traditional vocabulary of national power, purpose and interest.

In the context of this historical conception of traditional analysis, what was the impact of the Snyder scheme on the study of foreign policy? Mindful of the hazardous nature of this sort of assessment, it can be argued that this first systematic application of a decision-making framework to International Relations at least constituted a serious challenge to traditional assumptions. Others, indeed, might claim that the publication of this scheme was a crucial turning-point in the study of foreign policy. This author would argue that most commentators, by focusing almost exclusively on the inherent weaknesses of the approach, have erred on the side of understating the impact of the Snyder scheme and the decision-making approach as a whole. James Rosenau has argued that, in the context of increasing concern about the adequacy of a realist analysis of foreign policy prior to 1954, the Snyder scheme 'served to crystallize the ferment and to provide guidance – or at least legitimacy – for those who had become disenchanted with a world composed of abstract states and with a mystical quest for single-cause explanations of objective reality' (Rosenau 1967b, 202). Snyder himself

(1962, 2) later claimed that the heuristic value of the scheme was 'due less to its intrinsic properties than to a general need for and receptivity to it'. Unfortunately, Professor Snyder is not always so disarmingly modest. Much of his writing published since 1954 displays a quite excessive irritation that research in the field is not sufficiently geared to his own requirements (on this general point, see Pfaltzgraff 1974, 45).

The growing discontent with the traditional approach to the study of foreign policy came to focus upon the methodological adequacy of the realist critique, and thus constituted a key element in what came to be known as the behaviouralist 'protest' against the achievements of traditional political science (Dahl 1961a). While it was appreciated that the realists were primarily responsible for moving the study of International Relations away from a normative, Utopian bias and towards the attempt to describe the dynamics of the existing world, the realists in turn were criticized not only for their preoccupation with the concept of 'power', but also for their failure to subject such central concepts as 'power', 'balance of power' and 'national interest' to precise definition and rigorous analysis. The behaviouralists, for their part, were optimistic about the possibility of constructing empirically testable theories by the application of a scientific methodology. They argued that the lack of precision about the phenomena under investigation meant that traditional analysis could never rise above the level of the descriptive case study, which had little explanatory value and even less predictive potential.

Snyder's decision-making framework must be located, both historically and methodologically, within the behaviouralist movement. In terms of subject-matter and approach, the scheme represents the first attempt to apply the methodological rigour of the behavioural sciences to the study of foreign policy. The object of study is no longer a reified abstraction but the human decision-makers who act on behalf of the state. 'State X as actor is translated into its decision-makers as actors' (Snyder et al. 1962, 65). By definition, then, the state becomes its official decision-makers. The assumption that the state exists and acts in the way it does, only in so far as the people inhabiting it act as they do, clearly represents an important move away from traditional analysis. The fact that human beings, unlike abstractions, can be observed implies the possibility that the relevant political behaviour can be accurately observed and, therefore, rendered amenable to scientific analysis.

Certain other aspects of the 1954 scheme must be highlighted at this point. These are 'elements' which can be labelled innovatory in the context of foreign policy analysis. Not only do they represent a serious challenge to traditional analysis, but, as will be demonstrated, they also serve as key foci for future research efforts. Taken collectively, they measure the impact of the decision-making approach, which, in retrospect, precipitated a substantial reorientation in the study of foreign policy. The significant 'elements' which need to be isolated here are the following:

(*a*) the assumption that foreign policy consists of 'decisions', made by identifiable 'decision-makers'; the making of decisions, therefore, is the behavioural activity which requires explanation;
(*b*) the concept of the decision-makers 'definition of the situation';
(*c*) the emphasis on the domestic or societal sources of foreign policy decisions; and
(*d*) the clear implication that the decision-making process itself may be an important, independent source of decisions.

Relating the elements, in turn, to traditional analysis, the conception of foreign policy as a series of discrete decisions which can be analysed separately represented a distinctively new way of approaching the study of foreign policy – at least in the systematic way that the scheme implied. As noted earlier, the external behaviour of the state was not traditionally explained as a series of decisions made on behalf of the state, but in terms of the objective, environmental situation of that state; a situation which analysts, unless omniscient, could only assess in subjective terms. Snyder et al. (1962, 65) avoid this basic analytical quandary by asserting that 'the key to the explanation of why the state behaves the way it does lies in the way its decision-makers define their situation'. In other words, there is no need even to attempt to describe 'objective realities' if the subjective perceptions of decision-makers are the appropriate focus for any explanation of state behaviour. To take the example of the 'national interest', a problematic concept for traditional analysts, this can now be defined in terms of the subjective perceptions of the decision-makers.

The emphasis on the internal sources of foreign policy and the decision-making process itself also represent a significant departure from traditional analysis. As Kissinger (Rosenau 1969b, 261) succinctly notes, 'in the traditional conception the domestic structure is taken as given; foreign policy begins where domestic policy ends'. If the state boundary is assumed to be an effective barrier for both analytic and descriptive purposes, it is unnecessary, and clearly inconsistent with a systemic orientation, to look within the 'hard shell' of the billiard-ball state to account for its external behaviour. When, however, the object of study moves from the abstract state to its official decision-makers, external factors become one set of the range of factors which, collectively, comprise the 'situation' perceived and defined by the decision-makers. As demonstrated in the now famous box diagram, the salient features of the national and the international system, and the relationship between them, are located and classified under the headings of the internal and external 'settings' of decision-making (Snyder et al. 1962, 72). While this diagram graphically conveys the extent to which domestic sources of foreign policy had been neglected by traditional analysts, it also highlights, for the first time, the way in which the decision-making process is itself a key variable because it acts as a filter between internal and external stimuli, and decisional responses. The challenge here for traditional analysts is the clear implication that if policy outcome is, to a greater or lesser extent, a function of the processing stage, the institutional–organizational 'setting' within which decisions are made cannot simply be assumed merely to precede state action. The analyst must investigate the relationship between the process and the decisions which emerge from it.

If this is taken as a brief characterization of the extent to which the Snyder scheme challenged traditional analysis, it is necessary to add a qualifying rider – at least as far as this initial formulation of the decision-making approach is concerned. Following the distinction made earlier between 'state-centric' and 'state-as-actor' assumptions, it can be argued, with hindsight, that analyses of non-governmental and other 'transnational' actors rather than the application of the decision-making approach, have effectively challenged the assumption that national governments are, self-evidently, the most important actors in - International Relations (see in particular, the work of Keohane and Nye 1972). Decision-making analysts in the International Relations field appear to have accepted state-centricity for analytical purposes. Indeed, Snyder et al. (1962, 60) explicitly state that 'we believe that those who study international politics are mainly concerned with actions, reactions and interactions among political entities called national states'. However, as far as the state as actor assumption is concerned more recent developments in foreign policy analysis, which can be related to these elements within the Snyder scheme, have drawn attention to the restrictions inherent in the assumption that governments behave as monolithic, unitary actors in the formulation and execution of foreign policy. This is not to imply that the Snyder framework itself involves the rejection of this assumption; indeed, it can be argued that this scheme simply substitutes an 'official decision-makers as actor' assumption for the traditional 'state', with no necessary consequences for the ensuing analysis. Certainly, Snyder's 'decision-makers', who consciously make a series of discrete, calculated 'decisions' on behalf of the state, appear to behave in very much the same way as the purposeful, unitary 'government' of traditional analysis. The notion of an aggregation which acts on behalf of the state is still the dominant conception.

This analysis suggests that, while Snyder had clearly offered a serious challenge to traditionalists, the original formulation of the decision-making approach was still firmly rooted in traditional assumptions. This meant that the scheme was only mildly subversive in terms of its immediate impact. However, as noted above, certain 'elements' within the scheme did serve to encourage a gradial reorientation in the study of foreign policy. Therefore, without implying that every study after 1954 owes an intellectual debt to the original monograph, the rest of this section will attempt to highlight the influence of the decision-making approach, by reviewing the development of foreign policy analysis after this date. Despite a considerable overlap between categories, the literature will be classified in terms of the aforementioned 'elements'; case studies of foreign policy 'decisions', psychological and social–psychological studies suggested by the concept of the decision-makers 'definition of the situation', analyses of the internal or domestic environment of policy-making and related studies of the decision- or policy-making process (for an alternative classification which does not seek to highlight the influence of one particular approach, see Rosenau 1969b, 167ff).

Firstly, a wide range of foreign policy decisions has proved an important focus for research in the field. Dougherty and Pfaltzgraff (1971, 334) have observed that 'since the mid-1950s a considerable amount of literature has appeared on foreign policy decisions, primarily American and British. Most of it has been in the form of case studies of specific decisions which were telescoped in time and circumscribed as to the number of decision-makers'. Notable examples here of case studies on 'crisis' decisions would include the United States' decision to respond militarily to perceived communist aggression in Korea, June 1950 (Snyder and Paige 1958, Whiting 1960, Paige 1968), the British decision to intervene in Suez in 1956 (Childers 1962 and Thomas 1966), and the crucial decisions taken by both superpowers in the context of the Cuban missile crisis of October 1962 (Abel 1966, Allison 1969, 1971). Clearly, this type of decision, 'readily identifiable and isolable', is easier to analyse than the less dramatic and probably more typical, routine decision, which evolves over a more extended time period and is the concern of a larger group of decision-makers. The question of whether studies of such 'important' decisions illuminate the nature of the decision-making process or, more modestly, the particular decision situation, will be returned to later in this chapter (for a bibliography of both crisis and non-crisis case studies, consult Dougherty and Pfaltzgraff 1971, 334–5; Rosenau 1967a, 203–6; Robinson and Snyder 1965, 438–63).

A second category of research and publication has been stimulated by the concept of the decision-makers 'definition of the situation'. This concept, which served in the original study to structure elements from the internal, external and organizational 'settings', was the key to the Snyder et al. (1962, 7) attempt to 'combine in a single conceptual scheme two levels of analysis – the individual (psychological variables) and the group or organization (sociological variables)'. The assumption here is that any explanation of decision-making behaviour must include the attempt to reconstruct the subjective 'world' of the decision-maker(s) in an individual and a group context. The achievement of this objective clearly involves researching the range of psychological, social–psychological and sociological variables that condition and motivate individual and group behaviour. (The relevant organizational studies which stress the importance of sociological variables will be reviewed in the final category.) To inspect the research output which responds directly by this challenge is to be impressed by the contribution to foreign policy analysis of a distinctive set of concepts, research techniques and insights into both specific decisional events and more general policy orientations.

In particular, the decision-making perspective has brought within the scope of foreign policy analysis the concepts and the empirical research of social psychologists whose concern is to investigate the relationship between personality traits, situational variables and behaviour. (Some of the most relevant research has been reprinted in Kelman 1965, Singer 1965, 1968 and Rosenau 1969b. Kelman offers a clarifying discussion of the potential contribution of social psychological research, as well as stressing the limits of such a contribution, see in particular his introduction and conclusion.) At a minimum, empirical research in this area has served as a useful corrective to the rather 'cavalier' way in which traditional analysts, Morgenthau for example, tended to utilize psychological assumptions and concepts (Wolfers 1962, 10). However, the overall impact has been to increase the general awareness of the perceptual and attitudinal variables that condition the behaviour of individuals in a social situation, and therefore, the choices of decision-makers.

The concepts of 'image' (Boulding 1956, 1959) and 'belief system' (Holsti 1962), for example, have helped analysts to relate the perceptions of decision-makers to their foreign policy choices. It has become almost a truism to observe that decision-makers do not respond to the 'real' world, but to their 'images' of the world, which may or may not be accurate representations of that reality. In a study which investigates the possibility of misperception, the first hypothesis that Jervis (1969, 240) offers is that 'decision-makers tend to fit incoming information into their existing theories and images. Indeed, their theories and images play a large part in determining what they notice.' While Snyder is more concerned to stress the subjective perceptions of decision-makers, other analysts (following Sprout and Sprout 1956), have clearly distinguished between the psychological environment or 'psycho-milieu' of decision-making, and the 'operational milieu' or objective environment, which, though not perceived by decision-makers, may crucially affect the implementation of decisions. The concept of an 'objective environment' raises major epistemological problems which cannot be dealt with here.

Attempts to solve the problem of observing in as systematic and accurate a way as possible the behaviour of decision-making groups as they are actually engaged in decision-making, have resulted in the application of a range of research techniques borrowed from social psychology. These include quantitative content analyses of relevant statements and documents, which attempt to measure the relevant perceptions of decision-makers (Holsti 1962, Holsti et al. 1964, 1968), experimental simulation techniques (Guetzkow et al. 1963, Rosenau 1969b), and the intensive interviewing of 'key' decision-makers in order to reconstruct their definition of a particular decisional situation (Snyder and Paige, 1958).

Finally, the insights that social psychologists have generated with regard to both specific events and more general policy orientations, have been instructive. To exemplify the former, one notes again, in this context, the number of psychological studies of that specific decisional situation which can be defined as a 'crisis'. Empirical analyses of such variables as stress, cohesiveness and problem-solving efficiency, in the context of small-group behaviour, have convincingly demonstrated the extent to which a crisis situation significantly conditions the behaviour of the group and, thereby, the whole decision-making process (see, initially, Hermann 1969). Holsti's case study (1962) of John Foster Dulles, on the other hand, is an interesting example of a study which highlights the role of psychological variables in determining the foreign policy orientation of, in this case, the major 'architect' of American foreign policy between 1953 and 1959. The study investigates the relationship between Dulles' 'belief system' (defined as 'the complete world view') and his attitude towards the Soviet Union. By a content analysis of all Dulles' published statements relating to the Soviet Union made during his period as Secretary of State, Holsti is able to conclude that Dulles' belief system was 'closed'; particularly resistant, in other words, to new information which did not fit in with his existing 'image' of the Soviet Union. Thus a relationship is hypothesized between beliefs, images and foreign policy behaviour (Kelman 1965, 590).

Turning to the domestic and process categories in this classification the overlap problem becomes most evident. In the Snyder scheme, the 'internal setting' and the 'decision-making process' represent two sets of stimuli which give structure and content to the choices of decision-makers. Taken together, they suggest a hitherto neglected intrastate dimension to the explanation of foreign policy. However, a major analytical problem is to distinguish between these categories. For the purpose of this classification, the third category will contain those non-executive aspects of domestic politics which most studies have tended to parcel together and label 'the domestic environment' – these include political parties, pressure groups, public opinion, legislatures, the media, political culture and the domestic political system. The decision- or policy-making process, on the other hand, will refer to the executive or governmental actors who are involved in the making and implementation of policy decisions. However – and here the problem lies – the way in which the analyst characterizes the process, particularly with regard to the location and specification of key actors in the process, will determine how broadly or narrowly the 'government' is defined. In the absence of an explicit conception of the decision-making process, a foreign policy study of Congressional–Executive relations, for example, might be located in either category. The normative aspect of this sort of classification should, therefore, be noted.

It was, clearly, the response of foreign policy analysts to Snyder's emphasis on the 'internal setting' which prompted Rosenau to observe that 'one of the innovative virtues of the decision-making approach was that it provided a way of empirically tracing the role of domestic variables as sources of foreign policy behaviour (Rosenau 1967a, 198).[2] With the notable exception of the Almond (1950) study of the relationship between public opinion and American foreign policy, studies prior to the publication of the Snyder scheme had either 'black-boxed' the state, thus completely ignoring domestic variables, or merely paid lip service to internal factors by vague and unsystematic references to 'national character', 'national mood' or simply 'nationalism'. Since 1954, however, an increasing number of studies have been produced, though few explicitly comparative in scope, which share the common objective of establishing a connection between intrastate 'factors' and external state behaviour. A convenient distinction can be drawn here between those studies which investigate a range of potentially relevant domestic factors for their impact on foreign policy (e.g. Cohen 1957, Waltz 1967, Hanreider 1967, Rosenau 1967b, Kaiser and Morgan 1971), and those studies which focus on a single factor, such as public opinion (Rosenau 1961, Cohen 1973), strategic intelligence (Hilsman 1956), the press (Cohen 1963), or legislatures (Hilsman 1958, Robinson 1962, Richards 1967).

However, those analysts who have endeavoured to trace the domestic sources of foreign policy, have faced a complex set of conceptual and empirical problems, which relate back to traditional assumptions and serve to highlight the 'boundary' problems central to the study of foreign policy. If the latter was traditionally regarded as an aspect of International Relations, then the study of domestic politics was conceived as the proper concern of political science. This meant that the separation of foreign and domestic politics, 'central to the traditional concept of the nation-state' (Wallace 1971, 8), was 'institutionalized' in separate subjects, the boundaries of which were demarcated by the 'hard shell' of the billiard-ball state. Therefore, the relating of intrastate phenomena to external state behaviour forced analysts to cross subject boundaries; which, in turn, left them without appropriate analytical tools and concepts to describe and explain the focus of their concern.

Attempts to fill the conceptual vacuum thus exposed, can be seen in retrospect to have contributed to a fundamental reappraisal of the study of foreign policy and, indeed, International Relations as a whole. More specifically, the outcome has been to undermine both the 'state-centric' assumption and the 'security politics paradigm' outlined at the beginning of this chapter. Initially, it must be admitted, no explicit challenge was offered by the concept of 'linkage' between national and international systems, and the other theoretical concepts suggested by James Rosenau (1969a) for the study of those cross-national interactions relevant to the student of foreign policy (see also Hanreider 1967). Similarly, the borrowing of the concept of an 'issue area' from political science (Dahl 1961b), which enabled foreign policy to be analysed in terms of the domestic political process, seemed to reinforce the distinctiveness of foreign policy issues (Rosenau 1967b).

More recently, however, the empirical problems generated by the application of these concepts, how to establish the parameters of an 'issue' for example, together with a growing awareness of fundamental transformations at both state and international levels, have led certain scholars to reflect upon the restrictions inherent in 'state-centric realism' (Nye 1975). To take one example here, Morse (1970) has offered an analysis of these problems which is both clarifying and stimulating. He argues that changing intrastate demands, which are the product of 'modernization', combined with increasing levels of interdependence between states, have transformed the nature of foreign policy. As far as relations between modernized states are concerned, 'three general sets of conditions have developed' (Morse 1970, 371–2). Firstly, it has become increasingly difficult to separate foreign and domestic policy, 'even though the myths associated with sovereignty and the state' remain. Secondly, 'the distinction between "high policies" (those associated with security and the continued existence of the state) and "low policies" (those pertaining to the wealth and welfare of citizens) has become less important as low policies have assumed an increasingly large role in any society'. Finally, the ability of governments to control either domestic or foreign policy 'has decreased with the growth of interdependence, and is likely to decrease further'.

In effect, the conceptual and empirical 'boundary' has been crossed at two levels which need to be distinguished. At one level, analysts have been content to investigate the relationship between 'internal' and 'external' dimensions of foreign policy, thus assuming the impermeability of state boundaries, at least for analytical purposes. On the other hand, some scholars have drawn more radical conclusions and argued that analysts should now be concerned with the 'transnational systems of action and ideas' (Jones 1974, 11), which do not respect the boundaries of states, but which constitute the contemporary context within which foreign policy is made and implemented. A recent book on British foreign policy attempts to combine these perspectives, though the author does not explicitly make this point (Wallace 1975). Traditional 'high' policy issues, according to Wallace, are still handled in an intergovernmental framework, while the increasingly important non-security issues, which Morse refers to as 'low' and Wallace (1975, 11) rather confusingly labels 'sectoral policy issues', are handled in a variety of institutional contexts which cannot be wholly subsumed within a state-centric conception of International Relations.

Reference to Wallace, the first major study of the British foreign policy-making process, leads on to a consideration of the final category in this classification, the decision or policy-making process itself. In terms of the development of foreign policy analysis, Snyder's emphasis on the close relationship between the making of decisions and their content, has been of central importance and lasting concern. The original point was quite simple but the implications have transformed the study of foreign policy. In order to explain a foreign policy decision, the analyst must understand the process whereby that decision was made. The 'what' is, to a greater or lesser extent, determined by the 'how'. Thus, decision-making is defined as a process 'which results in the selection from a socially defined, limited number of problematical, alternative projects of one project intended to bring about the particular state of affairs envisaged by the decision-makers' (Snyder et al. 1962, 90). Decision-makers respond not only to internal and external 'settings', but to 'organizational–individual factors – the total relevant institutional environment; the reservoir of persons, roles, rules, agencies and functions from which a particular decisional unit is formed and within which it operates' (Snyder et al. 1962, 212). Much of the scheme is concerned with showing how organizational variables, in particular 'spheres of competence' (Snyder et al. 1962, 106), determine decisional behaviour.

Despite the reference to the 'total relevant institutional environment', Snyder, in fact, offers a restrictive conception of the decision-making process, which, again, suggests an adherence to the aggregative 'state-as-actor' assumption. As far as this scheme is concerned, 'only those who are government officials are to be viewed as decision-makers or actors' (Snyder et al. 1962, 99). Other analysts, however, though influenced by Snyder, have not restricted themselves to investigating the role of 'authoritative' actors in the decision-making process. As Hilsman (1969, 235) notes, 'many more people are involved in the process of government than merely those who hold the duly constituted official positions'. A review of process analyses since 1954 seems to reinforce the general point that the response to elements within the Snyder scheme, rather than the scheme itself, has contributed to the undermining of traditional assumptions, in this case, the 'state-as-actor'.

The response to the basic problem of how to understand the decision-making process has taken the form of subdividing the process, for analytical purposes, into its component parts. Different analysts have focused on different 'subprocesses' (Robinson and Majak 1967), thus highlighting a particular range of variables. Broadly, three such subprocesses have been identified: 'intellectual', 'social–organizational', and 'political'. These, in turn, have served to structure different conceptions or models of the process as a whole. The 'intellectual' subprocess has been defined by Robinson and Majak (1967, 180) as 'the analytic aspect of decision-making, which is performed largely by individual and group thought processes'. In this context, analysts have been concerned to ask why a typical decision-maker chooses to make a particular decision rather than another.

Attempts to answer what appears to be a simple question have been dominated by a complex multidisciplinary debate about rationality and choice. However, a common starting-point for this debate has been provided by the formal model of rational choice which is usually identified with classical economic theory. This model, and its variants explicitly sets out the stages which the rational decision-maker goes through in order to choose the most rational course of action; to produce the decision which, in economic terms, will maximize expected utilities. The perception of a problem requiring decisional action is followed by a listing of possible solutions. Having considered the consequences or 'utilities' of each course of action, the decision-maker proceeds to rank them in order of preference. The model assumes that, whenever possible, the decision finally made will be the one which maximizes expected benefits and minimizes expected costs.

In contrast, several analysts have argued that this sort of rationalistic conception of the process is a poor guide to actual decision-making situations, particularly in an organizational context (Verba, 1961). They assert that the assumptions implicit in such a model are unrealistic because decision-makers rarely have sufficient information or time to follow through this sort of process. Having observed the decision-making process in large organizations, Herbert Simon (1957) has coined the term 'bounded rationality', and suggested that the principle of 'satisficing' rather than 'optimizing' more realistically characterizes the process. This conception implies that a decision-maker will only search for alternatives until he finds one which meets certain minimum criteria. Braybrooke and Lindblom (1963) have postulated a continuum of decision process types, ranging from the rational economic model (the 'synoptic ideal') to much less rationalistic types. Of the four types outlined in this study, the one most practised, according to these authors, is the type they label 'disjointed incrementalism' (1963, 61); decision-makers are conceived as a socially fragmented group, making marginal adjustments to changing circumstances. This is the very non-rational process referred to less politely elsewhere by Lindblom (1959) as 'muddling through'.

The assumption of rational choice is elevated to a central place in the first 'conceptual model' of the decision-making process outlined by Graham Allison. In the very influential *Essence of Decision* (1971), Allison offers what is, in effect, an attempt 'to summarize the main features of three different bodies of literature' (Wagner 1974, 451), which relates closely to the subprocesses outlined here, particularly the 'social–organizational' and the 'political' The book as a whole represents a persuasive attempt to demonstrate the intimate relationship between the use of a particular mode of analysis and the resulting explanation of state behaviour. The first proposition asserts that 'professional analysts of foreign affairs (as well as ordinary laymen) think about problems of foreign and military policy in terms of largely implicit conceptual models that have significant consequences for the content of their thought' (Allison 1971, 3–4). Three such 'conceptual models' are distinguished, their 'organizing concepts' made explicit and used, in turn, to structure different accounts of the Cuban missile crisis.

The first model, called 'rational actor' or 'classical', is an important characterization of the traditional, 'state-as-actor' approach to the study of foreign policy. 'Most analysts and ordinary laymen attempt to understand happenings in foreign affairs as the more or less purposive acts of unified, national governments. Laymen personify rational actors and speak of their aims and choices' (Allison 1971, 4–5). Faced with an event which requires an explanation, the Model I analyst focuses on governmental choice. Having established the range of objectives and the possible choices involved, the analyst will try to relate the one to the other. The particular action is 'explained' when it appears to have been the rational thing to do, given specified objectives. Thus, state X did Y in order to achieve Z. In other words, the analyst puts himself in the position of the policy-maker and goes through the sort of calculations that he thinks the policy-maker has gone through.

In contrast to this type of explanation, two alternative models are introduced which radically change the analytical focus from governmental choice to the decision-making process and which, moreover, assume a disaggregated governmental actor. Though the traditional mode of explanation remains useful, Allison (1971, 5) contends that 'it must be supplemented, if not supplanted by frames of reference that focus on the governmental machine – the organizations and the political actors involved in the policy process'. The organizational context of decision-making, the subprocess highlighted by the Snyder scheme, reappears as Allison's 'organizational process' model (model 2). This model assumes that 'government consists of a conglomerate of semi-feudal, loosely allied organizations, each with a substantial life of its own' (Allison 1971, 67). Thus, foreign policy is understood to be the product, or the 'outputs of large organizations, functioning according to standard patterns of behaviour' (Allison 1971, 67), rather than the deliberate choices of a unified governmental actor. Explanation here consists of locating the organizational actors and relating their processes and procedures to the foreign policy event.

William Wallace, for example, in the study cited earlier, while denying the general applicability of either of Allison's process models to Britain, emphasizes the 'interrelationship between the structure of the policy-making machinery and the direction of policy' (Wallace 1975, 7). He points to the inflexibility which the administrative apparatus imposes on policy, and lists the organizational characteristics which reduce their responsiveness to political coordination and control. These include organizational loyalty, established routines, the attachment to tradition and continuity, and the existence of a separate Diplomatic Service with its élite status and norms of behaviour. Wallace (1975, 8) tentatively concludes that 'the high morale and prestige of the British Civil Service, and its successful resistance to the by-passing of its regular procedures by political channels, makes the problem of organizational inertia particularly acute for policy-makers in Britain'.

If the 'organizational process' Model attempts to apply the insights of organization theory to foreign policy analysis (Allison, 1971, 298ff), the third model, the 'governmental' or 'bureaucratic politics' model, clearly has its roots in political science. Again, in contrast to model 1, this model 'sees no unitary actor but rather many actors as players – players who focus not on a single strategic issue, but on many diverse international problems as well; players who act in terms of no consistent set of strategic objectives but rather according to various conceptions of national, organizational and personal goals; players who make government decisions not by a single, rational choice but by the pulling and hauling that is politics' (Allison 1971, 144). Instead of the traditional hard distinction between foreign and domestic politics, this model implies that the foreign policy-making process shares many of the characteristics of domestic policy formation, and, therefore, that political science analyses of domestic political processes are relevant to foreign policy analysis. Accordingly, foreign policy is conceived neither as governmental choice nor as organizational output, but as the 'resultant' of various bargaining games among key players within the government. In Allison's (1971, 7) phrase, 'a model 3 analyst has "explained" [a foreign policy action] when he has discovered who did what to whom that yielded the action in question'.

It is no exaggeration to claim that the study of foreign policy since 1971 has been dominated by *Essence of Decision* and the vigorous debate that has ensued about the utility of Allison's models. As indicated earlier, the point is not that Allison is saying anything strikingly new, though his inadequate appraisal of the political science tradition which is relevant to model 3 unfortunately gives this impression: rather, the attention is the product of the explicit construction of explanatory models combined with a convincing demonstration of their applicability to a particularly dramatic case study. Since the publication of this seminal work, Allison and, increasingly, Morton Halperin, in the attempt both to stimulate empirical studies and to highlight the policy implications of explanatory models, have 'merged' the second and third models and concentrated on the refinement of the bureaucratic politics model (Halperin 1971, 1974, Allison and Halperin 1972, Halperin and Kanter 1973). The focus on this hybrid model is justified, analytically, by arguing that 'organizations can be included as players in the game of bureaucratic politics, treating the factors emphasized by the organizational process approach as constraints' (Allison and Halperin 1972, 40).

A recent study of American involvement in Vietnam exemplifies the use of the bureaucratic politics model, as well as demonstrating the specific concern of American analysts with the quality of decisions in the wake of Vietnam (Gallucci 1975). This study begins with the premise that a convincing explanation of why Vietnam 'happened' must include an understanding of the process from which the relevant decisions emerged. Thus, having reviewed 'conventional' explanations, Gallucci (1975, 5) attempts to move towards 'a broader explanation', which focuses specifically on 'the link between the way the system worked and the outcomes that it produced'. The decision-making 'system' is, therefore, treated as a significant, independent variable. Gallucci concludes his study by asserting that the American involvement in Vietnam cannot be adequately explained solely in terms of broad historical factors or more immediate Cold War values and images, though these constitute the 'deepest roots of policy'. Explanation must focus on the character of the decision-making process which supplied 'the factors that were a good deal more proximate to the actual policy choices for Vietnam' (Gallucci 1975, 132). Prescription centres, therefore, on two general proposals for restructuring the decision-making process, which if implemented, are taken to offer the most promising way of preventing another Vietnam.

This brief reference to the Gallucci book, which serves here as one example of the increasing use of process models to account for foreign policy actions, concludes this attempt to locate the decision-making approach, both historically and methodologically, within the development of foreign policy analysis. Broadly, the point made originally by Arnold Wolfers, that the Snyder scheme represents a rather meagre departure from the traditional approach to the study of foreign policy, has been accepted here (Wolfers 1962). However, the burden of this analysis has been to highlight the more subversive impact of the decision-making approach over time, by attempting to relate important developments in the subject back to suggestive elements within the Snyder scheme. The specific focus has been on the contribution of this approach to the undermining of traditional assumptions, and thereby, to the gradual reorientation of the study of foreign policy, culminating in the contemporary emphasis on the decision or policy-making process and the self-conscious concern with the relationship between models, theory and explanation. This would seem to be an appropriate point at which to adopt a rather different perspective and to assess the theoretical status of the decision-making approach.

Decision-making as theory

In order to evaluate the theoretical status of any approach, some initial clarification is required, not only to distinguish between an 'approach' and a 'theory' in conceptual and functional terms, but also to establish evaluatory criteria. The term 'theory', according to Oran Young (1972, 180), has been 'used so imprecisely and indiscriminately by social scientists that it is in danger of losing any meaningful content'. The central problem is that there are as many definitions of 'theory' as there are theorists, and dogmatism, unfortunately, is the rule rather than the exception. The short history of International Relations has been punctuated by acrimonious debates about the nature of theory in this subject (for a historical overview of these debates see Pfaltzgraff 1974). Analysts might agree that there are different types of theory (e.g. normative, empirical, deductive and inductive), and different levels of theory (general or grand, 'middle-range', 'macro' and 'micro'). But, debates about what International Relations theory can or should achieve have been characterized by dissension and fundamental disagreements.

Having earlier located the decision-making framework within the behaviouralist movement, it seems reasonable to start by referring briefly to a social scientific theory of International Relations which establishes stringent criteria by which Snyder would wish his scheme to be evaluated. While there are significant differences between scholars, a scientific conception of theory is primarily concerned with explanation and prediction rather than 'mere' description. The focus is on recurring patterns of behaviour rather than unique occurrences. Thus, key variables must be isolated, hypotheses developed, operationalized and tested. The object of the exercise is the making of generalized statements and the establishment of rigorous cause–effect relationships as in the natural sciences (for a more detailed explication of this type of theory, see Ch. 10). Snyder et al. (1962, 3) clearly demonstrate their adherence to this conception of theory when they assert that the 'ultimate purpose' of repeated applications of their scheme 'is not historical reconstruction . . . but the development of adequate theory and testable hypotheses'. Jones (1970a, 12) infers from this sort of statement that the scheme 'was to be a general framework into which empirical research could be fitted and from which could emerge general theory of the broadest kind'.

It is notable that most critics have, implicitly, at least, adopted the criteria offered by this scientific conception of theory in order to highlight the theoretical paucity of the Snyder scheme and by implication the decision-making approach. McClosky (1962, 196) for example, an early critic, argues that 'until a greater measure of theory is introduced into the proposal and the relations among the variables are specified more concretely, it is likely to remain little more than a setting-out of categories, and, like any taxonomy, fairly limited in its utility'. Rosenau (1967a), though concerned in his critique to justify the lack of theory in the scheme, nevertheless draws attention to the absence of if–then propositions from which hypotheses might be constructed. Dougherty and Pfaltzgraff (1971, 27) having reviewed various types of theory conclude that the Snyder scheme can only be regarded as theory if the term is so broadly defined as to include a classifactory scheme 'which provides for the orderly arrangement and examination of data'. Perhaps the most serious criticism, from this perspective, is the evident failure of the scheme to spark empirical enquiries utilizing Snyder's categories, with the single unreplicated exception of the Korea study, started by Snyder and Paige and produced in its final form by Paige (1958, 1968). This study was clearly conceived as a contribution to scientific theory rather than a descriptive case study.

However, to criticize the shortcomings of the Snyder scheme in terms of the stringent requirements of scientific theory is not to deny the utility of either the scheme or the approach. Interestingly, Oran Young, in the chapter cited earlier, while defining theory in social scientific terms (1972, 180–1), specifically rejects the 'tendency to talk about the development of viable [scientific] theories as though they were the only objective worth pursuing' (1972, 187, my insert). This suggests that there might be a less demanding set of criteria by which decision-making might be evaluated. McClosky (1962, 198) qualifies his criticism by suggesting that 'the decision-making focus may also serve as a heuristic device for stimulating interest in questions that go beyond the categories of explanation traditionally employed in studies of international affairs'. This accords with the historical evaluation offered in the previous section, and can be compared with the variety of 'useful activities' which Young lists as alternatives to the development of scientific theory, in particular what he calls 'sensitization' and 'conceptualization'. The former consists of emphasizing 'concepts, questions and facts' that have been previously ignored or de-emphasized. As for 'conceptualization' Young (1972, 188) suggests that 'everyone views the world in terms of some conceptual framework or approach to analysis . . . [which constitutes] – an interrelated set of concepts, variables, and assumptions or premises – [and which] – determines what a person regards as worth explaining and what factors he will look for in the search for explanations' (my inserts).

To regard decision-making 'merely' as an approach from which one or more conceptual frameworks (called 'models' by Allison) can be derived, is not to demean decision-making, but rather to link the approach more usefully to a range of what might be called 'non-scientific' types of explanation. Thus, a more appropriate criterion by which the approach might be judged is whether or not it stimulates plausible explanations or, more accurately, accounts of foreign policy. This seems to be Pettman's point when he argues that 'substantive applications of an approach either realize its benefits independent of prior debate, or they do not and its explanatory potential is evident as a result' (Pettman 1975, 32). This sort of critique would ask, retrospectively, whether the concepts and categories offered by the approach have facilitated a 'better' understanding of foreign policy. From this critical perspective, the major problems with this approach have resulted directly from its central concern with decisions and decision-making processes.

As most critics have pointed out, a host of problems stem from the assumption that foreign policy consists of conscious, isolatable decisions. If it can be established that 'a good deal of activity . . . is not decisional in any precise sense' (Jones, 1970b, 37), then this assumption distorts the subject and, to that extent, does not advance our understanding of foreign policy. Ironically, studies of decision-making processes have themselves undermined rather than reinforced the centrality of decision-making in foreign policy formulation by highlighting such non-decisional factors as 'organizational inertia' and 'bureaucratic drift' (for the concept of a 'non-decision' in political science see Bachrach and Baratz 1963). If the approach can blind the analyst to relevant non-decisional activity, it can also have the unfortunate effect of encouraging analysts to look for 'key' decisions and important 'turning-points' in the evolution of foreign policy. However, the sheer quantity, variety and simultaneity of decisions made on behalf of the state raises two distinct questions here. Firstly, by what criteria are 'key' decisions to be identified and secondly, if the government is assumed to be disaggregated, at what levels within the policy-making machinery are different decisions made and by whom? (Jones, 1970b, 36–8).

In response to the problems outlined here, Wallace (1975, 5–6) begins his study by assuming that 'the process of policy-making is less one of a series of discrete and identifiable decisions than a continuous flow of policy – clear and final decisions are as rare in foreign policy making as in much domestic policy'. Though he identifies the major turning-points in postwar British foreign policy as the successive decisions to apply to join the EEC, the decision to devalue the pound sterling in November 1967, and the associated decision to withdraw from East of Suez, Wallace (1975, 7) asserts that 'in each case . . . the final decision was, at most, the culmination of a long series of smaller decisions and non-decisions, of considering and foreclosing options, and that this "final" decision itself was only the beginning of another series of consequential consideration of further alternatives'. This conception of foreign policy-making as a continuous process leads Wallace to reject the centrality of 'decisions' and 'decision-making' and to focus his account of British foreign policy on the relationship between the structure of the policy-making machinery and foreign policy output.

The more recent emphasis on the decision or policy-making process has also been problematical, despite the stimulating work that has followed *Essence of Decision.* Firstly, the overriding concern with the processes by which policy is made, has tended to produce studies which are more concerned with the mechanics of producing policy than with the actual content of policy. In this context, the Snyder scheme itself has been criticized by one scholar for casting the foreign policy analyst in the role of an 'efficiency expert to government' who, like the business efficiency expert, 'is not concerned with the product, or with the values that make it attractive . . . but . . . simply concerned with its production' (Jones 1970b, 35–6). Hoffman (1959, 364) makes essentially the same point when he accuses Snyder of 'proceduralism . . . the view of world politics as a series of procedures (easily represented by circles and arrows) irrespective of the substance of the messages carried or the decisions made'. Despite some concern recently with the quality of decisions, decision-making analysts have largely ignored important questions of values and the desirability or otherwise of policy objectives. Yet, as Reynolds (1971, 35) makes clear, the word 'policy' cannot be wholly divorced from its adjective 'politic' which 'carries' overtones of prudence or wisdom, and thus implies something about the purposes for which actions are taken'.

A second set of problems follows the conception of foreign policy as a series of decisions made by recognizable units or systems. For the 'system' analogy to be useful, the boundaries of systems and subsystems need to be clearly delineated in order to specify the relevant actors and to delimit the scope of the unit in question. However, the various conceptions of the process offered to date have been ambiguous and inadequately differentiated. To focus here on Allison's models, there is some confusion, for example, as to whether model 3 is independent of model 2 or merely an extension of it. Of more importance perhaps, the explanatory status of such models needs considerable clarification. Allison (1971, 4) for his part, warns his readers that he is using the term 'model' in the sense of 'conceptual scheme or framework', but this does not serve to clarify the relationship either between the models, or between the models and the notion of explanation. In what sense, we might legitimately ask, do models 2 and 3 increase the ability of analysts to explain and predict the decisions of governments?

In this context, Wagner (1974, 447) argues that, because Allison does not develop models in the formal sense of 'constructs yielding clear inferences that can be compared with the facts', he cannot be sure whether the models constitute 'alternative explanations of the same thing or simply different explanations of different things' (Wagner 1974, 447–8). Allison (1971, 329) relegates a discussion of this crucial problem to a footnote. Though Wagner does not make this point, part of the problem seems to be that Allison utilizes his models as empirical rather than conceptual frameworks. They appear, therefore, to be more relevant to the development of alternative descriptions (accounts) rather than explanations of foreign policy events, to the extent that description and explanation can be separated. Wagner (1974, 448–51) suggests that the next step should be the development of 'genuine' explanatory models, but asks whether these would necessarily follow Allison's 'guidelines'. The point is that Allison's models disaggregate governments in ways that seem, on reflection, both arbitrary and culture-bound. Models 2 and 3 may be heuristic in terms of American foreign policy-making (though easily caricatured, see Kohl, 1975), but they are unlikely to advance an understanding of less developed states, with less complex policy-making systems. Perhaps there is a prior need for a typology of policy-making systems to curb attractive but spurious universalistic conceptions of foreign policy-making processes?

Several references have been made in this chapter to the famous critique of decision-making by James Rosenau. Towards the end of that critique, Rosenau makes two points which appear to be contradictory. On the one hand, he asks rhetorically 'how can we explain the decision-making approach's apparent lack of durability?' (Rosenau 1967a, 207). Shortly afterwards, however, he concludes that 'the decision-making approach has been absorbed into the practice of Foreign Policy Analysis. The habits it challenged have been largely abandoned and the new ones it proposed have become so fully incorporated into the working assumptions of practitioners that they no longer need to be explicated or the original formulation from which they came cited' (Rosenau 1967a, 211). Despite this conclusion, the approach is deemed to have 'failed' because it has not made its promised contribution to the development of a scientific theory of foreign policy. This study, in contrast, by looking beyond the Snyder scheme and employing less demanding criteria, has offered a rather different evaluation. It has been argued that the approach, far from lacking durability, has made and continues to make a distinctive contribution to development of foreign policy analysis. Despite the major problems outlined above, the very fact that 'decision' and 'decision-making' are still used interchangeably with 'policy' and 'policy-making' only serves to underline the lasting impact of this approach.

Notes

1. Snyder, R.C., Bruck, H.W. and Sapin, B. (1954) 'Decision-making as an approach to the study of international politics', *Foreign Policy Analysis,* Series No. 3, Princeton, Princeton University Press. Reprinted in Snyder, et al. (1962).
2. However, see Rosenau (1971, 67–94) for a discussion of parallel developments in comparative politics in the 1950s, which influenced foreign policy analysis in a similar direction. On this point, see also Farrell (1966).

References and Further Reading

Asterisked items constitute a short bibliography for decision-making analysis.

Abel, E. (1966) *The Missile Crisis,* Philadelphia, Lippincott.

Allison, G.T. (1969) 'Conceptual models and the Cuban missile crisis', *American Political Science Review,* lxiii (September).

***Allison, G.T.** (1971) *Essence of Decision: Explaining the Cuban Missile Crisis,* Boston, Little, Brown.

Allison, G.T. and Halperin, M. (1972) 'Bureaucratic politics: A paradigm and some policy implications', in R. Tanter and R.H. Ullman (eds), *Theory and Policy in International Relations,* Princeton, NJ, Princeton Univ. Press.

Almond, G. (1950) *The American People and Foreign Policy,* New York, Harcourt Brace.

Bachrach, P. and Baratz, M.S. (1963) 'Decisions and non-decisions: An analytical framework', *American Political Science Review,* **57** (3), 632–42.

Boulding, K. (1956) *The Image,* Ann Arbor, Univ. of Michigan Press.

Boulding, K. (1959) 'National images and international images', *Journal of Conflict Resolution,* 3, 120–31.

Braybrooke, D. and Lindblom, C.E. (1963) *A Strategy of Decision,* New York, Free Press.

Castles, F.G., Murray, D.J. and Potter, D.C. (eds) (1971) *Decisions, Organisations and Society,* London, Penguin Books (Open University).

Childers, E.B. (1962) *The Road to Suez,* London, MacGibbon and Kee.

Cohen, B.C. (1957) *The Political Process and Foreign Policy,* Princeton, NJ, Princeton Univ. Press.

Cohen, B.C. (1963) *The Press and Foreign Policy,* Princeton, Princeton, NJ, Univ. Press.

Cohen, B.C. (1973) *The Public's Impact on Foreign Policy,* Boston, Little, Brown.

Dahl, R. (1961a) 'The behavioural approach in political science: Epitaph for a monument to a successful protest', *American Political Science Review,* (December).

Dahl, R. (1961b) *Who Governs?* New Haven, Yale Univ. Press.
Dougherty, J.E. and Pfaltzgraff, R.L. (1971) *Contending Theories of International Relations,* Philadelphia, Lippincott.
Downs, A. (1966) *Inside Bureaucracy,* Boston, Little, Brown.
Farrell, R. Barry, (ed.) (1966) *Approaches to Comparative and International Politics,* Evanston, Ill., Northwestern Univ. Press.
Frankel, J. (1959) 'Towards a decision-making model in foreign policy', *Political Studies,* vii (1) (February), 1–11.
Gallucci, R.L. (1975) *Neither Peace nor Honor: The Politics of American Military Policy in Vietnam,* Baltimore, Johns Hopkins Press.
Guetzgow, H., Alger, C.F., Brody, R.A., North, R.C. and Snyder, R.C. (1963) *Simulation in International Relations,* Englewood Cliffs, NJ, Prentice-Hall.
Halperin, M.H. (1971) 'Why bureaucrats play games', *Foreign Policy,* **2**.
Halperin, M.H. (1974) *Bureaucratic Politics and Foreign Policy,* Washington, DC, Brookings Institution.
Halperin, M.H. and Kanter, A. (eds) (1973) *Readings in American Foreign Policy: A Bureaucratic Perspective,* Boston, Little, Brown.
Hanreider, W.F. (1967) *West German Foreign Policy 1949–63,* Stanford, Calif., Stanford Univ. Press.
Hermann, C.F. (1969) 'International crisis as a situational variable', in J.N. Rosenau (ed.), *International Politics and Foreign Policy,* New York, Free Press.
Hilsman, R. (1956) *Strategic Intelligence and National Decisions,* Glencoe, Ill., Free Press,
Hilsman, R. (1958) 'Congressional-Executive relations and the foreign policy consensus', *American Political Science Review,* **52**, 725–44.
Hilsman, R. (1969) 'Policy-making is politics', in J.N. Rosenau (ed.) *International Politics and Foreign Policy,* (rev. edn), New York, Free Press.
Hoffman, S.H. (1959) 'International relations: The long road to theory', *World Politics,* xi (April).
*__Holsti, O.R.__ (1962) 'The belief system and national images, *Journal of Conflict Resolution,* vi (September), 244–52.
Holsti, O.R., Brody, R.A. and North, R.C. (1964) 'Measuring effect and action in the international reaction models: Empirical materials from the 1962 Cuban crisis', *Journal of Peace Research,* **1**.
Holsti, O.R., Brody, R.A. and North, R.C. (1968) 'Perception and action in the 1914 crisis', in J.D. Singer (ed.) *Quantitative International Politics,* New York, Free Press.
Jervis, R. (1968) 'Hypotheses on misperception', World Politics xx, 454–79. Reprinted in J.N. Rosenau (ed.), *International Politics and Foreign Policy,* 1969.
Jones, R.E. (1970a) 'Decision-making', *Political Studies* (March), 121–5.
Jones, R.E. (1970b) *Analysing Foreign Policy,* London, Routledge and Kegan Paul.
Jones, R.E. (1974) *The Changing Structure of British Foreign Policy,* London, Longman.
Kaiser, K. and Morgan, R. (eds)(1971) *Britain and West Germany: Changing Societies and the Future of Foreign Policy,* London, Oxford Univ. Press.
*__Kelman, H.C.__ (ed.) (1965) *International Behaviour: A Social–Psychological Analysis,* New York, Holt, Rinehart and Winston.
Keohane, R.O. and Nye, J.S. (eds) (1972) *Transnational Relations and World Politics,* Cambridge, Mass., Harvard Univ. Press.
Kohl, W.L. (1975) 'The Nixon–Kissinger foreign policy system and US–European relations: Patterns of policy-making, *World Politics* (December).
Krasner, S.D. (1972) 'Are bureaucracies important? (or Allison Wonderland)', *Foreign Policy,* **7**, 159–79.
Leoni, B. (1957) 'The meaning of 'political' in political decisions', *Political Studies,* v, 225–39.
Lijphart, A. (1974) 'The Structure of the theoretical revolution in international relations', *International Studies Quarterly* (March).
Lindblom, C.E. (1959) 'The Science of muddling through', *Public Administration Review,* **29** (2) (Spring).

March, J.G. and Simon, H.A. (1958) *Organisations,* New York, Wiley.
McClosky, H. (1962) 'Concerning strategies for a science of international politics', in R.C. Snyder, H.W. Bruck and B. Sapin (eds.). *Foreign Policy Decision-Making,* 1962.
***Morse, E.L.** (1970) 'The transformation of foreign policies: Modernization, interdependence and externalisation', *World Politics* **22** (April).
Nye, J.S. (1975) 'Transnational and transgovernmental relations', in G.L. Goodwin and A. Linklater (eds). *New Dimensions of World Politics,* London, Croom Helm.
***Paige, G.** (1968) *The Korean Decision,* New York, Free Press.
Perlmutter, A. (1974) 'The presidential political centre and foreign policy', *World World Politics,* (October).
Pettman, R. (1975) *Human Behaviour and World Politics,* London, Macmillan.
Pfaltzgraff, R.L. (1974) 'International relations theory: Retrospect and prospect', *International Affairs* **50** (1), (January), 28–48.
Puchala, D.J. and Fagan, S.I. (1974) 'International politics in the 1970s: The search for a perspective', *International Organization* **28** (2) (Spring).
Reynolds, P.A. (1971) *An Introduction to International Relations,* London, Longman.
Richards, P.G. (1967) *Parliament and Foreign Affairs,* London, Allen and Unwin.
Robinson, J. (1962) *Congress and Foreign Policy Making,* Homewood, Ill., Dorsey Press.
Robinson, J.A. and Majak, R.R. (1967) 'The theory of decision-making', in J.C. Charlesworth (ed.), *Contemporary Political Analysis,* New York, Free Press.
***Robinson, J.A. and Snyder, R.C.** (1965) 'Decision-making in international politics', in H.C. Kelman (ed.), *International Behaviour: A Social–Psychological Analysis,* New York, Holt, Rinehart and Winston.
Rosenau, J.N. (1961) *Public Opinion and Foreign Policy,* New York, Random House.
***Rosenau, J.N.** (1967a) 'The premises and Promises of decision-making analysis', in J.C. Charlesworth (ed.), *Contemporary Political Analysis,* New York, Free Press.
***Rosenau, J.N.** (ed.) (1967b) *Domestic Sources of Foreign Policy,* New York, Free Press.
Rosenau, J.N. (ed.) (1969a) *Linkage Politics,* New York, Free Press.
***Rosenau, J.N.** (ed.) (1969b) *International Politics and Foreign Policy, A Reader in Research and Theory* (rev. edn.), New York, Free Press.
***Rosenau, J.N.** (1971) *The Scientific Study of Foreign Policy,* New York, Free Press.
Simon, H.A. (1957) *Models of Man: Social and Rational,* New York, Wiley.
Singer, J.D. (ed.) (1965) *Human Behaviour and International Politics,* Chicago, Rand McNally.
Singer, J.D. (ed.) (1968) *Quantitative International Politics: Insights and Evidence,* New York, Free Press.
Singer, J.D. (1969) 'The level of analysis problem in international relations', in J.N. Rosenau (ed.), *International Politics and Foreign Policy* (rev. edn.), New York, Free Press.
***Snyder, R.C. and Paige, G.D.** (1958) 'The United States decision to resist aggression in Korea: The application of an analytical scheme, *Administrative Science Quarterly,* **3** (December), 342–78.
***Snyder, R.C., Bruck, H.W. and Sapin, B.** (eds) (1962) *Foreign Policy Decision-Making: An Approach to the Study of International Politics,* New York, Free Press.
Sprout, H. and M. (1956) *Man-Milieu Hypotheses in the Context of International Politics,* Princeton, Princeton Univ. Centre of International Studies.
Thomas, H. (1966) *Suez,* New York, Harper and Row.
Verba, S. (1961) 'Assumptions of rationality and non-rationality in models of the international system, in K. Knorr and S. Verba (eds), *The International System: Theoretical Essays,* Princeton, NJ, Princeton Univ. Press.
***Wagner, R. Harrison,** (1974) 'Dissolving the state: Three recent perspectives', *International Organization* **28** (3) (Summer).
Wallace, W. (1971) *Foreign Policy and the Political Process,* London, Macmillan.
***Wallace, W.** (1975) *The Foreign Policy Process in Britain,* London, RIIA.
Waltz, K. (1967) *Foreign Policy and Democratic Politics,* Boston, Little Brown.
Whiting, A.S. (1960) *China Crosses in Yalu: The Decision to Enter the Korean War,* New York, Macmillan.

Wolfers, A.M. (1962) *Discord and Collaboration.* Baltimore, Johns Hopkins Press.
***Young, O.R.** (1972) 'The perils of Odysseus: On constructing theories in international relations', in R. Tanter and R.H. Ullman (eds), *Theory and Policy in International Relations,* Princeton, NJ, Princeton Univ. Press.

Chapter 8

Military strategy

Peter Nailor

The extensive literature that exists on military affairs and, in particular on military strategy, reflects the importance of war in international affairs from the remotest historical periods of which we have knowledge down to the present day. It is not that war has always been the most significant factor in determining the fortunes of states or peoples, but it has recurred time after time and has persistently been engaged in as a deliberate act of policy to achieve objectives or to enforce compliance. It has, in fact, been a standard and common event in International Relations to a point where the absence of major wars can be remarked upon, in retrospect, as signifying something like a golden age. Not all wars, of course, are international: civil wars have been among the most protracted and bitterly contested and the distinction between what is a 'civil war' and an 'international war' depends sometimes upon the way that we choose to categorize the political units that take part. Were the conflicts in fifteenth century Italy tribal, civil or international wars, in so far as they occurred between formally organized political entities? The conflicts in Indo-China between 1951 and 1974 were clearly international wars at one level; but they were also, at another level of analysis, wars of 'national liberation', which is claimed to be another category. What is perhaps most useful to note about this typological difficulty is that the categorization of wars and the principal works relating to the analysis of their importance and utility stem primarily from European (or, to use the current distinction, 'Western') sources. Here the pattern of experience has been a development from feudal and warrior-dominated societies to centrally organized political institutions that have competed for political power and economic resources; in the eighteenth and nineteenth centuries this competition commonly extended beyond their own territories, and in the twentieth century has involved whole continents. Until the middle of the twentieth century at least, the game – and the rules of the game – was permeated by European values and goals.

As a rule of thumb, there have been four characteristics of the development that it will be useful to note. The first is that war has, historically, been so prevalent as to require the development and maintenance of a professional cadre, 'the military', on a social or an occupational basis. The second is that it has been seen as a traditional and legitimate tool of statecraft, in an international environment that has few control techniques or sanctions short of force. The third is that it is an apparently wasteful activity, consuming human and material resources in ways that may bear little relationship to the intrinsic importance of the object of policy. The parallel influences of these second and third characteristics have given rise from time to time to attempts to restrict the recourse to war, either by determining that some types of war are 'unjust' or unnecessary, or by setting some limiting rules about how war may be waged, or by offering some alternative method of resolving disputes. The last characteristic to note is that war has consistently created new demands for techniques that would ensure victory, and has since the late eighteenth century been a great stimulus to technological innovation.

It follows that the management of war has been a major preoccupation for political and military leaders and scholars, from their different standpoints. Success in waging war and accounting for the reasons for success – or failure – have been the foundations for many great reputations, from Alexander and Caesar, and Xenophon and Thucydides onwards. But military strategists have often had more restricted and specialized perspectives; many have contented themselves with analyses about the organization of armed forces and the *minutiae* of their deployment rather than about the purposes for which the organizations themselves are maintained and employed. The broader level of analysis – what Liddell Hart (1967, 335) has called 'the art of distributing and applying military means to fulfil the ends of policy' – has been seen as the level at which general principles can be deduced and examined so that the lessons of past experience may be placed in the desired context: and this is called 'strategy'. The narrower and more detailed analysis, about how to train, deploy and use forces in combat, is called 'tactics'. There is clearly an area for overlap in which considerations relating to tactics verge into strategy. And at an even broader level, there may well be concepts which are primarily related to military matters, which also affect political policies and affairs extending well beyond the use of force. This has conventionally been called 'grand strategy', but in the recent past, as we shall see, the distinction that the separate description infers has become more difficult to maintain.

Although the scope of writings on military strategy may vary quite widely, the great majority share one characteristic: they seek to interpret the interplay of factors that we can, loosely, identify as the international system of the time as an existing entity with conventions and usages that are both real and limiting. They tend therefore to accept the use of force or the threat of the use of force as a given entity, however much they might seek to constrain or alter its employment; from this point of view, military strategy tends to be explanatory, or prescriptive in a limited sense, rather than reformist in the sense in which most of the work of the peace researchers looks for alternative systems of conflict resolution (see Ch. 12 below). Many of the most substantial works in the field therefore are conventional, in the broad sense of the term, even though the interpretations or insights that they offer may be novel and even perhaps fundamentally innovative. They seek to distil the experience of past events, and to case them in a framework which may either be regarded as educative or, in some of the more grandly conceived works, didactic.

Thus Clausewitz and Mahan, in their separate ways, sought to impose upon the range of historical events with which they were concerned a pattern of analysis from which lessons could be derived to guide future habits of thought and action. In these two cases, the purpose which Mahan had was more specific, or at any rate more evident, since he lived to complete his work and to make his intentions more clear: he was concerned to demonstrate by inference the great importance of sea power to the United States and to show that for his own country as well as for the United Kingdom in the past 'he that commands the sea is at great liberty and may take as much and as little of the war as he will'.[1]

However, there are two major difficulties about this methodology. The first is a general problem by no means limited to military strategy and concerns the selection and interpretation of evidence. Depending upon the skill of the writer, and upon the state of knowledge of the historical period which is chosen, the deductions which are drawn from the material may be well founded, or may be highly selective; the selection may be that of the author or it may be dependent upon the random survival of recorded material. If the author's knowledge is extensive and his mode of analysis objective, a result may accrue that can be represented as 'reliable'; but if he determines to prove a preselected hypothesis by using only those examples which suit his case, the result may be rubbish, as well as unscholarly. If his aim is to influence future policy, it may be dangerous rubbish.[2] The second difficulty is again a universal one. The deductions that are made may be of such a general order as to be apophthegmatic, more suitable for a horoscope in a newspaper than for a manual of doctrine. The conclusions which they embody may be very well supported, but they will sound like general principles of applied common sense rather than the 'laws of war' which they have sometimes been called, or precepts to which particular courses of action can be fitted. They will, in fact, be better suited to providing a general range of knowledge about what has previously happened than to offering a key to action for political leaders or military commanders, who may face a specific and critical situation in which novel circumstances make the lessons of the past only partly useful. This does not, of course, diminish the importance of knowing – and understanding – what has gone on in the past; but it creates a requirement for a high quality of leadership and judgement as well as for good scholarship, so that the lessons of the past may be kept in their proper place, neither to be forgotten nor to be followed blindly.

It is a matter of judgement, for example, whether circumstances have so changed as to require a radical reaction; and it might even then require political and military skills of a very high order to carry out innovations which almost by definition will be experimental. So, we might argue, the circumstances of the First World War confounded soldiers and politicians; the trench warfare on the Western Front was sterile in political terms and horrific at every level, but its demands corroded what attempts were made to evade it. And it is questionable whether – either at the political or military levels – fundamental shifts of policy can be easily absorbed even under such urgent pressure. The social and political values that are involved in the making of war are frequently of a basic and fundamental appeal; national security, the survival of a way of life, the demand for vengeance, or at least victory, to justify the sacrifices that have been incurred, may all work towards rigidifying political attitudes and relationships, and produce slogans – like 'unconditional surrender' – rather than shifts of policy which can envisage major alterations in the objectives of the war, or negotiation and compromise. The coming of democratic forms of government has generally been held to have emphasized this trend; the active support of the people becomes more necessary to the government, and must be confirmed, or created, by establishing a clear purpose for the war, with a well-defined enemy exhibiting characteristics of an abhorrent nature, all of which at one and the same time precipitate support for the war and make it more difficult for the government to follow a path of compromise. It is a short step from here to attributions of 'war guilt' which, *ex hypothesi,* relate to the defeated. Nevertheless, the maintenance of morale at home has been seen to be essential, not only to the making of war, but also to the mobilization of the resources of the state.

This has been particularly true of the great wars of the twentieth century in which all of the major industrialized powers have been involved. The raising and maintaining of armed forces in the field has been at least as taxing as their successful deployment in battle; supplies of equipment and ammunition have first to be procured and then transported, and in both world wars this has called for immense efforts, amounting in some cases to virtually the total mobilization of the industrial and labour resources of the states concerned. Andrzejewski (1954, chapter 2 et seq) has noted that this high 'military participation ratio' gives rise to increased expectations about the better state of society after the struggle, and there is no doubt about the potency of some of the visions that have been created by the tensions of mass war – homes to be made fit for heroes and a level of social welfare of an unprecedented sort, besides substantial changes in the legal and social position of women in society. This may be partly due, in Western Europe at any rate, to the increased physical participation of the civilian population; especially in the Second World War, the great invasions and the vulnerability of the civil population to air attack made the distinction between 'the front line' and 'the home front' meaningless in any traditional way. Nevertheless by the close of the Second World War there was a consensus about the general nature of war; as Howard (1970, 49–50) said:

It was considered, first, that the mobilization of superior resources, together with the maintenance of civilian morale *at home, was a necessary condition for victory; a condition requiring a substantial domestic 'mobilization base' in terms of industrial potential and trained manpower. It was agreed that, in order to deploy these resources effectively it was necessary to secure command of the sea and command of the air. It was agreed that surface and air operations were totally interdependent. And it was agreed that strategic air power could do much – though* how *much remained a matter of controversy – to weaken the capacity of the adversary to resist. The general concept of war remained as it had been since the days of Napoleon: the contest of armed forces to obtain a position of such superiority that the victorious power would be in a position to impose its political will. And it was generally assumed that in the future, as in the immediate past, this would still be a very long-drawn-out process indeed.*

The development of nuclear weapons, and the rapid transition to thermonuclear weapons, has probably changed most, if not all, of these assumptions. There has to be an element of doubt about this judgement since nuclear weapons have not been used in war since 1945 (although the timing and extent of nuclear tests has certainly been planned 'strategically'); we simply cannot be sure precisely what the nature of a war between adversaries each equipped with these weapons would be like. Having said that, we know enough of the experimental effects of nuclear explosions to be able to deduce with a high level of confidence that the extensive use of large nuclear weapons would lead not only to a range but also a speed of devastation that is tantamount to the obliteration of civilization; even small, or 'tactical', nuclear weapons would lay waste great areas of densely settled territory, like the Central and Western European area, if they were used in quantity as battlefield weapons. Even if it were possible to take advantage of all the known methods of reducing damage to the home territory, by using extensive 'civil defence', the odds against surviving to enjoy what fruits there might be to victory have shortened dramatically. This, in the West at any rate, was an immediate popular deduction after nuclear weapons had been used at Hiroshima and Nagasaki. It was a view that was contested for a time; before the deployment of missiles with thermonuclear warheads was planned, the arsenals of 'atomic bombs' were relatively limited in size and their delivery had to be by bombers that were themselves vulnerable and were deployed from bases that had to be protected. Was war likely to be all that different? Perhaps there was not so much need now for massive fleets of bombers, but there might still be need for armies and navies, either to keep the war going if nuclear bombardment was not conclusive in the early stages or if the conflict was not closely enough related to issues of national survival to warrant the use of these weapons. The acquisition by the Soviet Union of nuclear weapons, in the 1949–51 period, also introduced a major new factor: mutuality.

Kissinger (1957, Ch. 11, section 6) endeavoured to synthesize the way in which states acquiring nuclear weapons viewed the process. He identified three stages in the cycle:

1. An initial period of learning the essential characteristics of the new weapons which is accompanied by protestations of the still dominant traditionalists that nuclear weapons cannot alter the basic principles of strategy and tactics; 2. as the power of modern weapons becomes better understood, this is usually followed by a complete reversal: an increasing reliance on the most absolute applications of the new technology and on an almost exclusive concern with offensive retaliatory power; 3. finally, as it is realized that all-out war involves risks out of proportion to most of the issues likely to be in dispute, an attempt is made to find intermediate applications for the new technology and to bring power into harmony with the objectives for which to contend.

As a general comment it can be said that much the same sort of response is likely in any innovatory process: assessment, assertion, assimilation, and the model seemed to fit the changes of policy that were known about in the Soviet Union quite well. Great Britain and France, and particularly China, do not conform quite as neatly; and the case of the United States seems to be different in some respects. The most notable is that from 1945 onwards there was a more evident urgency to develop a *rationale*; the 'atomic bomb' was already in being and had set the seal upon the place that the United States would have in postwar International Relations. In no more than five years the United States had been transformed from an *ingenue* to the actor-manager in the group of players forming the international system of the day; and in many of the writings of the succeeding period we can perceive attempts being made to explore and prescribe what the burdens and opportunities of this new leadership would be.

This perhaps in itself is not very remarkable – a thrusting, questing society like the United States was very likely to debate what its new circumstances would mean. What was remarkable was that a very great deal of the debate was conducted by non-military and indeed non-political writers; a preponderant number of the leading theorists were civilians of an academic cast of training, extending beyond the historians and political scientists, who might traditionally have been expected to concern themselves, to mathematicians, economists and natural scientists. Obviously there was a range of reasons why particular individuals became involved, but in general we can ascribe three general causes for the great proliferation of writings on strategy in the period. The first was that many of the scholars concerned had participated in the United States war effort and had both an interest and an expertise to apply to postwar problems. In particular the development of scientifically based investigations into operational matters created, in the United States and in the United Kingdom, new techniques of operational analysis and, as a corollary, new attitudes towards the arrangement and ordering of data. These opened up new avenues for the involvement of numerate and scientifically trained personnel in policy-making issues that had previously been the stalking-ground of diplomats, politicians and administrators, dependent rather more evidently upon intuition and experience than deduction.

The second cause was that, partly as a result of the wartime successes attending these new developments, the United States government itself encouraged the growth and use of non-governmental centres of investigation. Given the apparent novelty of some of the problems (and of restrictions upon employing more service officers and civil servants in the postwar environment of economy in the public service) there was a marked – but unsystematic – growth of interest in contractually linked 'think tanks', where both novelty and unconventional thought could be allowed to flourish and even perhaps encouraged. The best-known example is the RAND Corporation. This particular development owed a great deal to the desire of the newly formed independent US Air Force to consolidate its professional and bureaucratic position; but there was a general interest in military circles in evaluating the new technologies that were proliferating at the end of the war. Nuclear weapons (and nuclear power) were only the most dramatic; there were also jet engines for aircraft, radar and sonar, rockets and a wide range of new materials to be considered.

The third cause was an emerging realization that nuclear weapons might well be changing the nature of war, not least in so far as it was a factor in International Relations. The destructive power that they embodied forced attention to the concept of deterrence rather than defence as the first objective of policy, and this had two enormously important effects. The chief purpose of military forces must now be to avoid – to deter – war, rather than to win it when it happened; how would states prepare at one and the same time to deter war and then, if they failed, to win it, but only as a secondary objective: what would this mean for the organization and equipment of future forces? Secondly the change in purpose of military force required a much closer linkage between political and military leadership: the possession of nuclear weapons became a crucial diplomatic factor, as well as a military matter. Their usage, and therefore their control, would be likely to signify an important political judgement about the cruciality of the conflict; so the concept of 'the nuclear threshold' would transcend purely military considerations. Equally, this change in the nature of war meant that the particular claims to expertise that military leaders had – their skills and their training – were, in some important regards, downgraded; they were now not in any significant way better equipped than civilian analysts to know what form future crises and future wars might take and could not dispute the conclusions of hypothetical conjectures, or 'scenarios', about nuclear wars with anything like the same weight of experienced know-how that applied to what was now called 'conventional' or, sometimes 'limited', war.

These causes were enhanced in their effects by the development of the Cold War, in which the United States took the lead in standing up to the perceived threat of Soviet expansionist policies, which seemed in the years after 1948 as if they might extend to military adventurism in Western Europe and then, after the success of the Communist Revolution in China in 1949, in East Asia. The Korean War had a general effect of disappointing expectations that had been aroused that the development of nuclear weapons would make war obsolete between great powers, and emphasized three trends: the first was the alignment of many states into a bipolar pattern of hostility that highlighted the new role of leadership by the United States; the second was the need to establish a rational base appropriate for a long-term policy – the 'long haul' of the Eisenhower administration – and the third was to come to grips with the problems of a rapidly developing military technology in a way that would secure deterrence and enhance cohesion in the alliances which were formed, somewhat precipitately in the period between 1948 and 1955, to offset the physical and material advantages of the Soviet geopolitical position. If the United States dominated in nuclear air power, and maritime strength, and had enormous economic power, the Soviet Union had manpower reserves, physical contiguity, and an apparently cohesive operating ideology, which offered powerful counterweights. At a somewhat later stage, the emergence of 'wars by proxy' in which the two superpowers did not confront each other directly also began. As more became known about the collateral effects of nuclear explosions, and public concern about proliferation and usage grew too, so the development of 'tactical' nuclear weapons went some way to offset what seemed to be a persistent deficiency in NATO's conventional forces; it also seemed to imply some lowering of barriers of restraint that there might be to the early use of nuclear weapons in any war. Public concern therefore also arose about the prospects for nuclear war, and about the questions that would have to be answered if it was to be avoided.

There were occasional suggestions, based upon 'realist' perceptions, that the United States should attack and defeat the Soviet Union while it retained a favourable balance of military power, but they ignored both the war-weariness of the people and the idealistic strains in a governmental system that laid heavy emphasis upon legal concepts and moral constraints. The main stream of writings emphasizes the possibilities of applying rational analyses to a predicament in which victory was almost as cataclysmic as defeat; and in this sense rational models of state and governmental behaviour provided a basis for analysis and prescription in the way that the 'lessons of history' had provided a foundation for earlier writings.

Although the United States and the Soviet Union were quite quickly joined by the United Kingdom, and then France and China, as possessors of nuclear weapons, the scale of their resources identified these two states as 'superpowers', whose relationship could be presented as a bipolar structure. The effects of the behaviour of the one upon the other could therefore be assessed in a somewhat more straightforward way than a multilateral structure allowed. If this was a more convenient analytical device, it also seemed to reflect the dependence of many other states upon one or other of the giants for economic, military or political support in the postwar world, and to that extent was sufficiently realistic to support a rational framework of argument. But rationality extended beyond the purely internal logic of a particular set of propositions; it infused the general assumptions about state-directed actions. The basic rationale behind the concept of nuclear deterrence was that state A would be deterred from following policies inimical to state B if state B could demonstrate that it had the military power, and the political will, to take action against state A when its interests were threatened or attacked. This, of course, is the simplest form of the proposition, and it does not allow for the wide range of qualifications that had to be added. Not all of state B's interests are equally important; which is important enough to necessitate action? Which is important enough to necessitate the use of nuclear weapons? How is state A to know, in a sufficiently reliable and precise way, the rating which state B accords to all its interests? And what is state B going to do if state A sets out deliberately to test its resolve, and to probe a whole range of interests? If state B 'gives way' over one issue, what does this setback mean to state A's perception of state B's determination; and what is state B going to say to all its allies, who may be wondering what the setback means for their relationships with both B and A? Despite many difficulties like these, the concept of nuclear deterrence offered a way for both scholars and governments to grasp some of the fundamental issues in this new situation; and it is difficult to see how else a pattern of argument could have been built up except upon some broad assumption like the expectation that governments act rationally, that they endeavour to foresee the consequences of a policy before they commit themselves to following it. The utility of the framework was demonstrated by its widespread adoption, at the academic level of analysis as well as at the political level of declaration; it became an axiom.

But deterrence is not a new concept; it existed and operated long before nuclear weapons, and so far as military strategy is concerned was always a factor in conventional warfare. The principal difference seemed to be that in earlier days the armed forces that states maintained could both deter war and actually be used in fighting a war if deterrence failed and war occurred. Was this any longer the case? Nuclear weapons seemed to be an effective deterrent at one level, but it was by no means clear how they could usefully be used in war. They had quickly become so large and terrible in their effects that they could only be thought of as ultimate weapons: too gross to be a credible threat in minor disputes. Tactical nuclear weapons were developed partly to avoid this difficulty; but their very nature gave them, too, a special status. If they were used, a 'nuclear threshold' would be crossed and this might imply that the conflict was reaching the stage at which rationality was breaking down.

So, while theories of nuclear deterrence made it easier to visualize and debate the political and military problems facing a nuclear-armed power, their structure (and their novelty) also made it relatively easy to pick out the holes in the argument. Deterrence was, in essence, a negative proposition; it embodied an assertion that if an outcome that was feared did not happen, then the reason why it had been avoided was your own chosen policy. Thus, the avoidance of war in the 1948–55 period was due to the United States' diplomatic and military initiatives. This might well be true, and in all probability was true; but it was extremely difficult to *prove.* Moreover, the longer that a successful policy of deterrence worked, the more intricate the explanations became, and the more difficult it might be to explain to electorates that costly defence expenditures were necessary because the weapons that were being procured were not going to be used. They were intended to deter. The logic on which this sort of explanation depends is not the normal stuff of speeches and manifestos; it is more like poetry, in so far as it requires the suspension of disbelief.

It also requires elucidation, if it is to be used in an explanatory way for the formulation of policy. What was the linkage between tactical nuclear weapons and any more general nuclear exchange – even apart from the physical extension of the conflict to the United States and Soviet homelands? How could the employment of nuclear weapons be more rigorously controlled by political leaders: what would their selective usage mean, in terms of 'political signalling', and how could the adversary's intent be unequivocally determined? What was the logic of deterrence: how could you inhibit your adversary without also perturbing your allies, whose dependence upon your right judgement was critically constrained by the development of missile armouries that took no more than a few minutes to be launched and to reach their targets? How could the demands of the military, to take action in a professionally adequate way at a technically opportune time, be reconciled to the needs of the politician to be sure that an irrevocable decision was delayed as long as possible? How could you in fact be sure that the essentially negative and defensive nature of deterrence was credible to the adversary? And how, in areas where the confrontation with the Soviet Union was less direct, or less historically constrained than it was in Western Europe, could the phenomena of 'limited wars' be related to the range of American power and interests?

In the 1950s and early 1960s, prescriptions and diagnoses emerged in quantity. Some of the writings were elegant and powerful; Brodie had, as early as 1946, described the essential components of a policy of deterrence (Brodie 1946) and he was joined by a company of scholars, not all of whom followed his assumptions, but many of whom added significantly to the range of information about what might, or could, or should be done to avoid a direct conflict with the Soviet Union and maintain the United States' position. It is important to stress this preoccupation with analyses primarily related to the American condition; although some of the writings, especially those which endeavoured to extend the range of enquiry to include the para-psychological considerations that infused the hazy area of perceptions of intent, were cast in experimental and deductive terms many, especially those that sought to deal with the bridge between foreign policy and military strategy, were specific to the current problems and invariably concerned with United States perspectives. This sometimes had the effect of underplaying, or even ignoring, the concerns of America's allies – and either helped to create, or reflected, the governmental failing to observe the diplomatic niceties of consultation from time to time or the assumption, sometimes made without much feeling for political sensibility, that the concerns of the British or the West Germans or the Japanese were always parallel, if not identical, to those of the United States.

One of the most obvious examples of this preoccupation with the learning process of becoming an imperial or, more accurately, a global, power was the Cuban missile crisis of 1962, when the urgency of the matter precluded any extensive consultation with the allies in South America or Europe whose fates might nevertheless be bound up in the outcome. But crises are by definition times of unusual tension and, from some points of view, the successful resolution of this particular issue highlighted the resourcefulness and the range of resources on which the United States' claims to leadership were based; it also, however, emphasized the ways in which membership of an alliance dominated by such a leader might cut across some of the traditional interpretations of the benefits to be gained by adherence to an alliance – and gave rise, besides consequences at the political level, to reflections about the need for less claustrophobic military and political relationships. These reflections were most markedly embodied in French strategic writings and political policies of the time, but also arose in the United Kingdom where, paradoxically, the demonstration, in the Cuban missile crisis, that 'active deterrence' could be successful also cut away support for the Campaign for Nuclear Disarmament (Gallois 1961, Beaton and Maddox 1962 and Beaufre 1965a, 1965b, 1967).

Another example was the proposal to create a multilateral nuclear force of surface ships carrying intermediate range ballistic missiles which would be raised and maintained by some, if not all, of the United States' NATO partners. At the political level this policy may be seen as an attempt to gratify the wishes of some of the Western European allies who desired to share in the responsibility relating to nuclear weapons; but it was, in practice, a mechanistic device to allow participation in deploying nuclear weapons without doing anything in particular to resolve the extremely sensitive and difficult political issues concerning shared responsibility for authorizing their use. The concept of a multilaterally deployed force was originally conceived as a mechanism that would manage rather than solve such issues; but it had no distinctive basis or function in strategic terms and fizzled out eventually because it had no technical virtue or relevance, politically or militarily. To the extent that it owed a part of its origin to a mode of investigation that paid little attention to any military logic (or any really pressing political need to choose a 'hardware' solution) it illustrates some of the pitfalls which lie in wait for the scholar who enters the political arena. It also, incidentally, illustrates one of the difficulties of the period for a non-American observer. The MLF enthusiasts were only one of three or four groups of proponents who sought to deal with the difficulties of nuclear release in an alliance context; and even while senior officials of one persuasion were pressing their panaceas on the increasingly bewildered Europeans, others could easily be found who extolled other policies. Which was right was one pertinent question; but which spoke for the United States government was even more important. Was it the State Department lobby, making a virtue of the obscurities of the MLF: or was it the Pentagon, whose political head had made no bones about the politico-military necessity of centralizing the management of the nuclear forces of the Alliance under United States control? Each had their scholarly interpreters and supporters.

Part of the difficulty came from the fact that most of the scholars had government connections of one sort or another: Brodie, Kissinger, Schelling, Bowie, Kahn, Halperin, Wohlstetter and many others wrote with some knowledge at least of recent government business. For non-Americans, this was frequently taken to imply that they wrote with some sort of imprimatur, and that there was a connection between what they wrote and what 'the government' thought. It was therefore possible to construe each new pronouncement as if it might imply an impending change in government policy and, given the dominance of the United States in NATO, a consequential shift of emphasis to the Alliance's objectives, even though the specific ways in which the Allied governments conformed to the guidelines that are referred to as a collective NATO 'strategy' remained a unilateral state prerogative. It was more difficult than United States officials realized sometimes for Europeans to recognize that the alternative prescriptions remained, for the most part, suggestive, but unauthorized, contributions to a continuing debate. The other principal difficulty was that these contending views held virtually a monopoly in the market-place of ideas; there was relatively little in the way of similar activity in Western Europe until the later 1950s, although there is no reason to suppose that the British, French and West German governments were either insensitive to the problems which the nuclear age was producing or inactive in trying to find rationales by which to cope. It is worth remarking, however, that in these three states in particular, what significant contributions there were to strategic thought in the period came almost wholly from active politicians or retired military men; the universities hardly figured at all. In the United Kingdom the exceptions to this rule quickly run out after one has noted P.M.S. Blackett (1948, 1956) at the beginning of the period and Leonard Beaton (1972) towards its end. Apart from all the other differences one could list, it seems that one of the principal reasons for this difference was that, in Europe, the business of thinking about war was, importantly, already a professional preoccupation contained inside the apparatus of government; in the United States the shape of the profession to exercise power had still to be moulded, and still extended to scholarly activists who were eager to involve themselves with the working-out of the analyses to which they had contributed intellectually.

In this respect, two coincidental issues worked towards bringing this particular period of active debate, and active involvement, to an end: the Vietnam War and the anti-ballistic missile deployment. They were complementary in the sense that one was related principally to the exercise of military force to secure objectives that gradually lost political credibility, and the other to the development of a form of military power of a very specialized and costly sort, with a function that was inherently passive and uncertain, operating in a technical environment of almost theological complexity. The Vietnam War can hardly be called a war in a legal sense: but from every other point of view the period from 1965 to 1972 constituted a major war, with extensive international and domestic repercussions. Many experts were either proved to be misleading or misled. Over the ABM the dilemma was effectively resolved by an alternative political means that made some, at least, of the expert depositions irrelevant. An arms control agreement with the Soviet Union (the so-called 'SALT I Agreement') defined the technological competition between the two states in this area in something like the same way that the incipient naval competition between the United States and the United Kingdom had been averted in the 1920s. The late 1960s and early 1970s were chastening times, and although much of what had been written, especially about nuclear weapons and their consequences, is likely to be of more enduring value (since it represents so far our principal source of experience), there was no longer the same zest, or even perhaps the same need, to explore the American condition. Attention became more narrowly focused upon the problems of the specifically bilateral 'adversary partnership' with the Soviet Union. In saying this, one must note the apotheosis of Henry Kissinger, who has demonstrated that analysts can become successful executants if, in the first place, they assume accredited positions of real responsibility and, secondly, they have a resilience of temperament and character that goes with public office. So many others have found that to have a foot in both camps is to invite an excruciating dilemma when the camps do not march in consonance that he may be a lonely example.

What did all these outpourings achieve? In some ways it is difficult to identify the consequences because some of the writings have helped to create an intellectual environment which is likely to persist for some time, and in which the change from revelation to orthodoxy still limits our own attitudes. 'Writers like Kissinger himself, Brodie, Wohlstetter, Osgood, Tucker, Schelling and Kaufmann helped to put the advent of thermonuclear weapons into a political as well as a military context: arguing for a flexible posture, involving a range of choices however uncertain and even confusing that might be, more realistic than the dramatic doctrine of 'massive retaliation' which, even as it was enunciated by Secretary Dulles in 1954, was already inadequate. Not to put too fine a point on it, this type of intellectual activity substituted, so far as the United States government was concerned, for some of the pressures to accommodate to alternative viewpoints which it might have expected to get from Allied governments. Such pressures were not altogether absent: the British government attempted to influence American military and political conceptions in 1952; but they were relatively infrequent (Rosecrance 1968, 168 et seq.). Others, like Herman Kahn, opened up more brashly controversial areas of debate which nevertheless forced attention to the realities that nuclear war would entail. The fundamental assumptions underlying mutual nuclear deterrence went largely unchallenged,[3] but the ways in which such a posture could remain effective have been a constant source of concern to the United States' allies.

More detailed analyses about government operations and choice of policies, concerned with econometric measurements of efficiency and effectiveness, have had a more mixed effect. The contributions, in theory and in practice, of Hitch, McKean, Rowen, Enthoven and others, have had extensive consequences for administrative techniques, outside, as well as inside, the United States. But they have only had peripheral success in lessening the difficulties of selection and control in high technology investment in equipment: PPBS (planning, programming, budgeting systems) and systems analysis have probably done more for the computer industry than they have to incline governmental wisdom towards consistently better decisions. And there is no doubt that the collective activity, with its preoccupation with United States interests and its confident interest in novelty, contributed towards that 'arrogance of power' that Senator Fulbright denounced (Fulbright 1967): planning might be an inevitable and necessary condition for a superpower, but many thoughtful observers, and not a few United States allies, felt, with Mannheim, that even in a planned world diversity must be made possible.

As a part of this feeling, and partly as a response to the American example, more extensive interest in strategic studies was generated in Europe. In the United Kingdom, West Germany and France, formal organizations to conduct research into strategic issues were established in the later 1950s and early 1960s, and a few universities followed suit. Sweden set up an institute with a particular bias towards arms control and disarmament questions. However, these intiatives owed more to individuals than governments and were at least as much concerned with providing a counterweight to the United States' dominance as they were to emulate American achievements. The International Institute for Strategic Studies in London is the best known, and perhaps the most successful example, especially under its first director, Alastair Buchan, who not only produced substantial work himself but gave encouragement to a number of young scholars of promise.

The effects of the United States' strategic debate upon the Soviet

Union have also been important; a number of the more substantial books were quickly translated into Russian and became required reading in the military and political academies, and there seems little doubt that they have been studied carefully. Until the death of Stalin, professional debate about the strategic implications of the new weapons was muted (as Kissinger describes, in discussing his model of the 'learning process', referred to on p. 169), but it played an important part in the subsequent party arguments and struggles for power in the Malenkov–Khruschev transition. There were major difficulties in relating concepts of deterrence to Marxist–Leninist doctrines about the inevitability of war, and the emergence of an authoritative line of doctrine did not emerge until the late 1950s; it was embodied, most conveniently so far as Western readers are concerned, in Marshal Sokolovskii's book *Military Strategy* which was first published in 1962 (Sokolovskii 1975). The strategy heavily emphasized the expectation that future major wars would centre around the use of nuclear missiles as the decisive strike weapon, and although there have been some modifications to this expectation in the decade of emerging *detente,* the formal expositions of strategy that have been published still maintain this central position.

The relative dearth of open debate makes it difficult to provide any sort of comparison between developments in Soviet and United States official thinking, but it is clear that the absence of public debate does not mean either static or simplistic attitudes. Nor does it mean that Soviet writers and analysts have merely accepted, as well as absorbed, American assumptions and postulates. The growth of Soviet military capability, in nuclear weapons and in maritime power (which has been a particular matter of concern to NATO), as well as in other fields, indicates at the very least a continuing preoccupation with the instruments of military power, although Western experts in Soviet affairs continue to disagree about how these developments should be interpreted. There is now a voluminous interpretative literature; see, for example, Wolfe (1965, 1970), Garthoff (1966), Edmonds (1975) and Scott (1975). The growth of bilateral negotiations between the Soviet Union and the United States in the later 1960s, over a range of strategic issues related to nuclear weapons, has given a very particular importance, not only to the military balance between the two states, but also to the effects which this 'adversarial cooperation' might have upon their allies and clients. The discussion of areas of policy arising out of the series of Strategic Arms Limitation Talks has therefore spilled over to include wider political *fora,* like the European Conference on Security and Cooperation which was rounded off at Helsinki in the summer of 1975, and the multilateral negotiations on force reductions between the states of NATO and the Warsaw Pact; and the general effect, for analysts, has been once again to emphasize the relationship between military power and foreign policy, both in regard to the interests of individual states and to developments that might occur or be desirable in the alliance structures which, in form, sustain the policies of the first postwar decade.

It would be wrong to ascribe to the development of *detente* any strong influence in diminishing academic interest in aspects of military strategy; so far as European interests are concerned, it has perhaps stimulated rather than weakened concern. But in the United States, *detente* has certainly had an effect in changing the shape and extent of scholarly activity, bringing it rather more towards traditional aspects of diplomacy than innovative *schema* combining ideology, politics and military technology; and there is no doubt that the disillusionment, which the ending of the Vietnam intervention represented, made strategic studies in the United States, less fashionable, however illogically. In retrospect, however, it looks as if the period between about 1950 and 1965 represented a peak of activity, particularly and significantly in the United States, which was a response to the problems posed by a new position of prominence in international affairs. The rather different problems relating to the maintenance of a prominent position have not – so far – precipitated any comparable surge; and, to the extent that these problems represent a permanent preoccupation for all states, the cause that led for a time to United States dominance in the field has been overtaken.

Notes

1. Francis Bacon, *Essays: of the True Greatness of Kingdoms.*
2. For a discussion of some of the moral perspectives see Garnett (Ch. 1) in Baylis et al. (1975).
3. But see P. Green (1966) *Deadly Logic* as an example to the contrary.)

References and Further Reading

Andrzejewski, S. (1954) *Military Organisation and Society,* London, Routledge and Kegan Paul.

Baylis, J. et al. (1975) *Contemporary Strategy: Theories and Policies;* London, Croom Helm.

Beaton, L. and Maddox, J. (1962) *The Spread of Nuclear Weapons,* London, Chatto and Windus.

Beaton, L. (1972) *The Reform of Power,* London, Chatto and Windus.

Beaufre, A. (1965a) *An Introduction to Strategy,* London, Faber and Faber.

Beaufre, A. (1965b) *Deterrence and Strategy* London, Faber and Faber.

Beaufre, A. (1967) *Strategy of Action,* London, Faber and Faber.

Blackett, P.M.S. (1948) *Military and Political Consequences of Atomic Energy,* London, Turnstile Press.

Blackett, P.M.S. (1956) *Atomic Weapons and East-West Relations,* London, Cambridge Univ. Press.

Brodie, B. (ed.) (1946) *The Absolute Weapon,* New York, Harcourt Brace.

Brodie, B. (1965) *Strategy in the Missile Age,* Princeton, NJ, Princeton Univ. Press.

Clausewitz, C.M. von (1968) (introduction by A. Rapoport) *On War,* Harmondsworth, Penguin Classics.

Dickson, P. (1971) *Think Tanks,* New York, Ballantine Books.

Earle, E.M. (ed.) (1943) *Makers of Modern Strategy,* Princeton, NJ, Princeton Univ. Press.

Edmonds, R. (1975) *Soviet Foreign Policy 1962–73,* London, Oxford Univ. Press.

Fulbright, J.W. (1967) *The Arrogance of Power,* London, Jonathan Cape.

Gallois, P.M. (1961) *The Balance of Terror,* Boston, Houghton Mifflin.

Garthoff, R.L. (1966) *Soviet Military Policy,* London, Faber and Faber.

Green, P. (1966) *Deadly Logic,* Columbus, Ohio Univ. Press.

Howard, M.E. (1970) *The Classical Strategists* in *Problems of Modern Strategy,* A.F. Buchan, (ed.), London, Chatto and Windus.

Jukes, G. (1972) *The Development of Soviet Strategic Thinking Since 1945,* Camberra, Australian National Univ. Press (Canberra Fapers on Strategy and Defence, No. 14).

Kahn, H. (1960) *On Thermonuclear War,* Princeton, Princeton Univ. Press.

Kaufmann, W.W. (ed.) (1956) *Military Policy and National Security,* Princeton, NJ, Princeton Univ. Press.

Kissinger, H.A. (1957) *Nuclear Weapons and Foreign Policy,* New York, Harper and Row.

Knorr, K. (1966) *On the Uses of Military Power in the Nuclear Age,* Princeton, NJ, Princeton Univ. Press.

Liddell Hart, B.H. (1967) *Strategy, The Indirect Approach,* London, Faber and Faber.

Mahan, A.T. (1957) *The Influence of Sea Power upon History,* New York, Hill and Wang.

Nash, H.T. (1975) *Nuclear Weapons and International Behaviour,* Leyden, Sijthoff International Publishing Co. (Atlantic Series, No. 9).

Osgood, R.E. and Tucker, R.W. (1967) *Force, Order and Justice,* Baltimore, Johns Hopkins Press.

Rosecrance, R.N. (1968) *Defense of the Realm,* New York, Columbia Univ. Press.

Schelling, T.C. (1960) *The Strategy of Conflict,* Cambridge, Mass., Harvard Univ. Press.

Scott, W.F. (1975) 'Soviet Military Doctrine, Realities and Misunderstandings', *Strategic Review,* 3 (3), (Summer).

Smith, B.L.R. (1966) *The RAND Corporation,* Cambridge, Mass., Harvard Univ. Press.

Sokolovskii, M. (1975) *Soviet Military Strategy* (3rd edn, with commentary), H. Fast Scott (ed.), New York,, Crane and Russak.

Wolfe, T.W. (1965) *Soviet Strategy at The Crossroads,* Cambridge, Mass., Harvard Univ. Press.

Wolfe, T.W. (1970) *Soviet Power and Europe 1945–70,* Baltimore, Johns Hopkins Press.

Chapter 9

A systems approach

Richard Little

In contrast to social sciences such as sociology, economics and psychology, there has been a deep-seated prejudice against the idea of applying scientific method to the study of politics and International Relations until the last three decades. During the first half of the twentieth century when some of the core social sciences were engaged in the attempt to implement a more rigorous, analytical approach, except for the occasional 'maverick', all areas of politics were studied from a predominantly prescriptive and institutional framework. In International Relations, for example, there was an overwhelming concentration on international law and international institutions. It was the onset of behaviouralism which first precipitated the widespread acceptance in politics of the need to initiate research using the scientific method; but in International Relations, this development only occurred later after the introduction of a systems approach. Although the self-conscious attempt to encourage a scientific perspective provides an area of common ground between behaviouralism and a systems approach, their historical antecedents are quite distinct and an examination of the distinction can help to illuminate some of the essential characteristics of a systems approach and explain its impact on the development of International Relations.

Behaviouralism emerged after the Second World War and in so far as it represented a movement to encourage the application of scientific method to the study of human behaviour, it did not provide a radically new orientation for most social sciences, but in the case of politics, it precipitated a 'revolution'. For the first time, there were widespread and concerted efforts to use scientific method to study political activity. Its immediate affect on International Relations on the other hand, was much more restrained. The vast majority of writers, while occasionally acknowledging the need to develop a more rigorous approach, resolutely adhered to the traditional mode of research: providing sound, historical descriptions of events in the international arena.

For political science, however, behaviouralism not only changed the method of analysis, but it also altered the kind of material which was examined. There was a move away from the study of institutions towards an analysis of human behaviour; the emergence of voting studies denoted a new interest in the individual citizen, while community power studies extended the discussion of decision-making to the level of the individual operating in local politics. However, the emphasis in behaviouralism on the individual appeared to present the International Relations specialist, anxious to apply scientific method, with a fundamental problem. The individuals who seemed important were not readily accessible, and so the requisite data to implement behavioural analysis were unavailable. One way round the problem was to shift the emphasis to the individual citizen, and some of the earliest behavioural research did concentrate on individual stereotypes and attitudes formation towards other countries (Buchan and Cantril 1953).

Research of this kind, however, seemed remote from the areas of activity considered critical by most International Relations specialists. Their concern was with the behaviour of states, not the reactions of the 'man in the street'. Implicitly, however, behaviouralism seemed to indicate that scientific method should be applied at a micro-level of analysis. The introduction of a systems approach represented an attempt to refocus attention on the complex interactions between states, while retaining the scientific orientation propounded by behaviouralism. From this perspective, it can be seen why one of the early advocates made the otherwise surprising assertion that a systems approach provides the only possible method which can ensure the development of 'scientific politics' (Kaplan 1964).

The possibility of applying systems thinking to International Relations began to be discussed in the mid-1950s (McClelland 1955). At that time, the most striking consequence of this development was the emergence of the international system as a key concept in discussions of International Relations. The concept is now frequently used as the focal point for introductions to the subject, providing a reference point for works which are otherwise highly divergent in terms of style and approach (compare, e.g. Reynolds 1971 and Hopkins and Mansbach 1973). But when discussions of the international system first came into vogue, writers placed the term in italics (Sonderman 1961, 13) or in inverted commas (Brecher 1963, 214), a practice which, with the benefit of hindsight, can appear pedantic. At that time, however, it was considered novel and challenging to examine International Relations from the perspective of an international system which 'exists as a unique entity, separate – in a sense – from the behaviour it influences' (Sonderman 1961, 13).

Using a historical perspective, it is perhaps surprising that the concept should have been considered as an innovation, because holism, often regarded as the defining characteristic of a systems approach, has traditionally provided the dominant mode of analysis in International Relations. The balance of power, for example, an idea which has preoccupied thinkers since the time of the Treaty of Westphalia and before, was not considered from the perspective of any individual member, but was examined from a holistic perspective. Writers like Kant, for example, believed that the state system reflected a 'predetermined design to make harmony spring from human discord' (Gulick 1955, 21–2). Indeed, much of Western political thought has been written from this point of view. Churchman (1968) identifies Plato as a systems thinker and after examining a range of writers as different as Hobbes,

Hegel and Marx, Rapoport (1974, 13) argues that they all point to the same conclusion, that 'the "psychology" of the system may be entirely independent of the psychology of its human components'.

The concatenation between the systems approach and the application of scientific method can mask this line of historical continuity. But the early protagonists of the systems approach may also have failed to identify with this historical link because they found their inspiration in areas far removed from the traditional literature associated with International Relations. Modern biology and cybernetics provided the source of their ideas. To understand the role which systems thinking has played in the study of International Relations, therefore, it is more appropriate to examine the development of the systems approach in the context of modern science rather than looking for its philosophical origins which may be traced back to the ancient Greeks.

The antecedents of the systems approach

At first sight, it may appear strange that there is a discontinuity between behaviouralism and the systems approach, given the apparent commitment of both approaches to scientific method. The difference between the two rests on the assumption that in the history of Western science 'atomistic and holistic ways of thinking have alternated' (Laszlo 1972, 19). However, during the modern era of science since the seventeenth century, the atomistic mode of analysis has taken precedence. Although the issue is still contentious, many scientists now accept the desirability of adopting a holistic approach, and by tracing the route which has led to this acceptance we can find the antecedents of the systems approach.

Atomistic thinking encourages the idea that we can extend our understanding of reality by breaking down a complex whole into its component parts. Comprehension of the whole can then be achieved on a cumulative basis by adding together our understanding of the separate parts. The utility of the controlled experiment, an important ingredient of the scientific method, depends upon the validity of the atomistic approach. If scientists are interested in the durability of a particular material, for example, then they will systematically examine the behaviour of the material under a variety of controlled conditions which allow them to observe the rate of change in the material as the variable relating to the given condition is altered. In ideal circumstances, because all other factors are controlled for, any change in the material can be attributed to the variable being manipulated. According to the atomistic view of knowledge, each additional experiment adds to our understanding of the material. By analogy, when we read, each sentence adds to what we have already read. Knowledge of the whole accumulates as we aggregate our understanding of the parts.

The commitment of modern science to an epistemology based on atomistic thinking was accompanied by a model which depicts reality in mechanistic terms. The model assumes that the world around us is organized on the basis of rational principles and that nature fits together as do the parts of a machine, each part interacting with another on the basis of invariant laws. The behaviour of all gases, for example, can be described by the proposition that 'The volume of a gas at a constant temperature varies inversely with its pressure'. The behaviour of any gas can be described by this relationship between the three independent variables: temperature, pressure and volume. The relationship is deterministic and, as a consequence, the variables are not placed in an environment because it is assumed that there is no way the relationship between the three variables can be affected by environmental forces. The variables, therefore, are analysed in the context of a closed or isolated system. The deterministic relationship between the variables and the absence of an environment provide two important distinguishing properties of the mechanistic model.

The origins of a modern systems approach can be found in the reaction to the mechanistic and atomistic assumptions which underpinned the development of modern science. Biologists, in particular, felt constrained by the established view. It was argued that living matter generates behaviour different in kind from the behaviour observed by physical scientists, requiring a distinctive model and alternative epistemological assumptions. From the biologist's perspective there is a fundamental difference between the behaviour observed when the temperature of a gas is raised, and the behaviour observed when the colour of a flatfish changes to suit the background characteristics of its environment.

When biologists contemplated behaviour such as the changing colour of the flatfish, the relevance of the environment became apparent, and they began to examine living phenomena in the context of an environment. This led to the emergence of a new distinctive model. The conception of an environment provided one important difference with the mechanistic model, the potential for adaptation provided another. Before Darwin, it was generally believed that the extraordinary diversity displayed in nature occurred at one point in time, when the world was created. However, Darwin's theory of natural selection indicated that organic matter has undergone persistent change and the immense variety has emerged from a few simple organisms. This suggested, therefore, that when considering living phenomena, it must be accepted that adaptive behaviour constitutes a critical feature of the natural world (Smith, 1975, Ch. 1).

The ability of the flatfish to change colour reflects physiological versatility and demonstrates the ongoing capacity of an organism to adapt to its environment. By changing colour, the flatfish can increase its chances of survival, suggesting that this behaviour is a product of genetic adaptation: flatfish which did not develop this capacity failed to survive. The capacity to change colour, therefore, fulfils a vital function and, by extension, it can be argued that all structural features must perform functions for an organism. The introduction of a functional dimension into biological analysis marked a further departure from the mechanistic model, which deliberately eschews the idea that physical behaviour fulfils functions. Gas can expand under certain circumstances, but the physical scientist does not consider that any function is being performed as a consequence of the expansion. For behaviour to take a functional form, it must be purposeful, and physical scientists throughout the period of modern science have denied the validity of explanations based on the assumption of purposeful behaviour. Explanations of this kind are termed 'teleological' and are considered non-scientific. Nevertheless, the specification of functions was an essential element of the organic model.

The metaphysical idea of attributing conscious purpose to the behaviour of organisms was eventually eliminated when the concept of feedback mechanisms was understood. Ironically, the term 'feedback' originated in cybernetics, a branch of engineering devoted to communication machines, although biologists did independently come to understand the nature of the process (Cannon 1932). Communication machines, however, demonstrated quite clearly how the 'illusion' of purposeful behaviour can be developed, providing machines with 'the uncanny ability to simulate human behaviour' (Wiener 1950). For example, when an individual walks towards a door controlled by an 'electronic eye' the door appears to open in order to allow the individual to pass through. In reality, the door is controlled by a sensory receptor which is activated as the individual approaches the door. Information is then sent to the mechanism which controls the position of the door and the door opens because it has received a control message, not in order to allow the individual to go through. Using the same logic, the flatfish does not change colour in order to increase its chances of survival, but rather in reaction to a message from a sensory mechanism which is responsive to changes in the environment. With the emergence of feedback, therefore, the need for explanations based on the concept of purpose was eliminated, and, as a consequence, 'The sharp division between biological and physical systems has been broken' (Kay 1969, 9).

The discovery of feedback mechanisms provided an illustration for scientists of the possibility of developing concepts which can counteract the apparently inexorable tendency in modern science towards increasing specialization. Once the feedback process is understood, it is possible to see how the opening of a door and the changing colour of a fish reflects the presence of an identical process. Disturbed by the extent to which specialization in science has made it impossible for communication to take place between different disciplines, some scientists have argued that one way to counteract the tendency is to use both an atomistic and a holistic approach to examine phenomena. Bertalanffy, a leading advocate of this position, insists that it is necessary to study not only parts and processes in isolation, but also the 'dynamic interaction' between parts and processes' (1956, 1) because they look different when studied from the two perspectives. He believes that by using the holistic perspective, scientists will discover, behind the apparent diversity in the world around us, a limited number of organizing principles which will help to explain and relate a wide variety of different phenomena. Natural selection and feedback are examples of these principles.

Scientists who endorse this position have also come to feel that the notion of a system should be used as the central organizing concept because all phenomena can be viewed from a systems perspective and it therefore encourages the process of integrating knowledge. The mechanistic and organic models, for example, can both be described in systems terminology. The mechanistic model is simply a closed system, because it has no environment; the organic model, on the other hand, is an open system which can adapt to the environment with the aid of feedback mechanisms. If a system is identified as closed, it cannot adapt; whereas a capacity for adaptation demonstrates the existence of an open system.

The modern systems approach, therefore, can be identified with a movement in natural science. However, the founders also wanted the movement to embrace the social sciences. The idea of a system, they believe, is not restricted to physical behaviour; it can extend to social behaviour and it is necessary, therefore, to locate the organizing principles which underpin social systems. The modern systems approach, as a consequence, has provided a scientific legitimacy to holism, precipitating a resurgence of interest in the development of macro-models in social science.

The perspective of the systems approach

Despite its association with an apparently clearly defined movement in the natural sciences, it is not possible to provide a coherent and unambiguous statement about the essential characteristics of the systems approach. Although there is a large body of concepts, like feedback and adaptation, readily identifiable as 'systems' concepts, there is no body of rules indicating how a systems approach should be implemented. There is, therefore, no formal methodological procedure associated with the approach. Nevertheless, there is a systems perspective and it is normally quite clear when analysis is being written from this perspective. Before examining the systems literature in International Relations, it is worth while trying to trace some of its features.

So far, a formal definition of a system has been avoided. The omission is quite deliberate. Definitions of a system provide very little indication of the perspective associated with a systems approach. Instead, the definition simply provides an affirmation that behaviour in the world around us is not random and is therefore amenable to systematic study. After an analysis of systems thinking from a phenomenological point of view, for example, Jordan (1973, 61) concludes that in essence we call something a system 'when we wish to express the fact that the thing is perceived as consisting of a set of elements, of parts, that are interconnected with each other by a discriminable, distinguishable principle'. Therefore, one does not have to look far to find a system. This page of writing reflects the existence of a system for the reader because of the awareness that the letters on the page are interconnected by a 'discriminable, distinguishable principle', and the letters only have to be replaced in a random order for their relationship with the system to disappear. Language is a prime example of a system.

However, acknowledging the existence of a system does not necessarily indicate a willingness to use a systems approach. In linguistics, for example, there is considerable controversy surrounding the way an individual learns a language system. When behaviourist psychologists examine the process of communication, they assume that we learn language on an atomistic basis, building up slowly but surely from sounds to words and then learning how words are linked together. In structural linguistics, on the other hand, it is considered inconceivable that language is learned in this fashion. Although there are only forty-five basic sounds, or phonemes, in English, we hear about twenty phonemes per second during speech, and if we had to absorb each sound separately we should perceive only a 'steady buzz'. An alternative approach is to look at the structure of language and it is asserted that individuals have an innate capacity to discern this structure; we combine sounds into more complex units, so 'speech sounds unite into patterns as musical sounds unite into melodies' (Koestler 1967, 27). The second approach clearly reflects a systems perspective: a basic attempt is being made to understand the dynamic relationship between the parts.

It is the form of an analysis, therefore, not the conception of a system which distinguishes the systems approach, and the systems thinker argues that all areas of knowledge can be examined from a systems perspective. Whenever the systems thinker is asked to explain the behaviour of a particular 'unit', an organism, the delinquent child, a social class or the state, the explanation is always formulated at a higher level of analysis. The particular 'unit' is placed in the context of a broader system. It is assumed that the behaviour of the 'unit' is conditioned by the nature of the system. When Gunnar Myrdal (1942) examined the black–white relationship in the United States, he assumed that the two groups were part of a single system and that the plight of the black population was a product of the system and could not be explained by the 'inherent' characteristics of the black population. He demonstrated the existence of a vicious circle such that the standard of living for the black population was kept down because of white discrimination, but the white discrimination partially arose because of the low standard of living within the black population. The dynamic interaction between these two conditions made it impossible for the black population to raise its standard of living. In this case, the situation of the black population cannot be understood until it is placed in a broader context.

In social science, therefore, the systems thinker is committed to the view that social behaviour cannot be explained at the level of the individual. Society is not just a group of individuals, it is a systemic entity, described by a coherent set of interrelated structures. If one of these structures is changed, then the behaviour of individuals operating in the context of this system will be affected. Anthropologists, in particular, have been able to illustrate the affects of changing a societal structure. Turnbull (1973), discussing an African tribe called the Ik, describes how the tribe was radically transformed when the government stopped them hunting and they had to adopt an agrarian mode of existence. Hunting constituted an essential structure of the social system and when terminated, it altered the other structures in the social system, even affecting methods of child-rearing.

In International Relations, if a systems approach is not accepted, then the international system is no more than the totality of interactions between states. The systems approach, however, encourages the analyst to identify principles which explain the particular configuration of relationships which can be found in International Relations. It is assumed that despite the complexity and confusion displayed by the amalgam of interactions, there are a set of structures which describe the international system, and explain the behaviour of the individual states.

Systems thinkers, therefore, work from the premise that it is the international system which forms 'the key element in explaining why and how nations attempt to influence the behaviour of one another' (Singer 1963, 423). But before it is possible to see how the system influences behaviour, or find explanations of the behavioural regularities which can be observed, a logical precondition is considered to be the 'articulation of the structural order or form of a system whose actors have non-desultory relations with each other' (Brams 1969, 583). Satisfying this precondition is not at all easy if it is accepted that the international system is open and adaptive, with the structures in a constant process of modification. Nevertheless, research is now proceeding along these lines.

Most literature using the systems approach in International Relations has operated at the level of the international system, with the state still being regarded as the major actor in world politics. There is, however, another growing area of literature where it is argued that the 'state-centric' view of the world should either be supplemented or replaced by a conception of world society. This level of analysis is also global in orientation but the unit of analysis is the individual, not the state. It is argued that the role technology now plays in society makes it necessary to accept that there is in existence a complex web of transnational relations. These relations must be understood because state behaviour has been affected by this development. Although both these views of International Relations have been described from a systems perspective, they operate from very different premises and need to be examined separately.

The state-centric model and the systems approach

For many observers, the First World War marked the nadir of the balance-of-power system and after the war academics in the newly emerging field of International Relations rejected not only the balance of power system as a mode of organization for interstate relationships, but also the holistic perspective associated with it. Writing was prescriptive and reflected an institutional and legal approach. However, following the Second World War there was a strong reaction to the established framework, and writers like Morgenthau successfully undermined the idealist school of thought and replaced it with a realist's state-centric view of the world. In particular, Morgenthau (1973, 167) reasserted the importance of the balance of power which he elevated to a 'universal concept' determining the behaviour of any society of sovereign entities. He also identified the balance of power as a 'self-regulating mechanism' and thereby restored the traditional holistic orientation. From this standpoint, writers with views similar to Morgenthau can be considered to have heralded the modern systems approach.

Morgenthau revived the balance-of-power concept because he believed that it provided the basis for a general theory of International Relations, explaining why a society of independent, autonomous and amoral states has persisted. The persistence of the international society requires an explanation, according to Morgenthau, because all states are engaged in a constant pursuit for power, at the expense of the other members of the society; yet despite outbreaks of war, the system never disintegrates – a balance, or equilibrium, is always maintained or restored. Morgenthau's theory seeks to explain the maintenance of an equilibrium which ensures the survival of states in the international society. The theory, therefore, is essentially holistic; it is designed to explain the enduring structure of the international system.

The basic condition used by Morgenthau to characterize international society is the universal pursuit of power by its members: a condition depicted as the inevitable consequence of operating in an 'anarchic' system. Actors, in other words, are constrained by the nature of the system in which they find themselves (see Ch. 6). The logic and reasoning underlying this holistic viewpoint is vividly expressed in Rousseau's cautionary tale of the five hungry hunters who cooperate in order to catch a stag which will satisfy their hunger, only to fail in their endeavour because one of the hunters, seizing the opportunity to catch a hare which will assuage his own hunger, permits the stag to escape (Waltz 1959, 167–8). In an 'anarchic' system where rules do not exist because of the absence of an authority to enforce them, cooperation, therefore, becomes irrational, because of the danger that a 'deviant' will take advantage of the cooperation to further his own self-interest. In a state of anarchy, actors have no alternative but to use self-interest rather than group-interest to govern their actions.

Using the same logic at the international level, insecurity is an endemic feature, and it is irrational, therefore, for any state to do other than maximize its power potential. Power maximization is a product of the system and cannot be understood in terms of the intentions or the motivations of individual states. The system dictates the motivation. In such a system, Morgenthau asserts, a critical factor which prevents continuous conflict and disorder is the self-regulating balance of power mechanism. By a constantly shifting series of alliances formed between the members of the system, the power of any state or group of states can be prevented from threatening the survival of any individual actor, large or small, and consequently, the system will always persist. War is not eliminated from such a system, but it is minimized and stability is maintained in the sense that all the members of the system survive and no single state can ever dominate the system. At first sight, the idea of the balance of power is seductive because of its very simplicity: the system is preserved because each actor pursues its own self-interest. However, on closer inspection, as Claude (1962, Ch. 3) has skilfully demonstrated. Morgenthau is not at all consistent in the way he uses the concept of the balance of power and there are no clear specifications of the conditions which define the existence of a balance-of-power system. If there are no empirical referents with which to define the system, it becomes difficult to avoid the impression that Morgenthau's use of the term is purely metaphysical.

Holistic concepts have often been considered metaphysical, but when the attempt was made to apply a modern systems approach to International Relations, its advocates believed that because they were operating on the basis of a scientific framework they were thereby freed from this stigma. Kaplan, who produced one of the first major works using the systems approach, identified the existence of a system in terms of the occurrence of behavioural regularities between a defined set of variables (Kaplan, 1964, 4) and he thereby committed himself to a rigorously positivistic approach with the existence of the system depending upon observed behaviour.

Kaplan contends that states manifest different types of behaviour depending upon the structure of the international system. Unlike Morgenthau (although Morgenthau is ambivalent on this issue), Kaplan also considers that it is possible for the international system to take a variety of forms and that the task of the theorist is to show how the behaviour of states is determined by the structure of these different systems. In order to illustrate this argument, he establishes models of six different international systems, four of them purely hypothetical, and he outlines the characteristics of each on the basis of five sets of variables. By specifying these variables, Kaplan clearly aims to be much more rigorous than Morgenthau.

One set of variables, for example, is used to depict the behavioural attributes of an international system. The variables which characterize the behaviour of the balance of power system are stipulated as:

1. Act to increase capabilities but negotiate rather than fight.
2. Fight rather than pass up an opportunity in increase capabilities.

3. Stop fighting rather than eliminate a national actor.
4. Act to oppose any coalition or single actor which tends to assume a position of predominance with respect to the rest of the system.
5. Act to constrain actors who subscribe to supranational organizing principles.
6. Permit defeated or constrained essential national actors to re-enter the system as acceptable role partners or act to bring some previously inessential actor within the essential actor classification. Treat all essential actors as acceptable role partners.

According to Kaplan, all these variables must be present before a balance-of-power system can be identified, and as a consequence, he calls them the 'essential rules' of the system. The 'rules' play a critical role in his 'theory' of the balance of power and confirmation of the theory can be achieved, he argues, if it is shown that there is a high correlation between the variables which define the essential rules and the patterns of behaviour observed in the relations between states (Kaplan 1964, 24).

It can be argued, however, that the existence of a statistical relationship between these variables will only confirm a 'theory' if the relationship between the variables is established on the basis of a set of theoretical assumptions. Yet it appears that Kaplan can offer no significant theoretical basis on which the six variables are identified and related. The first three are included because they conform with 'classic philosophical standards' and the last three appear to be 'merely rational rules', necessary to maintain the system (Kaplan 1964 23–4). It is difficult not to accept Weltman's (1973, 24) assertion that these rules represent no more than 'a set of assumptions, commonly made about the state system in the eighteenth century'. They do not add up to a theory of a balance-of-power system.

Although Kaplan's work has had a very important influence on International Relations, in the sense that it has encouraged others to use the systems approach, its influence has been very limited in terms of generating empirical research. Writers who have tried to use and develop the models devised by Kaplan have worked either at a very impressionistic level (Chi 1968, Franke 1968) or at a highly abstract level, remote from empirical data (Reinken 1968), or have tested empirical propositions which are not specific to Kaplan (McGowan and Rood 1975). Therefore, elaborate specification of the rules which govern the behaviour of states has not elicited attempts at empirical verification, and ironically, as Jones (1970, 141) has pointed out, 'without clear verification, Kaplan's framework becomes metaphysical simply because it is self-defining'.

Although writers have continued to use the systems approach to establish general theoretical frameworks (Spiro 1966) and discussions of Kaplan, in the words of one caustic commentator, have precipitated an 'academic industry' (Pettman 1975, 138) there has been widespread criticism of writers who propound the virtues of the scientific method, yet have 'only engaged in elaborate "descriptions" of international systems and subsystems, descriptions that have been devoid of rigorous empirical foundation' (Russett 1969, 92). However, since Kaplan first popularized the idea of the international system, there has been an increasing volume of research based on a 'rigorous empirical foundation' which has examined the properties of the international system.

Given the influence of Morgenthau and Kaplan, it is not surprising to find that an important area of quantitative research has centred on attempts to define the structure of the international system from a power perspective. An important distinction, however, has been made between power defined by the capabilities possessed by a state and the power ascribed to the state by other actors in the international system. Ferris (1973), for example, examining the power structure of the international system defined over the period 1850–1966, restricts his analysis to objective power criteria. He uses six variables to identify and compare power capabilities: the size of the armed forces, the level of defence expenditure, the size of the population, the size of government revenue, the size of imports and exports and the area of the state. The scores for each of these variables are standardized and then aggregated and on the basis of the final result it is possible to rank the states in the international system according to their power capabilities. By standardizing the variables, the analysis incorporates the assumption that power is a relative commodity; if the power of one state increases, then it must be at the expense of other states in the systems. Power, therefore, is being defined from a holistic standpoint, because it follows that the power of any single state is determined by the distribution of power in the international system as a whole. It is only possible to consider the power of a state in the context of the power structure of the international system.

Traditionalists and behaviouralists agree that the power structure of the international system, defined by the power capabilities which each state 'achieves', has a major influence on behaviour within the system. Behaviouralists, however, are also committed to the idea that it is necessary to examine systematically the power structure defined in terms of perception; the rank of any state being determined by the power 'ascribed' to it by the other states in the system. However, indicators which identify the power status ascribed by an international consensus are not readily available. But there is at least one indicator which permits an examination of the perceptual aspect of the power structure, ingeniously devised by Singer. He has formulated a diplomatic index, based on the number and status of foreign representatives in each country's capital. The index can then be used to rank states and it is inferred that the resulting structure reflects an international consensus on the ascribed power of states in the international system (Singer and Small 1966). However, the utility attached to research which uses indicators of this kind rests on the assumption that an idea like 'ascribed power status' can be 'conceptualized as something immanent in the transactions nations have with each other, [and] can be abstracted from the flow of these transactions and operationally defined . . .' (Brams 1969, 582). This assumption, however, is common to most empirical analysis.

Research on the structure of the international system is a necessary preliminary to examining the relationship between the structure of the international system and the behaviour of actors within the system. However, once indicators have been operationalized, allowing the structure of the international system to be identified, it is possible to begin examining some of the theoretical disputes about the relationship between structure and behaviour. In the balance-of-power literature, for example, there has been a persistent debate between systems theorists who assert (*a*) that the level of conflict in the system declines when power is concentrated and there is a hierarchical distribution of power in the international system, and those who argue (*b*) that the level of conflict is minimized when there is an equal distribution of power among states in the system and power is consequently diffused. Persuasive theoretical arguments can be advanced to support both positions. Singer et al. (1972), after measuring the power capabilities of states during the nineteenth and twentieth centuries, developed an index which measured the degree of power concentration in the international system for each year. Power concentration was then related, using a variety of statistical techniques, to the amount of war which occurs each year. The findings suggest that while in the nineteenth century the amount of war increases as power capabilities in the international system become more concentrated, in the twentieth century, the concentration of power leads to a decline in the incidence of war.

This discrepancy in behaviour between the nineteenth and the twentieth century suggests that there are systemic processes at work which are as yet inadequately understood. This conclusion is reinforced by an examination of research carried out to test the theory which asserts that violence can be a product of status inconsistency (Galtung 1964). When applied to International Relations, status inconsistency can be identified by a discrepancy between ascribed and achieved power status. Using the kind of indicators already described, it has been possible to test the proposition that 'the greater the amount of status inconsistency in the international system as a whole, the greater the levels of conflict that will be experienced within it'. Findings by Rosecrance et al. (1974) suggest that the idea of status inconsistency has little relevance for International Relations and that it is necessary to develop more complex behavioural indicators to understand the factors which precipitate violence. However, both East (1972) and Wallace (1973) have found that the proposition can be given some support provided there is provision for a time-lag between the development of status inconsistency and the occurrence of violence. Wallace found that the best results were observed when the variables were separated by a fifteen-year time-lag. This suggests that there is a very slow feedback process operating in the international system which links change with the perception of change. A more thorough understanding of these processes is most likely to emerge as the result of studies using a systems framework which operates at the state rather than at the international level (Moul 1973). Work in this area has already been started by writers like McClelland (1964), Holsti and North (1965) and Young (1967).

However, the adoption of quantitative methods has not been the only possible way considered to develop a systems approach to International Relations. Some writers have turned away from an analysis of the general features of International Relations in favour of the unique, although still clinging to the concept of the international system. Under the influence of Aron's (1967) conception of 'historical sociology', writers working essentially within the traditionalist's framework have also probed the features of the international system, using the techniques of the historian. These writers are not opposed to the aims of the quantifiers, but rather to their methods (Kim 1965). They do try therefore to establish general propositions. So, for example, Kim (1970, 122) derives the hypothesis that 'A heterogeneous ideology tends to reduce international stability by sharply increasing the distortion in perception' on the basis of a historical analysis of the impact of the French Revolution on the international system. However, the amount of literature in this area is very limited.

World society and the systems approach

Systems thinkers working with the conception of an international system are operating within a framework which has long been accepted in the study of International Relations. The framework reflects a state-centric perspective; it asserts that the state is the primary actor in International Relations and it can be depicted as cohesive, autonomous and rational. Although this picture has now been extended by including a number of 'non-state actors', the basic outline of the framework remains unaltered and it is from this perspective that most analysis of International Relations is written. Even a writer like Reynolds, who develops a radical analytical view of the systems approach, is much more cautious when developing his conception of 'the significant interactions at the international level' (1971, 242) and he appears to be constrained by the state-centric perspective. There is, however, another strain to the systems approach in International Relations which has, at the very least, attempted to broaden the horizons of International Relations, some would say to a point where any idea of a boundary to the discipline has been lost altogether. The process of boundary extension, or dissolution, has taken place in three major areas, and each has tended to undermine the traditional conception of the international system. The common justification for these extensions has been that the state-centric model no longer corresponds to what is happening in the world.

The first area of attack has centred on the distinction which has traditionally been drawn between domestic and international politics. Activity which overlaps between the domestic and international system, it is argued, has not been adequately studied as a consequence. The international aspects of civil strife (Rosenau 1964) provides a specific example of this kind of activity, but the interaction between domestic and foreign politics, in general, is said to constitute an academic 'no-man's-land' (Farrell 1966, vi). An early attempt to use the international systems approach explicitly endeavoured to fill this breach (Rosecrance 1963), but most systems thinkers have moved away from analysis at the level of the international system when thinking about this area, and treat the state as an open system.

Herz (1959) developed the concept of 'permeability' to accommodate the development of nuclear weapons, suggesting that the state is no longer a defensible unit, and Scott (1965, 1967) considered the idea of a penetrated state system to take account of the tendency of the great powers to undermine the sovereignty of smaller states. Rosenau, on the other hand, saw the penetration process as part of a more general phenomenon, called 'linkage' which he defined by a 'recurrent sequence of behaviour that originates in one system and is reacted to in another' (Rosenau 1969, 45). He established three types of linkage: penetrative, reactive and emulative. A penetrative linkage process occurs when members of one 'polity' serve in the political process of a second 'polity'. A reactive process exists when events in one political system precipitate a reaction in another political system. (A good example is found in Milstein's (1973) study of involvement by the United States in South Vietnam. On the basis of public opinion data he demonstrates that by 1968 the United States and South Vietnamese political systems were linked: moves which undermined the South Vietnamese regime reinforced the domestic position of the United States President, while moves to bolster the South Vietnamese regime undermined the American President's position.) Finally, an emulative process is identified when, for example, a coup in one state precipitates a coup in another state. The original formulation of linkage politics was not very successful in generating further research. The conception of linkage, however, has now been broadened to include quantitative investigations of the relationship between internal and external conflict, an area of research which reflects, among other things, the traditional idea that international crises are sometimes used to divert attention from internal problems (Wilkenfeld 1973).

Examining the linkages between domestic political systems certainly confronts the International Relations specialist with unfamiliar terrain, which may explain the reluctance to explore this area: a result of the conservative desire to avoid unfamiliar avenues. Rosenau (1970) himself 'retreated' to a consideration of the individual state as an open system, with domestic and foreign policies being viewed as adaptive processes. Although an intriguing idea, this approval is compatible with a state-centric view of International Relations. More relevant, therefore, is

Rosenau's earlier distinction between vertical and horizontal systems which he devised to contend with the 'increasing obfuscation of the boundaries between national political systems and their international environment' (Rosenau 1966, 53). Traditionally, he argues, we have tended to think in horizontal terms, separating international, national and local politics. Now, there are issues which cut through these levels and define vertical systems. Berlin, civil rights and the population explosion are cited as examples which cut across the three horizontal levels and link individuals in ways which do not correspond to the horizontal boundaries.

The increase of issues which fail to respect state boundaries and have an impact on global politics, constitutes a second area being examined by systems thinkers. For the traditional theorist, a primary justification for studying International Relations is the failure of states to eliminate war from the international system. Now, it is difficult for any writer examining world politics from a holistic standpoint not to reflect the views of systems thinkers like Meadows et al. (1972), who argue that the survival of the human race is in jeopardy because of the refusal to take account of the finite nature of the earth. Concentrating on the dangers of war, to the exclusion of threats to the environment can, from perspective, represent a myopic view of the world. This position was justifiable in the past, according to Falk, because 'The parts did not interconnect with sufficient regularity and significance to require any continuing coordination of human activity over the whole globe.' But now, he argues, 'the interconnectedness of the networks of control and organization is a characteristic part of our world situation' (Falk 1972, 94–5). As a consequence, he believes that the threats to human existence are interconnected and 'cannot be successfully treated as separate and separable' (Falk 1972, 98). In addition to the global problem of war, therefore, Falk also identifies population pressure, insufficiency of resources, and the deterioration of the environment. If the subject-matter of International Relations is extended in this fashion, then it is clear that concepts associated with the state-centric perspective, like balance of power, deterrence and alliances, have very little relevance. You cannot deter, balance or form an alliance against environmental decay.

If we accept the 'power-politics' view of International Relations, the nation-state, through the medium of the balance of power, has been a tolerably successful mode of organization; it has minimized the level of violence both within and between states. However, from a wider perspective, it is clear that current global problems require a degree of cooperation which cannot be attained if states persist in evaluating situations from the perspective of their own national interests. The power-political conception of International Relations is not helpful on this point, since it asserts that the formation of a world society is incompatible with the conditions which describe the nation-state system. The reasoning which underlies this position has recently been reexamined by Modelski, using the systems framework developed by Forrester (1968). Modelski's systems model consists of two basic conditions, the nation-state and war which are 'causally and circularly interrelated', resulting in a vicious circle. Fear of war increases the commitment to the nation-state system, while the dominance of the nation-state system ensures that war is a persistent feature of the global system (Modelski 1972, 258). Each condition, therefore, feeds upon the other. Familiarity with this model has, according to Modelski, 'blinded' students of International Relations to facts and trends which suggest that the process described by the vicious circle can be reversed, permitting the emergence of world society. Decumulation, he suggests, can come about by accident or 'by design through conscious intervention' (Modelski 1972, 266).

However, in order to precipitate decumulation Modelski argues that it is necessary to move away from a conception of a state system and develop an understanding of world society, because the existing model of organization is inadequate as a basis for future organization. But to determine the nature of this organization, much more must be known about the needs of world society and this requires a greater understanding of the basic constituent, that is, the individual. Falk (1972, 351) suggests, for example, that smaller, more homogeneous units may be a prerequisite to the formation of a stable world society. This, however, makes an assumption about the relationship between human values and political organization which can at least be questioned, and a study of the individual is required to find an adequate answer. This line of argument, which follows inexorably from a belief in the systems approach, has been explicitly espoused by Burton (1972) and the commitment to study International Relations from the standpoint of the individual represents the third and most radical way in which the systems approach has extended the horizons of International Relations.

In contrast to writers who adopt a state-centric perspective, Burton asserts that we already operate in the context of a world society which is identified by the existence of a highly complex network of cross-cutting relationships. Some of these relationships have always been present, but their 'number and spread' have increased under the pressure of technological changes. In place of the billiard-ball model which reflects the state-centric perspective, Burton advocates the use of a cobweb model, each cobweb representing a system; the strands of the web represent the complex of relationships which make up the system. World society consists of millions of these 'cobwebs', which do not make reference to geographical boundaries. Because of the cross-cutting nature of the relationships, the 'expectations and values' of individuals and communities are diffused through the interlocking systems and, as a consequence, world society is characterized by an 'infectious process of social change' (Burton 1968, 5).

Burton's central concern is with the process of social change in world society, and he believes that the process is vitally affected by the existence of states, partly because of the impact which the existence of states has on people's perceptions of the world and partly because states can employ coercion to arrest or modify the forces of social change. He sees coercion as a form of behaviour which reflects a failure to understand the nature of the forces which precipitate conflict and change. In the past, the use of coercion was successful in curbing responses, defined from a state-centric perspective as 'deviant', but in the context of incipient world society, policies based on deterrence, balance of power and collective security, which depend on the use of force, are proving to be self-defeating. These policies generate the response they are designed to inhibit. The response of state authorities, therefore, whether they are dealing with 'delinquents' in the domestic or the international system tend to reflect a failure to understand the nature of contemporary world society. 'At all levels, the tendency is to respond to failure by applying more of the same medicine and not to acknowledge that the initial analysis was probably faulty. When 'law and order' fails, the level of coercion is increased' (Burton et al. 1974, 17).

For Burton, the failure to adopt new policies is a function of the prevailing state-centric view of the world, which 'promotes the status of state authorities', and policies then flow from this perspective which 'inhibit the process of political and social change' (Burton et al. 1974, 27). The task of the International Relations specialist, therefore, is not to perpetuate an analysis of the world which no longer reflects the reality of the situation, but to develop an understanding of the complex systems which make up world society, together with the values of the individuals who interact within these systems. On the basis of this understanding it should be possible to deal more successfully with the constant challenge precipitated by social change and conflict.

Conclusion

Despite the breadth and scope of literature associated with the systems approach, most analysis concerning International Relations is still written from a non-systems perspective. The literature is dominated by descriptions of the foreign policy of individual states, discussions about key concepts, ranging from non-alignment to arms control, and investigations into individual events, such as crisis and war. Although invaluable in their own right, these works provide very little insight into the dynamic processes which operate at the level of the international system. Nor do they generate concepts and ideas which allow us to compare one pattern of events in the international system with another. Still less does work of this kind give us the opportunity to relate international behaviour to behaviour at other system levels.

It was to rectify this situation that the systems approach was originally applied to International Relations. In recent years, however, there has been growing criticism levelled against the approach. It is argued that after twenty years, writers have still not got beyond the point of expounding the virtues of systems thinking. The work of Kaplan is often cited to illustrate that the application of systems thinking does not precipitate a scientific understanding of the international system. It merely generates a series of mechanistic models which have never received empirical verification. Vital (1969, 151) goes further and says that these macro-models represent exercises in 'latter-day scholasticism', because they are so far removed from diplomatic practice.

At this point, however, a potential split between behaviouralism and systems thinking becomes apparent. Vital argues, quite categorically, that there are 'no really convincing grounds' for supposing that the kind of macro-models established by Kaplan can be verified. This is because social science is said to be concerned with human behaviour and Vital cannot find any evidence that macro-systems analysis can be applied at this level. Vital here is expressing the fear which beset the early behaviouralists working in International Relations. Behaviouralism is being restricted to the analysis of human behaviour. It follows that any theory of International Relations must be developed at the level of the individual.

This position, of course, fails to understand that the systems thinker is searching for theories of behaviour which can apply at all levels: mechanical, biological and social. The systems thinker, in other words, has by-passed the original behaviouralist's objective of searching for a theory of human behaviour. Systems thinking is not restricted to human behaviour. In the context of International Relations, systems thinkers are searching for dynamic principles which can help to explain interstate behaviour, but they are, at the same time, trying to establish links with behaviour at other system levels (Galtung 1968).

As demonstrated in a previous section, systems thinkers in International Relations have succeeded in operationalizing the idea of behaviour in the context of the international system, although the success of this venture is dependent upon accepting that a concept like 'ascribed status' can be considered immanent in diplomatic representation. It is not surprising to find that Vital (1969, 148) considers Singer's 'exhaustive collation' of diplomats results in 'the illumination (if that is the right word) of one, small, marginal point in almost total isolation from all others'. In other words, he has not accepted the possibility that the process of diplomatic representation can be used to operationalize a theoretical construct. If Vital's position is adopted, it is not even possible to talk about state behaviour, only the behaviour of individuals representing the state. But many theorists would accept that there is no intrinsic problem about relating behaviour to an aggregate like the state. It does involve reification but there do seem to be good grounds to support this procedure. It is meaningful to stipulate that Germany and France went to war in 1870 and that Britain was involved in more civil wars than any other European state during the nineteenth century. These statements can be made without reference to individual decision-makers and it is on this basis that systems thinkers have proceeded.

A more damaging type of criticism has been levelled in the philosophy of science where the possibility of analyzing phenomena from a systems perspective has been specifically denied by Nagel, one of the major philosophers of science. He reaffirms that science can only advance if it is accepted that the behaviour of the 'part' can be studied separately from the 'whole'. Research based on this approach can give rise to 'expressions of genuine knowledge', whereas he believes that discussions from a systems perspective give rise to 'unenlightening statements liberally studded with locutions like 'wholeness', 'unifiedness' and 'indivisible unity', (Nagel 1961, 446). For Nagel, conceptualizing things in terms of an indivisible whole merely provides an obstacle to scientific advancement, and he asserts, moreover, that biologists who talk about 'indivisible unity' do not carry out research on this assumption.

A similar line of argument has been advanced by Weltman who argues that the use of 'system' in International Relations denotes no more than interrelation. He then stipulates that if the meaning of system cannot be extended beyond this limit, then the concept is both 'irrefutable and useless'. He bases this position on the fact that all social science rests on the assumption of interrelation and that it cannot proceed from any other base. He concludes that 'If system means only interrelation, systems theory loses any claim to uniqueness as a method of analysis of social events' (Weltman 1973, 100).

Again, the research described earlier does not seem to support these contentions. There have clearly been attempts to operationalize concepts which only have meaning in the context of the international system. Measures designed to assess the degree of power concentration, or the degree of alliance cohesion within the international system are not simply reflecting the idea of interrelation. They are measures which have been designed on the assumption that the international system is a meaningful concept and that it is reasonable to suppose that the behaviour of states can be explained by the structure of the international system. This statement is by no means uncontentious and some social scientists, methodological individualists, like Vital, do not accept the validity of explaining behaviour from a holistic perspective (O'Neill 1973).

It often appears difficult to avoid a sense of anticlimax when concluding a discussion of the systems approach in International Relations. The approach is derived from an exciting and developing movement in modern science; it advocates looking for dynamic rather than deterministic relationships and searching for principles of organization which identify uniformity in apparent diversity. Natural scientists can claim, with some justification, Nagel notwithstanding, that they have made progress along these lines. The development of the systems approach in International Relations must appear modest by comparison. There seem to be three reasons for attempting to counteract this lack of confidence. First, the systems approach has encouraged writers to think theoretically; second, the approach has precipitated attempts to test systems propositions at an empirical level; and finally, systems thinking has encouraged writers to extend the horizons of International Relations. These developments are far from negligible; they have transformed a narrow and inward-looking discipline into one of the most adventurous and outward-looking areas in the social sciences.

References and Further Reading

Asterisked items constitute a short bibliography or the systems approach.

Aron, R. (1967) *Peace and War: A Theory of International Relations,* trans. R. Howard and A.B. Fox, Praeger.

Bertalanffy, L. von (1956) 'General systems theory', *General Systems,* **1,** 1–10.

Brams, S.J. (1969) 'The structure of influence relationships in the international system', in J.N. Rosenau (ed.), *International Politics and Foreign Policy,* New York, Free Press.

Brecher, M. (1963) 'The subordinate state system in southern Asia', *World Politics,* **15,** 213–35.

*__Buckley, W.__ (1967) *Sociology and Modern Systems Theory,* Englewood Cliffs, Prentice-Hall.

Buchan, W. and Cantril, H. (1953) *How Nations See Each Other,* Urbana Illinois Univ. Press.

*__Burton, J.W.__ (1968) *Systems, States, Diplomacy and Rules,* Cambridge, Cambridge Univ. Press.

Burton, J.W. (1972) *World Society,* Cambridge, Cambridge Univ. Press.

Burton, J.W. et al. (1974) 'The study of world society: A London perspective', Occasional Paper No. 1, International Studies Association.

Cannon, W.B. (1932) *The Wisdom of the Body,* London, Norton.

Chi, H. (1968) 'The Chinese warlord system as an international system', in M.A. Kaplan (ed.), *New Approaches to International Relations,* New York, St Martin's Press.

*__Churchman, C.W.__ (1968) *The Systems Approach,* New York, Delacorte Press.

Claude, I.L. (1962) *Power and International Relations,* New York, Random House.

East, M.A. (1972) 'Status discrepancy and violence in the international system: An empirical analysis', in J.N. Rosenau et al. (eds.), *The Analysis of International Politics,* New York, Free Press.

Falk, R.A. (1972) *This Endangered Planet: Prospects and Proposals for Human Survival,* New York, Vintage Books.

Farrell, R.B. (1966) *Approaches to Comparative and International Politics,* Evanston, Northwestern Univ. Press.

Ferris, W.H. (1973) *The Power Capabilities of Nation-States,* Lexington, Lexington Books.

Forrester, J.W. (1968) *Principles of Systems,* Cambridge, Wright and Allen Press.

Franke, W. (1968) 'The Italian city-state system as an international system', in M.A. Kaplan (ed.), *New Approaches to International Relations,* New York, St Martin's Press.

Galtung, J. (1964) 'A structural theory of aggression', *Journal of Peace Research,* **1,** 95–119.

Galtung, J. (1968) 'Small group theory, and the theory of international relations', in M.A. Kaplan (ed.), *New Approaches to International Politics,* New York, St Martin's Press.

Gulick, E.V. (1955) *Europe's Classical Balance of Power,* Cornell Univ. Press.

Herz, J.H. (1959) *International Politics in the Atomic Age,* New York, Columbia Univ. Press.

Holsti, O.R. and North, R.C. (1965) 'The history of human conflict', in E.B. McNeil (ed.), *The Nature of Human Conflict,* Englewood Cliffs, Prentice-Hall.

Hopkins, R.F. and Mansbach, R.W. (1973) *Structure and Process in International Politics,* New York, Harper and Row.

Jones, R.E. (1970) *Analyzing Foreign Policy,* London, Routledge and Kegan Paul.

Jordan, N. (1973) 'Some thinking about "systems"', in S.L. Optner (ed.), *Systems Analysis,* Harmondsworth, Penguin Books.

***Kaplan, M.A.** (1964) *System and Process in International Politics,* New York, Wiley. First published 1957.

Kay, H. (1969) 'Introduction', in J. Annett, *Feedback and Human Behaviour,* Harmondsworth, Penguin Books.

Kim, K. (1965) 'The limits of behavioural explanation in politics', *The Canadian Journal of Economics and Political Science,* **31,** 315–27.

Kim, K. (1970) *Revolution and International System,* New York, Univ. Press.

Koestler, A. (1967) *The Ghost in the Machine,* London, Hutchinson.

***Laszlo, E.** (1972) *The System View of the World,* New York, Braziller.

McClelland, C.A. (1955) 'Applications of general systems theory in international relations', *Main Currents in Modern Thought,* **12,** 27–34.

McClelland, C.A. (1964) 'Action structures and communication in two international crises: Quemoy and Berlin', *Background,* **7,** 201–15.

McClelland, C.A. (1966) *Theory and the International System,* London, Macmillan.

McGowan, P.J. and Rood, R.M. (1975) 'Alliance behaviour in balance of power systems: Applying a Poisson model to nineteenth century Europe', *American Political Science Review,* **69,** 859–70.

Meadows, D.H., Randers, D.L. and Behrens, J. and W.W. (1972) *The Limits to Growth,* London, Potomac Associates Book.

Milstein, J.S. (1973) 'The Vietnam War from the 1968 Tet Offensive to the 1970 Cambodian Invasion: A quantitative analysis', in H.R. Alker et al. (eds). *Mathematical Approaches to Politics,* Amsterdam, Elsevier.

Modelski, G. (1972) *Principles of World Politics,* New York, Free Press.

Morgenthau, H.J. (1973) *Politics Among Nations: The Struggle for Power and Peace* (5th edn.), New York, Knopf.

Moul, W.B. (1973) 'The level of analysis problem revisited', *Canadian Journal of Political Science,* **6,** 494–513.

Myrdal, G. (1942) *An American Dilemma,* New York, Harper and Row.

Nagel, E. (1961) *Structure of Science Problems in the Logic of Scientific Explanation,* New York, Harcourt Brace.

O'Neill, J. (ed.), (1973) *Modes of Individualism and Collectivism,* London, Heinemann.

Pettman, R. (1975) *Human Behaviour and World Politics,* London, Macmillan Press.

Rapoport, A. (1974) *Conflict in Man-Made Environment,* Harmondsworth, Penguin Books.

Reinken, D.L. (1968) 'Computer explorations of the "Balance of Power"', in M.A. Kaplan (ed.), *New Approaches to International Politics,* New York, St Martin's Press.

Rosenau, J.N. (ed.) (1964) *The International Aspects of Civil Strife,* Princeton, Princeton Univ. Press.

Rosenau, J.N. (1966) 'Pre-theories and theories of foreign policy', in R.B. Farrell (ed.), *Approaches to Comparative and International Politics,* Evanston, Northwestern Univ. Press.

Rosenau, J.N. (1969) 'Toward the study of national-international linkages', in J.W. Rosenau (ed.), *Linkage Politics,* New York, Free Press.

Rosenau, J.N. (1970) *The Adaptation of National Societies,* Monograph MacCaleb-Seiler.

Reynolds, P.A. (1971) *An Introduction to International Relations,* London, Longman.

Rosecrance, R. (1963) *Action and Reaction in World Politics,* Boston, Little, Brown.

Rosecrance, R. et al. (1974) *Power, Balance of Power, and Status in Nineteenth Century International Relations,* Sage Professional Papers in International Studies, 02–029.

Russett, B.M. (1969) 'The young science of international politics', *World Politics,* **22,** 87–94.

Scott, A.M. (1965) *The Revolution in Statecraft: Informal Penetration,* New York, Random House.

*__Scott, A.M.__ (1967) *The Functioning of the International System,* New York, Macmillan.

Singer, J.D. (1963) 'Inter-nation influence model', *American Political Science Review,* **57,** 420–30.

Singer, J.D. and Small, M. (1966) 'The composition and status ordering of the international system', *World Politics,* **18,** 236–82.

*__Singer, J.D.__ (1971) *A General System Taxonomy for Political Science,* Monograph, New York, General Learning Press.

Singer, J.D., Bremer, S. and Stuckey, J. (1972) 'Capability distribution, uncertainty, and major power war, 1820–1965', in B. Russett, (ed.), *Peace, War, and Numbers,* Beverly Hills, Sage.

Smith, J.M. (1975) *The Theory of Evolution* (3rd edn.), Harmondsworth, Penguin Books.

Sonderman, F.A. (1961) 'The linkage between foreign policy and international politics', in J.N. Rosenau (ed.), *International Politics and Foreign Policy,* New York, The Free Press.

*__Spiro, H.J.__ (1966) *World Politics: The Global System,* Dorsey Press.

Turnbull, C. (1973) *The Mountain People,* London, Cape.

Vital, D. (1969) 'Back to Machiavelli', in K. Knorr, and J.N. Rosenau (eds.), *Contending Approaches to International Politics,* Princeton, Princeton Univ. Press.

Wallace, M. (1973) *War and Rank Among Nations,* Lexington, Heath.

Waltz, K.N. (1959) *Man, the State and War,* New York, Columbia Univ. Press.

*__Weltman, J.J.__ (1973) *Systems Theory in International Relations: A Study in Metaphoric Hypertrophy,* Lexington, D.C. Heath, Lexington Books.

Wiener, N. (1950) *The Human Use of Human Beings,* New York, Houghton Mifflin.

Wilkenfeld, J. (ed.) (1973) *Conflict Behaviour and Linkage Politics,* MacKay.

*__Young, D.R.__ (1968) *A Systemic Approach to International Politics,* Research Monograph No. 33, Center of International Studies, Princeton Univ.

Young, O.R. (1967) *The Intermediaries,* Princeton, Princeton Univ. Press.

Chapter 10

Communications theory

R.I. Tooze

Introduction

The nature of communications in International Relations

This chapter will attempt to identify and evaluate the set of writings in International Relations covered by the generic label of 'Communications theory'. As with any 'family' the differences between individuals may seem to be greater than the similarities and, consequently, the task of generalization is more difficult. In using the notion of a 'family' the intention is to emphasize the differentiated nature of the many writings in this field as well as to point out the common elements of the communications approach. At this point in the analysis the concept of an 'approach' will be substituted for 'theory', for, as will be shown, the communications literature can only be regarded as theory in a loose or limited sense.

The common element in the 'family' is the focus on the communication process, formulated by Lasswell (1948, 37) as 'Who, Says What, In Which Channel, To Whom, With What Effect'. Clearly each of these questions has a potential political relevance. A communications analysis would, therefore, seek to demonstrate the political aspects of international communications and the degree to which these flows of communication condition political behaviour. The term 'communications' has also come to include the concept of 'cybernetics' (steering), as developed by Norbert Wiener (1948), to signify the control of communication in political systems. For, if politics is envisaged as a 'system', the control of the system centres on communication and the ability of a state to control is related to its ability to deal with information. Weiner, in fact, equates communication and control; every time we communicate, we control.

Outline of the chapter

After discussing the difficulty of adequate generalization this introductory section will link the communications literature with the dominant theme of International Relations, hopefully providing a reference point from which the development of 'communications' and its impact on International Relations can be assessed. The chapter then falls into two main sections; the historical development of the field in three major phases is followed by an evaluation of 'communications' as theory.

The problems of generalization

The significance of the diverse range of studies of international political communication becomes clear when trying to evaluate the contribution of this literature to International Relations. The extent to which a particular analysis accepts the communications approach will logically determine the variables in the description and explanation of any phenomenon. A description of, say, political integration in Europe using the communications approach will consider the level and range of transactions as a critical indicator (Puchala 1970), whereas the functional approach would tend to emphasize the competence of European organizations to perform functional tasks (Pentland 1973, 76). In order to make statements about the usefulness or otherwise of the communications literature it seems preferable, therefore, to consider analyses according to whether they adopt the approach, utilize communications data as part of a wider analysis or are concerned with the general process of communication, in particular intergovernmental, in International Relations.

The assumptions of International Relations

A second initial task is to locate the communications literature within the broad framework of the development of the discipline of International Relations. In doing so the writings are related to the assumptions which characterize the discipline as a whole, with certain analyses clustering around particular assumptions. Bearing in mind the dangers of generalization, it is possible to isolate these assumptions, and, hence, show to what extent they 'determine in turn the range of facts sought, and the range of conclusions themselves' (Pettman 1975, 29).

As will be shown, the communications literature rested on what are regarded as the traditional assumptions of International Relations, namely:

'(1) significant relations (only) between states;
(2) states act as coherent units;
(3) political-military security concerns are the dominant objectives and motivations of states' (Nye 1975, 36).

Both Puchala and Fagan (1974) and Wagner (1974, 437) as well as Nye (1975), consider the problems of this 'state-centric realism' as a framework of analysis. The important point here is not that *every* analysis neatly fits into this framework but that the assumptions of this realist conception of 'security politics' are reflected in most writings on International Relations. Although initially based on state-centric realism the work on communications has contributed to a questioning of these traditional assumptions and, hence, has tended to weaken them, particularly the second.

The development of the study of communications in International Relations

The foregoing analysis has endeavoured to construct a background against which the evolution of the communications approach can be appraised. 'Evolution' suggests a growth over time which is organic and probably unilinear. With this conception it should be possible to locate particular analyses along a continuum, merely 'hanging' it on the line at some stage of the evolutionary process. Unfortunately for our purposes, but fortunately for the development of political science, such an exercise is both difficult and misleading. The imposition of a rigid historical scheme would obscure the nature of developments, particularly the 'hundred flowers' situation in contemporary International Relations where work based on the traditional assumptions is contemporaneous to work directly challenging these assumptions: compare the analysis in Martin, 'Propaganda in international affairs' (1971) to that in Bobrow, 'Transfer of meaning across national boundaries' (1972) who claims that International Relations is not a suitable domain for the development of an 'engineering theory' of communication. It is possible, however, to identify historical phases, albeit with a problem of arbitrary cut-off points, within which communication writings follow a broad pattern, exhibit certain common features and are based on similar assumptions.

Three such phases are identified here: (1) up to the early 1950s; (2) early 1950s to late 1960s; (3) from the late 1960s to date (1976).

First phase

Development

As is to be expected from a consideration of the traditional assumptions about the state-centric nature of the system, international political communication was initially solely concerned with formal relationships between state élites, seen as a two-way flow of messages, usually in a competitive or conflictual situation. Diplomacy functioned to mediate the effects of the international system and to achieve the objectives defined by the 'national interest' through the collection and evaluation of information and the presentation of information to other governments. In order to appreciate the precise nature of this type of communication it is helpful to describe it in terms of modern communication analysis. Any communication system is based on a message and three 'operating parts: a sender, a medium or channel, and a receiver' (Phillips 1974, 179 and Fig. 1). This is represented diagrammatically in Fig. 10.1. Here we must distinguish between the content of a message (what it means or, more correctly, what it is perceived to mean) and the medium or channel which transmits the message (radio, print, status of individual transmitting message). One further useful distinction is between communication and communications. According to Prosser (1973, 14), 'communications can be described as the networks and channels by which communication is transmitted'. For him, the act of communication is one of social interaction, whereas the channels of communication are determined by technology in its broadest sense.

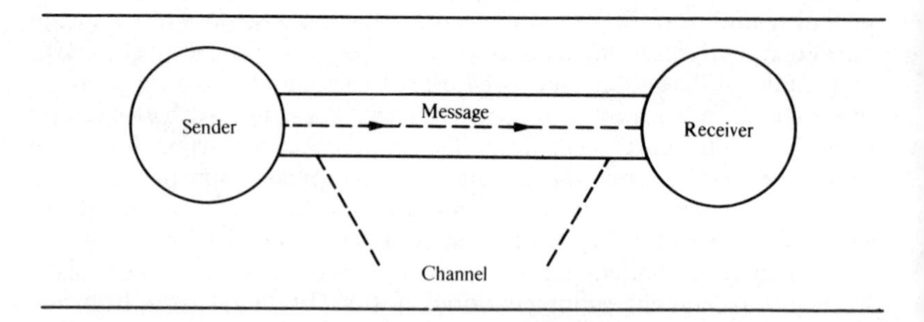

Fig. 10.1 A simple communications network.

The diplomat, then, is the channel through which governmental messages are transmitted, although he presumably has some influence on the content of the message. The number and location of a state's embassies, along with the number of individual diplomats, constitute the state's formal international communications network, which must of necessity limit the extent of interaction between states.

The scope and nature of international political communication has since expanded from this diplomatic focus, influenced by the development of social science, the effects of mass communications and the changing nature of International Relations. In a stimulating discussion Bobrow (1972a) traced the development of international political communication and the following account reflects his historical periods. The approach of total war politicized populations. From the viewpoint of communications, mass populations became channels of communication. Propaganda, as an instrument of war constituted a new form of influence from the government of one country to the public of another (Lasswell 1927). Inasmuch as the cause of the war was explained as a failure of communication (élite-to-élite) the prevention of future war, through the institutions of the League of Nations, was to depend on improved communications and world public opinion, which was assumed to be inherently desirous of peace. In our terms this conception can be represented in Fig. 10.2. Complementary to the traditional channel of diplomacy (Ag to Bg) we now have a multiplicity of channels. Propaganda (Ag→ Bc→ Bg) represents a modification to the 'state as actor' assumption in the penetration of the state. National public opinions are introduced as a force in international politics (Bc→ Ag), but the decisive actors are states: public opinion merely remains a constraint on government action.

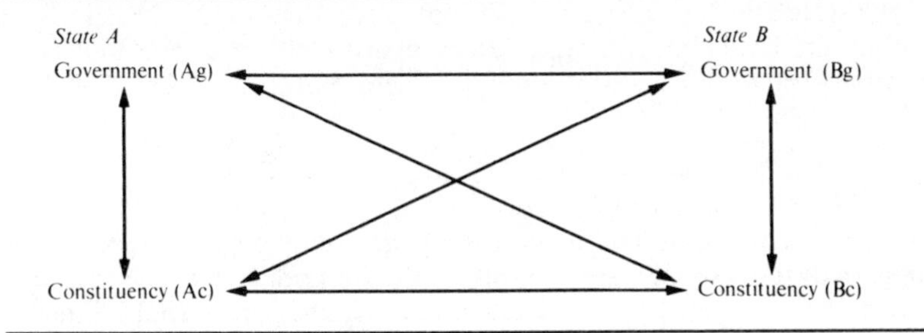

Fig. 10.2 Channels of international communication (from Wedge 1971, 42).

The development of communications technology coupled with the emergence of regimes willing.to use this technology as an instrument of foreign and domestic policy generated a growing concern, particularly in the United States. Consequently, the study of propaganda began to consider the content and the meaning of the symbols involved (Lasswell and Blumenstock 1939), the channels utilized and the particular strategies adopted. More importantly, the reaction to Utopian conceptions of International Relations in the form of 'the realist critique' (Carr 1939, 81ff) crushed the 'naïve' reliance on the efficacy of world public opinion as a constraint on state action. Public opinion becomes a power resource. This realist conception 'turned mass-to-élite communication within a nation from the peaceful constraint envisioned after World War 1 into an indicator of national war potential akin to production indicators' (Bobrow 1972a, 38). The experience of psychological warfare in the Second World War reinforced the focus on the interpretation of propaganda, naturally with an increasing use of psychological concepts (see, *interalia,* Lasswell and Leites 1949).

Evaluation of the first phase

The first phase is thus marked by a focus on international political communication from the perspective of the state; that is, the actions of government or the state élite are explained in terms of the single drive of 'national interest'.

Communication and communications are important in that they change the environment of the state, and, in doing so, challenge the ability of government to govern. They also provide new instruments of policy for governments and groups within states. Hence, although the state is no longer totally regarded as a monolithic sovereign body (assumption 2) governments remain the only important actors in international politics and 'security' concerns are paramount. International communication is political only when it relates to these concerns. This initial phase is also notable because developments in the study of communication and other ways of thinking about International Relations, principally functionalism, reject the traditional, legal conceptions of the state and the nature of sovereignty (de Vree 1972). The study of politics gradually becomes less tied to institutional structures and more of an abstract analysis dealing with general political processes.

Second phase

General 'behavioural' influences

The second phase is characterized by its complexity. As previously suggested, the idea of a single continuum does not reflect the 'real-life' convergence of many diverse influences. Any analysis of each influence and its probable results in isolation will of necessity underestimate their dynamic interaction. Nevertheless, some such analysis will be attempted, bearing in mind the above caveat. In this phase the communications literature, in common with other political science writings, exhibits a dissatisfaction with the realist explanations, both on a substantive and methodological level. Realist analyses are criticized as being limited in their understanding of international politics, restricted in their policy relevance and lacking in conceptual rigour. In particular the failure to investigate such key concepts as 'national interest' and 'power' restricts the analysis to specific historical situations. At the same time the growing use of psychological concepts increasingly focuses attention on the individual, in terms of the observation and measurement of behaviour. As Easton (1953, 202) points out, the premise of behavioural research 'is that the traditionalists have been reifying institutions, virtually looking at them as entities apart from their component individuals'. Clearly, the necessity of borrowing psychological and social-psychological concepts to explain International Relations reflects the perceived inadequacy of the existing terms. More importantly, the borrowing of concepts signified a desire to move away from the historically limited institutional emphasis, towards a more abstract analysis searching for patterns of behaviour susceptible to empirical testing. Dahl (1969, 767) has identified what became known as the behavioural approach as 'an attempt to improve our understanding of politics by seeking to explain the empirical aspects of political life by means of methods, theories and criteria of proof that are acceptable according to the canons, conventions and assumptions of modern empirical science'. Any attempt to account for the adoption of this 'approach' would have to consider the prestige of the 'queen' of the social sciences in America – economics, which had already undergone its behavioural revolution (for one analysis of the genesis of the behavioural approach see Dahl, 1969). It is sufficient here to note that the evolution of this approach has several implications for the development of communications analysis and its relationship with the field of International Relations in general.

Firstly, the focus on individuals tends to negate the unitary 'state-as-actor' assumption, although, as is suggested in Chapter 7 this may merely lead to the substitution of 'decision-makers' for 'state'. Similarly, the analysis of individuals in group or organizational situations tends to break down the monolithic nature of the state (see, e.g. Deutsch 1954). Secondly, the behavioural approach is inherently concerned with quantification. If the analysis deals with observable behaviour (between individuals, groups or larger entities) then the search for uniformities and patterns of behaviour centres on the indicators which measure this behaviour. Hence the problem of formulating indicators and gathering sufficient data based on the indicators to generate propositions about world politics (see Russett et al. 1964 for a discussion of the problems of formulating indicators). Thirdly, with the broadening of political analysis away from its former base the established concepts are revealed as inadequate. It is the search for new and relevant concepts that pushes politics into sciences and other social sciences, such as cybernetics, psychology and economics. Allied to the search for new concepts is an increasing awareness of the importance of methodology, particularly the conscious use of 'models' of political behaviour. A model is here taken to be any possible representation of political reality. According to Pettman (1975, 32), 'A model is a replica of the form of the system under scrutiny; it is a structural simulation that is held to correspond in some way to that system.' What is included in this 'replica' is closely influenced by the particular approach utilized. As will be seen a communications (or cybernetic) model isolates information flows as a prime determinant of political behaviour. A model is also related to theory. The essential difference between a model and a theory is one of inclusiveness. Alternative models of a particular system or process may exist side by side, whereas a theory has a certain exclusivity, a 'definitiveness of explanation' (see Davies and Lewis 1971, 19ff, for a discussion of this point). Although we shall return to this problem, it is important to point to the emergence of a cybernetic model as part of this general influence, particularly Karl Deutsch's (1948–49) initial work, 'The role of models in the natural and social sciences'.

Finally, one of the significant effects of the behavioural 'mood' is to break down the distinction between domestic and international politics. In the search for generalized statements international politics becomes just one case of political behaviour and not inherently *sui generis*. Related to this is the use of more than one level of explanation. Whereas the traditional assumptions provided 'an exclusively third-image' explanation (Lijphart 1974, 58) that is from the point of view of the international system as a whole, the breakdown of the 'state-as-actor' provides another level of explanation (but, for the problems this generates, see Singer 1961, Moul 1973). It is no longer sufficient to explain a particular phenomenon solely in terms of the imperatives and 'compulsions' of international politics. We now need to complement this level with an understanding of the behaviour of men in organizations, of which the state is but one of many. Recent communication-based studies of political integration, among others, have stressed the importance of this multilevel analysis (e.g. Cobb and Elder 1970, Puchala 1972).

Communications in the second phase
The result of this *mélange* of influences is to generate over a period of time and under the rubric of communications, diverse sets of writings clustering around certain themes, utilizing particular techniques and investigating particular topics. Because of the diffuse nature of these writings it is difficult to ascribe an order to them. Elsewhere it has been argued that any attempts to link the various modes of studying international political communication is 'tenous at best' (Bobrow 1972a, 55), because the topics have little commonality. What will be done here, therefore, is not to try to fit the work into any overarching framework, but to identify particular sets of writings that have emerged as categories of research and publication.

Two major categories have been evident, the 'instrumental' and the 'approach'. Two further subcategories have been derived from the work on communications as an 'approach', namely the attempt to map relationships between political units utilizing the concept of 'transaction', and the related focus on political integration. While not suggesting that these are in any way mutually exclusive, the two initial categories are particularly distinctive from the point of view developed in this chapter.

The instrumental category: development. 'Instrumental' is taken to mean those writings concerned to apply insights, concepts and techniques drawn mainly from psychology, social psychology, research on media and media technology to the existing state-centric analysis (assumption 1), largely within the 'security politics' framework (assumption 3). In a sense, then, these writings see communication and communications as a 'tool' of analysis and of foreign policy. For example, the insights generated by a communications analysis of the American mishandling of the attack on Pearl Harbor may be used to redesign the channels through which messages travel (Wohlstetter 1962). Alternatively, the rapid development of mass communications provides the state with new policy instruments through the increased number of channels (for propaganda) and better understanding of the effects of the content (see e.g., Martin 1971). As such the writings extensively reflect the traditional concerns of diplomacy (see the discussion of the first phase). However, the application of social-psychological concepts in itself generates new concerns, namely: 'A social-psychological analysis, in exploring the intersection between psychological processes and system processes, can contribute precisely because it makes problematic some of the propositions that are often taken for granted' (Kelman 1970, 4-5).

Various analyses have been concerned with how the changing nature of communications technology influences diplomacy (Hoffman 1968), the inefficiency of traditional diplomacy because it is 'an instrument of contest' in a power situation (Burton 1968, 264), with a related attempt to remedy the deficiencies through 'controlled communication' (Burton

1969); and prescriptive advice to diplomats (e.g. Fisher 1972). A common feature of these writings has been the need to modify and supplement traditional forms of interaction in the face of a rapidly changing world.

The increasing speed of technological innovation after the Second World War had two effects on communications analysis. In particular the development of nuclear weapons refocuses attention on communication between national élites, normally in a contest or bargaining situation (Ag→ Bg→ Ag in Fig. 10.2). It becomes imperative, not only to understand, but to control, the flow of signals from élite to élite, either in terms of borrowing models of abstract choice (Schelling 1960), or simulation techniques (Guetzkow et al. 1963), or in general ahistorical, social–psychological terms (see, for instance, the articles in Kelman 1965). In this process the scope of international communication is extended to mean 'all behaviours by one actor of which another could be aware' (Bobrow 1972a, 41). This moves the study of international political communication a long way from formal, governmental messages and channels. Secondly, and in a more general sense, the development of communication technology raises new political problems: for instance, what influences opinion on world affairs (Hero 1959), or how individuals perceive and react to their government's foreign policy (Kelman 1969). However, if the world is now seen as a multilevelled communication network then the problem for the study of International Relations is one of identifying relevant political communication. To say that *political* communication is that which 'significantly affects the power position of one actor relative to others' (Merritt 1972a, 11), tends to beg the question. Most of the studies considered within this phase seem to implicitly limit 'political' to our security politics assumption, or to the activities of states.

As part of the general adoption of psychological concepts, such as 'image', (particularly Boulding, 1956) 'belief system' and 'perception', concern with communication becomes linked with decision-making analysis. If the communication perspective emphasizes the receiver of a message, the perception of and response to this message is critical. Moreover, the receiver, almost by definition, is likely to be a member of a governmental organization and the response can be accounted for by the concept of 'decision'. Specifically, the application of stimulus–response model to crisis (security?) situations focuses on the perception of the stimulus by decision-makers (Holsti 1972). Robert North (1967, 307) claims a particular correspondence, 'In the nation state the perception of the stimulus (S) within a decision system corresponds to the "definition of the situation" in the decision-making literature'.

Here, the technique of content analysis is utilized because, as is implied, the intention is to discover the perceived content of the message (North et al. 1963) in the belief that it is the content which often determines which messages 'will be recognized and transmitted with special speed and attention, and which other messages will be neglected or rejected' (Deutsch and Rieselbach 1965, 152). A second technique is that of survey research, which is of particular use in studies of public opinion and élite attitudes (see particularly, Singer 1965, Part Two, section E).

The instrumental category: evaluation. In summary, writings in the 'instrumental' category display most of the influences discussed under the impact of behavioural analysis, namely, sender–receiver patterns occur at all levels, not only the state (see Alger, 1965, 1968, for a communication analysis within the UN); the individual and the individual in an organization become the principal foci; both messages and channels are quantifiable, and new concepts are utilized to break down the distinction between domestic politics and international politics. These influences have broadened the analysis out from its original concern with state institutions and formal interstate relationships. However, on the whole, they do not posit alternative explanations (for a discussion of the notion of explanation, see Reynolds 1973, 319ff). That is, they do not seek to replace the realist power model of International Relations (in terms of our three assumptions), but generally slot their new concepts, insights and techniques into a state-centric (assumption 1) and security-politics (assumption 3) world.

The communications approach: development. Our second category, the communications 'approach' promises to offer a different explanation of world politics in that it attempts to isolate particular variables and to establish a different set of cause–effect relationships. The key to this approach is the claim by Wiener (1968, 18), previously noted in the Introduction to this chapter, 'that society can only be understood through a study of the messages and the communication facilities which belong to it. . .' The communications approach consists of the application of the concepts of cybernetics, developed by Weiner (1948, 1968) and Ashby (1952, 1956) to politics. The principal exponent of this application has been Karl Deutsch and in this second phase we shall, therefore, concentrate on Deutsch's work in this field.

There seems to be three distinct processes involved in his application of cybernetics to politics:

1. 'Thinking about thinking': that is, the use of models in social science.
2. The development of a cybernetic model.
3. The application of this model to politics.

1. From our previous discussion of the impact of behaviouralism it should be reasonably clear what is meant by the term 'model'. Deutsch provides a similar interpretation. For him a model is 'a structure of symbols and operating rules which is supposed to match a set of relevant points in an existing structure or process' (Deutsch 1952,

357). In this sense a model helps us to understand more complex processes. The link between a (cybernetic) model and the process or structure it is modelling is by 'analogy' or 'metaphor': 'analogy means limited structural correspondence' (Deutsch 1963, 78). Deutsch (1948/9) was among the first to make explicit and implicit models of past explanations, and he was able to see the specific analogy between servo-mechanisms and human society, specifically human organizations, namely: 'Modern studies of communications engineering suggests that the behaviour of human organizations, peoples and societies has important relations in common with manmade communications networks, such as servomechanisism, switchboards and calculating machinery...' (Deutsch 1968 (1948), 389). Moreover, he was the first to attempt to apply cybernetic concepts to political behaviour, principally in his *Nationalism and Social Communication* (1953). The nature of the relationship between the model and 'reality' need not be fully understood for the model to be useful. According to Deutsch (1952, 361), 'If the model is related to the thing modelled by laws which are not clearly understood, the data it yields may serve as indicants'. This becomes particularly important when we consider the 'transaction' literature in International Relations. A second, related point is that the type of model developed by Deutsch is intended to give priority to certain variables in order to explain the political process. It determines the 'exclusion–inclusion of variables' (Teune 1964, 294) in that 'it suggests that the particular aspects to which it corresponds are in fact the important aspects of the thing for the purposes of the model makers or users' (Deutsch 1952, 358).

2. The second process has emanated from Deutsch's concern with the inability of existing models to 'effectively represent' crucial relationships in social science, such as problems of growth and adaptation involving learning and purpose (Deutsch 1952, 358 and similarly 1963, 38). By the use of cybernetic concepts these crucial relationships can be isolated, identified and 'treated in quantitative terms'. The development of cybernetics applied to society is difficult to separate from that of systems analysis. Both Deutsch and Easton (1965) utilize similar concepts, such as information and feedback, and both see the political process in similar terms; that is, in terms of demands that are converted into binding decisions in exchange for support. The distinction is that social sciences are concerned with systems that are steered. In de Vree's (1972, 60) terms, 'Cybernetics, one might say, is concerned with a particular kind of system, namely one that is steered and that is 'conceived in terms of communication and information'. Moreover, in strict cybernetic terms this communication is *political* if it involves the transmission of political messages: demands, support and binding decisions (de Vree 1972, 209).

It is also important to note that a cybernetic model is a very general, abstract one and its principal concepts may acquire different meanings according to the particular system to which they are applied, be it a computer, an irrigation system, the human brain or society. In its most abstract form, then, a cybernetic system is 'a set of communication processes through which certain impulses, information, which it receives from the environment, are processed into impulses which the system in its turn releases into the environment' (de Vree 1972, 91). In order to do this certain structures within the system must receive and transmit information (detectors and effectors). However, a cybernetic system is *steered* towards a particular goal, and as the system exists in a changing environment it needs structures to enable it to 'steer'. Deutsch (1964a, 61) characterizes these as 'decision areas'. Decisions are taken on the basis of information intake evaluated in terms of 'memory'. Hence, a 'decision area may be pictured as one where incoming messages are combined with recalled memories for determining the output of the system' (Deutsch 1964a, 62). As cybernetics stresses the 'full dynamics' of a system it must also allow for changes in organizational behaviour brought about by changes in the environment. In other words the organization 'learns' (Deutsch 1963, 91ff), via the process of 'feedback'. By 'feedback' is meant 'a communication network which produces action in response to an input of information and includes the results of its own action in the new information by which it modifies its subsequent behaviour' (Deutsch 1968 (1948), 390–1, and Deutsch 1963, 88). Instead of communication being linear, as in Fig. 10.1, the system is pictured as circular, with feedback from the receiver affecting the continued flow from the sender. The system's ability to learn and, therefore achieve its goals despite changes in the environment and within itself, is determined by its 'capacity', 'capability' or 'power', as well as four other factors: load, lag, gain and lead (for definitions, see Deutsch 1963, 187–8). Of particular interest is the relationship between 'load' and 'capability' because in this conception the 'balance between loads and capabilities' is critical to an understanding of the political system's ability to survive and grow. The basic concepts included thus far present a fairly simple notion of a cybernetic system. It now remains to apply the cybernetic model to society and politics.

3. Deutsch's application of the cybernetic model and its principal concepts to politics has been more than adequately described and evaluated elsewhere (see, *inter alia,* de Vree 1972, Young 1968a, Davies and Lewis 1971, and Lieber 1973). However, from the developmental perspective the formative years of 1952–4 are important. Most of the relevant and political applications are to be found in the early writings of Deutsch, principally 'On communication models in the social sciences' (1952), *Nationalism and Social Communication* (1953); and *Political Community at the International Level* (1954). His later works and those of his 'followers', often merely reformulate concepts and measurements without developing the approach (de Vree 1972, 173).

Starting with an enquiry into the basis of nationalism in terms of information and communication Deutsch develops a set of measurable definitions. He is concerned to focus on the concept of 'community'. For him 'a community consists of people who have learned to communicate with each other and to understand each other well beyond the mere interchange of goods and services' (Deutsch 1953, 91).

One result of the emphasis on communication is to point to the importance of boundaries as 'among members or parts of an organization there should be more rapid and effective communication than with outsiders' (Deutsch 1963, 205). These are not formal frontiers but result from the clustering of communication networks because 'the more effective a social communication system gets, the more sharply separate does it become from all those groups or languages which it cannot incorporate: unable to bear promiscuity, it must choose marriage or divorce' (Deutsch 1953, 175). Within this communication network exists a 'society' viewed as a 'group of individuals made interdependent by the division of labour, the production and distribution of goods and services' (Deutsch 1953, 87). Although the concept of interdependence is here used in a national context it later becomes central to a number of writings on international interdependence. Also of importance is the notion of 'transaction'. This is perhaps best characterized in Deutsch's later writings, although implicit at this stage, as thinking of communities 'partly in terms of the probability of mutual transactions between residents because their transactions would be more frequent or important within these communities than within any others' (Deutsch 1964a, 50). The cybernetic aspects of nationalism are considered as national consciousness and will, seen in terms of the process of autonomous control. It is the equation of communication with control that makes a communications network political.

Deutsch (1954) extends his application of these concepts to the international level and, as is perhaps to be expected from our security-politics assumption, is initially concerned with political community between states in the context of peace and war. His central concept is of a 'security community, a group which has developed the institutions and processes 'to assure peaceful change among (its) members . . . with "reasonable" certainty over a "long" period of time' (Deutsch 1954, 33). A security community then, is a product of 'integration', and the integration process includes psychological role-taking and processes leading to mutual interdependence and mutual responsiveness. He is particularly concerned to elucidate the relationship between the ability of a political community (defined as 'a community of social transaction supplemented by both enforcement and compliance' (Deutsch 1954, 40)) to balance its loads and capabilities, inasmuch as the stability of such a community 'depends on its continuing capabilities to produce peaceful adjustments against the growing load of social interaction and political friction' (Deutsch 1954, 42). Finally, recognizing that political integration is a multidimensional process he advocates a range of measures based on three main groupings, all of which are considered to be 'measurable'. These three groups are measures that test the compatability of autonomous groups, the distribution and balance of ranges of transaction and the volume and dimensions of transactions (Deutsch 1954, 51ff).

We have considered at some length Deutsch's early works in cybernetics and its initial application to politics because they contain the majority, if not all, of the important concepts which are later used or measured in different contexts. This is not to argue that all the following work stems directly from Deutsch but that his influence is central. The basis of his cybernetic model of politics is expanded to its most coherent statement in his *Nerves of Government* (1963), particularly in his elaboration of the model in the Appendix (1963, 259), while his later works, principally *The Analysis of International Relations* (1968a), and *Nationalism and its Alternatives* (1969) are wider ranging analyses incorporating contemporary research findings. Of particular interest is his characterization of the nation-state and the international system by a number of communication-based measures centred on the concept of interdependence. For Deutsch the major distinction between international and intranational relations is that 'interdependence among countries is spectacularly lower than interdependence with countries' (1968b, 89). In this phase, also, Deutsch's cybernetic model is used by Burton (1965) to formulate a general theory of International Relations prefaced on the assumption that the policy outcomes of such a perspective will better reflect the 'true' nature of world politics. For Burton, as for Deutsch, power becomes incidental, unimportant in terms of communication needs (1965, 47, for a critique of Burton, see Morse 1969, 314ff).

The communications approach: evaluation. In the historical sense the impact of Deutsch's work on the study of International Relations is threefold. Firstly, the communications approach no longer sees power as the key variable in the explanation of political phenomena. In communications 'power is . . . neither the center nor the essence of politics' (Deutsch 1963, 124). Instead of power the essence of politics becomes 'the dependable coordination of human efforts and expectations for the attainment of the goals of the society' (Deutsch 1963, 124). International politics, then, is not necessarily limited to security concerns (assumption 3). Secondly, there is a strong emphasis on the empirical nature of the concepts. The attempt is to 'operationalize' each concept through measurement and mapping. Quantitative data is not seen as a substitute for other types of analysis but as complementary in that it 'could do much to check, strengthen or confirm the judgement of the historian or political analyst' (Deutsch 1954, 48). Finally, the communications approach is not restricted to any one level of analysis. It is equally relevant to groups, peoples, organizations of any size, including the state, and relationships between these units. In other words, the unit of analysis is not necessarily the state, suggesting the possibility of non-state actors (assumption 1). The implication is that the processes and structures that the communications approach deals with have important similarities. The international system, then, is not intrinsically different and can be analysed using the same concepts as domestic politics. The language of communications can therefore provide a key to foreign policy as well as the working of the international system because it provides a possible common approach which transcends the traditional boundary of political science and International Relations (Wallace 1971, 7).

Concepts drawn from the model have since been applied to two very broad and overlapping fields, seen here as subcategories. In one sense both relate to the relative significance of interstate as opposed to intrastate politics (Morse 1969, 31). The data generated by the attempt to describe patterns of transaction and consequent levels of interdependence provide a map of interactions within the system as a prerequisite to judging the significance of these relationships. However, this leads to problems when we consider the phenomena of political integration because integration itself transcends both the boundary between the state and its environment, and in its study, the traditional subject boundary between political science and International Relations in that it is a general phenomenon, neither purely national or international in kind.

Integration. Chapter 11 of this book will consider 'Integration theory' in greater depth. What will be attempted here is briefly to trace the origins and development of a communications approach to integration and, in a later section, to examine the strengths and weaknesses of such an approach. Building on the conceptual framework of *Political Community at the International Level* (1954) Deutsch and his associates at Princeton apply these concepts to a historical study of the North Atlantic area (Deutsch et al. 1957), again with an emphasis on values, responsiveness, capabilities and loads. Using transactions as the principal indicator the authors suggest the following process of integration: an intensive flow of transactions will eventually establish mutual relevance between the important political actors, this will create patterns of interaction that will lead to the emergence of a 'security community' (Mally 1973, 34). This conception of integration represents a fundamental break with earlier institutional theories. Also Deutsch emphasizes the importance of the wider community; 'people-to-people' loyalties are important, not just the élite but all 'politically relevant strata'.

In what is essentially a dialectical process concepts and measurement have been modified over time, but the central concern has remained the study of transactions in the search for two broad patterns: (1) high absolute volumes of international transactions – social, economic, cultural and political – that would indicate international community; (2) community is also indicated by 'increasingly marked discontinuities in transactions between members of an emerging community and surrounding 'external populations' (Puchala 1970, 743).

Russett (1963, 1967) has developed a particular notion of integration based on loads, capabilities and responsiveness. He elaborates on the distinction between two kinds of capabilities (originally, Deutsch et al. (1957), 40). These are the capacity to act, corresponding to the traditional view of power, and capabilities for responsiveness, comprising the facilities in a particular system for attention, communication and mutual identification (Russett 1963, 27ff). In this study Russett (1971, 228) sees integration as 'the process of building capabilities for responsiveness relative to the loads put on the capabilities'. He also makes the important point that some factors which affect responsiveness are 'not measurable as transactions' (Russett 1963, 208), suggesting implicitly that other dimensions are necessary to understand the process of integration. Although he suggests the potential importance of 'non-transaction' factors he does not follow this up in *Community and Contention* (1963). This is left to Jacob (1964), in an important collection of essays on integration as a phenomenon. Jacob modifies the original communications process by stressing that in addition to social and economic factors, measured by transaction analysis, integration needs conscious decisions by policy-makers. Hence personal behaviour and the role of values are critical to any study of integration because it is people who decide to integrate or not.

Within this volume Deutsch restates the relevance of communication theory to political integration, including the use of transaction flows as indicators of political cohesion, without seeming to add much of substance to his original concepts except, perhaps, the notions of salience and convariance of rewards (Deutsch 1964a, 1964b). The problem remains to establish the importance of the various transaction measures to *political* integration. Social and economic transactions as such are not concerned with the traditional high politics of a security community and, moreover, the nature of integration may change over time. Once a security community is established institutions may become more important as the level of interaction increases and, therefore, demands an increased regulatory capacity. This difficulty is illustrated by Deutsch's study of *France, Germany and the Western Alliance* (1967) where he investigates five 'streams of evidence' to ascertain the scope and level of integration: élite interviews, mass-opinion polls, a content analysis of the Press, a survey of arms-control proposals and 'aggregate statistics of actual behaviour'. Based on the evidence from transactions indices (principally his RA Index) Deutsch (1967, 218) concludes that 'European integration has slowed since the mid-50s and it has stopped or reached a plateau since 1957–58'. While this conclusion and its methodology have been challenged (Inglehart 1967, Fisher 1969), Alker and Puchala (1968) offer a technical critique of Savage and Deutsch's RA Index and modify the original communications assumptions. Their argument rests on the claim that 'the level of economic interaction between nations can serve as a reliable *indicator* of the degree of political integration' (their emphasis, Alker and Puchala 1968, 288) thereby avoiding problems of cause–effect relationships and, indirectly answering the original criticism of the communications approach by Hoffman (1959). Here the use of an 'indicator' signifies that the relationship between 'transactions' and 'integration' is not clearly understood (Deutsch 1952, 361 and our earlier discussion).

Transaction analysis. Our final subcategory of research and publication is linked to the studies of integration, but is more directly concerned to map patterns of transactions and channels of communication between states. These patterns of transaction, variously interpreted, should enable us to make general statements about the international political system, such as 'The world is more/less interdependent now than in 1913'. The emphasis by Deutsch (1953) on transactions or communication flows in establishing boundaries implies the importance of the transactions of one unit of the system with other units in understanding the behaviour of that unit. The assumption is that if the transaction flows between units are aggregated for the relevant population in the system, then the resulting patterns can tell us something about the behaviour of the units in question. In terms of the international political system this involves a judgement of the relative significance of interstate politics and intrastate politics.

Deutsch (1954, 57) also implies a coincidence between transactions and the concept of interdependence, via intercommunication, but later makes this explicit (Deutsch 1966, 300). Interdependence and transactions are linked through the mutual predictability of behaviour within or between societies at different levels of transaction flows (Katzenstein 1975, 1022). High levels of transaction flows lead to consistent mutual predictability and therefore greater interdependence. Hence, the absolute volume and growth rates of transactions can signify changes in international interdependence, but to evaluate these changes Deutsch and others utilize the ratio between foreign and domestic transactions (Deutsch 1956, 1961, Deutsch and Eckstein 1961). The assertion of these studies, that national industralization, in its later stages, involves a decreasing reliance on external trade, affects International Relations in two ways. Firstly, it is precisely the industralized states that are 'important' in International Relations, and, secondly, if development means industralization then the world will become less interdependent as countries develop (Deutsch 1960b). Studies of various transactions, notably the trade/gross national product ratio, seem to indicate that 'international character of the world may have declined rather than increased during the last half-century' (Deutsch 1960a, 45). This has come about as a result of higher levels of integration and interdependence *within* states than between them (Deutsch 1968b).

Transactions analysis has also been used to measure patterns and identify channels and clusters of transactions that might signify groupings of states. Brams (1966) identifies various subsystems underlying the complex range of transactions of a group of states. Moreover, he makes the important theoretical point that transactions analysis is a systemic approach which 'deals specifically with the relations of nations: their substance and significance, the form they take *vis-à-vis* other nations, and *the effect of this form on national behaviour* (Brams 1966, 880, emphasis added, see also Singer 1961). The concern here is to focus attention on 'aggregated foreign state behaviour as a function of patterns of communication within and among states' (Haas 1974, 365). This type of analysis has been applied to airline traffic (Gleditsch 1967), the exchange of diplomats (Alger and Brams 1967) and to ranges of transactions, mainly economic, by Russett (1967, 1968) to establish regional subsystems. However, in all these studies the problem is to identify the significance of the transactions to the political behaviour studied.

Third phase

International Relations

The third phase of communications writing (late 1960s to date) reflects to a greater extent the concern of the discipline as a whole. These concerns have the effect of making the study of International Relations even more diffuse, and can briefly be characterized as follows:

(*a*) *Methodological concerns.* The discussion on methodology moves away from the attempt to construct a general or grand theory (McClelland 1972, 28) to consider concepts, approaches and models in a more self-conscious, eclectic and rigorous fashion. Young's careful analysis of the function and nature of an approach (1968) highlights the necessity of an explicit, rigorous analysis of concepts and models. This emphasis leads naturally to increased questioning of concepts, the empirical measures of these concepts, and the relationship between concept and 'measure' or 'indicator'.

However, the consequent identification and characterization of the traditional assumptions of International Relations as 'state-centric realism', and the inherent power of these assumptions to influence analyses, brings a possible unifying thread to what was thought to be two separate schools of thought. The 'great debate' in International Relations has usually been viewed as that between the 'traditionalists' and the 'behaviouralists' (Knorr and Rosenau 1969, Lijphart 1974), but from the point of view developed here the debate is perhaps spurious. Recent work suggests that, in the main, the 'behaviouralists', utilizing scientific approaches, have subsumed the assumptions of 'state-centric realism' (Handelman et al. 1973), only modifying one or other assumption rather than the focus as a whole.

(*b*) *Substantive concerns.* Here we have seen the emergence of problems in the international system that the state-centric approach does not help us to understand. These have variously been seen as involving the changing role of military force in International Relations, the increased role of communications across national borders and the degree of government involvement in economic welfare (Nye 1975), suggesting a more appropriate focus on cooperative as opposed to conflictural behaviour (see, particularly, Morse 1969, Puchala and Fagan 1974). As a result we are faced with an increase in the number and range of issues considered salient to international politics, particularly economic; a diversity of relevant actors, particularly multinational enterprises, and problems for the management of foreign policy arising from increased interdependence (Morse 1970, 1972a and b). These developments have been characterized in terms of interaction processes: 'vertical interaction (within the state) has made horizontal interaction (between states) relevant for political and government purposes' (Rosecrance and Stein 1973, 21). The general tenor is to emphasize the breaking down of the boundary between domestic and international politics.

Communications in the third phase

The development of the literature on communications can be clearly seen within this context. Increasing complexity and diversity of approaches and problems has blurred the boundaries of our analytical categories in the proliferation of research in this area. For instance, the contents of Prosser (1973) indicate wide variations in areas and techniques thought to be relevant (in some way) to International Relations. Moreover, other disciplines have come to offer a perspective on common problems of communication. Firth (1973) offers an anthropological perspective on symbols in communication. On a general level attempts have been made to summarize and integrate the diverse concepts into some overarching notions of communication in international politics (Merritt 1972, Prosser 1973). For example, the notions of content, expressed in terms of values or meaning, and transactions as developed by Deutsch, are brought together. As Merritt (1972a, 7) points out, if language and symbolism facilitates primary communication, 'flows or trade, mail and other transactions . . . create the "physical conditions for the communicative act"'. Meaning, then, can vary with patterns of transactions. Moreover, if communication is the transmissions of values then transactions themselves can redistribute values; for example, currency transfers. Merritt (1972a, 17) also acknowledges the importance of non-state actors, and in doing so highlights the potential political relevance of communication between multinational enterprises. Communication is now seen in the most general sense of 'any transmission of signs, signals or symbols between persons' (Merritt 1972a, 4), and at the highest level, as the transmission of ideas about the ends and means of social organizations (Prosser 1973).

These general overviews do not, however, isolate particular developments that are relevant. Within the writings here considered as 'instrumental' policy recommendations have involved behavioural techniques (Wedge 1971, Fisher 1972) and studies of specific channels consider the transnational impact of communication, particularly radio, as the 'only unstoppable medium of mass communication (Hale 1975, ix). The work falling within the communications 'approach' has principally applied Deutsch's communication model to specific situations. More importantly, Steinbruner (1974) has refined and extended the cybernetic analysis with concepts drawn from psychology to provide a rigorous decision-making analysis of policy-making at the state level. On the level of the international system, Bryen (1971, 26) has attempted to apply the cybernetic analysis through his concept of an action system, viewed as 'all the communications between two states'. It is the action system as an informal communications network which permits the notion of decision to be used in the analysis of the international political system, seen as involving communications between states aimed at producing decisions for that system. Finally, East has constructed a communications model of small state foreign policy behaviour. This study is important for two reasons – methodological and substantive. Firstly, it explicitly develops two contrasting models of foreign policy behaviour related to size; the 'conventional' and the 'communications', and proceeds to test these models with data based on the concept of a 'foreign policy event'. (For an elaboration of an 'event', see Hermann 1971, and Azar et al. 1972). Secondly, the general conclusions supports the communications model, namely: 'Small states act as they do precisely because of limitations on their organizational capacity and ability to monitor international affairs adequately. This leads to a lack of information, an inability to perceive situations at an early stage, and a tendency to employ high-commitment, high-risk types of behaviour' (East 1973, 576). This conclusion tends to reinforce Deutsch's and Russett's earlier concern with the relationship between capability and loads and the general problem of political systems, that of system overload.

The use of transactions in the study of political integration perhaps has shown greater changes. Here, again the concern is to analyse concepts' indicators and the relationship between them. In an important study based on the communications notion of mutual relevance Cobb and Elder (1970) develop a three-component model for the study of international collaboration. This model links various 'backgound' factors to the establishment of the 'mutual behavioural relevance' of two nations, through their transactions and interactions, and, thence, to levels of international collaboration. The model is empirically tested both in a global and regional context. Their findings challenge some of the previously held assumptions concerning integration, such as 'a necessary congruence among various integrative indicators'. That is, an increase in transactions is not necessarily linked to favourable perceptions (Cobb and Elder 1970, Ch. 8). After considering the different transaction indices, Puchala (1970) refines and widens the analysis by isolating 'indicative channels and patterns of *political* transaction' (1970, 755, his emphasis). Moreover, Russett (1971) continues the questioning of concepts by linking the relevance of transaction analysis to definitions of political integration. He also suggests that absolute volumes are not sufficient, that one 'must look for balance (in transaction flows), for their relationship to level of transactions with other, and for special political burdens' (Russett 1971, 240). The emphasis has been on identifying the political aspects of transactions, attempts to render transaction analysis more politically sensitive and the 'operational' and conceptual problems that this emphasis produces (see, particularly, Hughes 1971, 1972, Chadwick 1972). Apart from substantive findings which suggest that integration has continued (Puchala 1970), in contradistinction to Deutsch (1967), what has emerged is the importance of scrutinizing the assumed indicator/indicated relationships. That is, as transaction flow indices are limited to available quantitative data what do they *actually* indicate, and how is this linked to an understanding of political integration?

Similar problems are evident in the literature on transactions as indicators of international political system. Two themes have emerged. Given the increased salience of economic issues for governments, work on the notion of international interdependence has developed both a continuation and a critique of Deutsch's and Bram's original studies. For example, Katzenstein (1975), while accepting the critique of the transaction focus, has, nevertheless used transaction data in the analysis of interdependence: for him, 'Transaction data provide . . . one basis for inferring changes in international interdependence' (Katzenstein 1975, 1021). The application of Deutsch's indicators to recent (post-1951) data has reversed his and Kuznets (1966) assertion of a secular decline in international interdependence as measured by transactions. The relationship between transactions and interdependence is central to the critique of transaction analysis developed by Cooper (1968), Young (1968b), Morse (1969, 1972a), and Rosecrance and Stein (1973). The critique is both substantive, in that it challenges the assertion that international interdependence has been decreasing, and methodological, in that it suggests that transactions are 'not in themselves appropriate indicators of interdependence' (Morse 1972a, 39). The second theme has been the development of a complementary class of data to characterize the international behaviour of states. If transactions are numerous, commonplace and normally measured in aggregate (trade flows, immigration, etc.), then it is clear that other forms of behaviour are important to International Relations. These other forms have been characterized as 'event-interactions': 'single action events of nonroutine, extraordinary or newsworthy character that in some clear sense are directed across national boundaries and have in most instances a specific foreign target' (McClelland and Hoggard 1969, 713, and see Azar et al. 1972).

Communications in the third phase: evaluation

This diverse literature has both undermined and strengthened the traditional assumptions. Generally, work in communications has contributed towards a wider conception of the political process, particularly an awareness of the role of individual and group within the political framework of the state (assumption 2: states act as coherent units). Deutsch (1953) pointed to the potential importance of economic interdependencies to political processes and to a certain extent pre-empted the challenge to the 'realist' assumption ('political–military security concerns are the dominant objective and motivations of states'). However, it is only recently that the importance of non-state corporate actors, as suggested by Wolfers (1962, 19ff), has been specifically acknowledged (see e.g. Merritt 1972a). It is also important to note that much of the communications analysis has reinforced the focus on the state as the sole important actor in International Relations. Clearly, it is difficult to evaluate the precise contribution of the communications literature to the understanding of International Relations. To do so requires an explicit consideration of the criteria of evaluation. The foregoing has hopefully indicated the development of the field of communications analysis, its assumptions, methodology and conclusions and how it has formed part of the continuing endeavour to understand International Relations. In the final section we shall move to a consideration of the limitations and usefulness of the field in the complexity of contemporary world politics.

Communications as theory

The meanings of theory in International Relations

It is reasonable to suppose that any evaluation of communications will be based on a particular set of assumptions. In the past 'behavioural' phase these assumptions have emphasized the status of 'theory' and the contribution to 'theory' construction. However, it is now recognized that 'theory' production is not the sole criteria by which to judge the contribution of a body of concepts (Young 1972, Bobrow 1972b). Hence we need to establish the identity and status of the communications concepts before we can offer an evaluation: if the communications literature is indeed 'theory', then our evaluation will differ from that if it were not.

The initial problem is that the term 'theory' has no consistent usage, 'the word is used in a number of different senses, and it covers a whole range of somewhat different meanings' (de Vree 1972, 3). At one extreme theory is considered as any kind of abstract reasoning; at the other it is used in a specific sense, closely akin to its meaning in the natural sciences. Dougherty and Pfaltzgraff (1971, 27), for instance, have identified six usages of the term 'theory', apart from its natural science sense. The debate on the possibility and, if so, the desirability of a specific natural science meaning for International Relations theory has formed the backdrop to the development of the discipline (Knorr and Rosenau 1969, Reynolds 1973), but, in general, the behavioural use of 'theory' has been closely related to the use of the natural sciences. Hence, when a work is criticized for not being 'theory' two assumptions are involved. Firstly, the 'theory' it is not, is, in fact, a quite specific form of knowledge. Secondly, the activity of producing this specific form is preferable, more 'worthwhile', than other kinds of activity because the 'product', that is 'theory', is desirable. This specific sense of theory is characterized by Young (1972, 180): 'A theory is a set of general statements such that:

(1) some of the statements (the assumption or premises) logically imply the others (the theorems); and
(2) the theorems can be cast in the form of falsifiable predictive statements about the real world'.

Communications as theory

If this sense of theory is accepted then the bulk of the communications literature is patently not theory. It does not meet the criterion of ahistorical definition, nor the necessity for 'if . . . then' relationships between concepts, and, moreover, it is extremely difficult to state the situations in which the assumptions hold (its scope conditions). Given the difficulty of translating some of the communications concepts, such as autonomy, load, and perception into a 'testable' and causal form, it is not surprising that the 'theoretical import has been skimpy' (Haas 1974a, 365); despite Deutsch's aim 'to develop *eventually* a theory of politics, both national and international' (1963, xxv, emphasis added). Deutsch's own formulations were explicitly not theory but parts of an 'ongoing enterprise' to be developed into theory at some, unspecified, later stage. However, the attempts to arrive at theory using communications concepts, and hence produce a particular form of explanation (if . . . then), have foundered on the rock of cause and effect. For example, Puchala (1970, 762) specifically states, in regard to integration, '*transaction flows do not cause regional integration*' (his emphasis).

Communications, then, does not present theory, but that is not to say the concepts and findings of this literature are not useful. The explanations of phenomena that are produced may not be scientific explanations that are the products of behavioural theory, yet they may be the 'best' we have. It has been argued that we can regard a substantial part of the literature as forming an approach, and that an approach functions not only to isolate or select information considered relevant (the perceptual screen) but also to give order and assign priority to the screened information (Young 1968, 11ff). Secondly, it has also been suggested, in reference to Deutsch's work on models, that specific models are derived from the approach (that is, they are less general) because they help us to understand complex processes by isolating certain 'important' variables. Hence, we need to evaluate both the general approach and the specific derived models.

The communications approach: an evaluation

By its very nature an approach has no prior criteria of relevance. Its 'explanatory potential' is only evident after the approach has been applied (Pettman 1975). The adoption of a communications approach is largely a leap in the dark, an 'act of the faith' (perhaps as a result of 'professional' conditioning) about the possible advantage of its use. Bobrow (1972b, 206) has suggested that the term 'metatheory' is more appropriate because this suggests a perspective, 'often in the form of an analogy'. The only hope we have about the use of an approach, or a metatheory, is that we expect it to be helpful to our understanding. Generally, the development of an approach has the effect of 'sensitizing' us to facts, and thereby suggesting explanations that might have been previously ignored (Young 1972, 187, Bobrow 1972b, 207). Deutsch and his followers are explicit about this role, namely: 'recent models of communications and control may make us more sensitive to some aspects of politics that have often been overlooked or slighted in the past' (Deutsch 1967, 273 and Russett 1963, Preface). In sensitizing us to 'new' aspects of International Relations the communications approach contributes a vocabulary of political analysis. For instance, de Vree (1972, 167) characterizes Deutsch's work, particularly as 'one great attempt to develop a new language of politics'. This vocabulary enables us to conceptualize political processes in a particular way. Moreover, the claim is that 'communication theory [sic] further permits us to conceive of such elusive notions as consciousness and the political will as *observable* processes' (Deutsch and Rieselbach 1965, 157, emphasis added). 'Observable' in this context implies measurable, but the difficulty is what and how we actually measure 'national consciousness'. The concepts are suggestive, but no more.

In terms of the development of a new language, communications has indeed sensitized International Relations to a range of factors and phenomena. Minimally, a simple communication network, such as Fig. 10.1 suggests important considerations, both of understanding and improving the process of International Relations (see e.g. Scott 1967, Ch. 5). For example, 'does the receiver actually receive the message as the sender intended . . .?' (Phillips 1974, 179). At a different level the suggestion that we can explain the nature of a complex phenomenon, such as nationalism or international integration, through a study of social communication networks is a significant step in defining empirically the basis of a nation or the notion of integration. The important point, here, is that the majority of the communications concepts are heuristic. They suggest interesting conceptualizations of existing problems in International Relations and further suggest new problems which require further investigation. The concept of mutual relevance, for instance, suggests the importance of transactions and is successfully elaborated and 'indicated' by Cobb and Elder (1970) as part of a model of international collaboration.

It is, however, extremely difficult to point out 'better' explanations as a result of the application of the communications approach. At best we have a set of descriptions of particular processes and phenomena in International Relations. In some cases, notably integration, these provide generalizations that may be applicable to other situations, geographically and historically (see Seligson 1973, for one analysis outside Europe). North (1967, 30) emphasizes the systematic nature of description within the context of content analysis research: 'a well-designed communication study should measure systematically the correlation over time of *what is* said with *what is done,* and it should also uncover – impartially – consistencies and inconsistencies . . . in all that each actor for whom there is adequate data says and does'. The historical status of these descriptions is exemplified by *Political Community and the North Atlantic Area* (Deutsch 1957), which although developing a set of propositions (conditions) for integration, does so inductively from historical evidence. These propositions are limited to particular historical cases, which may be typical or untypical. In effect then, in most of the literature the communications approach provides a taxonomy, a framework for the orderly arrangement and examination of data (Dougherty and Pfaltzgraff 1971, 27). Concepts, such as 'loads', 'capabilities' and 'transactions' provide 'theoretical boxes in which to store empirical findings' (Gregor 1971, 581).

As previously mentioned a major difficulty is in measuring a political system's 'capability', 'load' or 'will', and because of this difficulty the application of the approach has been limited to describing the environment of the political system, seen as the state, and the focus on integration. The problems associated with the concept of 'transaction' are illustrative of the general difficulties of applying the approach. The basis of the problem is to establish the political salience of transactions. This arises from an ambiguity in Deutsch's original notion of communication, which, in strict cybernetic terms 'consists of the transmission of political messages: demands, support and binding decisions' (de Vree 1972, 209). The transmission of demands, support and binding decisions identifies with particular social communication system is the political system. A political analysis would, strictly speaking, have to identify and measure, through content analysis, these specific political messages. However, most of the empirical studies use the notion of communication in a wider sense. The volume and range of transactions, such as trade, capital flows, migration, travel, etc. form part of the communications environment of a political system and, to a certain extent, condition the demands of a certain population. Although all transactions are communications, transactions are not political in the strict sense; we need to know the message content of the transactions. Thus, the political salience of transactions needs to be demonstrated rather than assumed. Deutsch and Eckstein (1961, 271) attempt to link economic transactions to political outcomes, '(economic changes) constitute one relevant variable to influencing a political outcome through their effect on the resources and limitations in terms of which political choices are made'. The link between economics and politics is here through an 'interest group' which transforms economic demands into political decisions. The relaxation of the security-politics assumption (assumption 3) with the politicization of economic issues, and the consequent importance of economic interdependence, means that it is no longer necessary to construct this elaborate linkage. In this sense, economic transactions become more important to International Relations because they are not only a more salient part of the international environment, but also constitute the substance of political demands, support and decisions. A similar criticism has been aimed at the use of transactions in measuring integration: as transaction flows are not in themselves political how do they help us to understand political integration? Deutsch (1967) and others employ attitudinal findings as well, but the use of these merely begs the question of the relationship between transactions and attitudes (see Cobb and Elder 1970, Clark and Welch 1972). One solution is to return to Deutsch's original cybernetic sense of communication and to identify those transactions that are specifically political in that they constitute demands and support.

The problem remains, however, of establishing *what* communication is political. In the study of international communication what is political has usually been synonymous with the activities of states, either in the relationships between states or in the making of state foreign policy. Merritt (1972a, 11) suggests that communication is political if it 'significantly affects the power position of one actor relevant to others in a system'. In the international context the difficulties of applying such a test are manifold, and this notion seems to lead to more problems than it solves because power has tended to be associated with conflict. Hence, although the communications concepts are essentially transnational, they have been used mainly to relate to conflict issues (assumption 3), which is somewhat surprising given the emphasis on 'steering' rather than power.

The communication model

The derived cybernetic model (Deutsch 1963) can be evaluated on the same grounds as the approach, but as it explains less its explanations purport to be more precise. Two general points can be made. Firstly, the analogy is only justified to the extent that human processes and cybernetic processes are similar. Young's (1968a, 60) critique of the model is thorough, pointing out the logical consequences of the analogy, in that, for example, 'it does not deal adequately with the nuances of human thought processes . . . and the nebulous quality of many political relations'. Are political 'systems' simply goal-seeking entities? Here, Deutsch's (1963) model becomes so complex and formalized that it tends to negate its original purpose of helping to understand complex phenomena. Moreover, it has been suggested that such analogies as system and cybernetics merely '*simulate*' the transfer of knowledge from domains; 'we do know something of the system traits of servomechanical and cybernetic mechanisms; but we know next to nothing about the tolerance levels, feedback, loading and conversion properties of political "systems"' (Gregor 1971, 583). Secondly, given the generality of the model, its applicability to any organization and its emphasis on decision, how can it be applied to International Relations? Two possibilities are evident. The model can focus on the processes by which actors in International Relations make decisions affecting their international environments; or, it can be applied directly to communication flows in International Relations. Bryen (1971, 26) argues, however, that the latter cannot be attempted because there are 'only highly informal interfaces' between national systems. One area where the interfaces are less informal is, of course, the EEC, and, hence, the contined focus on integration. This leaves us with the application of the cybernetic model to the processes by which actors make decisions affecting their international environment, Bryen (1971) attempts to do this through his notion of an 'action system', whereas Steinbruner (1974) concentrates on the process of decision. While these works are open to the criticisms of the focus on decision (see Ch. 7), particularly if, as Bryen argues, 'cybernetic analysis is concerned with the making of *unusual* decisions' (Bryen 1971, 20, emphasis added), they do offer a different explanation of such processes. The critical point is made by Hoffman (1960, 47): 'The definition of values as the operating preferences according to which certain messages are transmitted first is a fine example of a statement which may be useful for cybernetics but is merely tautological in International Relations.'

Conclusion

In conclusion, the communications approach and its associated concepts offer one perspective on International Relations. This perspective has not yet provided theory but has provided a particular model of politics, the value of which needs to be demonstrated, and many useful empirically based descriptions of integration and the environment of states that have occasionally generated hypotheses. Despite the fact that the approach is essentially transnational, much work has concentrated on the state and/or conflict. Given the changing nature of contemporary International Relations the communications approach has significant potential.

References and Further Reading

Alger, C.F. and Brams, S.J. (1967) 'Patterns of representation in national capitals and inter-governmental organisations', *World Politics*,.

Alger, C.F. (1965) 'Personal contact in intergovernmental organisations', in H.C. Kelman (ed.), *International Behaviour: A Social-Psychological Analysis,* New York, Holt, Rinehart and Winston.

Alger, C.F. (1968) 'Interaction in a committee of the UN General Assembly', in J.D. Singer (ed.) *Quantitative International Politics: Insights and Evidence. International Yearbook of Political Behaviour Research,* vol. vi, New York, Free Press.

Alker, H. and Puchala, D. (1968) 'Trends in economic partnership: The North Atlantic Area, 1928–1963', in Singer, op. cit.

Azar, E.A., Brody, R.A. and McClelland, C.A. (1972) *International Events Interaction Analysis: Some Research Considerations,* Beverly Hills, Calif., Sage.

Ashby, W. Ross (1952) *Design for a Brain,* London, Methuen. 2nd edn, 1960, London, Chapman & Hall.

Ashby, W. Ross (1956) *An Introduction to Cybernetics,* London, Chapman & Hall; 2nd edn, 1964, London, Methuen.

Bobrow, D.B. (1972a) 'Transfer of meaning across national boundaries', in R.L. Merritt (ed.) *Communication in International Politics,* Urbana, Ill., Univ. of Illinois Press.

Bobrow, D.B. (1972b) 'The relevance potential of different products', in R. Tanter and R.H. Ullman (eds.), *Theory and Policy in International Relations,* Princeton, NJ, Princeton Univ. Press.

Boulding, K. (1956) *The Image,* Univ. of Michigan Press.

Brams, S.H. (1966) 'Transaction flows in the international system', *American Political Science Review,* **60** (4), (December) 880–98.

Bryen, S.D. (1971) *The Application of Cybernetic Analysis to the Study of International Politics,* The Hague, Nijhoff.

Burton, J.W. (1965) *International Relations: A General Theory,* London, Cambridge Univ. Press.

Burton, J.W. (1968) *Systems, States, Diplomacy and Rules,* London, Cambridge Univ. Press.

Burton, J.W. (1969) *Conflict and Communication,* London, Macmillan.

Carr, E.H. (1939) *The Twenty Years Crisis, 1919–39,* London, Macmillan.

Chadwick, R. (1972) 'A brief critique of "Transaction data and analysis: in search of concepte" by Barry Hughes', *International Organisation* xxvi, no 4 (Autumn) 1972.

Clark, C. and Welch, S. (1972) 'Western European trade as a measure of integration: untangling the interpretations', *Journal of Conflict Resolution,* **16,** 363–82.

Cobb, R.W. and Elder, C. (1970) *International Community: A Regional and Global Study,* New York, Holt, Rinehart & Winston.

Cooper, R.N. (1968) *The Economics of Interdependence: Economic Policy in the Atlantic Community.* New York, McGraw-Hill.

Dahl, R.A. (1969) 'The behavioural approach in political science: Epitaph for a monument to a successful protest' in H. Eulau (ed.) *Behaviouralism in Political Science,* New York, Atherton.

Davies, M.R. and Lewis, V.A. (1971) *Models of Political Systems,* London, Pall Mall.

Davison, W. Phillips, (1965) *International Political Communication,* New York, published for the Council on Foreign Relations by Praeger.

Deutsch, K.W. (1948–9) 'Some notes on research on the role of models in the national and social scenes', *Synthese,* **7,** 506–33.

Deutsch, K.W. (1952) 'On communication models in the social sciences'. *Public Opinion Quarterly,* **16** (Autumn), 356–80.

Deutsch, K.W. (1953) *Nationalism and Social Communication,* Cambridge, Mass., MIT Press.

Deutsch, K.W. (1954) *Political Community at the International Level: Problems of Definition and Measurement,* Hamden, Conn., Archon Books, 1970.

Deutsch, K.W. (1956) 'Shifts in the balance of international communication flows', *Public Opinion Quarterly,* xx (Spring), 143–60.

Deutsch, K.W. et al. (1957) *Political Community and the North Atlantic Area: International Organisation in the light of Historical Experience,* Princeton, NJ, Princeton Univ. Press.

Deutsch, K.W. (1960a) 'Towards an inventory of basic trends and patterns in comparative and international politics', *APSR* **54** (March).

Deutsch, K.W. (1960b) 'The propensity to international transactions', *Political Studies,* **8** (2), 147–55.

Deutsch, K.W. (1961) 'Social mobilisation and political development', *Americal Political Science Review,* **55** (3) (September).

Deutsch, K.W. (1963) *The Nerves of Government: Models of Political Communication and Control,* Glencoe, Ill., Free Press (2nd edn 1966).

Deutsch, K.W. (1964a) 'Communication theory and political integration', in P.E. Jacob and J.V. Toscano (eds.), *The Integration of Political Communities,* Philadelphia, Lippincott.

Deutsch, K.W. (1964b) 'Transaction flows as indicators of political cohesion', in Jacob and Toscano, op. cit.

Deutsch, K.W. (1966) 'Power and communication in international society', in A.V.S. de Reuek and J. Knights (eds.), *Ciba Foundation Symposium on Conflict in Society,* London, Churchill.

Deutsch, K.W. et al. (1967) *France, Germany, and the Western Alliance,* New York, Charles Scribner's Sons. 1967.

Deutsch, K.W. (1968a) *The Analysis of International Relations,* Englewood Cliffs, NJ, Prentice-Hall.

Deutsch, K.W. (1968b) 'The impact of communications upon international relations theory', in A. Said (ed.), *Theory of International Relations: The Crisis of Relevance,* Englewood Cliffs, NJ, Prentice-Hall.

Deutsch, K.W. (1969) *Nationalism and its Alternatives,* New York, Knopf, 1969.

Deutsch, K.W. and Eckstein, A. (1961) 'National industralization and the declining share of the international economic sector, 1890–1959', *World Politics,* **13** (January) 267–99.

Deutsch, K.W. and Rieselbach, L.N. (1965) 'Recent trends in political theory and political Philosophy', *Annals of the American Academy of Political and Social Science,* **360** (July) 139–62.

de Vree, J.D. (1972) *Political Integration: The Formation of Theory and its Problems,* The Hague, Montana.

Dougherty, J.E. and Pfaltzgraff, R.L. Jr. (1971) *Contending Theories of International Relations,* New York, Lippincott.

East, M.A. (1973) 'Size and foreign policy behaviour: A test of two models', *World Politics,* xxv (4) (July) 556–76.

Easton, D. (1953) *The Political System,* New York, Knofp (1971 edn.).

Easton, D. (1965) *A Framework for Political Analysis,* Englewood Cliffs, NJ, Prentice-Hall.

Firth, R. (1973) *Symbols – Public and Private,* London, Allen and Unwin.

Fisher, W.E. (1969) 'An analysis of the Deutsch sociocausal paradigm of political integration', *International Organisation,* **23** (2) (Spring), 254–90.

Fisher, G.H. (1972) *Public Diplomacy and the Behavioural Sciences,* Bloomington, Indiana Univ. Press.

Gleditsch, N.P. (1967) 'Trends in world airlines patterns', *Journal of Peace Research,* **4**, 366–407.

Gregor, A.J. (1971) 'Theory, metatheory and comparative politics', *Comparative Politics,* **3** (July), 575–85.

Guetzkow, H. et al. (1963) *Simulation in I.R.,* Englewood Cliffs, NJ, Prentice-Hall.

Haas, M. (1974a) *International Systems: A Behavioural Approach,* New York, Chandler.

Haas, M. (1974b) 'The future of international relations theory', in Haas, op. cit.

Handelman, J.R., Vasquez, J.A., O'Leary, M.K. and Coplin, W.D. (1973) 'Colour it Morgenthau: A data-based assessment of quantitative international relations', (mimeo), IR Program, Maxwell School, Syracuse, Syracuse University.

Hale, J. (1975) *Radio Power – Propaganda and International Broadcasting,* London, Elek.

Hermann, C.F. (1971) 'What is a foreign policy event', in W.F. Hanreider (ed.), *Comparative Foreign Policy,* New York, McKay, pp. 295–321.

Hero, A.O. (1959) *Mass Media and World Affairs,* Boston, World Peace Foundation.

Hoffman, S. (1959) 'International relations; the long road to theory'. *World Politics,* **3,** p. 346–377.

Hoffman, A.S. (ed.) (1968) *International Communication and the New Diplomacy,* London, Indiana Univ. Press.

Hoffmann, S. (1960) 'International relations as a discipline', in S. Hoffmann (ed.), *Contemporary Theory in International Relations,* Englewood Cliffs, Prentice-Hall.

Holsti, O.R. (1972) *Crisis, Escalation, War,* Montreal, McGill-Queen's Univ. Press.

Hughes, B.B. (1971) 'Transaction analysis: the impact of operationalization', *International Organisation,* xxv (1) (Winter), 132–45.

Hughes, B.B. (1972) 'Transaction data and analysis: In search of concepts', *International Organisation* xxvi (4) (Autumn).

Inglehart, R. (1967) 'An end to European integration?' *American Political Science Review,* **59** (1) (March), 91–105.

Jacob, P.E. (1964) 'The influence of values in political integration', in P.E. Jacob and J.V. Toscano (eds.), *The Integration of Political Communication,* Philadelphia, Lippincott.

Jacob, P.E. and Toscano, J.V. (eds.) (1964) *The Integration of Political Communities,* Philadelphia, Lippincott.

Katzenstein, P.J. (1975) 'International interdependence: Some long-term trends and recent changes', *International Organisation,* **29** (4) (Autumn) 1021–34.

Kelman, H.C. (ed.) (1965) *International Behaviour: A Social-Psychological Analysis,* New York, Holt, Rinehart and Winston.

Kelman, H.C. (1969) 'Patterns of personal involvement in the national System', in J.N. Rosenau (ed.), *International Politics and Foreign Policy,* London, Collier-Macmillan, pp. 276–88.

Kelman, H.C. (1970) 'The role of the individual in international relations: Some conceptual and methodological considerations', *Journal of International Affairs,* xxiv (1) 1–17.

Knorr, K. and Rosenau, J.N. (eds.) (1969) *Contending Approaches to International 'Politics',* Princeton, NJ, Princeton Univ. Press.

Kuznets, S. (1966) *Modern Economic Growth: Rate, Structure and Spread,* London, Yale Univ. Press.

Lasswell, H.D. (1927) *Propaganda Techniques in the World War,* New York, Knopf.

Lasswell, H.D. and Leites, N. (1949) Language of Politics in Stewart (ed.), *Studies in Quantitative Semantics,* New York.

Lasswell, H.D. (1948) 'The structure and function of communication in society', in L. Bryson (ed.), *The Communication of Ideas,* New York, Harper.

Lasswell, H.D. and Blumenstock, D. (1939) *World Revolutionary Propaganda,* New York, Knopf.

Lijphart, A. (1974) 'The structure of the theoretical revolution in international relations', *International Studies Quarterly,* **18** (1) (March).

McClelland, C.A. (1972) 'On the fourth wave: Past and future in the study of International systems', in J. Rosenau, V. Davis and M. East, *The Analysis of International Politics,* New York, Free Press.

McClelland, C.A. and Hoggard, G. (1969) 'Conflict patterns in the interactions among nations', in J.H. Rosenau (ed.), *International Politics and Foreign Policy,* New York, Free Press, pp. 711–24.

Mally, G. (1973) *The European Community in Perspective: The New Europe, the United States and the World,* London, D.C. Heath.

Martin, L.J. (ed.) (1971) 'Propaganda in international affairs', *Annals of the American Academy of Political and Social Science,* **398** (November).

Merritt, R.L. (1972a) 'Transmission of values across national boundaries', in R.L. Merritt (ed.), *Communication in International Politics,* Urbana, Ill., Univ. of Illinois Press.

Morse, E.L. (1969) 'The politics of interdependence, *International Organisation,* **23** (2) (Spring) 311–36.

Morse, E.L. (1970) 'The transformation of foreign policies: Modernization, interdependence, and externalization', *World Politics,* **22** (3) (April), 379–83.

Morse, E.L. (1972a) 'Transnational economic processes', *International Organisation*, xxv No. (3) (Summer); also in R.O. Keohane and J.S. Nye, Jr. (eds.), *Transnational Relations and World Politics,* Cambridge, Mass., Harvard Univ. Press.
Morse, E.L. (1972b) 'Crisis diplomacy, interdependence and the politics of international economic relations' in R. Tanter and R.H. Ullman (eds.), *Theory and Policy in International Relations,* Princeton, NJ, Princeton Univ. Press.
Moul, W.B. (1973) 'The level of analysis problem revisited', *Canadian Journal of Political Science,* **6.**
North, R.C. (et al.) (1963) *Content Analysis,* Evanston, Ill., Northwestern Univ. Press.
North, R.C. (1967) 'The analytical prospects of communications theory', in J.C. Charlesworth (ed.), *Contemporary Political Analysis,* London, Collier-Macmillan.
Nye, J.S. Jr. (1975) 'Transnational and transgovernmental relations', in G.L. Goodwin and A. Linklater (eds), *New Dimensions of World Politics,* London, Croom Helm.
Pentland, C. (1973) *International Theory and European Integration,* London, Faber & Faber.
Pettman, R. (1975) *Human Behaviour and World Politics,* London, Macmillan.
Phillips, W.R. (1974) 'International Communications', in M. Haas, *International Systems: A Behavioural Approach,* New York, Chandler.
Prosser, M.H. (ed.) (1973) *Intercommunication Among Nations and Peoples,* London, Harper and Row.
Puchala, D.J. (1970) 'International transactions and regional integration', *International Organisation,* xxiv (4), 732–63.
Puchala, D.J. (1972) 'Of blind men, elephants and international integration', *Journal of Common Market Studies,* **10** (3) (March), 267–84.
Puchala, D.J. and Fagan, S.I. (1974) 'International politics in the 1970s: The search for a perspective', *International Organisation,* **28** (3) (Summer).
Reynolds, C. (1973) *Theory and Explanation in International Politics,* London, Martin Robertson.
Rosecrance, R. and Stein, A. (1973) 'Interdependence: Myth or reality' *World Politics,* **26,** (1) (October) 1–27.
Russett, B.M. (1963) *Community and Contention: Britain and America in the 20th Century,* Cambridge, Mass., MIT Press.
Russett, B.M. et al. (1964) *World Handbook of Political and Social Indicators,* New Haven, Yale Univ. Press.
Russett, B.M. (1967) *International Regions and the International System,* Chicago, Rand McNally.
Russett, B.M. (1968) 'Delineating international regions', in J.D. Singer (ed.), *Quantitative International Politics: Insights and Evidence, International Yearbook of Political Behaviour Research,* vol. vi, New York, Free Press.
Russett, B.M. (1971) 'Transactions, community and international political integration', *Journal of Common Market Studies,* **9** (3) (March) 224–45, 22–919.
Scott, A.M. (1967) *The Functioning of the International Political System,* New York, Macmillan.
Schelling, T.C. (1960) *The Strategy of Conflict,* Cambridge, Mass., Harvard Univ. Press.
Seligson, M.A. (1973) 'Transactions and community formation: Fifteen years of growth and stagnations in Central America', *Journal of Common Market Studies,* **11** (3) (March), 173–90.
Singer, J.D. (1961) 'The level of analysis problem in international relations', *World Politics,* **14** (1) (October) 77–92.
Singer, J.D. (1965) *Human Behaviour and International Politics,* Chicago, Rand McNally.
Singer, J.D. (ed.) (1968) *Quantitative International Politics: Insights and Evidence. International Yearbook of Political Behaviour Research,* vol. vi, New York, Free Press.
Steinbruner, J.D. (1974) *The Cybernetic Theory of Decision: New Dimensions of Political Analysis,* Princeton, NJ, Princeton Univ. Press.
Tanter, R. and Ullman, R.H. (eds.) (1972) *Theory and Policy in International Relations,* Princeton, NJ, Princeton Univ. Press.

Teune, H. (1964) 'Models in the study of political integration', in P.E. Jacob and J.V. Toscano (eds.), *The Integration of Political Communities,* Philadelphia, Lippincott.

Wagner, R. Harrison, (1974) 'Dissolving the state: Three recent perspectives on international relations', *International Organisation,* **28** (3) (Summer), 435–66.

Wallace, W. (1971) *Foreign Policy and the Political Process',* London, Macmillan Press.

Wedge, Bryant, (1971) 'International propaganda and statecraft' in, L.J. Martin (ed.), 'Propaganda in international affairs', *Annals of the American Academy of Political and Social Science,* **398** (November).

Wiener, N. (1948) *Cybernetics,* Cambridge, Mass., MIT Press.

Wiener, N. (1968) *The Human Use of Human Beings,* London, Sphere Books (originally published New York, Houghton Mifflin, 1950).

Wohlstetter, R. (1962) *Pearl Harbor: Warning and Decision,* Stanford, Calif., Stanford Univ. Press.

Wolfers, A. (1962) *Discord and Collaboration,* Baltimore, Johns Hopkins Press.

Young, O.R. (1968a) *Systems of Political Science,* Englewood Cliffs, NJ, Prentice-Hall.

Young, O.R. (1968b) 'Interdependencies in world politics', *International Journal,* **24** (1) (Winter).

Young, O.R. (1972) 'The perils of Odysseus: On constructing theories of international relations, *World Politics,* xxiv (Spring).

Chapter 11

Integration theory

Michael Hodges

The origins of integration theory: Old wine in new bottles

As with many other contemporary theories of International Relations, integration theory is a relatively new and explicit way of looking at an old problem, namely the merger of two or more states to form a new and larger state – a phenomenon which has long been of interest to both students and practitioners of the occult arts of world politics. Although most of the significant attempts to theorize about supranational integration have been made only within the last two or three decades, it would be misleading to suggest that integration theory sprang full-formed from the brows of contemporary (and mainly American) political scientists. Indeed, as this chapter will make clear, the controversy surrounding the search for a form of organization transcending the nation-state is almost as old as the modern state system itself, and was generated by dissatisfaction with the working of that system and the conflict which appeared to be an intrinsic part of it.

Integration theory is controversial because, firstly, there is little agreement on how the dependent variable ('integration') is to be defined, or on whether it is a process or a condition. Is integration, like legal sovereignty, indivisible? Can a group of states come to be 'integrated' into a regional grouping without submerging their identities therein? In addition to the problems of definition and methodology, to be discussed below, we must add the difficulty of dealing with a body of theory which contains an appreciable dose of normative social engineering in addition to the guidelines it provides for empirical observation of integrative behaviour.

A brief glance at some definitions of integration will perhaps serve to indicate why regional integration has been the subject of controversy, largely because of the strong normative element which is present in most (if not all) of the various attempts to describe, explain and predict regional integration. Karl Deutsch, one of the founding fathers of modern integration theory, argues that integration is 'the attainment, within a territory, of a "sense of community" and of institutions and practices strong enough and widespread enough to assure, for a "long" time, dependable expectations of "peaceful change" among its population' (Deutsch, Burrell et al. 1957, 5). This emphasis upon peaceful change or reorientation of attitudes is reflected in a slightly different way by another pioneer integration theorist, Ernst Haas who has defined integration as 'the tendency toward the voluntary creation of larger political units, each of which self-consciously eschews the use of force in the relations between the participating units and groups' (Haas 1971, 4).

Joseph Nye carries this theme further when he asserts that regional political organizations 'have made modest contributions to the creation of islands of peace in the international system' (Nye 1971, 182).

As the quotations above make clear, regional integration has been seen as a means of promoting peaceful cooperation and reducing conflict between states in various parts of the world. However, this entirely laudable intention does sometimes tempt integration theorists to take themselves too seriously and to become exasperated when statesmen fail to grasp the expansive logic of integration. 'Academic enthusiasm for supranationality', as Inis Claude (1966, 103) has observed, 'reflects a tendency to rejoice in the possibility that spokesmen for states can be ignored, circumvented and overruled by representatives of a larger community'. This preoccupation with peaceful relations is something which integration theory has inherited, along with its manipulative pretensions, from classical federalism and a long line of schemes for promoting perpetual and universal peace. The argument that peace can only be secured by the merger of existing states into a single empire or federation has been made during (or shortly after) every major European conflict since the early seventeenth century, by writers as diverse as the Abbé de St Pierre and Harold Laski (Hinsley 1966, 196, 216).

Unfortunately, most schemes of this kind bore little correspondence to the historical realities of integration; indeed, plans for universal or regional federations were themselves a reaction to the coercive and distinctly non-pacific efforts which have marked the birth of nations and empires in the past. As Puchala (1974, 122) has noted, 'The bulk of historical cases of "national unification" are most appropriately labeled and studied as cases of amalgamation by imperialism rather than as examples of peaceful regional integration.' The integration theorist is therefore left a mere handful of examples of voluntary federation USA and Switzerland being the most important, but both predating the industrial age) at the national level, and a series of regional communities formed since 1945 at the supranational level – of which the European Communities are arguably the most developed.

Indeed, it was not until the era of reconstruction after the Second World War that integration theory and political practice began to converge. Prior to 1945 most schemes for regional integration were the product of political groups which blamed state sovereignty for conflict in the international system and which wished to replace the nation-state by 'fundamental social and political reorganization both below and beyond national boundaries' (Pentland 1973, 160). Norman Angell had pointed out as early as 1909 that increasing economic interdependence between the states of Europe had made conflict undesirable and unprofitable in material terms (Angell 1909), and Leonard Woolf was to argue in the midst of the First World War that 'complete independence today is merely a legal fiction, and if we are to make it a fact we shall have to destroy the international form of society which grew up in the last century and revert to the national isolation of a former age' (Woolf 1916, 217).

However, those who advocated international government found little support in the post-Versailles world of national self-determination and in an era when nationalism was at its height it is perhaps not surprising that proposals for liquidating the nation-state were often circumspect and even underhanded in their approach. The functionalists, of whom David Mitrany was probably the most influential, saw in the development of international organizations performing human welfare tasks a means of eroding popular support for nation-states and thus diminish the threat to world peace posed by nationalism. Mitrany, however, did not advocate a frontal assault upon nationalism; rather, he perceived that in modern states there were a proliferating range of technical, politically neutral, functions which the populations of those states expected their respective governments to perform.

Many of these tasks, such as the control of maritime traffic, or the international transmission of mail, or the allocation of radio broadcasting frequencies, could not be performed effectively at the national level, and international collaboration was vital if they were to be carried out at all. Mitrany and the functionalists therefore proposed that governments should be encouraged to delegate the performance of such tasks to non-political technical experts working within the framework of an international organization, for the benefit of the world community. Since the nation-state system is not immutable, and is the cause of violence, divisions and the undermining of the real needs and interests of mankind, the functionalist approach would build upon pre-existent interdependencies by taking on specific functional tasks of economic and welfare cooperation. This would avoid divisive political debate but at the same time create a community of interest which would ultimately render national frontiers meaningless (Mitrany 1966, 62).

Moreover, such a strategy would avoid a head-on confrontation with the principle of state sovereignty, or indeed any sterile constitutional debate; according to Mitrany, (1966, 73) the great virtue of the functional method is that of 'technical self-determination', in that the function concerned determines the institutions, powers and authority necessary for its performance, and that these might vary widely from function to function (Mitrany 1966, p. 73). Mitrany does not preclude the possibility that such functional beginnings could in time develop into a comprehensive political system through 'federalism by installments' (Mitrany 1966, p. 83). This federalism, however, would be based upon a web of overlapping systems of cooperation and welfare promotion, and would not be subject to the frailties of a federal constitution drawn up around a green baize table without the practical underpinnings of a successful tradition of functional cooperation. Thus nationalism would be replaced by allegiance to the world community, as men learned from their social environment that international cooperation could satisfy needs which the traditional rivalry of nation-states could not fulfil. Through functional endeavours the focus of human activity would be diverted from the divisive political issues to the technical problems which all states needed to solve.

The functionalist strategy, for all its initial appeal as an alternative to the assertive forms of nationalism which emerged prior to 1939, suffered from several major deficiencies. Firstly, it tended to assume that a global consensus on what constitutes 'welfare' is possible, but, as Reginald Harrison points out, the dissimilarity between states in their ideologies and levels of economic development would inhibit functional cooperation: 'Welfare spending, on a scale likely to be significant for building a community sense, would be reallocative and, therefore, unlikely to be agreed unless a profound community sentiment were *already in existence.*' (Harrison 1974, 36). In other words, welfare functions are predicated upon prior political consensus rather than being independent of it. Secondly, it would seem that the functionalist assumption that functional cooperation can be divorced from its political environment (and in particular the political objectives of national élites) and yet in the long run give rise to significant shifts in political loyalty, from the national to the global community, is not reflected in the experience of at least two functional international organizations – the International Labour Organization (Haas 1964) and the International Bank for Reconstruction and Development (Sewell 1966). However 'technical' the issue, the views of non-political functional experts seem to be shaped by the interests and political environment of the nation-state which they represent. During the 1960s, for example, Europeans failed to agree on a single colour television transmission system, partly because of the political preference of the Soviet Union for the French SECAM system over the technically superior PAL system developed by West Germany (Hodges 1972, 22).

It is not altogether surprising that functionalism, with its avoidance of direct 'political' questions, should have been developed at a time when European nationalism was at a peak, during the period between the two world wars. It is equally understandable that federalism, which assumes the primacy of politics as a means of tackling the problems of social and economic diversity, reached its apogee as a strategy for supranational community-building in the period immediately after the Second World War. The federalist approach offered a method of uniting hitherto separate states into a new supranational entity by means of a formal constitution, executed as a result of a common political commitment made by the parties involved. Federalism had long been an important component in the various institutional designs for pacifying the relations between states, as far back as the ancient Greeks, while the emergence of federal systems in North America and Switzerland provided a practical example of maintaining unity and diversity (Pentland 1975, 12). At the Hague Conference of 1948 and elsewhere, European federalists – many of whom had worked together in the resistance movement during the war – advocated the creation of a federal Europe, which would capitalize on the widespread destruction and disillusionment brought about by the war by providing an attractive alternative to the rebuilding of the nation-state system with its inherent rivalries (De Rougemont 1965).

Certainly federalism, with its model of government in which political power is divided between central and local institutions (each acting autonomously in its own sphere) is a very attractive strategy for uniting groups of states possessing diverse interests. Its advocates consider that federal government satisfies the twin criteria of efficiency (by creating central bodies to carry out certain functions, and to resolve disputes between the constituent parts) and democracy (by decentralizing other activities to ensure greater local control and autonomy). Moreover, the federation could be created relatively quickly, without the necessity for prior resolution of social, cultural and economic differences, provided that the political élites concerned were able to achieve a decisive act of collective political will to cut the Gordian knot of state sovereignty. Given the diminished capabilities of the nation-states of Western Europe in the period immediately after 1945, the hopes expressed by the federalists were not as unrealistic as they might now appear; in the face of the westward expansion of Soviet influence and American primacy in economic and strategic affairs, there were considerable attractions for the European states in hanging together lest they be hanged separately. Some European federalists saw the strategy as a step towards a 'United States of Europe' which would act as a balancer between the superpowers of the USA and USSR, while others saw it as an intermediate step in the task of democratizing society and eventually establishing a global federation (Forsyth 1967).

However, such differences as to the end-product of the federalist strategy were to remain academic; when the French Assembly rejected proposals for a European Defence Community in 1954, what had been called Europe's 'federalist phase' (Spinelli 1966, 19) was over. If the governments of Western Europe agreed on anything, it was to maintain the existing framework of national governments rather than to create supranational institutions, particularly since the threat of Soviet expansion in Europe had diminished after Stalin's death in 1953 and the Marshall Plan had enabled the national economies to regain and even surpass prewar levels. While federal institutions might well serve as a model for distributing and delimiting power in a regional community, it was clear that the European federalists could not provide the stimulus to political consensus which must precede the act of federal union. Federalism, therefore, provides a suitable strategy for only the final stage of integration, 'where the political will exists at the centre and where an alignment of interests has occurred' (Taylor 1971, 15). More recent federalist thinkers, pointing to the strains of federal systems operating in the absence of a broad sense of community – such as Nigeria, for example – have contended that less attention should be paid to legalistic definitions of institutional structures and more to the social and political consensus which determines what functions those institutions should perform (Friedrich 1968, 173).

If neither functionalism nor federalism provided a very satisfactory explanation for the presence (or absence) of integrative endeavours, it must be remembered that they were to have a profound influence upon the development of integration theory. From functionalism came the idea that certain welfare-oriented tasks might be delegated by states to an international organization, and that international decision-making is an incremental process, whereby participants in one international organization 'learn' from success in one field to apply the same techniques in another (Teune 1964, 258). From federalism has come the conception of a division of decision-making power between central (or supranational) and local (or national) institutions, and the balance between them; the federal model, therefore, remains an ideal type or paradigm against which to measure progress in the scope and level of decision-making in a putative supranational community.

Methodology and assumptions of integration theory: Pluralism and interdependence

Integration, like motherhood or apple pie, is a term which embodies certain values which few would care to reject in public; consequently it has suffered from over-use and vague or even mutually contradictory definitions of the concept. Some political scientists, such as Deutsch, regard it as a *condition* in which hitherto separate units have attained a relationship of mutual interdependence and jointly produce system properties which they would separately lack (Deutsch 1968, 159); others, such as Haas, consider that integration is a *process* by which the actors concerned begin voluntarily to give up certain sovereign powers and evolve new techniques for tackling common problems and resolving mutual conflict (Haas 1968, 11). As might be expected, therefore, the lack of consensus on the definition of the dependent variable has given rise to a number of theoretical approaches to the problem of regional integration.

Although integration theorists have not been blessed with an ecumenical urge, it is important to stress that there is general agreement among them that integration consists of a merger of separate institutions and communities, usually within a specific geographic region, into a larger unit. Where they differ is on the emphasis to be given to the role of institutions, élite and popular attitudes, and economic, political and social transactions in the creation of such a supranational community, and whether integration is brought about (to use the terms familiar to economists in their unending debate) by the invisible hand of mutual advantage or the conscious intervention and manipulation of an integrating élite.

The two major approaches to integration theory are the *transaction-*

alist approach, which emphasizes the role of transactions between people as both an indicator of their attitudes towards each other and as the begetters of interdependence within the community; and the *neofunctionalist* approach, which stresses the way in which supranational institutions possessing binding decision-making power emerge from a convergence of self-interest on the part of various significant groups in society. Although the two approaches differ in style and emphasis (with the neofunctionalists placing more stress on élite bargaining styles and strategies, and the transactionalists concentrating on the volume and rate of transactions or the ebb and flow of public opinion), both approaches agree on some broad elements. These are that certain background conditions must exist if integrative endeavours are to take root, that an élite group must be willing and able to set the integrative process in motion, and that the putative regional community must continue to expand its functions and attract increasing popular loyalty if the integrative momentum is to be maintained.

The transactionalist approach seeks to establish what characteristics distinguish an organized and interdependent community from a random grouping of individuals, and what conditions are necessary to promote and maintain a sense of community among the population of a given region. The major exponent of this approach, Karl Deutsch, began by examining the dynamics of nationalism and the role of social communication in forging national unity and consciousness (Deutsch 1953), and a few years later formed a team of historians and political scientists to examine the formation of integrated communities, or their disintegration, in ten historical cases – ranging from the successful integration of England in medieval times to the breakup of Austria-Hungary in the twentieth century (Deutsch, Burrell et al. 1957). The purpose of this latter study was to establish whether or not the so-called 'Atlantic Community' was an embryonic integrating region; Deutsch and his co-researchers assumed that integrative processes at the supranational or regional level are analogous to similar community-building activities at the national or even subnational level, and that the mutual relevance and responsiveness which are necessary for integrated communities to exist were brought about by a growth in transactions between members of the system. In other words, the transactionalists contend that the crucial variables for integration may be identified from community-building efforts in the past, and that by measuring changes in the intensity and scope of transactions between a given group of actors we can assess the growth of a sense of community in a given region.

Deutsch hypothesized that the more one nation-state interacts with another, the more relevant they become to each other; however, such an increase in mutual relevance may not lead to integration unless it is accompanied by mutual responsiveness, which was defined as the ability to respond satisfactorily to the demands contained in the transactions between the actors involved. Integration, according to the transactionalist view, is a *condition* in which the population of a given region have attained (as a result of their transactions with each other) a sense of community, in that they agree that common problems should be solved without resorting to violence. Instead, the members of the community support the creation of institutions and procedures which are capable of ensuring peaceful change. Deutsch did not assume that the end-stage of integration was necessarily a unitary supranational state; indeed, he specifically distinguished between the 'amalgamated security community', in which a common government presided over the merger of two or more previously independent units into a single larger unit, and the 'pluralistic security community', in which peaceful change was guaranteed and institutionalized in some respects, but in which the individual governments retained their legal independence. Deutsch cited the USA as a modern example of an amalgamated security community, and US–Canadian relations as typical of a pluralistic security community (Deutsch 1968, 194).

A community, in the transactionalist view, cannot exist unless its members are interdependent, and such interdependence can only be established by a network of mutual transactions. Transactions alone, however, do not guarantee that a community will come into existence, since communication can sometimes increase tension if it emphasizes divergent values and expectations rather than revealing an underlying identity of values and interests. Thus a certain level of transactions must also be accompanied by the development of mutual responsiveness, in the sense that the demands communicated through the system must receive an adequate response within an acceptable period of time.

The system will only be able to produce an adequate response if those controlling it are able to select the most important demands, combine them with information on past responses and available resources, and produce responses which promote integration by satisfying as many demands as possible. Since the level of demands made upon the system will usually increase if it is seen to work satisfactorily, it is crucial that the controlling institutions of the system increase their decision-making capacity to remain equal or superior to the load placed upon them. Failure to do so will bring about disintegration as was the case with British rule in Ireland in the nineteenth century (Deutsch 1964, 70).

Provided the capabilities of the system continue to balance the demands placed upon it, the transactionalists contend that as the intensity of communications increases, so will the development of a sense of community. The transactionalists, therefore, aim to use transaction flows between actors in a given region as indicators of interdependence ('mutual relevance') within that region, and to monitor changes in the levels of these transaction flows to discover if the actors meet favourable responses to their demands and thereafter increase and extend their use of the system ('mutual responsiveness'). Increases in mutual transactions can therefore be interpreted as the result of a learning process in which the actors involved become accustomed to using new common procedures for making demands and settling disputes, and to developing mutual recognition of certain stimuli and symbols within the region. In this way a structure of common values emerges as transaction flows create what Paul Taylor (1972, 205) has called a 'socio-psychological community'.

The methodology employed by the transactionalists leads them to look for two main patterns of communication which characterize emergent regional communities, namely a high volume of transactions within the region over a wide range of economic, political and social activities, and an increasing divergence between the volume and range of transactions within the putative community and transactions between that region and the outside world. Transaction flows can therefore be charted in order to determine the degree of interdependence prevailing within a region, and whether the constituent actors in the region are becoming more dependent on each other than they are on extra-regional actors.

Unlike transactionalism, which pays more attention to the symptoms of integration (i.e. transaction rates) than the causes of it, the neofunctionalists stress the motivation of the actors involved and the intended and unintended consequences of their individual pursuit of self-interest. The neofunctionalists stress not the development of communal values, but rather the pluralist nature of modern society, composed of competing élites and conflicting interests. Moreover, rather than treating integration as a condition in which political consensus and homogeneous values have already been developed, the neofunctionalists treat integration as a process in which politically significant élites (governmental and non-governmental) gradually redefine their interests in terms of a regional rather than a purely national orientation: '. . . the process whereby political actors in several distinct national settings are persuaded to shift their loyalties, expectations and political activities toward a new and larger center, whose institutions possess or demand jurisdiction over the pre-existing national states' (Haas 1966, 94).

This reorientation process, according to Haas, takes place not because of altruistic or idealistic motives on the part of the élites concerned, but because they perceive supranational institutions as the best way of satisfying their pragmatic interests. The neofunctionalists, therefore, concentrate on the development of processes of collective decision-making, and the way in which governmental and non-governmental élites change their tactics and organization as the decision-making process shifts from the national to the supranational level. Although the neofunctionalists have borrowed the functionalist concept of incremental decision-making, whereby participants in international organizations apply techniques of cooperation which have succeeded in one functional field to another such field, they reject the functionalist assumption that the performance of welfare tasks is essentially non-controversial and hence can be insulated from political conflict. Because power is inseparable from welfare, in that the performance of welfare tasks involves the political function of allocating scarce resources among competing demands, the integrative potential of international programmes of collaboration is likely to be high only if the tasks involved are economically significant, if the national representatives involved carry some weight in their national decision-making processes, and if the groups involved share a broad consensus on goals and procedures. Thus regional organizations are more likely to display integrative potential than global bodies in which a broad range of cultural values are represented (Haas 1964, 47–50).

The neofunctionalists view the integration process as one in which a group of actors decide to collaborate at the international level in order to further their individual and collective interest in the performance of some technical, relatively non-controversial, function. After a while, these actors discover that they can only fulfil their original purpose if they confer more authority on the collective decision-making apparatus and also act together in other related functional fields. Thus the initial collaborative endeavour gradually becomes politicized, as the scope of the enterprise widens and the choice between national autonomy and supranational decision-making becomes clearer. If such politicization is successful, and the national actors perceive that their interests are best served by delegation of national decision-making powers to the new supranational body in one field, it is likely that they will apply the lesson to integrative attempts in other fields.

This gradual expansion of integrative activity comes not because of an emerging ideological commitment to supranationalism, nor even a universal consensus on the collective goals to be pursued, but because the actors involved perceive their individual (and often competing) interests as being served by the extension of the competence of supranational institutions. This is the concept of 'spill-over', which is a central part of the neofunctionalist approach; the major assumption is that initial attempts to integrate in relatively non-controversial economic issue-areas will eventually spill over into more and more controversial (and hence political) spheres of activity – that political integration will follow on from economic integration. The major beneficiary of the spill-over may be the new supranational institution, which will increase its power and competence by acting as an 'honest broker' in putting together package deals which satisfy the various interests of the parties involved.

Neofunctionalists therefore tend to stress the individual motives and interests of the élite groups involved in the process, and emphasize the role of self-interest in shaping perceptions of integration. Far from proceeding, as the transactionalists do, from a bird's-eye view of the system (or lack of one), the neofunctionalists concentrate on the adaptation of élites as they reorient their activities and form new coalitions across existing national frontiers in order to pursue their interests at the regional level. As Haas noted, 'neo-functionalists rely on the primacy of incremental decision-making over grand designs', on the ground that most political actors stumble from one set of decisions to the next without having foreseen the implications and consequences of the earlier decisions, since they are 'incapable of long-range purposive behavior' (Haas 1971, 23). This assumption of myopic pursuit of short-term advantage was perhaps more applicable to neofunctional theorists than the élite groups they studied, as we shall discover.

Regional integration: Theory and reality

In general the record of integration theory in describing, explaining and predicting the course of regional integration in various parts of the world has been somewhat less than successful. Although the empirical studies of regional integration have produced a taxonomy of indicators and factors in integration, there is little agreement among theorists as to the relative influence of the various factors or conditions, and what combinations of them are necessary to achieve integration. This failure to agree on the ranking of integrative factors is due at least in part to the absence of an agreed definition of the very concept of integration itself. Indeed, it is difficult when surveying the empirical studies of integration to overcome the impression that the real world has been a source of continued disappointment to integration theorists.

The transactionalists have never claimed strong predictive power for their theoretical construct of integration, since the analysis of transaction flows can at best assume that what is past is prologue. The major difficulty in analysing transaction flows lies in determining which transactions are most significant in developing mutual relevance and potential cohesion within a region. Often there may be cross-pressures or divergences between various types of transaction flow; thus a study of Anglo-American relations during the period 1890–1954 demonstrated that the relative intensity of economic transactions between the two countries steadily diminished over time, yet there was a modest increase in political and military consultations (Russett 1963, 202). This type of cross-pressure or divergence in transaction flows may be useful in highlighting potential weaknesses in cohesion, but comparisons are difficult to make unless one can establish the relative importance of various types of transaction for promoting regional cohesion.

In one study of West European integration, Deutsch and his associates correlated transaction flows across national boundaries (such as trade, mail and telephone communications, student exchanges and tourist movements) with mass and élite attitudes surveyed through interviews, opinion polls and newspaper editorials. Deutsch concluded that European integration had slowed since the mid-1950s and since 1958 had reached a plateau; since then increases in transactions have been no greater than would be expected from random probability and the increase in prosperity in the countries concerned. Deutsch therefore thought it unlikely that Europe would integrate further within the forseeable future, since 'the spectacular development of formal European treaties and institutions since the mid-1950s has not been matched by any corresponding deeper integration of mutual behavior' (Deutsch, Edinger et al. 1967, 17). A more recent study of transactions and attitudes indicates that while transactions may promote relevance, mutual responsiveness either is not affected by changes in transaction flows or is subject to a very considerable time-lag (Cobb and Elder 1970, 138).

A somewhat different approach was adopted by Ronald Inglehart, whose study of public opinion in Western Europe led him to question the emphasis Deutsch placed upon structural integration (increases in trade, travel, mail, student exchanges and so on) rather than changes in attitude on the part of the groups concerned (Inglehart 1967, 197). Inglehart contends that there may be a threshold of structural integration which provides the foundation for political integration to take place, and that even if transactions such as tourism begin to level off this will not reflect anything more significant than a finite preference for holidays abroad. Thus the crucial factor is not the act of transaction, but the attitude which underlies it, and Inglehart's own research led him to conclude that a limited amount of attitudinal reorientation in favour of an integrated Europe had taken place since 1958 (the point at which Deutsch claimed integration had reached a plateau).

Inglehart argued that the most important change had occurred in the relatively more stable and enduring pro-European attitudes of the generation which had become socialized since 1945, as compared to the more nationalistic attitudes of earlier generations. If one accepts Inglehart's argument that the basic and enduring political attitudes are acquired in adolescence, and adds to it the demographic factor (that over half the electorate in West European countries in the 1980s will have been born since 1945), then it may well be that European integration will be an attractive goal for vote-seeking politicians to embrace. Inglehart's thesis of generational attitude change would therefore lead us to expect European integration to move into full gear in the 1980s, but although Deutsch himself found that younger members of French and German administrative élites tended to be more pro-European than their older superiors, the enthusiasm of the post-1945 generation for Europe might simply be a reaction against nationalism and the 'establishment' rather than support for the strengthening of the European Community.

Nevertheless, Donald Puchala provides some support for Inglehart's argument that European integration has continued since 1958, and that Deutsch's pessimism is therefore unjustified. Puchala makes the important observation that transaction flow indices are limited to available quantitative data, and that therefore they exclude many transactions which are not readily quantified, such as informal political consultation and coordination carried out between national governments. Moreover, the transaction flows themselves are but a reflection of integration rather than a cause of it, and are therefore useful to monitor the progress of integration in various fields, but not particularly reliable for predicting future systemic behaviour. Even so, Puchala's own findings indicate that since the formation of the EEC in 1958 the convergence in attitudes and a modest rise in transactions have continued, and that European integration had not stagnated as Deutsch had contended (Puchala 1971, 152–58).

One major flaw in the transactionalist approach is that (even if one accepts the proposition that transaction flows are an indicator of a sense of community) another aspect of the regional integration process is that of the growth of supranational decision-making procedures for conflict resolution. Since much of this regional dispute settlement is a function of high diplomacy, there are formidable problems in devising appropriate indicators. Even where adequate information exists – for example, joint membership in regional organizations as an indicator of the growth in the capacity of supranational institutions – it is difficult to weight individual transactions in order to indicate their relative significance. It is clear, for example, that membership in the EEC is more important than membership in the Western European Union, but by how much?

The transactionalist approach therefore is useful in delineating potential regions as suitable cases for integrative treatment, and may well be useful in indicating correlations between changes in various types of transaction flow, such as an increase in community formation preceding an increase in institutionalization. Such correlations may reveal patterns of priority in the integration process, but it is doubtful whether causal relationships can be demonstrated by the transactionalist approach. Political integration is not determined by the flow of transactions, but the network of intcrdependencies does create the environment within which statesmen must act. As Russett (1967, 227) noted, 'President de Gaulle may be able to throw some sand in the gears of political union on the continent, but President Nasser cannot, by an act of will, produce an Arab union.' The predictive power of the transactionalist approach may therefore be greatest in a negative sense – to indicate regions in which the absence of a network of mutual transactions make integration unlikely or unsuccessful.

Transactionalism warns us that we cannot make bricks without straw, and that regional integration must include a number of necessary elements if mutual relevance is to be accompanied by mutual responsiveness (though these need not be added in any fixed sequence). Neofunctionalism, to continue the metaphor, has us concentrate on the brickmakers rather than the bricks – and the heterogeneous interests which lead them to join the enterprise. In his study of economic and political élite activity in the European Coal and Steel Community (ECSC), from the Schuman Plan of 1950, which proposed establishing the ECSC, to the signing of the EEC and Euratom treaties in 1957, Haas (1968) found evidence of integration through spillover resulting from the interplay of competing interests.

While there was no consensus among the élites in the six member countries of the ECSC when it was established, in that there was no widespread ideological commitment to supranationalism, there was a convergence of individual short-term interests which permitted the Schuman Plan to be implemented. For the German CDU it represented a method of removing Allied controls over the Ruhr industrial area, while for some political parties in France the ECSC represented a chance to control German heavy industry and hence undermine Germany's capability to launch a future attack. For low-cost and efficient producers of coal and steel in all the member countries the ECSC was welcomed as a means of enlarging their markets, while most of the trade unions favoured the ECSC since collaboration at the supranational level improved their bargaining strength in national negotiations.

Because there were few divisive political issues, national élites had an incentive to seek out like-minded groups from other member countries of the ECSC. Trade union leaders from both socialist and Christian unions began lobbying jointly with their counterparts from other member countries, because they perceived their individual interests as being served by establishing through supranational organizations a regulated industrial economy in which labour interests had a permanent and significant influence. Élites in each member state found that economic integration through supranational institutions served their individual interests, and these converging practical goals provided the impetus for extending integration to sectors other than coal and steel.

While these changes of orientation were occurring among non-governmental élites, the perceptions of political élites were also changing – not only because interest-group activity was increasing at the supranational level, but also because the problems which grew out of the initial agreement to set up the ECSC required continuous and ever more extensive contact and consultation between the governmental élites. In these negotiations the High Authority of the ECSC acted as a supranational honest broker, upgrading common interests by producing package solutions which combined the maximum of short-term satisfaction of interests with the minimum of long-term sacrifice. In performing such a service, the High Authority gained in stature and significance, since it was at the very centre of the bargaining process, and in some cases even encouraged situations in which solutions were only possible through further increases in its competence and the creation of new central policies.

Although the neofunctionalist concept of spillover would seem to have been confirmed by the extension in 1958 of integrative activity into atomic energy and economic affairs in general, the development of the European Communities since that time has called into question many of the assumptions of the neofunctionalist approach. Studies of interest-group activity in the EEC found that some reorientation of the groups did take place, but that the bulk of their effort still remained oriented towards national goals (Lindberg 1963, 287) and that few interest groups were able to subscribe to a transnational consensus on general policy issues, as distinct from purely technical issues such as standard packaging sizes (Sidjanski 1967, 416).

In the case of general policy issues, interest groups in the European Community have generally found it more effective to operate at the national level by putting pressure on their respective governments, largely because by the time the member states come to the Council of Ministers meeting to establish a Community policy they have already formulated a national negotiating strategy and thereafter are relatively impervious to pressure from interest groups operating at the supranational level. However, as the activities and membership of the European Communities have enlarged, undisputed control over 'Community' issues has tended to slip away from foreign affairs ministries into the hands of ministries of trade, agriculture and so on, with the result that some transgovernmental lobbying has grown up to compete with or complement the activities of private interest groups (Wallace et al. 1977).

While the experience of the European Communities over the last two decades has cast serious doubt on the inevitability of economic integration spilling over into political integration, the weakness in the neofunctionalist approach is even more serious. Stanley Hoffmann has argued that the stagnation of European integration in the 1960s was due to the fundamental distinction between 'low' politics – involving calculable and relatively insignificant welfare issues – and 'high' politics, involving major foreign policy and defence issues which no government is willing to entrust to an untried supranational institution (Hoffman 1966, 882). The failure of the member states of the European Communities to achieve integration in high politics by means of spillover from economic integration is the result of the diversity of their national objectives, the differences in their national conditions, and the lack of any unifying and distinctively 'European' issues (as opposed to purely local or global ones).

Indeed, the rapid economic gains accruing to the member states after the formation of the EEC may actually have enabled them to undertake independent action in other areas of foreign policy (Hansen 1969, 249). As General de Gaulle's foreign policy made clear, the degree of independence which could be asserted without endangering the interlocking pyramid of bargains which constituted the European Communities was very considerable. The major pragmatic interests of the politically relevant groups could be satisfied by a relatively modest level of integration, and once this had been achieved there was no deep ideological commitment to go any further. De Gaulle's success in halting European integration in its tracks must thus be seen not so much as a singular achievement by a charismatic leader, but rather as an indication that European integration was not a cause more sacred to the Community's member states than the national interests of their fellow members. The result of the EEC's constitutional crisis of 1965–6 was an implicit agreement that integration in any given field would not be attempted if a member state considered that this contravened its vital interests – a confirmation of the veto power of member states (Newhouse 1967).

The evident discontinuity between economic and political integration has led Joseph Nye to suggest that the concept of integration should be broken down into economic, political and social components, and each should then be measured by the most appropriate indicators (mail flows as an indicator of social integration, for example). It would thus be possible to monitor situations in which integration of one type was accompanied by disintegration of another (Nye 1968, 865). Such disaggregation of the concept of integration sounds attractive, but one of the major problems is that of classifying each example of joint activity. Is trade an economic, social or political phenomenon?

An alternative approach is offered by Leon Lindberg and Stuart Scheingold, in which the key to political integration lies in the extent to which the authority to make decisions is transferred from the national level to the supranational level in various policy areas. They suggest that processes of collective or supranational decision-making may result in: (1) fulfilment of the original purpose agreed upon by member states (such as the establishment of the EEC's common agricultural policy); (2) retraction from the original purpose because acceptable common rules and policies fail to be produced (as in the case of the abortive EEC transport policy); or (3) extension of obligations beyond those originally envisaged, as happened when the Community expanded from a coverage of coal and steel in the ECSC to the general economy in the EEC and Euratom (Lindberg and Scheingold 1970, 180).

The attraction of this approach is that it emphasizes the transfer of authority and legitimacy from member states to Community institutions and procedures, and enables a composite picture to be built up of fulfilment, retraction and expansion in the various issue-areas in which integrative attempts have been made. The emphasis is on what Haas (1971, 29) has termed 'authority-legitimacy transfer' – on the way in which hitherto independent nation-states give up some attributes of their sovereignty – rather than on the shift of élite loyalty to a new centre, which the neofunctionalists had tended to stress in their earlier works. Another shift in the neofunctionalist approach has been to give at least some attention to the relations between the regional system and the outside world, rather than simply concentrating on the activities and aspirations of élites within the region. Amitai Etzioni's work on regional integration had stressed the importance of external élites in the process, and in the case of the EEC had shown that the diplomatic, economic and military pressures exerted by the United States had promoted European integration until the US support for British entry in 1962 came up against fundamental French objections. At that point the external élite had a distinctly disintegrative effect, as France's EEC partners had to weigh their European and Atlantic loyalties (Etzioni 1965, 238–46). Therefore, in many important respects it is necessary to consider the integrating region not only in terms of its general international environment, but also as a subordinate system subject to superpower influence (Cantori and Spiegel 1970, 381–92).

Integration, transnationalism and interdependence

It will now be apparent to those who have persevered thus far that integration theory and the real world came into closest contact in Western Europe some two decades ago. Although valiant efforts have been made to apply integration theory to other areas of the world, such as the East African Community (Nye 1965), Latin America (Haas and Schmitter, 1964) and South-East Asia (Levi, 1968), integration theory was developed in the industrialized, pluralistic West European laboratory, and the attempt of academic analysts to find functional equivalents to European groups or conditions has often taken on a Procrustean quality. In less developed countries there may not be very many technical, non-controversial tasks with which to push off the integrative bandwagon, since 'bread-and-butter' welfare issues are very definitely within the realm of high politics in a developing country. Chile's withdrawal from the Andean Pact at the end of 1976 was a recent example of economic integration melting in the face of intraregional political disputes, and the gradual disintegration of the once-thriving East African Community (which had achieved monetary union in colonial days, long before the EEC aspired to it) provided further evidence that integration is a fragile growth in regions where ideological differences are exacerbated by uneven economic development and excessive dependence on extraregional markets.

Even in the case of Western Europe, such instances as the undignified scramble for national protection in the 1973 Arab oil embargo, and the hesitant steps taken towards economic and monetary union indicate that the integration process had not become essentially bureaucratic and technocratic, operated by non-political actors who 'tend more and more to define their roles in terms of joint problem-solving rather than as agents of one system or another' (Lindberg and Scheingold 1970, 32). Indeed, General de Gaulle's major contribution to integration theory was to leave the stage in 1969, since which time integration theorists have lacked a scapegoat for the continued dominance of national interest politics in the European Communities.

And yet the European Communities have survived; buffeted by the waves of global interdependence, they failed either to disintegrate into the 'old order' of competing sovereign states or to make progress towards further transfer of authority and legitimacy to their supranational institutions. Perhaps, as Donald Puchala has suggested, we should look less at the institutions and more at the cooperative, non-competitive rules of the game in what he has characterized as a 'concordance system', one of many layers of decision-making in which states participate on a case-by-case basis where their interests can be usefully served (Puchala 1972, 267–85). Haas has indeed suggested that integration theory is now obsolescent in an era of increasing 'turbulence', which he defines as 'the confused and clashing perceptions of organizational actors which find themselves in a setting of great social complexity' (Haas 1976, 179). Integration, in the sense of the transfer of authority and legitimacy to a new, supranational set of institutions is one response to the condition of interdependence – a condition in which actors in the international system are sensitive and vulnerable to the acts of other entities, whether these be governments or transnational actors such as multinational corporations or terrorist groups (Keohane and Nye, 1972).

Integration, however, is not the only response to interdependence, and in certain circumstances it is probably a very undesirable one. There are, for example, strong arguments against the pursuit of a coherent energy policy in an EEC (as opposed to an OECD) context; as William Wallace (1977, 313) has noted, 'the Communities are not unique in offering governments a forum for managing the problems of interdependence'. Thus integration is unlikely to proceed in an orderly fashion within clearly delineated boundaries; rather, interdependence will lead to embattled national actors deciding to establish new layers of cooperation which will overlap with (and in some cases replace) what have now become the 'traditional' regional systems of cooperation. There are many ways to skin a cat, and there is no reason to expect that any one type of international regime enjoys a monopoly of virtue or validity, particularly in times of rapid economic, political or social change (Keohane and Nye 1977, 58–60). Just as integration theory was an attempt to correct an excessive emphasis by the realist school of International Relations on the primacy of the nation-state, so the emerging theories of transnationalism and interdependence serve to remind us that regional communities are not the only options available when we look beyond the nation-state.

References and Further Reading

Angell, N. (1909) *Europe's Optical Illusion,* London, Simpkin Marshall.

Cantori, L. and Spiegel, S.L. (1970) *The International Politics of Regions,* Englewood Cliffs, NJ, Prentice-Hall.

Claude, I.L. (1966) *Swords into Plowshares* (3rd edn.) New York, Random House.

Cobb, R.W. and Elder, C. (1970) *International Community: A Regional and Global Study,* New York, Holt, Rinehart and Winston.

De Rougemont, D. (1965) *The Meaning of Europe,* London, Sidgwick and Jackson.

Deutsch, K.W. (1953) *Nationalism and Social Communication,* Cambridge, Mass., MIT Press.

Deutsch, K.W. (1964) 'Communication theory and political integration', in Philip E. Jacob and James V. Toscano, (eds.), *The Integration of Political Communities,* Philadelphia, Lippincott, pp. 46–74.

Deutsch, K.W. (1968) *The Analysis of International Relations,* Englewood Cliffs, NJ, Prentice-Hall.

Deutsch, K.W., Burrell, S.A. et al. (1957) *Political Community and the North Atlantic Area,* Princeton, NJ, Princeton Univ. Press.

Deutsch, K.W., Edinger, L. et al. (1967) *France, Germany and the Western Alliance,* New York, Charles Scribner's Sons.

Etzioni, A. (1965) *Political Unification,* New York, Holt, Rinehart and Winston.

Forsyth, M. (1967) 'The political objectives of European integration', *International Affairs,* **43,** 483–97.

Friedrich, C.J. (1968) *Trends of Federalism in Theory and Practice,* New York, Praeger.

Haas, E.B. (1964) *Beyond the Nation-State,* Stanford, Calif., Stanford Univ. Press.

Haas, E.B. (1966) 'International integration: The European and the universal process', in *International Political Communities,* New York, Anchor Books, pp. 93–129.

Haas, E.B. (1968) *The Uniting of Europe* (2nd edn), Stanford Calif., Stanford Univ. Press.

Haas, E.B. (1971) 'The study of regional integration', in L.L. Lindberg and S.A. Scheingold (eds), *Regional Integration: Theory and Research,* Cambridge, Mass., Harvard Univ. Press, pp. 3–42.

Haas, E.B. (1976) 'Turbulent fields and the theory of regional integration', *International Organization,* **30,** 173–212.

Haas, E.B. and Schmitter, P.C. (1964) 'Economics and differential patterns of political integration: Projections about unity in Latin America', *International Organization,* **18,** 259–99.

Hansen, R. (1969) 'Regional integration: Reflections on a decade of theoretical efforts', *World Politics,* **21,** 242–71.

Harrison, R.J. (1974) *Europe in Question,* London, Allen and Unwin.

Hinsley, F.H. (1966) *Sovereignty,* London, Watts.

Hodges, M. (1972) *European Integration,* Harmondsworth, Middx., Penguin.

Hoffman, S. (1966) 'Obstinate or obsolete: The fate of the nation state and the case of Western Europe', *Daedalus,* 862–915.

Inglehart, R. (1967) 'An end to European integration?, *American Political Science Review,* **61,** 91–105.

Inglehart, R. (1971) 'Public opinion and regional integration', in Leon N. Lindberg and Stuart A. Scheingold, (eds.), *Regional Integration: Theory and Research,* Cambridge, Mass., Harvard Univ. Press, pp. 160–91.

Keohane, R.O. and Nye, J.S. (eds.) (1972) *Transnational Relations and World Politics,* Cambridge, Mass., Harvard Univ. Press.

Keohane, R.O. and Nye, J.S. (1977) *Power and Interdependence: World Politics in Transition,* Boston, Little, Brown.

Levi, W. (1968) *The Challenge of World Politics in South and Southeast Asia,* Englewood Cliffs, NJ, Prentice-Hall.

Lindberg, L.N. (1963) *The Political Dynamics of European Economic Integration,* Stanford, Calif., Stanford Univ. Press.

Lindberg, L.N. and Scheingold, S.A. (1970) *Europe's Would-Be Polity,* Englewood Cliffs, NJ, Prentice-Hall.

Mitrany, D. (1966) *A Working Peace System,* Chicago, Quadrangle.

Newhouse, J. (1967) *Collision in Brussels,* New York, W.W. Norton.

Nye, J.S. (1965) *Pan-Africanism and East African Integration,* Cambridge, Mass., Harvard Univ. Press.

Nye, J.S. (1968) 'Comparative regional integration: Concept and measurement', *International Organization,* **22,** 855–80.

Nye, J.S. (1971) *Peace in Parts: Integration and Conflict in Regional Organization,* Boston, Little, Brown.

Pentland, C. (1973) *International Theory and European Integration,* New York, Free Press.

Pentland, C. (1975) 'Functionalism and theories of international political integration', in Paul Taylor and A.J.R. Groom (eds.), *Functionalism: Theory and Practice in International Relations,* London, Univ. of London Press, pp. 9–24.

Puchala, D.J. (1971) 'International transactions and regional integration', in Leon L. Lindberg and Stuart A. Scheingold, (eds.), *Regional Integration: Theory and Research,* Cambridge, Mass., Harvard Univ. Press, pp. 128–59.

Puchala, D.J. (1972) 'Of blind men, elephants and international integration', *Journal of Common Market Studies,* **10,** 267–85.

Puchala, D.J. (1974) *International Pólitics Today,* New York, Dodd, Mead.

Russett, B.M. (1963) *Community and Contention: Britain and America in the Twentieth Century,* Cambridge, Mass., MIT Press.

Russett, B.M. (1967) *International Regions and the International System,* Chicago, Rand McNally.

Sewell, J.P. (1966) *Functionalism and World Politics,* Princeton, NJ, Princeton Univ. Press.

Sidjanski, D. (1967) 'Pressure groups and the European Economic Community', *Government and Opposition,* **2,** 397–416.

Spinelli, A. (1966) *The Eurocrats: Conflict and Crisis in the European Community,* Baltimore, Md, Johns Hopkins Press.

Taylor, P. (1971) *International Cooperation Today,* London, Elek Books.

Taylor, P. (1972) 'The concept of community and the European integration process', in Michael Hodges (ed.', *European Integration,* Harmondsworth, Middx, Penguin, pp. 203–23.

Teune, H. (1964) 'The learning of integrative habits', in Philip E. Jacob and James V. Toscano (eds.), *The Integration of Political Communities,* Philadelphia, Lippincott.

Wallace, H., Wallace, W. and Webb, C. (eds.) (1977) *Policy-Making in the European Communities,* London, Wiley.

Wallace, W. (1977) 'Walking backwards towards unity', in Helen Wallace, William Wallace and Carole Webb (eds.), *Policy-Making in the European Communities,* London, Wiley, pp. 301–24.

Woolf, L.S. (1916) *International Government,* London, Fabian Society/Allen and Unwin.

Chapter 12

Peace research

David J. Dunn

It might seem curious or paradoxical to define one's interest out of existence, to deny its right to appear in a book of this nature. Yet, strictly speaking, a survey and discussion of peace research has no place in a discussion of theories and approaches in International Relations. Why not? Because Peace Research is neither theory nor an approach; nor is its concern solely with International Relations. Defining a field as a theory implies that there is a set of interdependent, testable, tested and verified hypotheses that are logically linked one to the other. An approach implies that there is some degree of agreement in terms of definition, scope of the activity, methods and/or paradigms. Lest it be thought that such considerations are pedantic at this stage, it needs to be stated that peace research is, indeed, in a peculiar position. It is not based in, nor did it originate in, a particular academic discipline; there is no agreed methodology; there is no agreed research strategy. What, then, is peace research? It is an intellectual enterprise devoted to the study of peace and the bringing about of a state of peace in human society. That is, it is an intellectual enterprise built around an idea – peace. Even this agreed goal is a source of conflict, for what is peace to one man is repression and deprivation for another.

It is clear, even at this stage, then that though peace research is about peace – particularly about how to obtain it – nobody is clear that a universally accepted definition of that term exists, short of a Utopia. Thus stated, the idea of peace research appears to be naïve, the prospects for its survival rather slim. Succinctly, cynics might argue that Peace Research appears to be yet another refuge for those good people who habitually support life's good (i.e. lost) causes.

Set against this, however, is an enormous pile of evidence to suggest quite the contrary, to support the view that peace research is alive, vigorous, rapidly maturing (if not yet in the 'young adult' stage) and producing a good deal of work related to peace which conforms to generally accepted tenets of social science. What is the nature of this evidence? First, an increasing number of scholarly journals; second, a growing number of university and college departments, and research institutes, devoted in whole or in part to peace research; third, a fairly well-defined body of men and women known to each other, by reputation if nothing else, whose ideas are identified as the ongoing corpus of peace research; fourth, the institutionalization of the field in terms of a series of annual conferences where these people and ideas meet; and finally, there is evidence to suggest that peace research is increasingly identified, by people from outside its own confines, as being useful and worthy of financial support, surely an acid test of sorts. For example, the University of Bradford has, within the past few years, set up a Chair of Peace Studies, with the aid of outside finance, while in the 1960s the Stockholm International Peace Research Institute (SIPRI) was endowed by the Swedish government.

These initial comments, then, suggest an intellectual movement focused on an idea, an idea open to different interpretations, while at the same time hinting that two different conceptions of the peace research enterprise can arise from a survey of its present state. What follows is an attempt to demonstrate that though peace research might be in a particular, unique, position it has a symbiotic relationship with International Relations. Developments in peace research are capable of enlightening discussions of theory, methodology, value-free social science and relevance as these have manifested themselves in International Relations in recent years.

The development of peace research

The current state of peace research can only be properly understood if we are aware of its origins. Movements seldom develop codes, languages and procedures in the short term. Present divisions are often the product of conflict and controversy in the past and this is particularly apt in the case of peace research. At this point of the discussion, then, it is assumed that 'peace research' implies an intellectual activity, the aim of which is to achieve 'peace', utilizing social science methods. A more precise discussion of the term must wait until we have surveyed the origins of the field, as well as the changing conceptions of it. The idea of peace is hardly new. It has been seen as a problem from the early times, i.e. how to achieve a peace that was just, fair and equitable. The perennial concern for peace and the philosophical schools to which it has given rise are the bedrock of peace research. First, there is the idea that peace is a natural condition and, concomitantly, that war is not. This leads to the notion that, though war is sometimes a necessary evil, it is rational for man to seek peace. This line of reasoning is important; the power of reason and rationalism are of fundamental importance to contemporary peace researchers, for the premise is simple. If enough of the right sorts of information can be generated and presented properly to suggest that war leads to undesirable outcomes, it seems only reasonable that a man or group of men, acting rationally, will seek to avoid war and destructive conflicts. Second, there is a theistic view, that wars and conflicts harmful to man are undesirable and to be avoided. Though this is a generally held and widespread view, it is particularly associated with Quakerism. Third, and related to the second point, we need to consider pacifism, the view that above all else, peace is to be a cardinal virtue, a prime motive force in man's behaviour.

The three strata in the bedrock, though important, do not explain the genesis and growth of peace research. They merely suggest an intellectual or philosophical climate within which it might develop and prosper. Peace research has developed both by the efforts of men and the effects of events. There is no doubt that the carnage and slaughter of the First World War led to a groundswell of opinion in support of peace movements in particular and a widespread desire for peace in general. But the efforts of individuals are also important, though quite how important it is difficult to say with great precision. However, it is generally agreed nowadays that peace research owes an inestimable debt to two men active in the period between wars: Lewis Fry Richardson and Quincy Wright.

Lewis Richardson has the distinction of having two buildings named after him: the Richardson Wing at the Meteorological Office in Bracknell, Berkshire and the Richardson Institute for Conflict and Peace Research in London. This is not a coincidence; it reflects the nature of Richardson's mind in trying to come to terms with two major unpredictables that had plagued man for centuries, the weather and war. It had, of course, always been assumed that both the weather and war were phenomena that took their own course, subjecting man to their whims. Tolstoy certainly held to the view that war was one of the forces with which man would have to live out his days. Richardson was not content with this. Professionally he was a meteorologist; in his spare time he, a Quaker, studied war. Only after his death did his works on war reach a wider audience (Richardson 1960a, 1960b). Yet they stand as works of seminal value. In them, and in earlier articles, Richardson sought to examine the dynamics of conflicts, and arms races in particular, simply to find out what stages they went through. what patterns they followed. Why? Hardly, one would have thought for a Quaker, for the fun of it nor just as a hobby: rather, to identify the precise nature of the problem at hand as a prelude to trying to control it.

At the same time that Richardson was working in England, Quincy Wright was working at the University of Chicago on a project to understand war. Begun in 1926, Wright's study was published in 1942 as *A Study of War* and ran to more than 1,600 pages (Wright 1965). Wright shared with Richardson a common aim: to understand war as a means to control it. With this end in view, Wright tried to come to terms with war in all its aspects; he catalogued and classified war; counted deaths; identified issues over which states fought, and so on. Such was the magnitude of Wright's efforts (without a computer) that even when the second edition appeared in 1965, Karl Deutsch could write in the preface that the work was still 'indispensable for the serious graduate student . . . scholars and teachers in political science, international relations and all sectors of the social sciences that deal with war and peace' (Wright 1965, xviii). Here is a major point – important as these works were in their time, their significance lies in the fact that they acted as stimuli to further development; the undergraduates of the 1930s were to become the teachers of the 1950s and 1960s.

By the time of the Second World War, then, it could be argued that some seeds had been sown, some fertilization was taking place. In terms of the developing influences that were to shape peace research, a major factor was the harnessing of atomic power as a weapon of war. While the war was going on it was held to be imperative that the Allies develop an atomic bomb before the Germans did. In the event, estimates of German development were exaggerated. At the war's end, however, the scientists whose task it had been to develop the bomb apparently come to terms with the immense ramifications of their discovery. Not only were these ramifications scientific, they were also moral and political. A perusal of war memoirs of the politicians involved suggests that, to all intents and purposes, the atomic bomb was deemed to be yet another weapon of war, qualitatively different in terms of its destructive power, yet not so different as to be in a unique category. The issues surrounding the dropping of the first bombs on Japan in 1945 are fairly complex; significant in the present context is the fact that there was a developing consensus within the scientific community which, regarding the consequences of nuclear war, saw a clear threat to mankind. Einstein, for example, argued in the autumn of 1945 that

The scientists of Cambridge, as well as those throughout the world, need help urgently in these days of turmoil and unprecedented tension. What makes the present atomic power situation so full of anguish for all of us is the cruel irony wherein one of the greatest and most joyful triumphs of scientific intellect may bring frustration and death rather than spiritual uplifting and more audacious life (Nathan and Norden 1968, 341–2).

Such concerns, as expressed by Einstein, were widely shared. At the very genesis of the nuclear era in New Mexico, Robert Oppenheimer had expressed grave doubts about the prospects of a nuclear world. The concern among the natural scientists developed and grew; they began to discuss issues, hold conferences and try to come to terms with the full implications of the political uses of nuclear power. A clear expression of the commitment of the atomic scientists is their own journal founded shortly after the Second World War, *The Bulletin of Atomic Scientists,* in which much of the ongoing debate took place. A second spur to the mobilization of the natural science community came at the initiative of Bertrand Russell in 1955. Russell drew up a resolution calling for states to concentrate on using peaceful means of conflict resolution and asked eminent scientists to join with him in asking governments to heed the warning contained therein. Many did, and some were eminent, recognized scientists, including Nobel prize-winners, who tried to draw attention to the very central problem of nuclear power as it existed in a strained political environment, such as the Cold War. From the Russell resolution there developed the Pugwash movement. Scientists met at Pugwash in Nova Scotia to explore further the major issues and, from there, developed a series of conferences (which still continues) focusing on world peace.

Apart from the intrinsic importance of the Pugwash movement and the importance of scientists in politics, why was this development important for peace research? In the first place it demonstrated that peace was being discussed not just by minority groups, but by eminent and sensible men who had something to say. Secondly, this served to stimulate (by how much, of course, it is hard to say) others to join in the discussion of the issues and to become committed to the peace-research ethic in the longer term. Several eminent members of the peace research movement have acknowledged the importance of these stimuli in their own development. Thirdly, Pugwash did begin to produce hard information, both crucial to the policy process and to discussions of nuclear war.

Though Pugwash had a role to play, it was not the only movement evolving. In the social sciences there was developing, particularly in the United States, a mood, critical of conventional structural approaches to social science analysis, that came later to be called the behavioural approach. Quite why and how the approach developed in American institutes and universities at about this time is not strictly within our compass, but its net effects are important. In the first place, discussion of social problems (and war and peace were held to be within the sphere of discussion) was less in terms of structures and more in terms of actual behaviour; not just how people ought to behave but how they actually did. Furthermore, behavioural science was avowedly and self-consciously interdisciplinary. Not only the lawyer and the political scientist, but also psychologists, sociologists, economists, might have something to say about political processes. As this mood developed in the field of International Relations, it led to the rise of a school quite clearly critical of prevailing analyses cast in terms of power politics (the premises and criticisms of which are discussed elsewhere in this book). It is not an exaggeration to say that some analyses of International Relations in the 1950s accepted that, if a power-politics model of International Relations were adopted nuclear weapons might be used. It was partly as a response to this mode of analysis that there developed the search for an alternative conventional wisdom. The story of its development is significant in several respects for the historian of peace research, but at this stage we need only acknowledge that, as with Pugwash, a mood of dissatisfaction and innovation was developing.

The development of an alternative mood or consensus in turn provided an environment which, while not exactly conducive to hot-house growth, tolerated and mildly encouraged different approaches. This ought not to imply that academic heretics were somehow sought out and burned at stakes, but it is to say that intellectual movements have frequently appeared not as from a magician's hat, but when individuals and groups with a common concern are able to come together and institutionalize their effort.

As regards peace research, this developed in the mid-1950s: a few social scientists, gathering together and discussing major issues, committing themselves to a mode of study in an area and then searching for funds to continue the enterprise. In the academic year 1954–5 at the Center for Advanced Study in the Behavioural Sciences, based at Stanford University in California, there came together a group of people whose role in peace research is now variously acknowledged but which was then seminal: Kenneth Boulding (an economist), Anatol Rapoport (a mathematical biologist), Harold Lasswell (a political scientist and a colleague of Quincy Wright), Herbert Kelman (a social psychologist) and Clyde Kluckhohn (an anthropologist). Also at the Center in 1954–5 was Stephen Richardson, Lewis Richardson's son who 'had his father's works with him in microfilm, the only form in which they were then available' (Kerman 1974, 48). Clearly, these people did not sit down and 'invent' peace research, but they did come together to give focus and impetus to the movement, bringing together all the previous trends; i.e. a recognition of the work of Richardson and Wright; a concern for behavioural science, 1954–5 being the inaugural year of the Stanford Center and a commitment to the idea that peace was a topic open to analysis.

As a consequence of this meeting of minds (though not a direct consequence) there developed the idea of establishing a centre for the study of conflict and its resolution, as well as a journal. A bulletin, *Research Exchange on Prevention of War,* was already in existence, but it was to be improved, to become 'a more ambitious interdisciplinary journal' (Kerman 1974, 68). Thus, in 1955–6, at the University of Michigan, the *Journal of Conflict Resolution* was founded and it became and remains a central place for debate in the field. Soon on the heels of the journal there developed at Michigan the Centre for Research on Conflict Resolution, though its foundation and financing were not without problems.

Though activity at Stanford and Michigan was intense, there were several other centres of intense activity; and not all the major contributions to peace research were the product of groups. In this respect, the effort of Theodore Lenz is of special significance. Given the efforts of others, some might quibble with the view that Lenz was the 'father of peace research', but in fact Lenz's monograph *Towards a Science of Peace* (1955), ought not to be underestimated. The title of the work gives a clue to the major thrust of the argument contained therein; Lenz's premise was deceptively simple; bring together science and democracy to produce a harmonious ordering of human affairs. It might be argued that there is nothing strikingly original in this, but Lenz's path to this situation was couched in terms that demonstrate his centrality in the foundation of peace research. There are, he argued five 'features of faith' that could achieve the goal of peace. First, the goal is faith in human harmony; second, the means is provided by the faith in facts, the tool being faith in human intelligence. Fourth, the method is faith in science, with faith in democratic or humanistic motivation being the fifth feature. Now there is in this brief tabulation of a new kind of faith the statement of a view which has both a long tradition and a current constituency. It was referred to earlier, but it deserves restatement because it is adherence to this faith which, by and large, marks out many peace researchers from their colleagues in other fields: Believe that a basic harmony is possible and let it permeate your work; accumulate scientific data as to the nature of current and future forms of social order, on the assumption that intelligent minds, when confronted by it, will try to change structures.

As with the Michigan venture and Pugwash, the impact of Lenz's work was widely felt. To those looking for a possible way out of the Cold War syndrome, it represented one. At the same time, as one might expect, the peace research movement was developing in a fashion so obvious that it is frequently overlooked. Since many of the pioneers of the formative period were in universities, much of their work was permeating, even at an early stage, to graduate and undergraduate levels, the effect being to stimulate younger minds, perhaps even converting them to thinking about peace as a positive goal. We ought to remember that the 'Young Turks' or second generation that came along in the 1960s were the undergraduates of the 1950s.

By and large, much of the early work was done in North America; Lenz had been working at Washington University in St Louis, while the Michigan group was developing in various centres prior to their coming together. Though the work was primarily American, it was not uniquely so. In England various groups, taking a route as a supplement or alternative to the Campaign for Nuclear Disarmament, began to found peace groups whose prime aim was the accumulation of information and a raising of consciousness in regard to nuclear weapons in particular. In retrospect these efforts – which produced, among others, the Peace Research Centre in Lancaster – were the early days of the organizations now acknowledged to be foci of research activity. The pattern was to be repeated elsewhere.

What sort of work did the peace researchers actually do? They addressed themselves primarily to the situation which they faced immediately: the nuclear environment. Apart from being the period when peace research took off into sustained growth, the postwar period was also the period of Cold War politics. There were intermittent crises in Formosa, China, Berlin, Germany, Greece, Korea, Hungary and elsewhere, as well as the conspicuous development of nuclear weapons, with the attendant publicity associated with weapons tests. It is hardly surprising, then, to find that the peace research movement addressed itself to these issues. A survey of the early issues of the *Journal of Conflict Resolution* reveals the major preoccupations: What is deterrence? How does it function? How do Soviet and American decision-makers perceive each other? How important is public opinion in the making of foreign policy? How might disarmament be achieved? What are the prospects for arms control? If these were the preoccupations, the means of attack of the peace researchers is also amply demonstrated in the early days; they did not, necessarily, eschew direct action (i.e. signing of petitions, demonstrations, etc.), but as an intellectual group they relied on the Lenzian premise – faith in science. Not a simple, blind faith, but a belief that if data were gathered and assembled in such a way as to conform to the accepted tenets of science to produce bona-fide hypotheses relating political phenomena (e.g. disarmament) to antecedent conditions, then changes might be effected. So in addition to direct analysis and observation, formal analyses of bargaining situations and economic analyses were also included in the ambit of peace research; such studies would try to find recurrent patterns of choices and behaviour that, though theoretical, might produce insights for consideration in concrete situations. The editorial policy of the *Journal of Conflict Resolution* might be taken as a statement of the initial ethic of the movement: the journal

is designed to stimulate and communicate systematic research and thinking on international processes, including the total international system, the interactions among governments and among nationals of different states, and the processes by which nations make and execute foreign policy. It is our hope that theoretical and empirical efforts in this area will help in minimizing the use of violence in resolving international conflicts.

Furthermore, the nature of the problem was made even more explicit:

(*a*) the most important practical problem facing mankind is in International Relations, i.e. the threat of global war;
(*b*) if intellectual progress is to be made, it must be on the basis of interdisciplinary action and work (*Journal of Conflict Resolution,* (1957), **1** (1), 1).

The developing pace of innovation in the social sciences meant that the means of implementing the aim were available or being prepared. Behaviouralism was firmly established, computer applications in social science were sufficiently well developed to permit data-gathering on an unprecedented scale as well as sophisticated model-building. Furthermore, the peace-research constituency was expanding; the *JCR* had a readership and served as a focus; the number of people involved was expanding and so was the geographical scope. The Conflict Research Society was established in Great Britain in 1963, the Canadian Peace Research Institute had been founded by Alan and Hannah Newcombe while, at about the same time, monographs exploring both the possibilities of peace research and its relationship with International Relations began to appear (e.g. Burton 1962, 1965). Though few research efforts were financially sound from the outset, money – so important in the new field of behavioural science, dependent as much of it was on team research and computers – was found from various sources. However, to counterbalance this view it needs to be said that many of the initial efforts were treated with suspicion on the grounds of both novelty and unconventionality, and consequently were financially strained. Nevertheless, of peace research in the early 1960s it could be said that there was a developing corpus of knowledge, an identifiable community of scholars, a relatively small number of journals, newsletters and mimeographed research reports circulating and that peace research had begun to accumulate knowledge about peace.

It may be thought surprising, then, to learn that by 1964 the peace research establishment came in for a degree of criticism on precisely this point; that it was, despite evidence of early suspicion and birth pangs in some areas, too 'establishment' orientated. These early criticisms, in retrospect, were only the first in a series of recurrent waves of criticism, some from within the peace research mainstream, some from without, which were profoundly to affect the nature and direction of further peace research development. Whether these waves of criticism were necessary or desirable is debatable; one view is that, despite some undoubted benefits, the net effect of what came to be called the 'radical critique' was to divert peace research from its initial and still primary aim, the avoidance of international war. Contrary to this is the contention that the critics precipitated a period of introspection and self-analysis which has served to expand and enrich the very essence of the peace research movement, thus endowing it with a greater significance. As time went on, the critics began to appear in areas thought to be outside the geographical mainstream, but in the first instance the critiques appeared in the very countries where peace research had developed and, therefore, become established.

In 1963, Hayden (1963) contended, in acknowledging that peace research was now established, that this was not necessarily a beneficial influence, since most of the work being done was sterile, remote and conservative. In searching for an answer, Hayden agreed that the economic facts of life were largely influential, since peace researchers had to cut their coat according to the available cloth; that is, since money to fund research was coming from governments, industry and foundations, then research would have to fit in with some sorts of demands, implied or explicit, in order to ensure the continued supply of cash. Oppenheimer (1963), on the other hand, approached the notion of the establishment from another related perspective. Oppenheimer agreed that in so far as peace researchers assumed societies to be coherent, integrated wholes capable, by and large, of remaining in a steady state, their work was being tailored to help societies simply to pass through periods of stress and, therefore, aided the system. To some extent these forms of criticism were part of a wider critique of American social science in general, and sociology in particular, for it was in the period of the early 1960s that the dominant model in American sociology, that of Parsonian functionalism, came under fire. The basic premise was that the model used by Talcott Parsons and others was too static in its assumptions, giving little credence to the notions of conflict, change and system transformation. Consequently, one of the major changes effected, in the post-Parsonian-dominance period, was to send researchers and students further in the direction of conflict as a feature in human societies; a change of direction which undoubtedly gave a fillip to the developing area of conflict and peace research.

These were only the first signs of change. In 1964, in Oslo, the *Journal of Peace Research* was established under the editorship of Johan Galtung. It is surely not without significance that the first line to appear in a new journal was in the form of a question: What is peace research? To ask such a question may indicate one of two things: that the initial undertaking and its premises were either incomplete or not self-evident; or that events had changed the nature of the problem to be studied. More light is cast on the issue by Galtung's (1964, 1) discussion of the notion of peace. 'One may look upon peace research as research into the conditions for moving closer to the state we have called GCP (i.e. general and complete peace) or at least not drifting towards GCW (i.e. general and complete war).' Correspondingly, therefore, Galtung distinguished two sorts of peace: negative peace – the absence of violence and war; and positive peace – the integration of human society. Though, in making this distinction Galtung shared the commitment to interdisciplinary work made by the *JCR,* he did posit that the distinction required there to be two sorts of peace research. This is a significant departure; why did it come about? Perhaps because, as a sociologist, Galtung was wanting to see the idea of peace and violence set in the wider context of socio-economic processes, of which political processes (long held to be the paramount among many) was only one. In this sense, therefore, political violence might be simply a manifestation of deeper social or economic cleavages or imbalances. Alternatively, it might be argued that international relations had changed so as to render the older preoccupation with nuclear war rather obsolete. What evidence would support this view? The world had indeed avoided nuclear holocaust and forms of crisis diplomacy evolved to manage nuclear threats. Moreover, the character of international war was seemingly altering. Classic forms of interstate war were being superseded by an increasing number of internal wars and external interventions, conflicts that were classified as guerrilla rather than conventional conflicts. The process of decolonization – or its absence in some areas – had much to do with this. In addition, the reappearance, in the wake of decolonization, of theses relating to neocolonialism and imperialism, coupled with the growing popularity of Marxist analyses of economic and political relations (especially among the New Left) served to effect a change of emphasis in the study of conflict in some quarters, both at the level of the state and international society.

It is in the context of these sorts of changes that the radical critique gained momentum. Not all of the new work being done was akin to firebrand radicalism; in a survey of the early issues of the *Journal of Peace Research* it is clear that the work being done was of a more sociological nature, perhaps adding to rather than threatening the established approaches. However, whereas in 1964, Galtung had hinted that peace research should concern itself as much with the conditions that generate a long-term stable peace as much as preventing war, by 1968 a fellow Scandinavian took this discussion further. A sociologist at the University of Lund, in Sweden, Herman Schmid (1968, 219) took the view that the primary focus of peace research was wrong and proposed an alternative:

Peace research should formulate its problems not in terms meaningful to international and supranational institutions but to suppressed and exploited groups and nations. It should explain not how manifest conflicts are brought under control but how latent conflicts are manifested. It should explain not how integration is brought about, but how conflicts are polarised to a degree where the present international system is seriously challenged or broken down

The article by Schmid stands as a landmark of sorts, since it tried to link the changing patterns of political relations to the changing concerns of peace researchers, bringing the two together with a clear and unambiguous plea for new direction. In this he was successful, since the plea was rapidly taken up. Deprivation, racial inequality and violence (which had rapidly stimulated an interest in analyses of urban unrest in the United States after 1968) soon became – with imperialism, stratification and development – issues for debate and research, often for the first time. Not only did Schmid's prompt lead to new research, it helped to change people's way of looking at peace. Galtung stands as a case in point, for in 1969 he argued:

I used to see [*positive peace*] *in terms of cooperation and integration, but I now agree fully with Herman Schmid that this expresses a much too integrated and symmetric view of conflict groups and probably reflects the east–west conflict or a certàin ideology in connection with that conflict. I would now identify 'positive' peace with 'social justice'* (Galtung 1969, 190).

In the same article he took the discussion of social justice and violence a stage further, introducing the notion of structural violence. Personal violence, as a term, implies the direct infliction of pain and harm by one individual on another in a direct, unequivocal sense; for example, if one member of a gang kicks or stabs an opponent he is inflicting personal violence. Structural violence, on the other hand, implies something rather different; structural violence occurs not as a direct result of an attack or assault, but rather as a product of a social relationship, where one person (or group, or class, or country) is able to maintain a relationship over another, such that the latter is unable to attain a degree of self-attainment or self-realization. In this sense, the case of the master-slave relationship best exemplifies the notion of structural violence: even though the slave-owner may be benevolent and trusting, in so far as he maintains the system of slavery he is doing violence to another.

The implications of this shift in emphasis as it relates to violence are discussed in detail below, but at this stage it is clear that it heralded a new phase of debate; if violence was not just the physical doing of harm in the traditional sense, where was peace research to go? How was future research to be directed and into which areas first?

To dwell, thus far, on the growth of the radical critique is not to imply that the transformations of the 1960s and early 1970s produced only a mishmash of competing reinterpretations and 'great debates'. While these events did frequently occur, the field progressed in spite of them. There was a rapid growth of centres of research in North America and Europe (the 'traditional' centres), and also in Eastern Europe, Asia and the Third World. In 1966, for example, the Stockholm International Peace Research Institute (SIPRI) was established, funded by the Swedish Parliament, and very rapidly established itself as a centre producing work of relevance and high quality. Its annual *Yearbook of World Armaments and Disarmament* soon became an established authoritative source of data, consulted by international organizations and governments. Research also came closer to another audience – university and college students. It is a remarkable feature of the developments in social sciences, generally, that their rapid growth in the 1960s coincided with the rapid growth in university student populations, this serving to facilitate the wider dissemination of relatively new material. Hence, the readership of the established and newer journals expanded and in the longer term graduate courses in peace research, conflict analysis and related fields began to appear (on the wider significance of this development, see below). The major effect of the growth of the field – and the accounts critical of it – was to expand the broad spectrum of peace research; the older, conventional wisdom that had motivated the pioneers of Pugwash and the early social scientists was not displaced. It took its place in the spectrum, now being only one band in it.

Current issues in peace research

Most of the issues raised in the transitional decade of the 1960s are still being discussed. Why has progress not been made? Why have these issues not been dealt with and either assimilated or discarded? Perhaps for two reasons; it might be argued that the persistence of these issues is testimony to the fact that though peace research 'took-off' in the early days, its journey was bound to be short until it had put its own crew in order. But this is to say no more than that peace research is, if nothing else, still an essentially young venture. More importantly, it can be argued that the issues raised are so fundamental and so difficult to answer that no easy answers will suffice; that the difficult transition period is bound to persist until the answers are worked out, but that until then 'transition' or 'debate' are terms that need not carry pejorative associations.

The nature of the difficulties faced may be illuminated simply by investigating the concept of peace. What the term meant in 1960 was not the same as it meant in 1970 for many peace researchers. If we look at the extreme interpretations first, the topic becomes clearer. On the one hand there is the view that peace researchers should confine themselves in the first instance to a particular view of peace; namely, that which is concerned with the problem of international war. A proponent of this view is Karl Deutsch (1975, 246) who contends that 'Peace research seeks to identify the conditions which make large-scale war less probable . . . this is a minimal definition of peace [which] calls peace merely the absence of large-scale war.' This need not imply that a conservative position is being propounded or that those who favour a minimalist position somehow abjure the possibility of social justice. What it does mean is that peace and social justice are best achieved if priority is first given to the initial problem; the logic of this is clear – those people killed in (nuclear) war do not even have the possibility of participating in a just social order. This is to assign the first order of priority to a particular form of problem, based on the premise that elimination of war precedes peace.

The alternative view is based on the idea that peace is to be equated with social justice; put another way, violence does not mean killing and suffering in war, but deprivation, starvation, repression and hunger in times normally described as 'peace' – i.e. where there is no war being fought, but where structural violence is endemic in socio-economic structures. Thus, as Schmid argued above, the aim, in the view of the maximalists, is to find out why some latent conflicts become manifest. Turning round the minimalist logic, the reason why there are wars, it is said, is because there is no peace; if there were peace, in the maximalist sense, then the resort to war would be unnecessary. Now if we argue that the minimalist and maximalist interpretations are the extremities of a peace continuum, we admit, logically, that a middle ground is possible, where there is a major concern with the problems of transition from a world where war and violence are facts of life to be acknowledged (because, unfortunately, they will not go away), to a world where their employment as tools or means in pursuit of ends becomes unlikely. Here, the view is taken that the middle grounders (e.g. Kenneth Boulding) acknowledge that coercion and threat systems exist, but they try to find ways of circumventing them. This 'middle ground' rests on the assumption that concrete data about the incidence of war are required, as well as schemes regarding the nature of a warless world, speculative as these might seem. Hence, the concern for, say, the economic effects of disarmament, or the search for superordinate goals.

But, it may be asked, what does it matter if there are different interpretations of peace; peace, like 'good' and 'moral', is a term that the individual must come to terms with himself. On one level, of course, this is undeniable. Yet for the development of peace research, as a committed social science venture, the adoption of a particular perspective on peace is crucial since it is likely to determine not only an individual world-view as to the desirable ends, but also the research strategy (or action strategy) that is likely to be adopted. This, in turn, will help determine the nature of the future development of peace research itself. Consider again the minimalist view; if the aim is to curtail the incidence of 'large-scale war', to use Deutsch's term, then a particular research strategy is implied. Try to identify the phenomenon of war by accumulating data on the nature of war, its duration, its observable causes, the nature of the transition from small-scale to large-scale wars. Having identified the phenomenon and tried to measure it, the task then is to explain it; in what circumstances do wars begin, how do they end, how do they change in character, when does peace give way to war. But what if a perfectly valid explanation of war is developed? Then what? This is where one reverts to the initial premise of peace research; the aim is to do something with the accumulated knowledge. It does not stand as an edifice to truth, pure and simple, but it is meant to be used to determine policy. In this way, it is contended that if evidence is presented to decision-makers it may tell them something about the desirability of certain sorts of policy and, perhaps, help effect suitable (peaceful) alternatives. To reiterate the *JCR* commitment, 'it is our hope that theoretical and empirical efforts in this area will help in minimising the use of violence in resolving international conflicts'. To this extent, the aim is to establish peace research as an applied science. In addition, new institutes have committed themselves to this line of attack – to provide information with a clear relevance to contemporary issues. The journal *Instant Research on Peace and Violence,* based at the Tampere Peace Research Institute in Finland, firmly declares in its statement of aim that, 'To be of practical interest, it is considered important that the journal contains conclusions as well as discussions, implications and recommendations.' However, there still remains a major problem; it is still not clear as to who are the best recipients of accumulated knowledge. For example, if decision-makers are in the habit of using force and defining it as useful, how can they be made receptive to views that challenge that basic premise?

It is here that we find the link forged by the middle grounders (e.g. Lenz, Boulding) between the maximalists and the minimalists. By itself, new information may not change perceptions and attitudes, but if decision-making structures could be changed and linked to changed perceptions, then in the longer term the prospects for peace might be materially improved. (But this is not to say that decision-makers are always oblivious to new information, as the SIPRI venture has amply demonstrated.) Hence, one of the issues much discussed by the middle-grounders has been concerned with the integration of two variables: changing perceptions and changing structures. Structural change is the obvious point which unites the maximalists; only by changing these present structures can the long-term goal of peace and harmony be achieved. As part of the radical critique of peace research it was proposed in some quarters that peace research, in so far as it was concerned with the attainment of justice, should include within its ambit the idea of revolution research. This raises serious questions, not least – is it just to use violence to eradicate violence to achieve peace? In a sense this is simply a restatement of the traditional just-war concept; that in certain circumstances violence in pursuit of moral ends is justifiable. Unfortunately, though the distinction has some validity in the realm of the metaphysical, it has been notoriously difficult to implement in practice. In the early days of civil unrest in Ulster, for example, the Civil Rights movement was acknowledged to be acting in pursuance of just and legitimate demands; unfortunately the initial stimulus of fairness and justice became lost in a welter of other conflicts. For the most part, then, the maximalists have tried to come to terms not with how best to achieve revolutionary change, but how to effect long-term changes in social structures and processes that might effect peace. In this realm, the idea of a 'technology of peace' has become established, especially among European peace researchers.

One clear avenue of advance has been in the field of peace education. This involves not a direct input into a particular policy process, but the gradual development of a new consciousness that leads, in turn, to a different perception of what peace might mean, in accordance with changes in research (e.g. Galtung, Curle). Thus, at the University of Bradford there exists a Department of Peace Studies, finance for which was rapidly found when the idea for the creation of a professorial chair and department were first mooted in the early 1970s. The course is not vocational in the strict sense; people cannot be trained and then go out to 'do peace'. Rather, the venture, along with others in schools and colleges all over the world, aims to raise the level of consciousness; to try to alter attitudes regarding peace in the hope that this will stimulate changes in structures. It is perhaps significant that the first professor of peace studies at Bradford was formerly associated with the fields of education and development (Curle 1971). Couched in terms of maximalist–minimalist approaches to peace, this discussion of a major substantive issue has hinted at the existence of a second issue, that related to value-commitment and the application of peace research. In 1970 Anatol Rapoport asked, 'Can peace research be applied?' and, though the ensuing discussion was not of a stature sufficient to warrant the term 'great debate', it did prompt an enquiry into the essential nature of applied peace research. The net effect of the dialogue (Rapoport 1970, Kent 1971, Stohl and Chamberlain 1972) was to demonstrate that application of findings was not nearly so easy as might be imagined, even though peace research aimed to be an applied science. In one sense, however, an answer to the question posed by Rapoport depends upon one's interpretation of the notion of peace. If the minimalist position is preferred, then the aim might be simply to accumulate data on specific issue areas, to be brought to the notice of decision-makers, an informed public, or both. An answer to Rapoport's question would then be 'Yes, but not all potential consumers of information would want the same sorts of information.'

Moreover, a crucial question remains open: Which is the best target audience for any new information? If the extreme maximalist position is chosen, then it is unlikely that it will become 'applied' in the accepted sense for, as Rapoport indicates, it is unlikely that a government will fund research to subvert its own values. Nevertheless, to acknowledge that work in the maximalist school has developed and coexists with other approaches need not imply that it is bound to fold up. Rather, as with peace education courses, it is likely to develop in places where longer-term changes are the major focus of discussion, rather than more pressing policy-relevant issues. Though this is something of a general picture and inevitably simplified, it does give a clue as to the flavour of the applied science debate. The evidence suggests, again, that various schools can be accommodated; SIPRI goes from strength to strength, university departments are taking up the peace-research themes and, though many have problems relating to finance, independent institutes persist.

The extent to which one seeks to apply the findings of peace research depend in part on the relationship between two variables: personal commitment (i.e. a value premise) and the requirements of methodological rigour (Kelman 1968). This is a thorny issue related to a basic question; if I am interested in amassing useful information in an effort to try to eradicate a major social problem, how much heed needs to be paid to intellectual rigour? Again, it may be argued that this is a case for personal choice, but the point has been made that there has, in some quarters, been a retreat into the defences of methodology in the face of the range of difficulties presented by commitment. This may be an overstatement, but in recent years a good deal of work in the field has appeared, the immediate relevance of which is unclear. This is not to argue that every new research communication should be accompanied by an oath of commitment, but that the aim of the movement is not just to produce sophisticated technical models for their own sake. The most that the motivated scholar can do is to make clear his basic premises that have led him to research into a field and then go on to undertake his work and do his best. A good example of the way this can be done is demonstrated by Bruce Russett's work on American defence; Russett's commitment is clear, since he argues in a preface, 'I wrote this book because I am concerned for my country' (Russett 1970). Yet his findings are perhaps more likely to be taken up since his method of analysis is scientific and explicit.

In 1970, two Danish scholars argued that the utilization of science had produced a negative effect, an effect that served to elevate technical sophistication at the expense of value premises (Olsen and Jarvad 1970). In the first instance the remarks were aimed at North American academics in the context of the war in Indo-China and, to be sure, it is no more than a statement of the obvious to say that some academics incurred the wrath of their colleagues due to the adoption of political stances in relation to Vietnam. On the other hand, to argue from this that it somehow portrays a general and widespread mood is an overstatement; the concern to bring the thorny issue of value commitment into social science, to explore the limits and strengths of 'value-free' science remains an enduring preoccupation (some would say *the* major issue) in social science. Moreover, in the case of peace research, it has already amassed a wealth of experience in confronting the issue of relevance, an issue only now being faced (in the light of the Vietnam experience) by some of the more established academic disciplines.

The third leg of the peace research tripod, implied in discussions of the first two (substance and values), is methodology. Whereas in the first instance the commitment was to an interdisciplinary effort, the results of the growth have been spectacular. In the early days there was a reliance on certain limited ways of knowing, for example informed speculation, but the availability of complementary and competing modes of analysis have served to enrich the field. In a discussion of research findings, methodological considerations – how we know what we know and how we have accumulated data – are crucial. One effect of the widening of the scope of peace research has been to create berths where different methodologies can rest. Thus, while peace research may now be as much about development as deterrence, population as much as proliferation of nuclear weapons, this concern for wider issues has given rise to innovations in methodology. Data can now be collected from several levels of analysis – group, class, person, state, system – on the assumption that there are general, recurring patterns of behaviour, with conflict and violence not necessarily made unique by their appearance in only a few social contexts. Experimental data (e.g. simulations, surveys, etc.) complement findings from history, and so on. Economic analyses and formal, abstract models are also employed in increasing numbers, reflecting the increasing interdependence of socio-political issues. Thus, one of the major developments associated with – but not confined to – peace research has been methodological sophistication, a concern for understanding how we know what we know. This represents both a natural development in the progress of social sciences and a means of bridging the rigour–vigour issue.

Yet in another sense, it can be agreed that the concern for methodology is either overstressed or not as important as first assumed. As far back as 1936 Mannheim argued that

New forms of knowledge, in the last analysis, grow out of the conditions of collective life and do not depend for their emergence upon the prior demonstration by a theory of knowledge that they are possible; they do not, therefore, need to be legitimised by an epistemology. The relationship is actually quite the reverse; the development of theories of scientific knowledge takes place in the preoccupation with empirical data and the fortunes of the former vary with those of the latter (Mannheim 1936).

Liberally interpreted, then, it could be said that one of the points made by Mannheim is that the asking of the questions 'Why?' and 'How?' should follow the actual impetus to undertake the work. This is a subtle way of resolving the dilemma between commitment and science, and also a way of avoiding it: the basic impetus should be to get the work done, because it is felt to be necessary, then to enquire into the foundations of methodology. By so doing, Wallace (1972, 28) argues, peace research may be able to prove the validity of the enterprise. 'It is often difficult to realize that concepts, generalizations and findings which are inadequate or incomplete from the point of view of our theoretical concerns may be entirely sufficient to deal with practical problems.' Moreover, by getting on with the work, peace researchers may shed the cloak of humility that many of them still seem to wear.

Where, then, does this leave peace research? The survey of the historical evolution of the enterprise, it is hoped, has indicated its distinctive features, of which there are three. Thus, peace research may be defined as the area contained in the triangle, the sides of which constitute: (*a*) the *substantive* issues of peace and violence; (*b*) the *methodological* issues involved in amassing good data about a complex social phenomenon; (*c*) basic concern for a value *commitment* in the study of peace. To recap, peace researchers do not seek knowledge for its own sake, nor do they approach the study of peace in a detached manner; they do it in order to enlighten the topic in the hope of achieving some positive benefit. In so doing, they are distinguished from propagandists and action groups by their commitment to achieve a knowledge that conforms to accepted criteria of 'good knowledge'. Adherence to these criteria means that peace research is able to accommodate a wide population; it includes sophisticated model-builders and those who claim to be thoroughly innumerate; it includes radicals and moderates, in terms of both research outlook and political persuasion; it includes political scientists, anthropologists, biologists, economists, historians and psychologists. Moreover, and in spite of often difficult confrontations (particularly between Americans and Europeans), the field persists and continues to grow in a relatively coherent fashion, expanding in terms of numbers involved, intellectual compass and geographical scope. International organizations are taking up the peace-research cause, and it is surely a point of significance that the United Nations General Assembly has twice in the last ten years commissioned reports designed to catalogue the growth of the field.

Despite these signs of health, vigorous debate and stimulus, critics might argue that the entire field of peace research is nothing more than a rag-bag of well-intentioned academics trying to attain the unattainable. They would do well to remember two things; intellectual innovation often looks messy in the early days. Peace research, in its present form, has been with us for only a couple of decades and, therefore, can expect to make major mistakes and waste some time. Second, the comments often levelled at peace research were aimed at another new field less than twenty years ago, when it was argued that International Relations was in a dreadful mess. As the other chapters in this book make clear, the development of theoretical approaches within International Relations and in fields akin to it has been nothing short of remarkable. It is to the affinity between International Relations and peace research that we now turn.

Peace research and International Relations

In the first instance, the relationship between peace research and International Relations depends upon not only how one perceives peace research but how one identifies the quintessence of International Relations. If it is argued that the nature of the international system is such as to make it unique because it comprises primarily states who acknowledge no authority higher than themselves, then it can also be argued that the likelihood of a link between the fields is remote. But as the other contributions to this book have demonstrated, International Relations is not simply about power-politics and states; it is also about non-state actions, communications flows, systems analysis and so on. There have been, as in peace research, innovations related to both the analysis and substance of International Relations.

The questioning of the traditional concepts of International Relations and the consequent shift away from a strict state-centric model, means that the study of international structures and processes is even more closely linked to the study of socio-political systems in general. Even though some of the work done in the field of systems theory may ultimately prove to be of doubtful value, the shift away from state to system as unit of analysis is surely something more than an academic fad. The trend towards more sophisticated and complex analysis is, moreover, evident in other areas of the field. Foreign policy analysts are crossing traditional boundaries when they discuss linkage politics and the notion of 'coupling'. The point is clear; no longer is it possible to assume the strict validity of a state-centric model. Why is this significant in a discussion of peace research? Peace research as an approach to the general problems of human behaviour and the specific goal of peace is characterized by a relatively eclectic style of attack; that is, even though it is concerned with the goal of world peace, it is concerned to apply the findings from social processes other than the global to the effecting of a global solution, i.e. even though the essence of international politics may be said to be the problem of world power concentrations, it is also important to say that in so far as international politics is giving way to world society, then the findings that stress the similarity of social processes may become fundamental to the study of the global milieu. That being the case, and the view is open to criticism, then, logically, the way is open for the field of peace research to contribute to the study of world society. Thus, it is admitted that in terms of essential concerns there is a degree of overlap between peace research and International Relations. This is not to say that the academic disciplines are inseparable; there is a clear boundary between the areas. International Relations is concerned to understand the structures and processes in world politics and in this it draws on other fields, such as politics, economics, strategic studies and peace research. Yet it is clear that certain of the issues central to peace research are not strictly relevant to the academic field of International Relations, for example Marxist analyses of social deprivation or schemes for peace education. They are akin to, not separate from, International Relations. The physical manifestation of the degree of overlap lies in the fact that many International Relations scholars are also peace researchers, for example Bruce Russett, John Burton, Karl Deutsch and David Singer.

Sharing some of the same issues of substance means that there is often a similarity of approach and method. Thus, Herbert Kelman (1968, 298), in highlighting the very close links between the fields, contends that

Peace research does not differ – and rightly so – from any other research on International Relations or political behaviour, in terms of the criteria for scientific objectivity and validity that it tries to meet, just as cancer research does not differ in these respects from other biochemical or microbiological investigations. Yet the selection of problems to which the peace researcher addresses himself is based, at least in part, on his desire to contribute to a peaceful world order.

Hence, there is an obvious overlap in terms of common methodology. But there is a crucial distinction. Whereas International Relations, as a bona-fide academic discipline, does not necessarily seek to produce knowledge that is always relevant to policy, but rather is, in part, knowledge about international systems for its own sake, peace researchers eschew this stance since they are defined to be committed. This represents nothing more than an academic division of labour, and a proper one at that; the seeker of the truth, for its own sake, may perform the very valuable function of revealing that 'the truth' may be unpleasant and does not necessarily convey the image of reality held by the committed or relevance-orientated scholar. In this, there is an affinity between peace research and strategic studies; both seek to unearth and apply knowledge and though their essential concerns are different (one takes the existence of and possibility of conflict for granted and the other tries to eliminate it) they stand in a similar position in relation to International Relations, i.e. as an essential adjunct to, but distinct from, the academic core. Moreover, the careers of the International Relations scholars/peace researchers may serve to demonstrate that the sparks set off by the clash of roles may serve the innovative function of perceiving the same issues differently; this in turn may unlock long-shut doors, simply by means of different perceptions, for example that international relationships based on economic or social matters may, in fact, be more important than political issues, despite the traditional assumption that the latter is, by definition, the more important. In another respect, International Relations has much to learn from a survey of peace research. As has been often repeated, peace research involves commitment and relevance. Yet in International Relations, recently the idea of policy orientation has come to the fore. Vietnam and the crisis it precipitated in American academic circles has much to do with this, as well as the entry into policy-making circles of former scholars, such as Kissinger, Brzezinski and Rostow. Whether and how International Relations scholars can reach an accommodation on the issue is still to be decided, but in making up their minds they might be well advised to review the debates about commitment that have had a central role in the development of peace research. To want to be relevant and taken seriously in government or official circles does not always mean that one always is. Furthermore, serious issues regarding the status of funding and contract research might also be involved.

Peace research and International Relations share the same style of analysis; they are both interdisciplinary, but for different reasons, and in this area peace research is far in advance of International Relations. Whereas, in the formative stages of the behavioural revolution, there were numerous pleas that International Relations should be about political science, psychology, anthropology, etc. in short that the discipline should be less of a historical field and more eclectic, in the case of peace research the researchers, when they came together, were from different disciplines; they did not decide to become interdisciplinary, they were. Hence, peace research has found room for physicists, chemists, botanists, biologists, economists, anthropologists and the like. They are united in their focus on peace, diversified in their approach to it. The different premises, assumptions, styles of approach and perceptions of reality are as much a source of strength and innovation as diversity and disagreement. General agreement is not necessarily a good thing in itself. If we follow the premise of Feyerabend (1975), we may come down in favour of the view that innovation and breakthrough are likely to occur in the absence of agreed method, often by chance, in an atmosphere akin to intellectual anarchy. To that extent, the view that 'anything goes' *might* be a major source of strength.

To say, in conclusion, that the focus of peace research is on the causes of war and the conditions of peace is to admit of a logical overlap between it and International Relations, which is concerned with the study of the general patterns of behaviour to be found in world society. The fields are not the same – but they do share a commonality in terms of both subject-matter and methodology. There is also evidence of further points of contact in so far as policy problems come more into the reckoning in International Relations and foreign policy analysis. The *Concise Oxford Dictionary* defines symbiosis as the permanent union between organisms, each of which depends for its existence on the other; though one might not go so far as to say that peace research could not exist without International Relations, or vice versa, there is enough in common to suggest that the relationship approaches one of symbiosis, with each feeding from the other. It is to be hoped, therefore, that the progressive, lively and often controversial development of these fields might contribute to a greater understanding of the notion of peace. Indeed in conjunction with the developments in other areas catalogued here, there is perhaps every reason to believe that peace research can stake a legitimate claim to have something of import to say in the development of International Relations, informing it with a sense of importance, urgency and vigour.

References and Further Reading

Burton, J.W. (1962) *Peace Theory, the Preconditions of Disarmament.* New York, Knopf.
Burton, J.W. (1965) 'Peace research and international relations', *Journal of Conflict Resolution,* viii (3) 282–6.
Curle, A. (1971) *Making Peace,* London, Tavistock.
Deutsch, K.W. (1975) 'Peace research', in *International Yearbook of Foreign Policy Analysis,* Vol. II, P. Jones (ed.), London, Croom Helm.
Feyerabend, P. (1975) *Against Method,* London, New Left Books.
Galtung, J. (1964) 'Editorial', *Journal of Peace Research,* **1** (1).
Galtung, J. (1969) 'Violence, peace and peace research', *Journal of Peace Research* No. 3, 167–92.
Hayden, T. (1963) 'Peace research USA', *Our Generation Against Nuclear War,* Special Peace Research Supplement, Volume 3.2, p. 55–61.
Kelman, H.C. (1968) *A Time to Speak: Values and Social Research,* San Francisco, Jossey-Bass.
Kent, G. (1971) 'The application of peace studies' *Journal of Conflict Resolution,* xv (1), 47–53.
Kerman, C.E. (1974) *Creative Tension: The Life and Thought of Kenneth Boulding,* Ann Arbor, Univ. of Michigan.
Lenz, T. (1955) *Towards a Science of Peace,* London, Halcyon Press.
Mannheim, K. (1936) *Ideology and Utopia,* London, Routledge and Kegan Paul.
Nathan, O. and Norden, H. (1968) *Einstein on Peace,* New York, Schocken Books.
Olsen, O.J. and Jarvad, I.M. (1970) 'The Vietnam Confererence papers: A case study in the failure of peace research', in *Peace Research Society (International) Papers* Vol. xiv.
Oppenheimer, M. (1963) 'Peace research: A criticism', *American Behavioural Scientist* (October).
Rapoport A. (1970) 'Can peace research be applied?' *Journal of Conflict Resolution,* **14** (2), 277–86.
Richardson, L.F. (1960a) *Statistics of Deadly Quarrels,* Chicago, Quadrangle.
Richardson, L.F. (1960b) *Arms and Insecurity,* Pittsburgh, Boxwood Press.
Russett, B.M. (1970) *What Price Vigilance?* New Haven, Yale Univ. Press.
Schmid, H. (1968) 'Politics and peace research', *Journal of Peace Research,* No. 3, 217–32.
Stohl, M. and Chamberlain, M. (1972) 'Alternative futures for peace research', *Journal of Conflict Resolution,* xvi (4), 523–30.
Wallace, M. (1972) 'The radical critique of peace research: An exposition and interpretation, in *Peace Research Reviews,* iv (4).
Wright, Q. (1965) *A Study of War* (2nd edn.), Chicago, Univ. of Chicago Press.

Further reading

N.B. The available literature is, of course, vast. These few titles relate to works that synthesise the major issues current in peace research and work presently going on. Most have lengthy bibliographies that can be consulted by those wishing to follow the detailed evolution of peace research.

Dedring, Juergen, (1976) *Recent Advances in Peace and Conflict Research: A Critical Survey,* London and Beverly Hills, Sage.

Fink, C.F. and Boulding, E. (eds.) (1972) 'Peace research in transition: A symposium', special issue of *Journal of Conflict Resolution,* xvi (4).

Newcombe, A and Newcombe, H. (1969) *Peace Research Around the World,* CPRI, Oakville, Ontario.

Peace Research Reviews (1972) iv (4). Special issue devoted to 'Alternative approaches to Peace research.'

United Nations, General Assembly, Document A/10199 (30th Session). Report of the Secretary-General, *Scientific Work on Peace Research.*

Chapter 13

Theories of International Relations: the normative and policy dimensions*

G.L. Goodwin

Theories of International Relations abound. Yet neither their exact epistemological status nor their educational value is always obvious, while their relevance to the day-to-day activities of diplomatic life is often hotly contested. Perhaps the first thing is to define, if only for the purposes of this article, what is meant by theory. Here theory is defined as a set of interrelated and logically consistent propositions, either about international phenomena in general or about the nature, structure and processes of particular aspects of international relations, which in principle are subject to empirical testing. The appetite for theorizing can vary. Theories may be mainly heuristic devices intended to aid our understanding of the nature and texture of international life; they may have an eirenic purpose intended to help identify the kinds of arrangements which might conduce to a more peaceful international society; or they may be accorded a predictive or prescriptive role aimed at delineating the parameters of choice open to the policy-maker. The main concern of this article is with the normative and policy dimensions of theory. However, whatever the particular concern, most theoretical studies in International Relations fall into one or other of six branches: the historical, the clarificatory, the classificatory, the explanatory, the predictive and the prescriptive. These six branches are not, of course, mutually exclusive. Most theorizing partakes of more than one. And the normative and policy dimensions of each can be illuminated whether the approach is in a mainly traditional vein (as is adopted here) or from a more 'scientific' viewpoint.

The first branch of international theory is concerned with what has historically been said on some of the perennial issues of International Relations; for instance, on the origins and characteristics of the states system; on the ideas underlying the legal and diplomatic practices of post-Westphalian Europe and the balance of power, that 'most solid foundation of lasting concord' in the system; or on the persistent tension between the notions of peace, justice and order. This historical dimen-

---

*I am indebted to my colleagues, Christopher Hill and James Mayall, for some helpful comments on an earlier version of this article.

sion of international theory is undertaken not so much as an end in itself, though it can be that, but as an essential part of the exploration of some central and persistent questions of International Relations. It is not primarily a study of the 'texts', but rather an exploration of these questions in the belief that not only have they been asked whenever and wherever the condition of International Relations has obtained but also that they continue to be of contemporary concern. The aim then is to examine the traditions of thought on these questions, to trace the historical antecedents of concepts, assumptions and explanatory theories, through the memoirs of statesmen and the writings of historians, political theorists and international lawyers. By so doing, seemingly new approaches to the questions can be put in perspective by eliciting the debt to be paid to some established line of thought. A particular merit of this approach is that it can help bring to light, or make more explicit, the presuppositions of thought – and also the value judgements – which colour the perceptions of the scholar and the practitioner alike. The concern here is thus with illuminating the present by drawing on the wisdom and experience of the past, not merely in the form of a history of international thought – valuable as that can be – but rather in the spirit of political theory where the exploration of certain perennial issues of political relations proceeds in conjunction with allusions to the answers that have been given to these issues both in the past and more contemporaneously. It is 'a tradition of speculation about relations between states, a tradition imagined as the twin of speculation about the state to which the name "political theory" is appropriated' (Wight 1966, 17).

The second branch is the clarificatory.[1] Much confusion arises both in diplomatic life and in the academic study of International Relations from the fuzziness of many of the central concepts, such as power, interest, justice, rights and legitimacy. The vocabulary of international politics cannot achieve the measure of precision to be found in the natural sciences or indeed in such social sciences as economics, but if diplomatic life is to be less scarred by the use of these concepts as political slogans and if the academic study of International Relations is to gain in rigour and coherence then they need to be used with greater care and not as means for deception or concealment or as excuses for stereotyped thinking. The key concepts of 'power' and 'interest', for instance, are often insufficiently thought through and tend, therefore, to obscure rather than to clarify.

The limits of clarifications must, of course, be recognized. Many of these concepts are shot through with inescapable ambiguities, while others, such as justice, order and legitimacy, are normative concepts which are particularly resistant to being neatly encapsulated in clear-cut definitions. They are what Professor Gallie (1964) has called 'essentially contested concepts'. Controversy about their 'meaning' is part of their very life-blood. Nevertheless, it is incumbent upon the scholar as well as the practitioner to pay heed to the common usage of such terms – where such exists – or at least to indicate as precisely as possible in what sense a term is being used in a particular context. Moreover, the clarification of the way in which some of these terms first entered the academic and diplomatic vocabulary, of the differing senses in which they have been and are used, of the corresponding terms in other languages and the extent to which different nuances are rooted in different cultural traditions, might be helpful both for the scholar and for the practitioner. A scholar's penchant for drawing fine distinctions may not always be to the practitioner's taste, yet the latter can also benefit. 'I am told', Lord Balfour is once reported to have said, 'people complain that I am given to drawing fine distinctions. I am. High policy depends upon fine distinctions; and, if people find they cannot understand them, they should entrust their affairs to those who do' (Manning 1962, 64).

The third branch is the classificatory. Theories are also, it has been said, 'nets to catch what we call "the world"' (Popper), a means of identifying and marshalling, as a preliminary to explaining, relevant data. Much of this branch of international theory takes the form of taxonomies, that is, classificatory structures for helping to identify and order differing patterns of transactions in international relations and to indicate their origins and main characteristics. Classificatory structures cannot reconcile their inevitably static nature with the evidently dynamic nature of the patterns of transactions which have been classified (Dawisha 1976). Nevertheless, taxonomies can help to rank and order the key variables, trace some typical interconnections, and perhaps posit some tentative hypotheses about recurrent patterns of transactions and interactions which can on occasion provide a basis for modest comparative analysis. There is of course a close link here with the clarificatory branch, as Martin Wight has illustrated in his categorization of the concept of the balance of power into eleven distinct meanings and his delineation of the characteristics of each (Wight 1966, 151), a categorization which greatly helps to clarify the concept. Again, in the field of foreign policy analysis the taxonomic approach could be particularly valuable in decision-making theory and input–output theory, both of which may yet prove a rewarding preliminary to the more exacting exercise of comparative analysis, an exercise of potential value to the academic and policy-maker alike.

The explanatory branch of international theory is not only considerably more ambitious, it is central to the whole academic enterprise. It is concerned not merely with ordering the data and identifying the critical variables, but also with explaining possible causal connections between events and suggesting explanatory hypotheses about why certain patterns of transactions and interactions have developed within the international system and why the members of that system, above all the sovereign states, behave as they do. The appetite for explanatory theories, both general and particular, is naturally almost insatiable. Yet the status and validity of any general explanatory theory, that is, one which purports to offer a unified explanation of international phenomena, must be open to question. The enterprise is too redolent of the ancient quest for the philosopher's stone. The search for particular – or partial – theories, that is, those addressed to particular issues, is more promising. There are theories about the nature of the interstate system (or society); is it analogous to domestic political systems or has it its own distinctive characteristics; if so what are these characteristics and, in particular, why is a modicum of order sustained despite recurrent conflict? There are the exogenous explanatory theories which stress the response of states to pressures external to themselves, that is, emanating from the interstate system; for instance, the geographical, the economic and the strategic. There are the indigenous explanatory theories which focus on the internal make-up of states which are seen as the main determinants of the external behaviour of states, for instance, the cultural, the psychological, the economic, the ideological and the bureaucratic politics theories.

Indigenous theories are apt to attribute a greater range of choice than states usually possess, and exogeneous theories tend to underplay the idiosyncratic element in state behaviour; both are prone to fall into the reductionist trap by elevating single-factor explanations into more general explanatory theory. One of the most difficult questions in any analysis is, in fact, the relative weight to be accorded to this theory or that. There are other methodological problems. How far has a theory been adequately tested – and what does that mean? With what degree of reliability has it emerged – what is its status? To what range of occurrences geographically – the horizontal dimension – and over what period of time – the vertical dimension – it is applicable? And throughout there is the need to reconcile – or at least to hold in a fruitful tension – the historical and the 'scientific' dimensions of analysis (Goodwin 1973, 243), to allow for the subjective element present in most theoretical insights, and to recognize that international life, like life itself, is invariably so shot through with the incongruous and paradoxical that it rarely fits neatly into rigorously constructed and logically consistent theoretical frameworks. Nevertheless, in so far as almost any kind of analysis presupposes a set of theoretical preconceptions of likely causal relationships, explanatory theories can help to make what is implicit more explicit, to refine and check differing explanatory hypotheses and generally to sharpen the everyday tools of political and historical analysis of both academics and practitioners.

The predictive branch of international theory is beset with the most serious problems. Even when prediction is limited to the enunciation of a range of possibilities ranked in a hierarchy of probabilities, the play of the contingent (Singer 1973) and of radical and strategic uncertainty (Burns 1968) can wreak havoc with even the most confident probabilistic assertions. Extrapolations from the past are notoriously unreliable, while the vulnerability of the international system to bouts of cataclysmic change has been vividly illustrated more than once this century.

More often than not 'Forecasting is the art of saying what will happen, then explaining why it didn't' (*Economist* 21 August 1976, 67). Nevertheless, some measure of prediction is intrinsic to any policy-oriented studies or discussion of contemporary events, whether, for instance, in the fields of strategy or economic relations. 'In the strategic field, lead time for modern weapons systems is now anything from ten to fifteen years' (Edmonds 1975, 151). Consequently, some attempt has to be made to try to envisage the kind of political environment in which a particular weapon system may have to operate. Or in the field of contemporary economic relations some consideration of the future pattern of the production of and demand for raw materials, mineral and energy resources, and of the shifting configurations of economic power of states and the extent to which it is likely to be translated into political influence, is inescapable. What merits further exploration is the epistemological status of various predictive theories and the assumptions – cultural, psychological, methodological – implicit in most prognostications of the future.

The prescriptive branch of theory is closely related. The boundaries are elastic and can embrace both the 'milieu' and 'possessional' goals of states – to use Wolfers' terminology (Wolfers 1962) – and men's search for a 'better' world. Whatever the policy orientation, one of the basic concerns is to illumine means/ends relationships and to ensure that the normative dimensions of policy choices are made quite explicit and subject to careful scrutiny. Some academics may, of course, hold that *qua* academics, their task is not to prescribe for the future but to cherish and diffuse the intellectual heritage of the past. And that is certainly a task on which they can properly choose to concentrate. Yet it may still be argued that heritage can only be preserved if the values and institutions of the societies which it has helped to shape survive present-day challenges. To attempt, for instance, to illumine the normative dimension of contemporary policy choices (which is one of the aims of this essay) is also a perfectly proper academic responsibility – and usually an intellectually rewarding one.

What follows, therefore, is an attempt to elicit and make more articulate the normative as well as the pragmatic dimensions of the traditions of thought about three selected issues in contemporary International Relations, selected both because of their intrinsic intellectual interest and because of their policy relevance. The three issues are: the relevance of moral norms and of the concept of justice in international society; the validity and implications of the concept of interdependence in that society; and the relevance of differing concepts of European unity to the normative values that unity is intended to promote. The approach adopted here is complementary to, and draws upon, the approaches already mentioned, but its main aim is to disentangle the different traditions of thought into three main schools: the realist, the reformist and the radical.[2] Classifications of this type can offer no more than a kind of rough summation into any one of which no one theorist or practitioner neatly fits. Yet they do provide useful conceptual categories for disentangling the main threads of thought, and though their main purpose is heuristic they may also help us better to appreciate 'the role actually played by values and rules in international society and the legitimacy of raising questions about them in considering questions of policy' (Bull).

The place of moral norms in International Relations

The realists hold that the distinctive characteristic of the interstate system is the absence of any overarching system of government. Consequently, the realist image of international society is an exemplar of the Hobbesian predicament of mankind, of that state of nature characterized by a 'perpetual and restless desire for power' and 'by that condition which is called war'. That condition of war is not necessarily one of overt conflict; it is a condition of incipient conflict arising out of the lack of a common authority to impose order. This is the line of thought in Rousseau's 'The state of war'. in which he writes (Rousseau 1755) that

'just as war presupposes the existence of the state, so the existence of the state presupposes the existence of a state of war... Because the grandeur of the state is purely relative it is forced to compare itself with that of the other... It is in vain that it wishes to keep itself to itself, it becomes small or great, weak or strong, according to whether its neighbour expands or contracts, becomes stronger or declines... war is born of peace or at least of the precautions which men have taken for the purpose of achieving durable peace'.

Moreover, no way out of this predicament can be foreseen. Nothing less than a federation of all states would eliminate war, but nothing less than the international system prevents the conclusion of the federation. In any case why should a federation be 'more to be desired than feared'? Nor is the state of war as intolerable for states as it is for individuals, if only because the very existence of the state is something of a guarantee for the security of its citizens, while the very strength of states makes the fear of annihilation much less pressing than for the individual. The continued existence of the state is therefore a mitigating force in an anarchical system and realists have generally been insistent upon the desirability of the perpetuation of the sovereign state. It could be contended that this realist position is in fact saturated with normative presuppositions, that it is, in fact, a moral position in that it accords moral primacy to the state and to its security interests. Nevertheless, realists of this school can be expected to be sceptical about the relevance of moral and legal rules and of notions of justice which are external to the state. They may accept that the interstate system must be accompanied by some form of diplomatic system if only to ease the process of communication (by which is often meant spying upon possible adversaries!) and by legal rules which can inject a certain amount of predictability and reliability into interstate relations. But these are usually seen as mere conveniences that can be set aside if they conflict with the interests, particularly the security interests, of the state. There is relatively little sense of *pacta sunt servanda* – that is, promises are made to be kept – of law being a repository or expression of norms derived from a natural or divine source, or of a justice 'constituency' beyond the bounds of the nation-state.

Other realists, in the Machiavellian tradition, hold that at the international level the political life and the moral life do not interpenetrate and that moral rules do not therefore impinge on the sphere of interstate action. 'To this war of everyman, against everyman, this also is consequent, that nothing can be unjust. Notions of right and wrong, justice and injustice have there no place. Where there is no common power, there is no law; where no law, no injustice' (Hobbes, 1651). Or as Hobbes might have put it: 'Clubs are trumps.' All that might be allowed is the quality of prudence; this quality may, especially in a nuclear age, have a moral content, but it is seen mainly in terms of enhancing the safety and security of the state.

Never let any government imagine that it can choose perfectly safe courses; rather let it expect to have to take very doubtful ones, because it is found in ordinary affairs that one never seeks to avoid one trouble without running into another; prudence consists in knowing how to distinguish the character of trouble, and for choice to take the lesser evil (Machiavelli, 1513, 127).

Or there is the more extreme realist view that states are complete and morally self-sufficient entities, that the state alone is 'the universe of the ethic' (Hegel). The perils implicit in this latter view have lead some realists to assert that the main need is to curb the moral pretensions of states, to curb for instance the propensity of states to 'oppose each other as the standard bearers of moral systems, each of national origin, and each of them claiming to provide universal moral and political standards which all the other nations ought to accept' (Morgenthau 1966). The main threat to a fragile international order is the heat of moral indignation which makes each side in a dispute or conflict so conscious of its own rectitude as not to consider compromise, an attitude only too well exemplified in twentieth century war.

Lastly, there are the realists who believe in the existence of ethical and moral principles, such as justice or good faith, and admit their relevance to political behaviour. There is a necessary dialectic of ethics and politics 'which prevents the latter, in spite of itself, from escaping the former's judgement and normative direction' (Morgenthau 1944, 176). However, the application of the principles is bound to be relative, for 'universal moral principles cannot be applied to the actions of states in their abstract universal formulations . . . they must be, as it were, filtered through the concrete circumstances of time and place' (Morgenthau

1958, 83). The call here is for a situational morality, one which considers not only what states *ought* to do but what in a given situation they *can* do. Moreover: 'To know that states are subject to the moral law is one thing; to pretend to know what is morally required of states in a particular situation is quite another.' There is, for instance, little agreement as to what human rights are or in what hierarchy of priorities they should be ranked. In any case they are accorded 'only a selective protection that is not determined by the merits of the case but by the vagaries of international politics' (Bull 1971, 278). Inconsistencies of attitude are legion. In much of Asia and Africa the realist critic might claim that the most vociferous cries for justice internationally often come from those least sensitive to the claims of justice domestically. Even when it is admitted that some concern for justice is a necessary ingredient of order, what of situations where the issue is justice *or* order? For most realists a relatively stable balance of power is a prerequisite of a modicum of order in the international system. Yet the maintenance of that balance was invoked to excuse the injustices inflicted by the partitions of Poland and Turkey at the end of the eighteenth century and of Turkey, Africa and China at the end of the nineteenth (Wight 1966, 156). Among the major nuclear powers there is little inclination, in a nuclear age, to subordinate the requirements of order to the dictates of justice (especially when those dictates in themselves can be so contentious). In 1956 and 1968 in Eastern Europe coexistence was primary, justice secondary. For most realists and in most situations the best guarantee of justice for the weak is still the sense of justice of the great – even though the premiums for the weak are apt to be high. This is not an attractive picture of the interstate system but it is – a realist would argue – an accurate picture. It is a system which sustains a modicum of order while enabling states to maintain their freedom. It has its faults, but it may have fewer faults than any alternative upon which the world could agree (Northedge 1976, 323).

For the reformist the fact that a better system has not yet been found is no reason for supposing that a better system cannot be found. Reformist thought is marked by the insistence on the bankruptcy of realism. It sees the system of states as constituting not a mere anarchy but a society of states. This society remains a plurality of states, but it embodies a common diplomatic system, common standards of propriety and legal rules, and to some extent common institutions (James 1976). Consequently it is well on the way to becoming, in Tonnies' term, a *Gemeinschaft,* to displaying a degree of solidarity which allows of a shared sense of moral purpose. The reformist, therefore, looks to ways of strengthening this sense of solidarity, of fostering a sense of obligation as well of rights among the members of international society, and of encouraging them to accept the relevance of moral principles such as equal political rights, equal economic opportunities, the outlawing of the use of force 'save in the common interest', and of the role of international law in consolidating and expressing them. Reformists tend to stress not only what states *actually do* but also what states *ought to do*. And there is the conviction that most states most of the time do show a sensitivity to moral precepts not merely out of diplomatic expediency but because they recognize in them an obligatory character. Moreover, the recognition of rights extends not only to states but to the men, women and children that people them, whether in the protection of human rights, the eradication of racial discrimination or the achievement of social justice. There is the belief here not only in the validity of the ethical in the realm of politics, but also that international society constitutes, in some admittedly rather ill-defined form, a 'justice constituency', justice does not stop short at the 'waterfront'.

That there are difficulties in defining justice and in its application are not denied by reformists. The dictates of justice may conflict, the relative weight to be given to the requirements of justice domestically and internationally may be in dispute, the costs of achieving justice in terms of possible damage to the existing order or to peace itself, may be very difficult to assess. Yet these problems are somewhat analogous to the problem of 'natural justice' within domestic society. Thus at both levels there is the question whether justice is to be seen primarily in terms of equality: equality of rights, equality of opportunities, equality of obligations. Demands for justice in international society are usually demands for 'the removal of privilege or discrimination, for equality in the distribution or in the application of rights as between the strong and the weak, the large and the small, the rich and the poor, the black and the white, or the victors and the vanquished' (Bull 1971, 273). Yet justice may not be served by equality: 'injustice arises when equals are treated unequally and also when unequals are treated equally' (Aristotle quoted in Bull 1971, 273). Justice needs at times to be not arithmetically equal but proportionate, in the sense that the weak may need special protection that the strong can provide for themselves. In GATT negotiations the principle of reciprocity has been discarded in recognition that those with little bargaining power inevitably found themselves at a severe disadvantage if they had to give equal concessions to the strong.

Reformists generally draw a distinction between 'reciprocal' justice[3] and 'distributive' justice. By reciprocal justice is meant the recognition of 'rights and duties by a process of exchange or bargaining, whereby one individual or group recognises the rights of others in return for their recognition of its own' (Bull 1971, 274). The stress is on the responsibility of the members of international society to act justly towards each other, whereas 'distributive justice' emanates from international society as a whole, the implication being that that society constitutes at least a quasi-*Gemeinschaft* and that the institutions it possesses have a major responsibility for defining and securing the application of commonly agreed notions of justice as reflected for instance in United Nations resolutions on Southern Africa or the New International Economic Order. Finally, most reformists appreciate the dangers of pursuing justice *à outrance* – 'fiat justitia et pereat mundus'. Yet order shot through with glaring injustices is not an order that is likely to survive. Indeed the righting of massive injustices may be the most effective means of strengthening international order, or at least of providing a way of avoiding a resort to violence as the only means of change in international society. Reformists do not exclude the propriety of intervention in order to secure the remedy of gross injustice. They point out that collective interventions for humanitarian reasons were not uncommon in the nineteenth century (e.g. in favour of Greek insurgents in 1827, in Naples in 1856, in the Lebanon in 1860, in the Congo in 1885, Wight 1966, 120–1). Consequently the notion of collective intervention on behalf of persecuted black majorities in white minority-ruled regimes in Southern Africa is not necessarily unthinkable so long as the legitimacy of intervention has been endorsed by that instrument – however imperfect – of the 'world's' conscience, the United Nations.

The third school, the radicals, fall into two overlapping groups: the first consists of the more militant leaders of the so-called Third and Fourth worlds and the second of the revolutionary and more doctrinaire Marxists–Leninists and Maoists. The first group's notions of radical justice have come increasingly to dominate the United Nations, which with its expanding membership no longer reflects the values and political vocabulary of the West as it did in its first decade. Its debates are now dominated by demands for economic justice for the poverty-stricken peoples of developing countries and demands for racial justice for the black African peoples in Southern Africa. The notion of distributive justice is to be found in the demand that the application of what is held to be the emerging consensus on such notions of justice is seen as the responsibility of representative institutions such as the United Nations. There is some ambivalence about the relation between order and justice. There is little desire to upset that level of international order stemming from a relatively stable central balance of power – 'where the elephants fight the grass gets trampled' – but where their own particular racist issues are involved 'the tendency of the majority of the United Nations is to pursue justice at some risk of war' (Connor Cruse O'Brien and Felix Topolski 1968, 67). Thus justice is seen as conferring legitimacy on the use of force against recalcitrant white minority regimes in Southern Africa. That such use of force might cause intensified suffering for the African peoples concerned and spark off widespread bloodshed does not derogate from the Kantian imperative to realize the dictates of justice. Moreover, violence itself is sometimes seen as both a unifying force and a cleansing and purifying force which can help 'tear the mask of hypocrisy from the face of the enemy' (Fanon). It is a necessary instrument for the eradication of injustice. Such notions of justice are often, as has already been remarked, highly selective, but they are passionately held.

The demands for justice of this group are also reflected in assertions of the need for a New International Economic Order, both as a restitution for past economic exploitation and as a means of securing a more 'just' distribution of the world's resources. The transfer of resources from the rich to the poor may, in the longer run, prove to be to the mutual economic advantage of both and help to allay political animosities,[4] but it is first and foremost a form of distributive justice that is demanded by the poor and weak of the rich and powerful; that it may be difficult to reconcile with assertions of 'permanent sovereignty over natural resources' likely to inhibit the private foreign investors through whom the bulk of such transfers of resources would be likely to take place, is rarely acknowledged. Nevertheless, behind the rhetoric lies a very real need; and perhaps the rhetoric itself is a necessary ploy for forging that level of unity which is necessary to achieve more effective bargaining strength.

In line with the preoccupation with justice there is a certain scepticism about much of the content of international law which is seen as still reflecting the interests of rich Western ex-colonial powers. Claims to respect legal obligations or rules more often than not merely display the hypocrisy and self-righteousness of these powers, the 'successful burglars now trying to settle down as country gentlemen, making intermittent appearances on the magistrate's bench' (Martin Wight quoted in Bull 1976, 108). The need rather is to enunciate a refashioned body of international law which, by reflecting more closely the precepts of both political and economic justice, already enshrined in the Charter and spelt out in resolutions of the General Assembly, will acquire greater relevance and moral standing.

The second radical group, the doctrinaire Marxist–Leninists or Maoists are not concerned to preserve an interstate system or an international society; rather it sees 'an inherent conflict between the present framework of international order and the achievement of justice' (Bull 1971, 281). The goal is to refashion the world in the image of the proletariat. The vision is of a classless society in which the horizontal splitting of mankind into antagonistic classes – the 'root cause of all evil in society' – gives way to the dictatorship of the proletariat and the withering away of the state. However, Marxian ambiguity regarding the disappearance of the state is well brought out in Waltz (1959) and, particularly, Berki (1971). The state might have great durability, but it is still a historical and ephemeral entity: 'Internally, the state's function as "the managing committee of the ruling class" is to maintain the system of exploitation; externally, its main preoccupations is to facilitate the expansion of its own bourgeoisie' (Berki 1971, 82). 'To the extent that antagonisms between classes within the nation vanishes, the hostility of one nation to another will come to an end' (*Communist Manifesto*). Progress towards social justice lies in that which helps, retrogression in that which hinders, the socialist revolution of the proletariat; for 'real social justice can only come in the last stages of Communism'. Economic justice will only come when the ownership of the means of production passes from capitalist into proletarian hands. Moreover, the individual has no innate rights, but only such rights as derive from, and are recognized by, a socialist society and these rights will therefore be most effectively secured by the achievement of a classless society in which men's sense of 'alienation' will finally be surmounted. Consequently, everything which hastens the victory of the proletariat is morally right: 'Everything is right which serves the revolution' (Lenin). The logical corollary is that no truly socialist state can be an aggressor or an imperialist state, as these are attributes of non-socialist, bourgeois capitalist states. Also 'the question of the rights of nations (to self-determination) is not an isolated, self-sufficient question; it is part of the general problem of the proletarian revolution, subordinate to the whole...' (Stalin, quoted in Berri 1971). Socialist states should assist in emancipating the oppressed peoples in the dependent countries from the yoke of imperialism, but support should only be given 'to such national movements as tend to weaken, to overthrow imperialism, and not to strengthen and support it'.

These claims are in principle absolute and universalistic. 'Today's revolution is one, its goals and techniques are everywhere similar, the goal being to overthrow world capitalist imperialism' (Schram 1969, 271). Tactical adjustments may be necessary. The existing correlation of forces may dictate a policy of 'peaceful coexistence of countries with differing social systems', but that coexistence is only a transitory phase; 'it does not mean conciliation of the socialist and bourgeois ideologies. On the contrary, it implies intensification of the struggle of the working class, of all the communist parties, for the triumph of socialist ideas' (Statement of the Conference of Eighty-one Communist and Workers' Parties, Moscow, 6 December 1960). That struggle, whether by the property-less against the property-owning, by the alienated against the 'bourgeois bureaucracy' or by liberation movements against colonial or racist oppression, is represented as that of the new and progressive against the old and the moribund. In a nuclear age the struggle is to be conducted mainly by peaceful means. But the necessities of survival only condition, and do not negate, the ideological imperatives.

There is little place here for notions of 'justice' derived from 'natural law' or the 'general principles of international law recognized by civilized nations'. Regard for legal obligations is a matter of reciprocal convenience or interest, and the premise of *pacta sunt servanda* is tempered by the dictates of proletarian internationalism and by the precedence given to an emerging system of socialist international law predicated upon a durable base of socialist solidarity over a system of general international law based upon a transitory period of coexistence between competing ideological systems (Lapenna 1975).

Although the system of values reflected in the goals of the proletarian revolution are still publicly affirmed and the perceptions of Soviet leaders may still be coloured by their ideological preconceptions, Soviet diplomatic practice has in recent years conformed so closely to more realist notions of great-power behaviour as to call into question the continued relevance of the doctrinal commitment. The tactics imposed by a realistic appreciation of the perilous correlation of forces in a nuclear age may overshadow longer-term strategic goals. The modes of behaviour induced by tactical necessities could be striking deeper roots and induce a process of assimilation to more traditional, though mainly *Realpolitik,* patterns. Calculations of political expediency may even induce some outward regard for the prescriptive norms of international society. If so, where might the process lead? Such issues are not irrelevant to, for instance, the prospects for identifying possible areas of collaboration within a prolonged period of competitive coexistence.

This was precisely one of Mao Tse-Tung's fears. For him doctrinal purity was a moral imperative as a safeguard against the corrupting influence of bourgeois revisionism and bureaucratic routinization. Within the framework of Marxism-Leninism the stress was on 'the continuing revolution': 'Altering the economic base of society by expropriating the private owners of the means of production only establishes the basic *possibility* of socialism. Bourgeois habits of thought, bourgeois motivation, the whole bourgeois world outlook still have to be fought and conquered ideologically to bring into existence socialist man' (Schram 1971, 228–9). Moreover, the traditional Chinese view of the world, which sees China as the centre, the sole upholder of true civilization, the law-giver to the barbarians, makes for the rejection of the norms of an international society which are so evidently imbued with the political vocabulary and the political heritage and values embedded in their 'Western' heritage (Fitzgerald 1964). Yet 'external events are strong' and they may in time evoke a process of assimilation to a more conventional and 'realist' great-power stance. Whether this is likely to happen, and at what pace, is a question of great practical significance in trying to predict both what world role Communist China may come to play and the outlines of future world order.

What moral norms are likely to prevail depends less, it should be stressed, on their ontological validity than on their prevalence (and on the intensity with which they are held). But the prevalence of this or that set of norms is in turn very largely a function of the prevalence of a sense of interdependence, or – in Tonnies' phrase – of a sense of *Gemeinschaft.* In other words if the world is seen as increasingly interdependent, the growth of a genuine if minimal moral consensus is not to be excluded. If, on the contrary, the world is held to be an increasingly pluralistic one, moral norms will be generally regarded as highly relative and it would be imprudent to look for any sensitivity to moral norms except at the level of rhetoric or among like-minded states. The concept of an interdependent world therefore merits closer scrutiny.

The concept of interdependence

Theories of interdependence do, in fact, continue to proliferate with often markedly differing realist and reformist diagnoses.[5] The concept of interdependence is, of course, shot through with no less ambiguities and contradictions than the concepts of justice and order. For most realists interdependence denotes little more than that states coexist in an interstate system in which no one member can for long remain unaffected by the policies pursued by its neighbours or near-neighbours. For the realists, however, states are mainly concerned to maintain their independence and they only intermittently portray a sense of mutual dependence in any wider sense, the extent and intensity of which is likely in any case to vary considerably from one state or group of states to another; indeed, an interdependent relationship may seem to some more like: 'I depend; you rule' – or vice versa.

The reformist, by contrast, sees interdependence as a function of an emergent world society, even an incipient world community, the members of which share a mutuality of interest in the general well-being of that society, whether in excluding the use of force 'save in the common interest', in preserving the ecological health of the society, or in securing a more 'just' international economic order. This reformist view is, in effect, the contemporary version of the solidarist conviction that the world is increasingly tied together in 'an intimacy of conduct, an interdependence of welfare, and a mutuality of vulnerability'.

One difficulty in testing theories of interdependence is that there is contradictory evidence as to the facts of interdependence. Looked at historically the world may have become more closely knit, as reformists assert, in terms of the ease and speed of communication – psychologically, the world may have become a 'global village' – of the spread of industrial and electronic technologies and in terms possibly of a thickening pattern of international economic transactions. Yet contrary trends making for greater fragmentation are stressed by realists. The world has in most respects become politically, culturally and ideologically more fragmented. In 1914 there were 44 sovereign states; by 1976 United Nations' membership had risen to well over 140. Moreover, an interstate system that had been shaped and dominated until the early decades of this century by a European vocabulary of diplomacy, by European concepts of the balance of power, and by European norms of political behaviour has had to adjust, it is claimed, to 'the political emancipation of the non-Western nations and the resurrection of their native civilizations – both processes that had been instigated by the diffusion of Western values – [but which] had the effect, eventually, of evoking and activating long-dormant memories of earlier approaches to foreign affairs' (Bozeman 1960, 498). It is true that in some parts (e.g. in much of Africa) such memories are often either rather patchy or they lack genuine historical roots. And it could be contended that there as elsewhere they are being overlaid by a spreading ethos of 'industrialization' (Gellner 1964). Nevertheless, in many instances there has been a revival of indigenous cultural systems and outlooks, a revival accelerated, in many cases, by the supersession of Western-trained élites. At the same time, albeit with fluctuating vehemence, the clash of ideologies calls into question some of the fundamental premises of the existing interstate system. For the realist, far from becoming increasingly integrated, the world is in many respects more fragmented, more pluralistic.

Nor is it self-evident that a greater measure of interdependence would make for closer cooperation rather than for greater friction. On the contrary, for the contemporary realists, as for Rousseau, the most reliable way of mitigating conflict is to keep states apart. The more contact there is between states, the more potentialities for friction may be engendered. Neighbourliness is as likely to produce a sense of rivalry as a sense of vicinage. Interdependence may thus have negative as well as positive connotations, or it can contain both positive and negative elements. This is most vividly demonstrated in the adversary–partner relationship – as Henry Kissinger has called it – between the two superpowers. What can make for the stability of this central nuclear balance – the 'delicate balance of terror' – has for realists and most reformists alike been crucial to the survival of civilized man. Strategic theorists in bodies such as the International Institute for Strategic Studies have been concerned, for instance, to identify the ingredients of stability and instability in the 'deterrence' relationship, to highlight the normative issues involved in the use of force, and to subject the shibboleths – and 'buzz' words – of the Cold War and of 'detente' to critical examination. There have, of course, been marked differences of emphasis and approach, but generally on this adversary–partner dimension of interdependence the separate strands of realist diagnostic and reformist prescriptive thought converge to become not readily distinguishable in an ongoing discussion involving people of many different nationalities and from many different walks of life. Whether policies have been much modified directly as a result is a moot point; but the level of informed discussion has been transformed.

However, theories of interdependence have been applied in recent years, mainly to the non-security field, and here realists and reformists tend to part company more frequently. For example, most reformists claim that, even apart from nuclear weapons, scientific and technological advances pose a threat to the human environment and to the use of natural resources which could endanger man's survival unless more effective control is exercised over them. They argue that the nation-state has lost the capacity to handle the problems of oceanic and atmospheric pollution or of the pressure of unchecked population growth on limited food, raw materials, and energy resources, and that effective control can only be exercised on a global scale through international – or 'world' – institutions which, instead of being mainly instruments for asserting and – hopefully – reconciling national interests, will serve as organs of management for exercising collectively, on behalf of world society, what have hitherto been the prerogatives of nation-states. It is an approach which is dismissive of cautionary realist pleas that the impact – and so the alleged threat – of scientific and technological advances is far from clear, that if there indeed be a threat it affects different states and peoples very differently, and that so far the predominant response of states has been to attempt to strengthen their own powers of control rather than to hand them over to international agencies.

The differences between realists and reformists are in this context mainly those of emphasis. Yet they are not unimportant at both the theoretical and the practical level. A basic postulate of most reformist thinking is that the forces making for interdependence will steadily grow stronger. There is an implicit assumption of linear progress even though the pace, and indeed the modalities, of change in any particular realm, may be difficult to predict with any confidence. A further premise is that as élite perceptions come to appreciate that the challenges of interdependence are beyond the capacity of states to meet them, modalities of collective management will evolve which, over time, will assume many of the responsibilities at present exercised by states (Haas 1975).

Theories of general application are, therefore, sought as to how élite perceptions can be modified accordingly, about the structural changes in the present interstate system needed to secure more effective modalities of collective management and about the 'norms' of 'global responsibility' (e.g. of distributive justice) to which they should give affect. These theories are reflected in the spate of multilateral conferences over the early 1970s dealing with environmental, population, food and commodity problems and with the law of the seas; in the proposals for a collective approach to their management which the conferences generated; and in the recommendations for structural improvements to the United Nations' system currently under discussion (Goodwin 1976).

Realists have some reason for being scornful of the rhetoric of interdependence which customarily so clouds the mind in these conferences and for being critical of the dramatic oversimplifications of reformist diagnoses and prescriptions. Given the primacy still accorded by realists to power-politics, 'cobweb' theories of functional interdependence are brushed aside as near-irrelevancies. States may in some aspects of their affairs feel themselves to be more interdependent than they like; in which case they will be primarily concerned with reducing what they regard as a dangerous degree of dependence at vulnerable points, both as a means of protecting specifically national interests in the short term and of acquiring a higher degree of national self-sufficiency and autonomy in the long term.

In short, for realists the sovereign state is still the basic decision-making and operational unit in the international system; it is moved far more by shortish-term domestic interests and concerns than by longer-term global needs; and rather than eroding the capacity of states to manage their own affairs international institutions tend to strengthen it by providing, when desired, modes of collaboration which can enable them to do so at less cost and with less friction. Hitherto such collective management as has been exercised has taken the form of the covert but pervasive influence of a single dominant power (e.g. the USA working mainly through the Bretton Woods system) or of a small congerie of the industrially powerful (e.g. the Rambouillet and Puerto Rico 'Six'). The OPEC countries now have aspirations to enter this managerial circle, as have some of the leading members of the UNCTAD 'Group of 77'. Here may be the embryo of new forms of collective management, but the role accorded to the United Nations system would be quite secondary.

Moreover, in a more 'pluralistic' world of still egocentric states the scope for 'norms' of interstate behaviour is more closely circumscribed. In such a world the need is not so much to secure 'positive' agreement on such 'norms', certainly not on such Western 'rules of the game' as were embodied in the Bretton Woods system. The need rather is to encourage 'passive' cooperation on a pragmatic basis, a form of cooperation which 'responds to events rather than seeking to control them', (Morse 1975), which encourages restraint by states in both their domestic and foreign economic policies, so as to ensure the avoidance of 'beggar-my-neighbour' policies, of actions perceived to be damaging to others. In other words, the need is for modes of cooperation which take full account of the widening diversity of expectations and objectives and of the rise of new sources of political and economic influence and pressure in a fragmented world. The modalities of such cooperation will reflect the political and economic weight – and the bargaining strength – of the powers most directly concerned – and this is precisely what the weaker developing countries fear. Yet if concepts of economic 'justice' are to enter in it, it is the political backing they can command that is bound very largely to determine the influence they carry. Illusory voting victories cannot obscure this basic fact.

These issues, and the realist–reformist distinctions, have only been very lightly sketched in. The aim has been to indicate how an analysis of the theoretical assumptions, the preconceptions, even 'inarticulate major premises', of those caught up in the 'interdependence' debate could – if carried further – make some modest contribution to a more perceptive understanding of policy choices. What is the significance of new forms of interdependence both for national policy-makers and for the emergence of new norms of international behaviour? Are there signs of a shift in élite perceptions in the direction of consensus on the facts and needs of interdependence? In what areas may there be a call for the collective 'management' of interdependence and is it to be exercised by a power cabal or more representative United Nations bodies – and exercised positively or passively? And what may be the role of 'Europe' – or more exactly of the Europe of the Nine in all this?

European unity[6]

To claim that 'Europe's' role in an interdependent world will turn mainly on the extent to which the Nine become steadily more integrated into a true Community is almost a truism. But what light does experience so far throw on the type of Community that may be emerging, in terms both of the values it embodies and of the part it may play in strengthening or weakening the forces making for interdependence in the world at large? How far do contrasting theories of European integration help to clarify both the pragmatic and normative dimensions of this central issue?

Among these competing theories there are the historical, tracing the past history and present relevance of the European idea; the clarficatory, addressed to the ambiguities of the very concept of Europe – Carolingian Europe? 'from the Atlantic to the Urals'? the European Communities with or without the Mediterranean and Scandinavian appendages? – or to the different political forms that closer European political integration might take; the explanatory, attempting to identify the sources of dynamism – and of regression – in the integration process; and the predictive and prescriptive, usually implicit in the foregoing, but at times directed more explicitly to forecasting and influencing the thrust and direction of European integration, whether in specifics (e.g. monetary policy) or in more general terms of the why and wherefore of the integration process and its goals (e.g. the neofunctionalists). Again the different theoretical interests often overlap and are certainly not easily separable. Nor do the three schools of thought already utilized – realist, reformist and radicalist – provide quite such a serviceable means of identifying the different approaches and their characteristics. Yet the three to be used here – the prophets, the priests and the pragmatists – do correspond in a rough-and-ready fashion to the radical, the reformist and the realist, respectively.

The prophets – and radicals – were the federalists of the early 1950s, up to the demise of the European Defence Community and its accompanying European Political Community in 1954. Their most sophisticated representative was Jean Monnet. Their goal was to put an end to the fratricidal strife between France and Germany, the two contenders for the supremacy of 'Europe', and to create an economic system capable of competing successfully with the USA. They were usually anti-nationalist – 'Nous ne coalissons des etats, nous unissons des hommes' (Jean Monnet) – and European Union was seen both as an end in itself and, by some, as a means to the wider end of a world federation (Forsyth 1967, 490). There was considerable stress on the institutions which were to be the practical embodiment of the idea and the 'motor' for the 'concrete action necessary to bring that idea [European unity] to reality' (Jean Monnet, quoted in Duroselle 1966, 196). Consequently, the supranational character of the truly European body, the High Authority of the European Coal and Steel Community, was seen as crucial, as was the development of a 'community spirit' among not only the member governments but also among their business enterprises, trade unions and political élites generally. The initial approach was functionalist, building 'Europe' brick by brick. The exact nature of the eventual 'federal' Europe was left unclear though there was a good deal of talk of a 'new type of political entity'; but the stress was on 'the necessary logic' of an integration process in which the successful exercise of their supranational powers by the High Authority of the ECSC and other such bodies would pave the way for political integration. It was a courageous goal, but it lacked a sufficiently discerning and penetrating dimension of political analysis, particularly of the addiction of states to retaining – or regaining – their sovereignty and of the changing and ambivalent nature of the Franco-German axis underlying the whole enterprise (Goodwin 1972, 7–9).

However, several of the aspirations of the radical-minded prophets have persisted into the thinking of the priests, the more soberly reformist school, but the still rather dogmatic guardians and ritualists of the Rome Treaty and of the collective European 'interest' said to be embodied in it. This reformist – or priestly – approach mingled with the more radical, prophetic school for the first few years of the European Economic Community up to the 1965 crisis. Thereafter the integrationist goals persisted, but the determination of member governments to defend their interests as integration proceeded could not be gainsaid. Nevertheless, neofunctionalist theories proliferated, looking to the gradual accretion of authority to largely technocratic but increasingly supranational institutions, particularly the Commission. Despite the 1965–6 setback, for the greater part of the 1960s the Commission was, indeed, self-consciously attempting to define a European interest and active in initiating policies for European integration and creating the norms of the European would-be policy. The Rome Treaty appeared at first to have identified a feasible approach to closer European integration; but actual economic and political practice soon revealed the fragility of the underlying premises. With the completion of the Customs Union in 1968 the Community moved from the relatively clearly demarcated process of 'negative' integration into the little-explored and much more sensitive area of 'positive' integration (Pinder 1972).[7] Moreover, not only was the relative weight within the Bonn–Paris axis shifting, but the major preoccupations were less with the 'deepening' of integration than with the 'enlargement' of the Community. Here – and in delineating the practical requirements of 'positive' integration – the Treaty of Rome, a *traité cadre,* had less to offer and the Commission's role within the institutional structure was correspondingly diminished as governments reasserted their particular national interests.

The 1970s have seen the increasing ascendancy of governments, of the pragmatists, perhaps of the realists. Incrementalism *à la carte* by somewhat agnostic practitioners is the keynote. The value and durability of the sovereign state is rarely challenged and there is little inclination (though there are differences of priorities) among the member states to contemplate their absorption into something of a supranational character. Economic integration (e.g. in monetary and fiscal matters) may still in principle be an accepted long-term goal, but the main preoccupation has been with surviving the successive economic crises of the 1970s and generally with creating an intergovernmental negotitating network, with the Commission as an *interlocuteur valable,* but the European Council providing 'managerial' direction, which will allow the members to concert policies that are within the purview of the Treaty and to speak, if not in unison at least in harmony, on a limited range of foreign-policy issues. It is a far cry from the prophetic predictions of the early 1950s; it may be a viable system, but so far it lacks a sense of direction, of purpose.

The European Community faces what is in fact both a severely practical question and one of considerable theoretical interest. Events, both external and internal to its member states will be the prime factors in shaping its future, but the differing conceptions and perceptions of its members as to the direction the Community should take could also be crucial. It is far from clear whether the Rome Treaty provides appropriate guidelines for this future. This is for four main reasons. The first is that the Treaty was drafted some twenty years ago and tailored to a world substantially different from the present. Inevitably it gives only limited guidance to how the Community should develop in the late 1970s and 1980s. The second is that one of the major challenges for most, if not all, members is not merely the economic well-being of their electorates but also the need to protect and underpin the democratic institutions, values and way of life which it has been one of the main purposes of the Community to uphold. Their membership of the Community can open up possibilities of mutual help – a sense of interdependence – in both these tasks, but any increase in the powers of Community institutions runs the risk of deepening the sense of alienation from parliamentary democratic institutions already so rife in several member countries. It *need* not do so, but it *could* do so if it were to be thought that accountability for major policy decisions was being taken out of the hands of national legislatures in favour of a remote – and what is rapidly becoming a 'closed' – European system. Hence, the importance not only of a directly 'elected' European Parliament with real powers (e.g. of areas of co-decision-making with the Council of Ministers), but also of more effective scrutiny arrangements at the level of domestic legislatures; in short, of a more 'transparent' Community system which can help to give greater legitimacy to the democratic process.

The third reason is that the Community faces a new process of enlargement which could have far-reaching implications for its future: after Greece, probably Portugal, then maybe Spain and possibly Turkey, and even perhaps Malta and Cyprus? This would be a pluralistic Community indeed, not only with wide structural differences mirrored in *per capita* incomes and levels of development, but also with varying degrees of commitment to the democratic values the European movement was intended to safeguard. Fears have already arisen of a 'two-tier' community within the present Community of Nine, particularly in the context of monetary relations. A Community of twelve or more might raise the bogy of a 'three-tier' Community. What would then be the prospects for 'conjunctural management' of the national economies let alone for full economic integration? The model then might be more that of a Commonwealth of European states, which would have to make a virtue of diversity, rather than be a vehicle of integration – a goal very different from that of the founding fathers of the European Union.

The fourth is that the value of Community initiatives, and of a collective Community negotiating position, on issues of special Community concern (e.g. Gatt, Lomé Convention, Euro-Arab dialogue, 'Helsinki') has been accepted by its members, as has the importance of asserting a Community identity and enhancing the representational role of the Presidents of the Commission and of the Council of Ministers. Yet the Community is hampered not only by continued internal divisions but also by the fact that in some issue areas it is too large and in others too small. For instance, it is too large for the intimate 'summit' meetings of the key industrialized countries (as at Rambouillet and Puerto Rico when only four of the Nine were present). By contrast, it is too small in that, not only does the OECD often offer a more relevant circle for consultation and action (Camps 1975, 48–50), but that on a whole range of issues relations with the USA are so central as to make it, in effect, a tenth member. This latter relationship is inevitably an ambivalent one. American indifference (e.g. 'Helsinki') or heavy-handedness (e.g. 1973/4) conduces to the cohesion of the Nine, but the symbiotic relationship in security matters spills over into other fields to the point where at times it overshadows intra-Community ties. In short, the developing pattern of relations between the USA and the Community, both as a collective entity and with its individual members, is likely to be crucial for the Community's future.

Yet theoretical studies of the European Communities have so far been dominated by integration theories which have tended to focus on the internal processes of the Community in implementing the tasks, both explicit and implicit, in the Paris and Rome treaties. New kinds of questions have now arisen to which integration theory must be addressed if it is to retain theoretical interest and practical relevance. How can integration theories be modified to accommodate a more pluralistic Community system, to accept the primacy of politics over more 'functional' processes, to allow that the continuing cohesion of the Community may stem as much, if not more, from external pressures and opportunities as from internal processes? How – above all – can we ensure that theory gives more heed both to the Community's role in preserving the democratic values and institutions which is its ultimate *raison d'être* and to the definition of a role in an interdependent world which will help to heal present divisions and not mainly reflect a nostalgia for past glories.

Martin Wight once argued that there was an inescapable disharmony between international theory and diplomatic practice, that there is 'a kind of recalcitrance of international politics to being theorized about' (Wight 1966, 33). One suspects that he had in mind mainly the 'scientific' theories of the behaviouralist schools; for he himself was, of course, an outstanding theorist not only of the balance of power but of the differing schools of thought about the growth and characteristic features of the international system. Some of the merits of more 'scientific' theories have been displayed in earlier contributions to this volume. That they may have useful insights to contribute within their own particular field of enquiry is not seriously questioned (Goodwin 1973, 16–22). The assumption here, however, has been that theoretical analyses, in the Martin Wight vein, embracing the three patterns of thought[8] outlined above and focusing on the normative dimensions of international life also have a good deal to offer, particularly in helping scholars and practitioners alike to acquire a keener sense of their own ethical and moral bearings within the diplomatic 'cosmos'. It is an enterprise which calls for a feeling for history, which can lend a sense of perspective and of the 'true relation and proportion of events'; for the exercise of imaginative insight, of the quality of empathy into views other than one's own; and for a recognition of the ambiguities and paradoxes of the human condition (the existential dimension of international life), only imperfectly reflected here (Goodwin 1973, 244).

A further assumption is that collaboration between academic theorists and practitioners can often be mutually beneficial. Theory does after all find in practice, both past and present, its main testing ground, while practice is itself, it has been argued, not wholly pragmatic if only because it is inevitably impregnated with the preconceptions and value judgements of the practitioners. Admittedly, the mere elucidation of practitioners' values does not necessarily give a direct clue to the policies they will choose – or even should choose – but it can help to bring the normative dimensions of their choices out into the open; it is only too easy for these to be submerged within the organizational ethos to which bureaucrats are so vulnerable or within the party doctrines which can entrap even the most sophisticated politician. Neither technical discussion nor dialectical niceties should be allowed to disguise the conflicts over values which are the essence of politics.

Such collaboration is not easy. Collaboration between academic specialists is often difficult enough. Each specialism develops its own vocabulary of analytical concepts and modes of thought which make sense to fellow specialists but which outsiders can have difficulty in following. Similarly, different professional people (e.g. the diplomat, the financier, the industrialist, the journalist and the academic) display differing styles of thought, of vocabulary and of conversation which can constitute awkward barriers to interprofessional communication. Moreover, the perspectives of, for instance, the diplomat and the academic are bound to differ. The former is properly concerned with the more immediate problems of the day and his time scale is apt to be a foreshortened one – decisions have to be taken and cannot indefinitely be deferred; his vantage point is that of one who has the responsibility to protect and foster specific interests – bureaucratic and organizational as well as 'national' – and he is likely to be more sensitive to the limited range of choice – to the logic of most situations – with which policy-makers are usually faced.

The academic's aim is to add to the understanding of policy choices, not to decide policy. Absorption in the policy-making process for a period can be a salutary and rewarding experience, but the kind of understanding to which the academic aspires demands a degree of detachment from particular concerns and interests, the cultivation so far as possible of at least a 'scientific spirit' – coupled with a determination to see problems in their historical perspective and not to be imprisoned by the immediacy of day-to-day events. Again these contrasts are put too harshly; but the potentialities for mutual incomprehension, even mistrust, will be evident. Yet collaboration can, over time, establish the kind of personal relations which can make for mutual education. Academic analysts of contemporary international politics can be encouraged to break out of narrow specialist confines as they learn to appreciate the many-sidedness of most policy issues – economic policy, for example, is neither economics nor politics, but both – and more. They can acquire a deeper appreciation of the ambiguities and contradictions of most of the situations with which policy-makers are faced. Practitioners' minds can be opened to their own, and others', intellectual assumptions, to a concern for ends as well as means, and to an appreciation of the longer-term needs and evolution of the societies which they serve. Above all, and perhaps most directly, it could help to raise the general level of informed public discussion on the major international issues of the day. Foreign policy is no longer an élitist sanctuary. One may regret that it is no longer so and that so many international issues are debated with so little mutual understanding – and compassion. But it is just possible, though by no means certain, that continued ignorance about – often coupled with active dislike of – 'foreign' affairs among the much wider circle of those now caught up in them may be a partial explanation of this lack of mutual understanding. Greater understanding could at times at least bring greater mutual comprehension of divergent views – possibly even greater mutual forbearance, a quality of which the world is sadly in need.

Notes

1. It could be argued that, on a strict adherence to the definition of theory given on p. 280, the 'clarificatory' and 'classificatory' branches should be regarded as pre-theories, i.e. as necessary preliminaries to theory, but this distinction is in practice difficult to maintain, and if only as a matter of convenience is not pressed here.

2. This classification follows somewhat similar classifications by Kenneth Waltz (1959) and Martin Wight (Bull 1976, 104).
3. Bull uses the term 'commutative' justice.
4. Whether the resources will trickle down effectively to the poorest within the 'poor' states may be questioned.
5. There is not space to consider radical views. In summary the radicalist so-called 'Third World' school tends both to merge with the reformist and to draw upon the Marxist view that interdependence is little more than a euphemism for the dependence of the poor on the rich and that an interdependent world is necessarily an exploitative world, since 'the random distribution of natural resources does not merely lead to the development of differentials in living standards, wealth, armed strength, and, in turn, to warfare and ultimately relations of domination among the separate units . . . [but] these relations of domination also reflect the exploitation, by the owner of the means of production, of those who have in the last resort, nothing but their labour-power to sell' (Berki 1971, 101, also Galtung 1973).
6. European unity has been taken as the third issue area, partly because of the author's own interests but mainly because the forms of collective management with which the Nine are experimenting are both novel and interesting and the outcome of this experiment will have a direct bearing on the kind of role that Europe of the Nine may be able to play in the world at large.
7. This distinction is not, of course, as neat as this in practice; for instance, the baneful effects of the introduction of a common market (i.e. negative integration) may have to be countered by measures of positive integration (e.g. regional policies).
8. Hedley Bull rightly points out that 'the essence of (Martin Wight's) teaching was that the truth about international politics had to be sought not in any one of these patterns of thought (i.e. *the Machiavellian, the Grotian or the Kantian*) but in the debate among them'. The same applies, *mutatis mutandis,* here (Bull 1976, 110).

References and Further Reading

Berki, R.N. (1971) 'On Marxian thought and the problem of international relations', *World Politics,* October. Vol. xxiv, No. 1, pp. 80–105.

Bozeman, A.B. (1960) *Politics and Culture in International History,* Princeton Univ. Press, Princeton.

Bull, H. (1971) 'Order vs. justice in international society', *Political Studies,* September. Vol. xix, no. 3, p. 269–283.

Bull, H. (1976) 'Martin Wight and the theory of international relations', *British Journal of International Studies,* July. Vol. 2, no. 2, p. 101–116.

Burns, A.L. (1968) *Of Powers and Their Politics,* Eaglewood Cliffs, Prentice-Hall.

Camps, M. (1975) 'First World Relationships', the role of the OECD, The Atlantic Papers 2, Insitute for International Affairs, Paris and Council on Foreign Relations, New York.

Dawisha, A.I. (1976) 'Foreign Policy models and the problem of dynamism', *British Journal of International Studies,* July. Vol. 2, no. 2, p. 128–137.

Duroselle, J.-B. (1966) 'General de Gaulle's Europe and Jean Monnet's Europe', *The World Today,* January. Vol. 22, no. 1, p. 1–13.

Edmonds, R. (1975) *Soviet Foreign Policy, 1962–73,* London, Oxford University Press.

Fitzgerald, C.P. (1964) *The Chinese View of their Place in the World,* London, Oxford University Press.

Forsyth, M. (1967) 'The political objectives of European integration', *International Affairs,* July.

Gallie, W.B. (1964) *Philosophy and the Historical Understanding.*

Galtung, J. (1973) *The European Community: A Superpower in the Making,* Allen and Unwin.

Gellner, E. (1964) *Thought and Change,* London, Weidenfeld and Nicolson.

Goodwin, G.L. (1972) 'European unity – a return to realities', *University of Leeds Review,* May. Vol. 15, no. 1, p. 57–79.

Goodwin, G.L. (1973) 'International relations and international studies', in *The Yearbook of World Affairs 1973,* Stevens.

Goodwin, G.L. (1976) 'International institutions and the limits of interdependence', in A. Schlaim (ed.), *International Organisations in World Politics, Yearbook, 1975,* London, Croom Helm.

Haas, E. (1975) 'An international "scientific society"', in G. Goodwin and A. Linklater (eds.), *New Dimensions of World Politics,* London, Croom Helm.

Hobbes, Thomas, (1651) *Leviathan,* Basil Blackwell, 1955.

James, A. (1976) 'International society: An inaugural lecture', University of Keele.

Lapenna, I. (1975) 'The Soviet concept of "socialist" international law', in *Yearbook of World Affairs,* Stevens.

Machiavelli, Nicolo, (1513) *The Prince,* Everyman Library, 1952.

Manning, C.A.W. (1962) *The Nature of International Society,* London, Bell.

Morgenthau, H.J.(1944) *Scientific Man versus Power-Politics.*

Morgenthau, H.J. (1958) *Dilemmas of Politics,* Chicago, Univ. Chicago Press.

Morgenthau, H.J. (1966) Introduction to D. Mitrany, *A Working Peace System,* New York, Quadrangle Books.

Morse, Sir Jeremy, (1975) 'The international monetary kaleidoscope', The Mercantile Credit Lecture delivered at Reading University, 11 November.

Northedge, F.S. (1976) *The International Political System,* London, Faber.

O'Brien, Conor Cruse and Topolski, Felix, (1968) *The United Nations: Sacred Drama,* London, Hutchinson.

Pinder, J. (1972) 'Positive integration and negative integration: Some problems of economic union in the EEC', in M. Hodges (ed.), *European Integration,* Middlesex, Penguin.

Rousseau, J.J. (1755) 'L'Etat de Guerre' in C.E. Vaughan, *The Political Writings of Rousseau,* Cambridge 1915.

Schram, S.R. (1969) *The Political Thought of Mao Tse-Tung,* Penguin, (rev. ed.).

Schram, S.R. (1971) 'Mao Tse-Tung and the theory of the permanent revolution, 1958–69', *The China Quarterly,* April/June.

Singer, D.J. (1973) 'The peace researcher and foreign policy prediction', *The Papers of the Peace Science Society (International),* **21.**

Waltz, K. (1959) *Man, the State and War,* Colombia.

Wight, M. (1966) 'Why is there no international theory', and 'Western values in international relations', in H. Butterfield and M. Wight (eds.), *Diplomatic Investigations,* London, Unwin.

Wolfers, A. (1962) *Discord and Collaboration,* Baltimore.

Index